This is a most welcome volume. There is no better place to b those seeking a sense of the evangelical perspective on the range tions emerging in the current dialogue between Christianity and t ural sciences.

RANDY L. MADDOX, PHD
Professor of Theology and Wesleyan Studies
Duke Divinity School

For Christians—whether students or their teachers—accustomed to holding the worlds of science and faith apart, Chappell and Cook have performed an invaluable service. With an impressive assembly of balanced and informed contributors, they show that God's ways cannot be segregated, that believers need to learn from and engage the sciences, and that we have the resources to move forward into this conversation faithfully as Christians.

JOEL B. GREEN, Professor of New Testament Interpretation
Vice President of Academic Affairs and Provost
Asbury Theological Seminary

With an honest approach to critical questions, *Not Just Science* fills a gap in the discussion about the relationship between faith and reason. This is a most welcome addition to these significant scholarly conversations.

RON MAHURIN, PHD
VP, Professional Development and Research
Council for Christian Colleges and Universities

Finally, Chappell and Cook have edited a book that grapples with important questions that intellectually curious students are asking about the intersection of Christian faith and natural science. The distinctive contribution of this work is how faculty contributors who are Christians reveal the importance of critical thinking skills and the interdependency of the disciplines as vital to understanding the Creator and His creation. This book is a "must read" for students in introductory science courses in higher education.

JEANETTE L. HSIEH
Executive Vice President and Provost
Trinity International University

NOT JUST
SCIENCE

QUESTIONS WHERE

CHRISTIAN FAITH AND

NATURAL SCIENCE INTERSECT

NOT JUST
SCIENCE

general editors

Dorothy F. Chappell & E. David Cook

GRAND RAPIDS, MICHIGAN 49530 USA

ZONDERVAN™

Not Just Science
Copyright © 2005 by E. David Cook and Dorothy F. Chappell

Requests for information should be addressed to:
Zondervan, *Grand Rapids, Michigan 49530*

Library of Congress Cataloging-in-Publication Data

Not just science : questions where Christian faith and natural science intersect / Dorothy F. Chappell and E.
    David Cook, general editors.
            p. cm.
        Summary: "A look at some of the questions students should be asking as they study the natural sciences
            in relation to the Christian worldview and think critically about God's creation"—Provided by
            publisher.
        Includes bibliographical references.
        ISBN-10: 0-310-26383-2 (pbk.)
        ISBN-13: 978-0-310-26383-2
        1. Religion and science. I. Chappell, Dorothy F., 1947- II. Cook, E. David (Edward David), 1947-
    BL240.3.N68 2005
    261.5'5—dc22

Interior design by Tracey Walker

Printed in the United States of America

---

05 06 07 08 09 10 11 12 /❖ DCI/ 10 9 8 7 6 5 4 3 2 1

For Christ and His Kingdom

CONTENTS

FOREWORD

Many years ago, when I was an undergraduate at Goshen College, I was faced with a difficult career choice. The college had a sustained tradition of Christian service, and in fact its motto was "Culture for Service." My major was chemistry, and I knew that chemists could invent safer tires, more durable fabrics, or effective medicines. But I had a long-standing attraction to astronomy, which seemed about as useless as poetry. Could I, as a Christian, devote myself in good conscience to something as seemingly esoteric as the study of the heavens?

At this point my math teacher weighed in with some advice: "If you feel a calling for astronomy, you should go for it. After all, we shouldn't let the atheists take over any field of study."

And thus it was that I elected to go on to graduate school in astronomy. At the time I felt that I was the lucky recipient of a unique piece of counseling. Only much later did I appreciate that this was part of a general awakening within conservative Christian circles. After half a century or more of suspicion regarding higher education, church leaders had begun to realize that to be competitive in the modern intellectual world, it was necessary to have trained specialists in a broad swath of disciplines, including the sciences.

Today this is true more than ever. Within America the two largest cultural blocks are religion and science, and it is high time that these two groups should be in dialogue with each other. Their respective approaches to understanding the world and evaluating what is important are often very different, and all too frequently members of one group hold a shallow and simplistic caricature of the other group's extensively integrated viewpoint. These differences and lack of mutual understanding can generate a volatile clash of judgments on the national political scene—for instance, on how biological evolution should be addressed in public schools. This debate is simply the most conspicuous of a number of issues where science and religion cross paths.

Not Just Science is a subtle and thoughtful examination of this common ground. Here I found new insights on topics I thought I understood well, and I found provocative areas that I had never thought much about. Nevertheless, I am sure this book will irritate and outrage many potential readers.

Take, for example, the incendiary issue of Intelligent Design. Virtually all Christians, who accept a Creator God as a fundamental tenet of their beliefs, will agree that creation is intelligently designed because the world proves to be such a congenial place for the existence of intelligent, self-reflective life. The more scientists learn about the intricate interconnections of the natural world and the incredible "fine tuning" of its physical and chemical details, the more astonishing it appears that we are here. But simply to say that we exist because of God's awesome designing power is a showstopper for science. Scientists want to build a coherent picture of *how* it could be done, what the principles are behind the origin of life. The amazing similarities of the DNA structures in all life forms demand an explanation that goes beyond the simple statement, "God did it!"

Not Just Science does not take a stand on the *political* issue of whether Intelligent Design should be given time in science classrooms. (Note that Intelligent Design in the political sense is an anti-evolution movement, as opposed to the more general Christian belief that in some way God did provide for a well-designed cosmos.) Since many religious persons who have little background in science feel that their views are being shortchanged by not having design explicitly discussed in biology classes, they will no doubt be disappointed by a book such as this. On the other hand, a hard core of scientists who feel that science and religion must never mix will no doubt dismiss this book with disdain because it treats the idea of design sympathetically.

Fortunately, the two great cultural groups, religion and science, are not mutually exclusive. There is a large cadre, including Nobel laureates, deans, professors, and laboratory leaders, who are equally at home in both cultures. Recently the American Association for the Advancement of Science set up a program for a Dialogue on Science, Ethics, and Religion, with leading scientists and theologians on its advisory committee. The mere existence of such a program was bitterly fought by some members of the association, but when the program was publically challenged in an open council meeting, one section president after another took the floor to say how relevant and important such a program was. Curiously, this aspect of the confrontation went essentially unreported in the media.

Clearly, more education on the science-religion interface is needed. *Not Just Science* will help delineate the areas of intersection and provide a basis for integration. It includes a discussion of topics, such as the age of the earth, where the advancing frontiers of scientific knowledge suggest that a strictly literal interpretation of biblical texts is no longer appropriate. Here also are considered scripturally based theological constructions—for example, the richly symbolic role of Adam and the question of what it means to be human. Finally, brought to the table is a variety of ethical issues such as species extinction and global warming, where even persons who do not identify with Christianity are essentially being morally bankrolled by the conscience of the Christian tradition.

No one book can ever aspire to have the last word on issues of science and religion, but in *Not Just Science* a number of voices bring their expertise to bear on issues of common concern, and in so doing they propel the discussion forward. I commend their thoughtful reflections to you.

Owen Gingerich
Harvard Smithsonian Center for Astrophysics
Cambridge, Massachusetts
May 2005

INTRODUCTION

Dorothy F. Chappell and E. David Cook

WHY HAVE WE PRODUCED THIS BOOK?

The wonder and ecstasy in discovery and study of the mysteries of the natural world are not limited to professional scientists. Casual observers and those who interact with the material world and technology also share in the delight of beauty, elegance, intricacy, and ordered efficiency of creation. Humans as a part of creation intervene in some of its processes. Such interventions often occur through the practice of science when we study and manipulate the material world and our proficiencies in doing good are increased through curing diseases, feeding the hungry, stewarding resources, and alleviating suffering. Likewise, interventions in science can give humankind means to support greed, selfishness, hatred, and other vices detrimental to human welfare and God's purposes. Hence the initiative for this book is taken because, for Christians, it is "not just science" that concerns them. They are also concerned about the development of moral character and a deep sense of responsibility to know the Creator, to know the purposes of creation, and to steward portions of creation.

Why did we undertake this project together?

One of us is a philosopher, theologian, and ethicist, and the other is a biologist with interests in theology and ethics. The expertise we bring to this task provides insights that are integrative and enrich the discussion of central conceptual matters. As professional Christian educators, we are committed to the intellectual development of students and others interested in issues where their faith and the academic disciplines converge. In this book, we are addressing some questions at the intersection of Christian faith and natural sciences. We delight in the outcomes of the interactions generated through such discussions, and as part of our stewardship, we desire to pass on those treasures to other learners.

The vast deficits in discussions in this area of convergence shortchange the education of Christian first-year nonscience and science students entering higher education science classes. Some of these deficits are addressed through the design of this book and the topics undertaken. Faculty who serve as authors in this book, with expertise in scientific investigation and experience in teaching, use demonstrable critical-thinking skills in raising questions to challenge students. This book is useful for reading and discussion not only for introductory-level students but also for many other readers who enjoy studying and thinking about the natural sciences.

The academic disciplines do not exist as islands—they are interdependent. This interdependency among the natural sciences opens stimulating opportunities to research and understanding. Some of that intrigue is captured in this book. The mysteries revealed in creation and the development of exciting technologies demand that informed decisions about the natural sciences and their effects in the world be given treatment by more perspectives than we can address in this book. History, philosophy, theology, and the social sciences help contextualize the natural sciences, but these disciplines do not address the whole picture. The nature of the individual natural science interdependencies also affects how each science is practiced. For instance, understanding some chemistry is essential to gaining insights into biology. Similarly, when some types of chemistry, like pharmacology, are effectively applied, knowledge of biological cells and systems is essential. The interdisciplinary nature between the natural sciences and mathematics is also extensive. Mathematics influences the natural sciences in many ways. Scientific inquiry requires the collective intellectual approaches to gain glimpses into the workings of the natural world. By discussing interdisciplinary web-like interfaces of these disciplines with the Christian faith, students of science may gain new insights into their relationship with the Creator.

Christianity is not an island either, and as Christians grow, their whole being is permeated with a drive to serve God with the greatest sphere of their abilities. The challenge of being living sacrifices includes transformation and renewal of the mind to discern God's good and perfect will, even in studying the natural sciences. This is a huge undertaking and deserves Christians' best attention. We hope that students, in the broadest sense, will be inspired to develop excellent critical-thinking skills about science and unselfishly apply what they know to the world.

Of extensive value to Christian students is the recognition of ultimate meaning about phenomena in nature and formulation of moral guidelines for the practice and use of science in creation. Questions about God's purposes for and in creation dominate public and private discussions. Christians can lend great insights to these discussions and the practices of the natural sciences because their lives are transformed within the meaning of the grand narrative of the creation, fall, redemption, and glory. Chapter 3 discusses this narrative. This book sheds light on the roles of Christians who study and use the natural sciences.

A broad view of science is shaped in the following chapters by faculty authors from a wide range of natural science disciplines. Readers will perceive the diversity of expertise and experiences of these faculty who engage the nature of science and some biblical theological perspectives. They disclose some truths at the intersection of natural sciences and Christian faith where philosophical discussions then help formulate the ultimate questions. It is at this intersection where ultimate truths are derived, humanitarian applications of science are conceived, and ethics can be brought to bear on scientific practice and the use of the products of science throughout the world. Our confidence is that as a philosopher and a natural scientist, we editors can bring light to some of these things. This book serves as an example of critical thinking for those who consider science in its various roles. We make no claims that our approach to critical thinking is the only way to address difficult issues. Readers should not expect that all questions are asked or that all questions are answered. In fact, we anticipate that we are only part way on our lifelong journey of asking questions.

How should the natural sciences be contextualized for Christians?

Natural science, as a means of knowing, provides an active process that exposes the remarkable empirical characteristics of creation. It does not explain phenomena beyond the natural realm. We make a theological assumption that our contextualization lies in the presumption that all truth is God's truth and that Christ Himself is the Creator and Sustainer of the cosmos of which we are a part. As we are exposed to the effects of studies and developments in the natural sciences, the influence of the scientific community increases in our everyday lives. The natural sciences also are academic disciplines engaged by large segments of learned populations. They provide legitimate courses of study and are taught widely in universities, technical schools, and colleges—secular and Christian. When Christians study the natural sciences and are informed by reflection on the Creator, the incarnate and written Word, the Holy Spirit, and the application of biblical virtues, they tap into the richness of understanding purpose and accountability in their relationship to creation. To Christians informed in this way, science has proper authority and is not the ultimate hope for humanity.

The natural sciences are not to be feared, and they do not define the ultimate human existence as emptiness and meaninglessness where all of existence is reduced to matter and energy. In fact, the most honest attempts to contextualize natural science involve defining it and the scope of its capabilities and limitations. Applications of science considered individually and systematically rest on worldviews. Christians should take intellectual responsibility for making sense of and understanding issues important in making decisions influencing both the practice of science and the use of scientific advances.

Does the process of inquiry provide any advantages to learning?

The heart of educational pedagogy in higher learning is critical thinking, and the art of asking excellent questions is central to learning. Asking questions moves individuals from subconscious thinking to gaining command of concepts and phenomena. Inquiry engages the intellect and emotions, and the biblical mandate requires that we be transformed in the renewal of our minds and that we understand our roles in stewardship. As emotions and intellect are stirred through knowledge gained through inquiry, the cultivation of attitudes and motivation to applications of knowledge occurs. In fact, as we renew our minds, we are to attempt to determine the will of God, which is good and acceptable and perfect. For the editors of this book, part of the educational task is to challenge students to maximize the quality of their thinking because an enlivened mind engaged in critical thinking will motivate and inform them how to serve God. Serving God involves action in God's world.

Intellectual engagement is an essential quality of Christians, and it is sometimes painful. In addressing the intersection we describe, Christians should apply critical thinking as they engage the art of asking well-formulated questions as an *embedded and integrative task*. Usually it is not added on. It is a lifelong skill that can be improved only through practice. The Christians who give attention to critical thinking in every area of their lives will discover meaningful applications of their knowledge because they can have created awareness of the consequences of their actions. On a personal level, critical thinking helps individuals wrestle with virtues and vices, and in a more collective sense, it assists them in doing justice, loving kindness, and walking humbly with God. Obviously, the lifelong acquisition of knowledge is a process that is constantly adjusted, bringing new insights and corrections to applications of knowledge.

This book is about some important questions at the intersection of natural sciences and Christian faith. Raising the right questions as part of the process of inquiry allows participants to wrestle through issues and formulate opinions about topics. Since inquiry is an excellent tool in critical thinking, it helps motivate humans to conduct themselves within certain parameters. In this case, when studies of the natural sciences and Christian worldview intersect, tough questions must be posed regarding attitudes toward creation and the practice of the natural sciences within the creation mandate. Through our attempts to present some foundational concepts in a question format, we are encouraging Christians to formulate their roles in meditating on and administering God's mandate for care of creation.

Has the process of asking questions as a valid learning technique withstood the test of history?

The oracle at Delphi was where the ancient Greeks went to find answers to difficult questions. When they asked the oracle who was the wisest man in the world, the answer was Socrates. When he was told the news, Socrates suggested that the reason he was the wisest man was that he knew how little he really knew. The more we learn about the world—and indeed, any subject—the more there is to learn. As Alexander the Great wept when there were no more kingdoms to be won, so humanity understands that none of us will or can know everything. But that doesn't mean that we can't know anything, and science helps us do just that.

Children like to ask, "Why?" and that is a good question. Human beings want and need to understand themselves and the world they occupy. Questions and answers help us do just that. Francis Bacon described science as "asking questions" or even "torturing Nature." As we discover answers to our questions, we not only understand the world better, but we are able to refine and improve our questions and answers.

Real questions have a point. They are not just hypothetical or for fun. The answers to good questions elicit change and transform how we live, whether that is how we treat the world, how we deal with it and with each other, or how we understand ourselves and our nature and destiny.

Philosophy and theology ask a different level of question than that of any particular discipline such as science and the various forms of science. Philosophy and theology help us understand the *why* rather than the *how*. Science can give us a great deal of knowledge about how the world operates and how we relate to that world in its many expressions, but that information won't tell us what we should do in light of that knowledge and what is important and valuable. One can give a scientific expression of how the body reacts to another body of the opposite sex, but that in itself will reveal nothing about the relationship, affection, fear, or care involved. Even the social and psychological sciences offer descriptions, but providing an evaluation requires some kind of worldview of values and beliefs.

We can see the influence of worldviews in the things scientists choose to study, for they reflect the beliefs and concerns of their different cultures and ages. The history of science reveals very different areas of interest and concern. Christianity inspires questions and raises issues of fundamental importance as to who we are, what we are doing, why we and the world exist at all, and where everything is headed. It also helps us focus on the responsibility we have for what we learn about the world. Environmental studies show that we are literally exhausting resources in the world. To continue living in this world, humanity must behave differently. The ways that HIV and AIDS are transmitted warn us that if humanity is not more careful about sexual behavior, then even more millions will die. Medical sciences reveal what is going on with our bodies but not why we should care for them or why life is important and has meaning.

Society as a whole should ask and answer these fundamental questions that underlie and are exposed by science and its findings. In the face of the complexity of life and the world, we need humility to realize our human weakness and to realize that our scientific knowledge can be put to good and evil uses. The horrors of Nazi Germany remind us of what can happen when science is put to work for a cruel and inhumane totalitarian regime. Scientific questioning requires a clear understanding of values and goals. Christianity is not the only value system or worldview that provides these moral and theological guidelines, but we believe that history shows, and good scientific practice supports, the truth and value of Christianity working hand in hand with the sciences.

What kinds of questions should be posed at the intersection of Christian faith and science?

When we ask questions, we reveal something about ourselves and our view of the world. If one asks someone else whether he has stopped beating his wife, the assumptions exist that he both has a wife and is or was a wife beater. Questions at the intersection of Christian faith and science will vary and depend on whether they are asked by a Christian, a scientist, a Christian who is a scientist, or someone who is neither. Everyone has common questions about the meaning of life, the existence of God, and the veracity of purpose and design in the world as well as about issues that arise as the various sciences are practiced and knowledge about the world is discovered. Then one begins to face what can and cannot be done and should or should not be done with that knowledge.

Ultimate questions about the Creator, His creation, and human responsibility to and for the world and all that is in it are clearly the kinds of questions asked by everyone. Christians have unique perspectives in offering answers. These questions are part and parcel of knowing God and knowing what He is like and what He has done in creation and history. The knowledge gained from the study of these questions leads us to more than just a better understanding of God and His world. It forces us to our knees in worship and praise of the great God who has made and upholds such a wonderful world.

The questions posed by Christians are very different from those raised by people outside Christianity who seek to find reasons not to believe in God and evidence in the world that points to different conclusions about the origin, nature, and direction of the natural realm and all that is in it.

Likewise, scientists, whether Christians or not, find their study leads to yet more questions, and they build their knowledge and grasp of reality and its functioning on what humans already know. Science and its progressive work are the context for and the means of asking and answering such questions.

In contrast, the borderline between faith and science raises questions about the significance of what we have learned, the value and purpose of that reality and knowledge, and ethical reflection on what should be done with scientific knowledge. We can describe the different species of plants and animals, but they do not provide us with information about whether they should be conserved, or experimented upon and used for food or medicine, or simply enjoyed in gardens, zoos, and wildlife parks. Dealing with these kinds of questions helps us discern the responsibility we have for the world where we live, move, and have our being and for every aspect of the created order of which we are a part. Good questions lead to good answers and right actions. Science transforms what humans do because it gives them better understanding and sets that understanding in the context of human beliefs and values so decisions can be made about how to live in relation to the world and everything in it.

Have there been any conflicts at the intersection of Christian faith and the natural sciences?

Struggles with issues where Christian faith and natural science intersect have accentuated the relationship of science and Christianity through the centuries. Questions about certain topics have heightened the debate of the relationship of science and the Christian faith. Some have attempted to solve these struggles through intellectual debate. Others have compartmentalized the issues into religion and science categories without ever sharing scrutiny that could lead to richer understanding. Thus some of the conflicts remain as disparate as desert is from sea. To serious thinkers who attempt to integrate science and a Christian belief system, tough questions are debated head-on and with the rigor of thorough investigation found in the finest intellectual pursuit.

Good examples of the questions about the compatibility of the Christian faith and science are often seen through historical windows where interactions of Christianity and science are deeply embedded in specific cultural situations. Encounters between Christianity and science have not always been positive. You can read about some of those conflicts in this book in the chapter on the history of science (chapter 1) and in the sections on ethics, environmental studies, and societal impacts of the natural sciences, among others. Profound questions in the practice of ethics relating human activity to creation assume the role of the oxymoron "perpetual frontier," which is likely to accompany human existence until the end of time. The history of science reveals that conflicts over important theological issues based on erroneous interpretations of Scripture and/or science have been resolved over time. Even the area of "compatibility" of scientific issues with Christian religious beliefs is often a conflict, and the issues are always in tension.

Scientific excellence is compatible with devout, biblically grounded Christian faith. Challenges to this principle are met by Christians with rigorous study to seek truth and the discernment to draw humans to reason together on issues that cause conflict. Although the individual and larger good may seem in conflict, there are reasonable ways to negotiate through conflicts. Often, as in the case of medical ethics, conflicts are resolved for individuals and medical institutions/constituencies through boards of specialist ethicists who bring valued principles from many perspectives to conflicts.

Are there limits to human knowledge and an end to questioning?

Confidence and humility weave a fabric in the thinking of Christians who are effective critical thinkers. Not all questions can be answered, and answered questions can stop the flow of critical thinking. The creative thinker takes every opportunity to ask more questions. The limits to human knowledge are especially evident to Christians. They acknowledge that they are made and given an ability, to discern to a small degree the rational mind of God. They also recognize that they have fallible minds and seemingly infinite capacities for inquiry. But all human inquiry generates an incomplete grasp of reality. Humility is the result of the Christians' consciousness of the fallible outcomes of their own efforts.

It is claimed that Aristotle was the last person who knew everything. We do well to be skeptical even of that claim because there is too much to know and too little time to know it, and our human capacity for knowledge is far too limited. Real knowledge recognizes its limits and leads to the desire for more and better understanding.

If science pretends to "think God's thoughts after Him," then humans will never be able to understand all that God knows, does, and has done. Christians and non-Christians understand that human intellects are limited in what can be grasped, understood, and retained. What there is to be explored, experimented upon, known, understood, and applied by technology is endless. This combination of our limits and the richness and limitlessness of the created order at every level, from the subatomic to the ecosystem and cosmos, means that all questions cannot be answered and answered questions should not stop the flow of critical thought but open up more aspects for research and development.

Christians realize that before the sheer immensity of all there is to know and the wonder and complexity of reality, the only proper human response must be humility, careful recognition of our frailty, and the essential incompleteness of our knowledge. The doctrine of sin also indicates that every aspect of our life and being has been affected by sin, which should make us realize that our conclusions are never final and must always be open to revision and refinement. In this book and in the practice of science, we believe that good answers do not end discussion and understanding but are opportunities for more work in better understanding reality. Unanswered questions are invitations for further discovery, study, and classification. That is part of what is meant by critical thinking that reveals what we know and do not know and what we do with that knowledge.

How is ethics related to the intersection of Christian faith and the natural sciences?

Scientific knowledge in itself is neither moral nor immoral, but scientists and all who benefit from that knowledge and its application are people who have ethical standards and particular values that fundamentally affect how scientific work is done and what is done with its results. Morality is shaped by many different factors, ranging from education to family life to cultural settings. There are also different bases for ethics and morality, and people have different ideas of what is right and wrong. These values relate closely to beliefs about the nature of the world and whether or not one believes that there is a God who made humanity in His image and both created and continues to sustain the world. Simply put, humans either discover an objective moral base or have to create their own morality. Christians firmly believe that God reveals moral standards that are a reflection of who He is and what is both good in itself and for human beings.

Debates about how and why we do science and how we are to use scientific discoveries are a part of our life together. Genetic and environmental sciences have helped us understand the link between disease and genes and the impact of human behavior on climate and the ecosystem. But such scientific knowledge raises ethical questions about whether we should test people from when they are in the womb to when they are adults for genetic disease and whether we should abort, manipulate, replace, or euthanize those who are carrying so-called defective genes and will suffer from disease or handicaps because of those genes. That our fuel consumption is affecting our atmosphere and polluting our environment will not tell us how we should respond until and unless we bring our ethical perspectives to bear on the problem and decide what we value and what we should do about that in modifying or adapting our behavior.

Christians recognize that this world belongs to God and that He has a purpose for it and for humanity's role and responsibility for our scientific work and our behavior in light of and because of scientific discovery. The challenge, as we look at the different natural sciences, is to discover and obey God's moral laws and His biblical commands as we try to know and do God's will.

How should readers apply what they learn through study of the concepts presented in this book?

Student essays and oral presentations on moral, philosophical, and theological questions are usually evaluated on their description and critique. What is often sadly missing is any application of what has been learned. The whole point of this book is not to leave readers in the same state they were in before reading it. Learning, like science, requires that we do something with what we have learned.

So far we have recognized that humanity does not and cannot know the answers to all scientific questions in the here and now and that good critical questioning leads to further questions and search for knowledge. We also have seen that scientific questions are framed in and depend on our worldviews, beliefs, and moral values. Our hope and prayer are that this book will show how we can discern the questions at the intersection of faith and science, how we should approach them, and how we should respond to them. That means we will learn a great deal about science and about our Christian faith, God and His will, and values. Such knowledge should lead to a different attitude toward science, understanding and knowledge, and the uses of that science and the technologies we develop. Education embedded in a strong Christian worldview shapes our attitude to science, inquiry, and the lifelong learning and activity in which we engage. Good Christian education results in well-informed, balanced people who are able to do their work with a better grasp of science and of their Christian faith and how each informs, affects, and interacts with the other.

We want to encourage confident Christians to engage responsibly in the scientific enterprise. And we want nonscientists to know how to go about positively critical reflection on the issues and questions science raises for faith and faith raises for science, and especially to know how to act and behave in a thoroughly Christian way in the practice, application, and regulation of science.

Does the fall affect the power of the intellect?

The authors of this book acknowledge that the effects of the fall adversely affect our own capacities to know truth. The corrupting influence of sin affects the ability to see the world as it is. Christians expectantly work as stewards in the renewal of the physical world with a deep commitment to faithfulness to God and in response to his command to rule over creation. In studying creation through scientific inquiry, humility and consciousness of the fallible outcomes of human efforts remain a constant reality.

God has created humans with great capacities for curiosity and has created a marvelous world for humans to explore. This temporal world bears the mark of the Creator. Christians can see the creation as evidence of God's majesty and power. They are motivated to worship God because of the revelations they understand and enjoy, realizing that the full scope of knowledge of the whole complexity of creation exceeds the limits of human understanding. Chapters 2 and 3, on philosophy and theology, deal with these concepts in greater detail.

To whom is this book written?

The fine faculty contributors to this book are deeply committed to scientifically literate nonscientists and to those scientists who continue to learn and build careers in the scientifically grounded professions in God's kingdom worldwide. General education students, science majors, members of church and parachurch groups, pastors and priests, and many others will find in this book trustworthy approaches to some fundamental questions Christians ask when searching for truth through investigations in the natural sciences.

Our intent is to take seriously the task of bringing such issues into focus. We trust that people of Christian faith can honestly engage issues and that integration will inform understanding. The teacher-scholars who have written for this book are deeply committed to the pursuit of truth in theory and in the person of Jesus Christ. They frequently engage students and their church communities in the discourses presented here.

Does this book address all natural sciences?

Investigations in empirical and theoretical natural science disciplines have been very successful in discovering new truths about the natural world. This book samples only a few of those disciplines. It addresses some traditional established sciences like biology, chemistry, geology, and physics. Some applied areas like computer science, engineering, medicine, and agriculture are also part of our efforts here. It is important to note that mathematicians, like natural scientists, view God as the source of their knowledge. Mathematics is often developed as an abstraction apart from the observable world.

This book encourages readers to examine the scientific method, frameworks of the traditional natural sciences and the recently emerging sciences, and the conceptual assumptions that guide excellent scientific practice. As scientists who are Christians, we engage in the study of science to discern truth in God's general revelation in creation.

The Editors

PART 1

PRESUPPOSITIONS

1

HOW HAVE CHRISTIAN FAITH AND NATURAL SCIENCE INTERACTED IN HISTORY?

Joseph L. Spradley

Many authors have noted the close interaction between Christianity and science.[1] Although the two are often assumed to be in conflict, a more positive relationship between science and faith is evident from their overlapping histories. The direct influences of Christian ideas on the success of science are often difficult to assess.[2] However, their mutually supporting roles are evident in history, even when they sometimes appear to be in conflict. In fact, the roots of modern science can be traced to early Christian thought, and both science and faith can be seen as historically interrelated efforts to understand the physical universe and its creative source.

Are natural science and Christian faith locked in conflict, or is there evidence of cooperation between the two?

Perhaps the most typical view of the relationship between science and faith is one of conflict or confrontation, even though the emphasis on this "warfare" model has greatly diminished at the scholarly level. Historically, the idea of warfare between science and Christianity developed during the latter half of the nineteenth century with the rise of positivism and evolutionary theories. Before this time, a close relationship between the two was evident from the number of pioneering scientists who were Christians and the number of clergymen who participated in scientific activities. The growing professionalism of science in the nineteenth century led to a spirit of competition and confrontation with the religious establishment.

The increasing conflict and the formulation of a warfare model were supported by two influential books.[3] John William Draper published the first edition of his *History of the Conflict between Religion and Science* in 1874. Andrew Dickson White published his two-volume *History of the Warfare of Science and Theology in Christendom* in 1896. Both books had a strongly positivist and antireligious view of history, and both portrayed the natural sciences as the champions of academic freedom and the liberators of humanity from religious oppression. The popular interpretation of Darwinian theory in terms of the "survival of the fittest" seemed to support this warfare model, with science replacing religious authoritarian claims in the struggle for cultural supremacy.

In the first half of the twentieth century, logical positivism claimed victory in the supposed warfare between science and Christianity. The positivist's view was that only empirically verifiable knowledge is valid and that all other kinds of knowledge are opinion and emotion, literally "non-sense." Of course, this view itself was not empirically verifiable, but it became the dominant view for nearly fifty years. In the second half of the century, increasing historical analysis of science began to show the close relationship between science and culture and the way science changes with shifting cultural ideas and values.

In the twentieth century, certain fundamentalist Christian groups who saw the natural sciences in opposition to a more literal interpretation of the Bible embraced the warfare model. For example, a recent book by Henry Morris, president of the Institute for Creation Research, that attacks the theory of evolution is entitled *The Long War against God*.[4] The book treats modern evolutionary theory as the continuation of Satan's attempt to dethrone God. At times the popular media assume the conflict view in discussing the relation between science and religion, often concluding that science disproves religion.

Do cooperation and convergence offer a legitimate model of understanding issues at the intersection of natural science and Christian faith?

A more fruitful and historically accurate approach to the relation between science and Christianity is one of cooperation and convergence rather than confrontation and conflict. This view emphasizes the Augustinian idea that "all truth is God's truth" and that advances in science should be seen as adding to God's revelation in nature. In such a view, the content of Christian theology will sometimes influence and motivate scientific work, and discoveries in the natural sciences will sometimes clarify and correct Christian thought.

Some of the most important features that distinguish modern science from its ancient Greek heritage can be identified in the early centuries of the Christian church, especially in the christological controversies that dominated Christian theology for more than a millennium. Christian ideas have influenced scientific thinking at several points in history. Such ideas are also essential in any attempt to understand science from a Christian perspective.

An understanding of the divinity of Christ emerged early in Christian thought, leading to a stronger foundation for theoretical science. Starting from biblical sources,[5] Christian thinkers developed the Greek *Logos* concept and applied it to Christ as the divine reason and Word of God in the creation of the world. The Logos doctrine together with the doctrine of creation provided a basis for the assumption in science that nature is an ordered cosmos, which is in some degree intelligible to human understanding. It reinforced the growing Christian conviction of the unity of creation, which led to the eventual defeat of the pagan tendency to deify nature and the Greek view of celestial perfection, both of which had hindered the full development of science.

The humanity of Christ and its relation to His divinity took longer to work out but was no less important for a Christian understanding of nature. The doctrine of the incarnation reinforced a new appreciation for the dignity of labor, the reality of matter, and the goodness of creation—themes that eventually provided support for the development of experimental science. In the scientific revolution of the sixteenth and seventeenth centuries, several mediating and sometimes heretical views of Christ were used to explain scientific ideas concerning the unity and vitality of nature. These views also served to motivate the practice of science and its application to social needs.

1. EARLY CHRISTIANITY AND SCIENTIFIC ORDER

What did early Christian thought contribute to the acceptance of Greek science and the origins of modern science, and how does modern science differ from Greek science?

Did the concept of Logos have anything to do with the acceptance of Greek science? In late antiquity, the rational traditions of Greek science and philosophy were shifting toward ethics and theology, with an increasing emphasis on mysticism and magic. Neoplatonic authors were adding esoteric religious ideas to the Greek emphasis on the unchanging perfection of the celestial realm beyond the moon. Early Christian thinkers began to develop their own intellectual tradition to counter these pagan ideas, leading eventually to a Christian assimilation and development of Greek science. They based their idea of the divinity of Christ on John 1:1–14, where Jesus is revealed as the Logos or "Word" of God. The Logos concept had a long history in the Greco-Roman world, beginning with Heraclitus in the fifth century BC as the principle of harmony and order in a universe of continual flux. In Stoic teaching, the Logos was the divine power that orders and maintains the cosmos.

The first major Christian apologist was Justin Martyr (c. AD 100–c. 165), who was a student of Greek philosophy. After converting to Christianity (c. 130), he rejected pagan polytheism but welcomed Platonic metaphysics and Stoic ethics as being compatible with Christian truth. He taught in Rome where he was eventually martyred. Justin viewed Jesus as the incarnate Logos whose divine power and reason in creation ensures an ordered cosmos as developed in Greek science. He taught that where truth existed, in both the Old Testament writers and the Greek philosophers, it was grounded in the universal rational power of the divine Logos: "Whatever has been uttered aright by any men in any place belongs to us Christians; for, next to God, we worship and love the reason (Word) which is from the unbegotten and ineffable God; since on our account He has been made man. . . ."[6] The divinity of Christ as expressed in the Logos theology ensured that the rational tradition of the Greeks would be adopted by Christian thinkers and even strengthened by the biblical conviction of the order and intelligibility of creation freed from magical elements.

Justin's example of reasoned discourse applied to Christian theology was followed by several of the early Christian apologists, including Athenagoras of Athens,

Theophilus of Antioch, Clement of Alexandria, and Origen. Tertullian (c. 155—c. 230) appears to break with this tradition in his celebrated denunciation of Greek philosophy: "What is there in common between Athens and Jerusalem? What between the Academy and the Church? What between heretics and Christians? . . . Away with all projects for a 'Stoic,' a 'Platonic,' or a 'dialectic' Christianity!"[7] But even he embraced the Logos theology of Justin: "God made this universe by his word and reason and power. Your philosophers also are agreed that the artificer of the universe seems to be Logos. . . . This Word, we have learned, was produced from God, and was generated by being produced, and therefore is called the Son of God, and God, from unity of substance with God."[8]

How did Augustine regard the natural and spiritual worlds?

The most influential statement of the Christian attitude toward reason and science, especially in the West, was that of Augustine (354–430), bishop of Hippo in North Africa. Although Augustine clearly gave a higher priority to the spiritual world, he always had a high regard for the natural world and believed that the temporal could serve the eternal. He viewed creation as a revelation of God. "Some people read books in order to find God. Yet there is a great book, the very appearance of created things. Look above you; look below you! Note it; read it! . . . Can you ask for a louder voice than that? Why, heaven and earth cry out to you: 'God made me!'"[9] Augustine's attitude toward scientific knowledge, both theoretical and empirical, is well expressed in his work entitled *De Genesi ad litteram* (The Literal Meaning of Genesis).

> Usually, even a non-Christian knows something about the earth, the heavens, and the other elements of the world, about the motion and orbit of the stars and even their size and relative positions, about the predictable eclipses of the sun and moon, the cycles of the years and the seasons, about the kinds of animals, shrubs, stones, and so forth, and this knowledge he holds to as being certain from reason and experience. Now it is a disgraceful and dangerous thing for an infidel to hear a Christian, presumably giving the meaning of Holy Scripture, talking nonsense on these topics; and we should take all means to prevent such an embarrassing situation, in which people show up vast ignorance in a Christian and laugh it to scorn.[10]

From his writing, it is clear that Augustine accepted the best science of his day and believed that interpretation of the Bible must take into account what can be learned from reason and experience. He also used rational arguments against Stoic determinism and rejected casual astrology, pointing out that astrologers "have never been able to explain why twins have been so different in what they do and achieve. In their professions and skills, in the honors they receive, and in other aspects of their lives and deaths."[11]

Has anyone provided a comprehensive critique of Aristotelian science?

The strong emphasis on the Logos concept and the deity of Christ in the early church influenced one of the last philosophers of the Alexandrian academy, who was also the first Christian to qualify as a major scientist. John Philoponus, also called John the Grammarian, flourished in the first half of the sixth century. The name Philoponus means "industrious" and may have been the class name for a group of active Christian laymen. After his conversion to Christianity, he wrote theological works on the Trinity and the nature of Christ, as well as influential scientific works, which in translation contributed to Arabic and medieval Western thought. His strong emphasis on the deity of Christ led him to develop the first philosophy of nature that combined scientific cosmology and monotheism.[12] His work included the first comprehensive critique of Aristotelian science, which became a strong influence on Galileo.[13]

Building on the biblical doctrine of the creation of the universe by one God who transcends nature, Philoponus concluded that matter was created *ex nihilo* with all the necessary properties for its development from an original chaotic state to the present ordered structure of the universe. This Creator-Logos conception of a world governed by natural law broke with the classical Greek view in which the gods never reigned above nature but were viewed as acting within it. By making a radical distinction between the Creator and all of his creation, Philoponus was led to a view of the unity of heaven and earth in contrast with Aristotle's dichotomy between celestial perfection and terrestrial imperfection. This also led to an attack on Aristotle's doctrine of the eternity of the world and a rejection of the imperishable and divine nature of the stars:

> "One star differeth from another star in glory," says Paulus. Indeed, there is much difference in them in magnitude, colour and brightness, and I think that the reason for this is to be found in nothing else than the composition of the matter of which the stars are constituted. They cannot be simple bodies, for how could they differ but for their different constitution?[14]

Since composite bodies imply decomposition and decay, Philoponus concluded that celestial bodies are subject to decay and must have had a finite beginning. He denied that the sun is made of the indestructible fifth element, the ether, and gave evidence that it is made of fire: "The sun is not white, of the kind of color which many stars possess; it obviously appears yellow, like the color of a flame produced by dry and finely chopped wood. However, even if the sun were white, this would not prove that it is not of fire, for the color of fire changes with the nature of the fuel."[15]

Philoponus did not restrict his critique of Aristotle to cosmological issues such as the eternity of the world and the dichotomy between heaven and earth. He rejected much of Aristotelian dynamics, anticipating Galileo in emphasizing experience to show that "if one lets fall simultaneously from the same height two bodies differing in weight, one will find that the ratio of their times of motion does not correspond to the ratio of their weights, but that the difference in time is a very small one." Contrary to Aristotle, he accepted the possibility of a void and suggested that air can move downward as well as upward. Especially important is his criticism of Aristotle's theory of forced motion, particularly his denial that projectile motion requires the action of circulating air to push it along. Philoponus concluded that "some incorporeal kinetic power is imparted by the thrower to the object thrown" and that "if an arrow or a stone is projected by force in a void, the same thing will happen much more easily, nothing being necessary except the thrower."[16] This came to be known as the "impetus" theory after further development of the ideas of Philoponus by Islamic and Western medieval scholars, leading to the inertia concept of Galileo, Descartes, and Newton.

Philoponus applied the idea of impetus to the motion of the heavens, suggesting that God imparted it at Creation. In fact, creation holds a central position in the development and interconnection of his ideas. It permits the expansion of impetus theory to celestial motions. It supports his attack on natural places, his argument for space as extension, and the abolition of the divinity of the heavens. It allows him to unify dynamics in a book devoted to biblical creation, *De opificio mundi* (On the Creation of the World). In several of these cases, his theology influenced his scientific theory to an extent unparalleled in antiquity. It would later have a similar influence on Galileo in ushering in the scientific revolution.

By the end of antiquity, most of the implications of the divinity of Christ for science had been worked out. The Logos theology had ensured that the rational tradition of Greek science would not be rejected by most Christian thinkers. It established a solid foundation for the scientific belief in the order and intelligibility of creation, surpassing the Greek view that order was only partially and imperfectly realized in the material world and could only be apprehended by rational contemplation of eternal forms. The Creator-Logos conception of Christocentric monotheism also led to a new vision of the unity of the created order in which natural laws apply uniformly throughout the universe.

Although the thirteenth-century medieval synthesis of Christian theology and Aristotelian cosmology by Thomas Aquinas would revive the dichotomy between the celestial and terrestrial realms, the order and intelligibility of the universe would be reinforced and the unifying concepts of Philoponus would finally prevail in the

---

Impetus theory was applied to projectile motion in Islamic science beginning with the work of Avicenna (*ibn Sina*) in the eleventh century. They used the Arabic word *mayl* for the "inclination" of a projectile to keep moving. However, they viewed *mayl* as self-dissipating and did not apply it to creation and the motion of the celestial spheres, being reluctant to deviate very much from Aristotle. Their use of the impetus concept has been traced to a ninth-century Arabic source that apparently draws directly from the work of Philoponus, although he is only identified as *Yahya* (John).*

*Fritz Zimmermann, "Philoponus' Impetus Theory in the Arabic Tradition," in Richard Sorabji, ed., *Philoponus and the Rejection of Aristotelian Science* (London: Duckworth, 1987), 121–29.

work of Galileo and in the scientific revolution that followed. In the meantime, new implications of the humanity of Christ would emerge and provide added support for the growth of Western science.

2. MEDIEVAL CHRISTIANITY AND SCIENTIFIC VALUES

How did medieval Christianity help foster empirical science?

The early church recognized both the deity of Christ as the Creator-Logos and the humanity of Christ as the incarnate Word become flesh (John 1:1–14). The Chalcedonian Definition of 451 placed equal emphasis on the deity and the humanity of Jesus Christ as one person in two natures: "Therefore, following the holy fathers, we all . . . acknowledge one and the same Son, our Lord Jesus Christ, at once complete in Godhead and complete in manhood, truly God and truly man."[17] The humanity of Christ found expression in several new emphases that contributed to attitudes and values that were important in the later development of Western science. The monastic movement and the Benedictine Rule gave rise to a new emphasis on the dignity of labor, which went beyond the Greek concentration on rational contemplation and speculation. New Eucharistic teachings and incarnational insights recognized the reality of matter, in contrast with the Greek tendency to view the material world as mere appearance, the source of opinion and illusion. The Franciscan movement celebrated the goodness of nature, leading to a new interest in the particulars of experience rather than the Greek idea of the terrestrial world as chaotic, imperfect, and evil.

Intellectuals in the ancient world had a low regard for manual labor, relegating most of it to artisans and slaves at the lower end of the social scale. With a few exceptions, such as that of Aristotle, philosophers and scientists avoided any physical manipulation of nature and thus failed to develop any significant experimental tradition. Among Christian thinkers, the humanity of Christ offered a clear example of the dignity of manual labor and menial service. When the Creator-Logos became flesh, He worked with His hands as a carpenter until His ministry began, and then He continued to serve through such acts as healing, feeding the hungry, and even washing the feet of His disciples. This example became an important element in the development of monasticism, especially in the West where it had a more practical and communal expression than the ascetic and hermit monasticism of the Eastern church. Western monasticism preserved Roman civilization and developed centers of learning in which new attitudes toward labor and nature could grow.

How did Western monasticism contribute to the foundations of experimental science?

The greatest leader of communal monasticism in the West was Benedict of Nursia (c. 480–c. 547), the chief exponent for joining labor with learning. In 529 he founded the monastery of Monte Cassino and established the Benedictine order.

The Rule of St. Benedict became a practical guide to communal living that gave equal value to worship and work.

Benedict himself helped in cultivating the soil, feeding the poor, caring for the sick, teaching children, and organizing monastic life. Following his example, Benedictine monasteries combined the preservation of knowledge and scholarship with manual labor in clearing the forests, draining the marshes, breeding new seeds and livestock, and building roads. They experimented with better methods of agriculture and established a tradition that would eventually contribute to more systematic efforts in experimental science.

Another contribution of Western monasticism to the foundations of experimental science was a new emphasis on the reality of matter growing out of incarnational and Eucharistic themes. Greek science was hindered by the Platonic view of matter as chaotic and illusory, an imperfect reflection of the real world of eternal ideas. The incarnation, revealing God through Jesus Christ as fully human with a material body, held little meaning if matter is a mere appearance. The sharpest contrast between Greek and Christian attitudes toward the physical world is seen in the Greek view of death as escape from the material body, while the Christian hope is related to the resurrection of the body.

Although differing views of the Eucharist have arisen, they all affirm the reality and importance of the material level of being. This concern with physicality was in part a move against heresy. Aberrant forms of mysticism sometimes allowed bodily license because matter was viewed as basically unreal. By the twelfth century, several theologians argued that denial of the notion that God becomes flesh and food in the Eucharist is one of the most dangerous kinds of heresy.[18]

> "Idleness is the enemy of the soul. And therefore, at fixed times, the brothers ought to be occupied in manual labor; and again, at fixed times in sacred reading. . . . But, if the needs of the place or poverty demand that they labor at the harvest, they shall not grieve at this: for then they are truly monks if they live by the labors of their hands; as did also our fathers and the apostles."
>
> —The Rule of St. Benedict*
>
> *Benedict of Nursia, The Rule of St. Benedict XLVIII, as quoted in Henry Bettenson, ed., *Documents of the Christian Church* (London: Oxford Univ. Press, 1960), 173–74.

Did any women theologians contribute to Western science during the development of medieval Christianity?

Working in the Benedictine tradition that combined labor and learning, Hildegard of Bingen (1098–1179) was not only the first great woman theologian, but she was also the first important scientist in the awakening of Western Europe. Harvard historian George Sarton called her "the most distinguished naturalist" and "the most original medical writer of Latindom in the twelfth century."[19] She is among the first to benefit from Latin translations of Arabic sources. Hildegard argued that the divinity and the humanity of Christ are complementary and that both are needed in our salvation just as male and female are both necessary in procreation.[20]

Hildegard's affirmative attitude toward the material world, based on the humanity of Christ as reflected in the physicality of female experience, found further expression in much of her scientific work. While serving as the abbess of a Benedictine convent that she founded near Bingen, Germany, she began to record her scientific and theological ideas, many revealed in visions, which led to her first book in 1151 with the abbreviated title *Scivias* (*Sci Vias Dei*: Know Thou the Ways of God). She offered imaginative theories for observed phenomena in the physical world that were influential with many of her medieval contemporaries and affected scientific thought well into the Renaissance.

In a second book, the encyclopedic *Liber Simplicis Medicinae* of 1160, Hildegard described 230 plants and 60 trees with their medical applications, as well as many animals, stones, and metals. When this book was edited by a man named Schott for publication in Strasbourg in 1533, he renamed it *Physica* (Natural Arts). It became a popular scientific work and was used as a text at the medical school in Montpellier, France. In *Physica*, Hildegard gave German terms instead of Latin for each botanical entry, along with its medical applications, developing a German botanical nomenclature that is still in use. Her printed works were widely distributed and contributed to scientific thought well into the Renaissance.[21]

How did ancient views of the terrestrial realm move from imperfect and evil to "good" and enjoyable in the medieval period?

In the thirteenth century, the monastic Benedictines were largely succeeded by the mendicant religious orders, whose monks begged or worked for a living. These included the Franciscans and Dominicans, who provided most of the great university teachers. According to Charles Singer, "The work of the Franciscans led up more clearly to the scientific revival."[22] The incarnational emphasis of monasticism led to a new affirmation and celebration of the goodness of nature in contrast with much of Greek thought, which viewed the terrestrial realm as the lowest level of reality and often associated it with evil. Especially in the Franciscan tradition, the goodness of creation was explicitly related to the incarnation and humanity of Christ.

In Francis of Assisi (c. 1181–1226), the imitation of the life of Jesus and obedience to His teachings reached a level that would earn him the title of "the second Christ." Although Francis committed himself to a life of poverty, he did not reject the material and natural world. Jaroslav Pelikan's evaluation suggests "Quite the opposite: Francis of Assisi was responsible for the rediscovery of nature, and he introduced into medieval Christianity a positive enjoyment of the natural realm for which there were few precedents."[23] His was a simple love of nature in which he celebrated all God's creatures, preaching to the birds and calling fire, wind, and sun his brothers, earth and moon his sisters. In his biography of Francis, G. K. Chesterton suggests that Europe had finally purged itself of the degrading nature worship it had inherited from its classical and barbarian origins, and now in Francis, "man has stripped from his soul the last rag of nature-worship, and can return to nature."[24]

How did medieval values support experimental science?

The friars (brothers) of the Franciscan order carried the ideals of their founder into the secular world, especially the emerging universities, since their vows of poverty, chastity, and obedience did not include isolation in monastic communities. The order had many scholars who began to apply the ideas of Francis in ways that supported experimental science, including Robert Grosseteste, Roger Bacon, and William of Ockham. Grosseteste (1175–1253) founded the Oxford Franciscan school and served as the Bishop of Lincoln. He recognized the gap in Aristotelian science between the intuitive leap from induction to universal definition and suggested that experiments are needed to verify or falsify inductive hypotheses. Through observation and experiment, both definitions and deductions can be grounded in the actual world.

Roger Bacon (c. 1214–94) carried on the experimental emphasis of Grosseteste at Oxford in the tradition of the faction known as the "Spiritual" Franciscans, who adhered to the original ideas of Francis. He emphasized mathematics as "the gate and key" of the sciences, enhancing and utilizing the accuracy of observations and experiments: "And similarly in mathematics it is possible for a sensible example to be given for everything, and a sensible test in figuring and counting, in order that everything should be clear to the sense; consequently there can be no uncertainty in it."[25] Bacon applied this approach in his optical studies, extending the ideas of Grosseteste and borrowing from the translated works of the great Arabic scientist Alhazen (965–c. 1040). Using geometric diagrams, Bacon showed how the light rays of a burning mirror are multiplied and how lenses magnify. He believed that even alchemy and magic could be tested and corrected by more careful experimentation, and he speculated on the possibility of circumnavigating the earth and on such inventions as automobiles and flying machines.

How sharp was Ockham's Razor?

The Spiritual Franciscans were among the first to challenge the synthesis of Aristotelian science with Christian theology as formulated by Thomas Aquinas in his *Summa Theologica* (1265–73). Their appeal to the Bishop of Paris, Etienne Tempier, led to the Condemnation of 1277, consisting of 219 condemned errors that could lead to excommunication. A number of errors relevant to Aristotelian science were condemned in order to preserve the absolute power of God: for example, that God could not create several worlds, that He could not make a void space by moving the world, and that He could not make an accident exist without a subject (a direct challenge to the doctrine of transubstantiation). Although the condemnation was not universally applied, it forced scientists and philosophers to think in new ways and to question Aristotelian ideas. The result was a profound critique of knowledge led by such Spiritual Franciscans as William of Ockham (c. 1285–1349), whose philosophy is known as nominalism or radical empiricism.

Ockham denied the existence of universals except as names. His emphasis on the particulars of experience and the independence of logic from metaphysics provided strong support for empirical science. Ockham's famous "razor" introduced a new economy into the analysis of nature: "It is vain to do with more what can be done with less." He also cast doubt on any absolute evidence for theological propositions apart from the testimony of Christ and the saints. According to Ockham, "Nothing is to be assumed as evident, unless it is known per se, or is evident by experience, or is proved by the authority of Scripture."[26] This skepticism of the fourteenth century opened up new hypothetical possibilities in both theology and science.

Ockham's nominalism had a strong influence on the renewed study of motion in the fourteenth century. With the emphasis on particulars, the study of motion shifted from the essence of movement to the intensity of change in the motion of a body. Thus nominalism led to quantification and the mathematical analysis of change and motion. At the University of Paris, Jean Buridan (c. 1295–c. 1358) developed this tradition. In accordance with the Condemnation of 1277, he agreed that God could intervene in the causal order and alter the "common course of nature" at any time; but he insisted that science should act as if nature always followed its "common course" if order was to have any meaning. According to Buridan, although scientific principles cannot be demonstrated, "they are accepted because they have been observed to be true in many instances and false in none."[27]

The influence of Philoponus began to emerge in Europe after the translation of Arabic sources such as Avicenna, a Persian Muslim philosopher (980–1037). In 1322 Buridan attended lectures on Philoponus's theory of an impressed force to explain projectile motion, lectures given by the Franciscan scholar Franciscus de Marchia. He followed Arabic sources suggesting that this force imparted by the mover was self-dissipating in the projectile so that it eventually fell.[28] Buridan developed the idea, closer to that of Philoponus, that the mover imparted a permanent power of motion, which he called impetus. Air and gravity usually act as resistance to the motion, causing a decrease in impetus. But in the absence of such resistance, impetus would persist.

> And thus one could imagine that it is unnecessary to posit intelligences as the movers of celestial bodies since the Holy Scriptures do not inform us that intelligences must be posited. For it could be said that when God created the celestial spheres, He began to move each of them as He wished, and they are still moved by the impetus which He gave to them because, there being no resistance, the impetus is neither corrupted nor diminished.[29]

Thus he suggested that God imparted a permanent impetus to the celestial spheres at Creation so that they could rotate forever without the need for the immaterial intelligences or unmoved mover of Aristotle. In this respect, his views again resemble those of Philoponus in challenging the divinity of the heavens. It would appear that many of Philoponus's ideas filtered through apart from known translations until the sixteenth century, when the main work of translation from original Greek sources into Latin was done and Philoponus became more widely known in the West.[30] Buridan also viewed impetus as quantifiable in terms of the amount of matter in a body and its speed in a manner similar to the inertia and momentum concepts of Galileo, Descartes, and Newton.

Other possibilities opened up by the Condemnation of 1277 were those of void spaces and other worlds. Buridan considered the idea of an infinite void and suggested that God as infinite spirit is omnipresent in infinite space.

Both Ockham and Buridan died of the plague, which along with the Hundred Years' War had ravaged the fourteenth century. Nicholas of Cusa (1401–64), a German cardinal and Bishop of Brixen in the Tyrol, marks this transition from the Middle Ages to the Renaissance. He explored the limits of nominalist thought and tried to describe the relation between finite experience and the infinite God in his book *Learned Ignorance* (1440). Extrapolating the geometry of the circle to infinity, he concluded that there can be neither absolute center nor circumference of the universe except God Himself, and thus the earth must be in motion. For Nicholas the structure of the Aristotelian cosmos with its separation of heaven and earth loses all meaning.

3. The Scientific Revolution

What did Christians contribute to the scientific revolution?

The idea of an infinite universe became a more explicit and realistic possibility after the displacement of the earth from its central position into an orbit around the sun in Copernican theory (1543). Nicolaus Copernicus (1473–1543) was a faithful canon at the Cathedral of Frauenberg in what is now Poland, but he never became a priest. Although cautious about challenging the geocentric theology of Aquinas, he was encouraged to publish his ideas by a Lutheran scholar from the University of Wittenberg, Joachim Rheticus (1514–74), who actually published the earliest account of the heliocentric theory in 1540. In 1576 the Puritan Thomas Digges (c. 1546–95) published the first English account of the Copernican system. His description of an infinite universe included a gap between the planets and the stars designated as "the habitacle for the elect." He seemed to be indicating a deeper symbolic meaning for the new heliocentric universe.

The Dominican monk Giordano Bruno (1548–1600) believed that the power of an infinite God cannot be restricted to a finite world and that an infinite number of stars would support an infinite number of populated planets, each requiring the redeeming action of Christ through infinite time.[31] In 1576 he left his order in Naples and went to Geneva where the Calvinists ejected him. He traveled about Europe teaching a Hermetic (Gnostic) philosophy in which the omnipresence of God is the factor uniting the universe rather than a hierarchy of beings. After spending some time at Oxford and Wittenberg, he returned to Italy where he was arrested by the Office of the Inquisition, charged with pantheistic heresies and burned at the stake in 1600. He is known as the first martyr to science, although this is somewhat inaccurate, since his conviction was based on his theological ideas.

The sixteenth century saw the publication of the scientific work of Philoponus as well as that of Hildegard. The first printing of the Greek text of *De aeternitate mundi contra proclum* came in 1535, edited by Vittore Trincavelli, who praises the work for refuting the teaching of Proclus on the eternity of the world. It appears that Philoponus was given favorable treatment among rediscovered Greek writers because of his Christianity. His *Physica* was published in 1535 and reprinted nine times by 1581. The first among several Latin writers to recognize the full implications of Philoponus's writings was Gianfrancesco Pico della Mirandola (1469–1533), who used them to attack Aristotle but not to develop alternatives to Aristotle.[32]

What were the risks in supporting the Copernican theory?

The Copernican theory was finally established by the work of Galileo and Johannes Kepler. In his early writings, Galileo Galilei (1564–1642) mentions Philoponus more often than Plato, Ockham, or Duns Scotus, another fourteenth-century critic of Aristotle and Aquinas.[33] In his early notebooks, Galileo used Philoponus's arguments for creation, easing the way for his ideas on matter, space, motion, and the vacuum. He uses Philoponus's arguments for finite velocity in a vacuum in his *De motu*, and his early ideas on impetus are very similar to those of Philoponus and Buridan. Thomas Kuhn, without mentioning Philoponus, notes that Galileo was trained to analyze motions in terms of the impetus theory, which Kuhn sees as a paradigm shift in the study of motion that led to the scientific revolution.[34] Galileo remained a faithful son of the Roman Catholic Church to the end, in spite of his condemnation by the Office of the Inquisition in 1633 for challenging the official view of the church on the centrality and immobility of the earth. His idea that God's revelations in both Scripture and nature cannot disagree led to the recognition that some biblical passages—such as the statement in Psalm 93:1 that the earth "cannot not be moved"—cannot be interpreted literally. He spent his last years under house arrest at his villa completing and publishing his ideas on matter and motion in his *Discourses on Two New Sciences* (1638).

The first great Protestant scientist was Kepler (1571–1630), who finally broke the grip of the circle with his discovery of the elliptical orbits of the planets. As a passionate Lutheran and Pythagorean mystic, he mixed theology, mathematics, and mysticism in his lifelong search for the inner coherence and harmony of the heliocentric system. He believed that the unity and simplicity of the universe revealed the mind of God. In his *Epitome astronomie Copernicanae* (1621), he suggested that the sun rotates and carries the planets along by its *anima motrix*, although he thought of *anima* (soul) as a kind of force (*vis*). For Kepler the Copernican universe illustrated the mystery of the Trinity. He compared the sun to God the Father, source of light and power; the fixed stars stood for God the Son; and the all-pervading force of the sun in the space in between was the Holy Spirit. However, he rejected infinite space, because he believed that order and harmony cannot be found in an infinite and therefore formless universe.

What was involved in the Christian revival of atomism?

The rediscovery in 1417 of the great Latin poem *De rerum natura* by Lucretius, based on the atomism of Epicurus, led to increasing interest in atomism as an alternative to both Aristotle's theory of matter and the mystical tendencies of the Renaissance. Atomism was the view that all physical phenomena can be explained by the order and arrangement of indivisible particles moving in space. At first this theory was viewed as too atheistic to be given serious consideration, compounded by the difficulty of accounting for the order of nature from chance encounters of atoms moving in a void. Among the first to revive atomism was the French Catholic priest Pierre Gassendi (1592–1655) in his *Philosophiae Epicuri syntagma* (1649). He followed Epicurus in accepting the void but rejected his idea that motion was inherent in matter. Gassendi baptized atomism by holding that God imposed motion on atoms at the creation, denying the independence of nature and establishing its contingency on God. The Christianized atomic theory of Gassendi was popularized in England by Walter Charleton (1620–1707), who later became physician to Charles II. Gassendi attributed the motion of atoms to God, but Charleton suggested that the motion of such inert atomic particles was a proof of the existence of God. In *The Darkness of Atheism Refuted by the Light of Nature* (1652), Charleton argued that atheistic atomism cannot account for the activity and order of the atoms that are apparent in the universe.

Applications of the atomic theory were begun in England by Robert Boyle (1627–91), who referred to it as the "corpuscular philosophy" to avoid any identification with atheistic Epicurean atomism. He strongly supported the Reformation thought of Martin Luther and John Calvin on the radical sovereignty of God and the view that nature is passive apart from God's supervision. "In place of the Aristotelian definition of nature as 'the principle of motion and change,' the Reformers conceived of nature as entirely passive."[35] Boyle joined in the criticism of Aristotle's concept of nature as a living and active being and insisted that it is subject to the command of God as the only active principle in the world. Thus, in his corpuscular philosophy, material bodies are completely passive and totally dependent on God. In his *Excellency and Grounds of the Mechanical Hypothesis* (1665), he describes the role of God in his mechanical view of the world.

> "... not only that God gave motion to matter, but that in the beginning he so guided, the various motions of the parts of it, as to contrive them into the world he designed they should compose ... and established those rules of motion, and that order amongst things corporeal, which we are wont to call the laws of nature."
>
> —Robert Boyle*

*Robert Boyle, *Some Occasional Thoughts about the Excellency and Grounds of the Mechanical Hypothesis* (1665), Annexed to the *Excellence of Theology*, 3:450, quoted by Eugene M. Klaaren in *Religious Origins of Modern Science* (Grand Rapids: Eerdmans, 1977), 166.

In spite of Boyle's Reformed sympathies, the emphasis was shifting from the Reformation view of God as Sovereign Redeemer to God as Universal Ruler of the world machine.

What question did Newton have trouble answering?

The culmination of the mechanical view of the world was the product of Isaac Newton (1642–1727) in the *Principia* (*Mathematical Principles of Natural Philosophy*, 1687). An early notebook at Cambridge shows a commitment to the mechanical philosophy of Charleton and Boyle. He extended the dependence of nature on God to space as well as matter, arguing that space is a necessary effect of God's existence while matter is contingent on His creative will. Newton's view that matter is completely passive and that God is the source of activity in the world was complicated by his discovery of the law of universal gravitation, which unified the world but seemed to imply that matter has the active power of attraction. He attempted to resolve this problem in the *Opticks* (1704) by separating natural phenomena into two principles: a "passive" principle associated with matter and an "active" principle associated with God. Active principles were identified with phenomena such as motion, gravitation, cohesion, and fermentation. Thus Newton saw matter as inert and lifeless but animated by God with both space and gravity manifesting His presence in the world. For the Reformers, the sovereignty of God led to a personal Savior, but for the mechanists, it led to a cosmic Clockmaker.

In his published works, Newton appears to be motivated by orthodox religious convictions. He concludes the *Principia* with a General Scholium that expresses traditional Christian piety.

Newton's profound theism is clear, but his private manuscripts, which were unknown to most of his contemporaries, reveal a rejection of orthodox views of the death of Christ. In his letters collected under the title *Notable Corruptions of the Scripture* (1690), Newton claims that passages in the Bible on the Trinity were inserted in the fourth and fifth century and that the true form of Christianity is represented by Arius.[36]

Newton's Arian views seem to be an effort to purge Christianity of mystery and superstition. For Newton, the heart of the Bible is prophecy, revealing God's dominion over history rather than His redeeming love.

In the eighteenth century, Newtonian Christianity degenerated into Deism supported by Freemasonry (established in 1717 in London) and liberal Anglicanism. The God of Deism does not interfere in either nature or human history, thus the incarnation and trinitarian theology are nullified. One result associated with

"This most beautiful system of the sun, planets, and comets could only proceed from the counsel and dominion of an intelligent and powerful Being. This Being governs all things, not as a Soul of the World, but as Lord over all.... He is eternal and infinite, omnipotent and omniscient; that is, his duration reaches from eternity to eternity; his presence from infinity to infinity; he governs all things, and knows all things that are or can be done."

—General Scholium of Newton's *Principia* (1687)*

*Isaac Newton, *Principia* (Mathematical Principles of Natural Philosophy), 3rd ed. (1726), ed. Florian Cajori, trans. Andrew Motte (Berkeley: Univ. of California Press, 1934), 544–46.

the mechanical worldview was the rapid growth of technology, from improvements in the clock to the development of the steam engine and factory. But applied science and the idea of progress had much deeper roots in Christian theology and practice. In the perspective of the ancient world, time is circular and the changing events of history cannot give life permanent significance and meaning. This cyclical view is antithetical to human purposes and progress, since no goals can be achieved without vanishing again. The defeat of this deadly concept of circular time was one of the most important developments of Christian thought and Western culture, ending the pessimism of the ancient world.[37]

Do linear views of time have anything to do with Christianity?

The biblical understanding of history can be traced back to the Hebrew view of the exodus from Egypt, but it had its most complete formulation by Augustine. His concept of linear time is based on both creation and redemption. God created time with a beginning and an end, and the incarnation introduced new and eternally significant events into history. Augustine's two great works, the *Confessions* and the *City of God*, illustrate purpose and meaning in both personal experience and human history. The Benedictine emphasis on manual labor and the Franciscan interest in nature revealed new possibilities of progress. The linear view of history was applied to human responsibility in the Reformation doctrine of vocation. Both Calvin and Luther emphasized the importance of secular vocations as a way of serving God. Calvinism encouraged diligent work and thrifty habits to promote the general welfare and glorify God. This "Protestant ethic" was especially endorsed by Puritanism and applied to scientific work.[38] The study of nature was divinely sanctioned, because it would reveal God's handiwork and exemplify orderly activity.

The eighteenth-century idea of progress can be understood as a secularized version of the Christian view of historical purpose and redemption. The success of science opened up the prospect of indefinite improvement of this life by application of scientific methods, slowly displacing the Christian vision of God's will and kingdom. Thus the idea of progress was a perversion of the doctrine of redemption, with a new faith in human goodness and the efficacy of reason. As technological developments in the Industrial Revolution improved the outward conditions of life, faith in applied science and the idea of progress were reinforced; but too often this was without a sense of redeeming purpose or Christian stewardship to protect against meaninglessness and exploitation.

4. MODERN SCIENCE

What led to increasing separation between science and Christian faith?

By the nineteenth century, science was beginning to distance itself from its historic relation to religious ideas and motivations, first on the Continent and later in Great Britain and the United States. Even though some of the greatest scientists of the period were devout Christians, including Michael Faraday, Joseph Henry, James Clerk Maxwell, and William Thomson (Lord Kelvin), the newly accepted practice was to avoid any explicit mention of their religious convictions in their scientific writings. However, many of the scientific ideas that emerged in the nineteenth and twentieth centuries have reflected Christian themes. Thus the monotheistic unity of the triune Godhead, the relationship of the Persons of God within the Trinity, and the mystery of God in Christ being both divine and human in the incarnation resonate with new scientific discoveries that reveal the unity of creation, the interrelatedness of nature, and the paradoxical dimensions of reality.

Although the Newtonian synthesis established the universality of natural laws, especially in the law of universal gravitation, the emphasis on material particles separated in absolute space resulted in a mechanistic worldview of isolated and independent entities. This led to the deistic view of a clock-maker God who is no longer needed. Several scientific developments in the nineteenth century showed the inadequacy of this Newtonian view and revealed a new degree of unity and interdependence in nature, reflecting the Christian truth that "all things have been created through him and for him . . . and in him all things hold together" (Col. 1:16–17 TNIV). The energy concept was found to apply to all natural phenomena, relating them by the principle of conservation of energy in all its forms, including mechanical, heat, chemical, electromagnetic, biological, and nuclear. The field concept of Faraday and Maxwell unified electromagnetism and optics, showing that all particles are interconnected by electromagnetic fields and waves. The theory of evolution suggested that all forms of life are connected by a common ancestry.[39]

In the early nineteenth century, it was thought that God wasn't needed for the operation of the physical universe but that His design and activity were still evident in living organisms. Later in the century, Darwin's theory of evolution challenged this view and the prevailing idea of the "fixity of species" that seemed to reflect a literal reading of the Genesis account of creation. To account for such facts as the extinction of species in the fossil record and the geographical variations of life forms, Darwin introduced the ideas of competition between species, "natural selection" and "survival of the fittest" acting over long periods of time, leading to the emergence of new species. Although this appeared to many Christians as a contradiction of the Genesis record, others saw the processes of evolution to be one of the means of God's creative activity in nature. In his book *Darwin's Forgotten Defenders*, David Livingstone documents many Christian thinkers at the turn of the century who saw no threat from evolution, including some who helped establish the doctrine of scriptural inerrancy.[40]

The relational dimensions of nature have been further confirmed in the twentieth century by relativity and quantum theories, connecting space with time, matter with energy, and particles with waves.[41] But these discoveries have also revealed a paradoxical dualism that is most evident in quantum theory. This dualism that physicists now see at the heart of matter raises intriguing possibilities with respect to the dual nature of Christ as both human and divine: "Who, being in very nature God, did not consider equality with God something to be used to his own advantage; rather he made himself nothing by taking the very nature of a servant, being made in human likeness" (Phil. 2:6–7 TNIV). According to Niels Bohr, the classically incompatible concepts of "wave" and "particle" become "complementary" descriptions of atomic events in quantum theory. This duality not only reveals an integral relation between particles and waves that explains many aspects of matter, but it also illustrates how two apparently distinct natures can inhere in a single entity without compromising its integrity.

With the separation of science from its Christian roots, it has become increasingly difficult to identify Christian contributions to science. However, several Christians who have contributed to recent scientific advances are worthy of mention. In 1912 Henrietta Leavitt (1868–1921), daughter of a Congregational minister, discovered the period-luminosity law for certain variables, leading to the discovery of the expansion of the universe. In 1923 Arthur H. Compton (1892–1962), a Presbyterian churchman who later won a Nobel Prize, demonstrated the wave-particle duality of quantum theory. In 1931 the Belgian priest-astronomer Georges Lemaitre (1894–1996) developed the first "Big Bang" theory to explain the expanding universe, although he resisted its implication of evidence for the creation of the universe. American Protestant Charles Townes (b. 1915) shared the 1964 Nobel Prize in physics for work in quantum electronics, leading to the invention of the laser. Barbara McClintock (1902–92), who discovered genetic transpositions ("jumping genes") in plants, is the only American woman with a Protestant background to win a Nobel Prize (1983). American Protestant Francis Collins, director of the Human Genome Project of the National Institutes of Health, led the 1990s effort to map the entire human genome.

Do ideas of modern science support or conflict with Christian thinking?

Modern science has ignored its Christian roots and has substituted the idea of progress as a secularized version of redemption. Although the mechanical view raised new problems about meaning and purpose, leading to Deism, it aided in the growing emphasis on applied science. This was supported by the Protestant ethic and Puritan values, but the resulting idea of progress was often seen as a substitute for Christian redemption. In the nineteenth century, mechanistic science was largely replaced by relational emphases in new ideas associated with energy, evolution, and electromagnetic fields. Much of twentieth-century science has been based on dualistic relationships associating space with time, mass with energy, and particles with waves. These concepts can provide illuminating parallels with christological ideas and trinitarian relationships.

The interaction between science and Christianity over two millennia has been mutually enriching for both in spite of occasional conflict. Christian theology has provided new values and attitudes to free science from polytheistic confusion and motivate it to new levels of understanding and application. Science has led to a new appreciation of the wisdom of God and the unity of His creation. It also has helped to show the interrelationship between all things, which is supremely revealed in the Trinity of God and the incarnation of His Son.

QUESTIONS

1. Why did the scientific revolution emerge in Western civilization?

2. What unique attitudes and values were present in Western Europe to foster the birth and growth of modern science?

3. What were the positive and negative results in Western culture from the development of modern science?

4. What are the greatest areas of conflict and of cooperation between science and faith?

5. What responsibilities does a Christian have in relation to science and technology?

NOTES

1. See, e.g., Ian Barbour, *Religion in an Age of Science* (New York: HarperCollins, 1990); John Hedley Brooke, *Science and Religion: Some Historical Perspectives* (Cambridge: Cambridge Univ. Press, 1991); John Dillenberger, *Protestant Thought and Natural Science* (Garden City, N.Y.: Doubleday, 1960); David Lindberg and Ronald Numbers, eds., *God and Nature: Historical Essays on the Encounter between Christianity and Science* (Berkeley: Univ. of California Press, 1986).

2. Attempts to show how Christianity contributed to the growth of science include R. Hooykaas, *Religion and the Rise of Modern Science* (Grand Rapids: Eerdmans, 1972); Eugene Klaaren, *Religious Origins of Modern Science: Belief in Creation in Seventeenth-Century Thought* (Grand Rapids: Eerdmans, 1977); Robert K. Merton, "Science, Technology and Society in Seventeenth-Century England," *Osiris* 4 (1938); and Collin A. Russell, *Cross-Currents: Interactions between Science and Faith* (Grand Rapids: Eerdmans, 1985).

3. John William Draper, *History of the Conflict between Religion and Science*, 7th ed. (London: Henry S. King, 1876); Andrew Dickson White, *A History of the Warfare of Science and Theology in Christendom*, 2 vols. (New York: Applegon, 1896).

4. Henry Morris, *The Long War against God: The History and Impact of the Creation/Evolution Conflict* (Grand Rapids: Baker, 1990).

5. See especially John 1:1–14; Phil. 2:5–11; Col. 1:15–20.

6. Justin Martyr, *Apology* (c. 150 AD), II.xiii.4, reprinted in Henry Bettenson, ed., *Documents of the Christian Church* (London: Oxford Univ. Press, 1960), 8–9.

7. Tertullian, *De Praescriptione haereticorum* (c. 200 AD), vii, reprinted in Bettenson, *Documents of the Christian Church*, 10.

8. Tertullian, *Apology* (197 AD), xii, reprinted in Bettenson, *Documents of the Christian Church*, 44.

9. Augustine, *Sermon*, Mai 126, 6, in Vernon J. Bourke, ed., *The Essential Augustine* (Indianapolis: Hackett, 1974), 123.

10. Augustine, *The Literal Meaning of Genesis*, 1.19.39 (401–15 AD), quoted by Mark A. Noll, *The Scandal of the Evangelical Mind* (Grand Rapids: Eerdmans, 1994), 202–3.

11. Augustine, *The City of God*, 5.1 (413–26 AD), quoted by David Lindberg, "Science and the Early Church," in Lindberg and Numbers, *God and Nature*, 38.

12. Samuel Sambursky, "John Philoponus," in *Dictionary of Scientific Biography*, ed. Charles Gillispie (New York: Scribner, 1970), 7:134.

13. David Lindberg, *The Beginnings of Western Science* (Chicago: Univ. of Chicago Press, 1992), 302–6.

14. Philoponus, *De Opificio Mundi*, IV, 12 (c. 548 AD), quoted in Samuel Sambursky, *Physical Thought from the Presocratics to the Quantum Physicists* (New York: Pica, 1975), 117.

15. Philoponus, *In Meteorologica*, 47, 18, quoted by Sambursky in "John Philoponus," 135.

16. Philoponus, *In Physica*, 683, 17 and 641, 29 (517 AD), quoted by Sambursky in "John Philoponus," 135.

17. *Council of Chalcedon*, Actio V, Mansi, vii.116 f (451 AD), as quoted in Bettenson, *Documents of the Christian Church*, 72–73.

18. Caroline Walker Bynum, *Holy Feast and Holy Fast* (Berkeley: Univ. of California Press, 1987), 252.

19. George Sarton, *Introduction to the History of Science*, 3 vols. (Baltimore: Williams & Wilkins, 1927–48), 2:70, 310, quoted by Margaret Alic in *Hypatia's Heritage* (Boston: Beacon, 1986), 74, 198.

20. Hildegard of Bingen, *Liber Divinorum Operum Simplicis Hominis and Liber Vitae Meritorum*, quoted in Bynum, *Holy Feast and Holy Fast*, 260.

21. Alic, *Hypatia's Heritage*, 66, 74.

22. Charles Singer, *From Magic to Science* (New York: Boni and Liveright, 1928), 88.

23. Jaroslav Pelikan, *Jesus through the Centuries* (New Haven, Conn.: Yale Univ. Press, 1985), 138.

24. Gilbert Keith Chesterton, *Saint Francis of Assisi* (Garden City, N.Y.: Doubleday, 1931), 51, as quoted in Pelikan, *Jesus through the Centuries*, 138.

25. Roger Bacon, *Opus Majus* (1268), quoted in Sambursky, *Physical Thought*, 154.

26. William of Ockham, *Sentences* I, d. 30, q. 1, trans. Ernest A. Moody, in *Dictionary of Scientific Biography*, 10:173.

27. Jean Buridan, *Questions on the Metaphysics*, bk. 2, q. 2, trans. Ernest A. Moody, in *Dictionary of Scientific Biography*, 2:605.

28. Marshall Claggett, *The Science of Mechanics in the Middle Ages* (Madison: Univ. of Wisconsin Press, 1959), 519–30.

29. Jean Buridan, *Questions on the Four Books on the Heavens and the World of Aristotle*, bk. 2, q. 12 (7); trans. from the Latin by Marshall Clagett in *The Science of Mechanics in the Middle Ages* (Madison: Univ. of Wisconsin Press, 1959), 562.

30. Charles Schmitt, "Philoponus' Commentary on Aristotle's *Physics* in the Sixteenth Century," in *Philoponus and the Rejection of Aristotelian Science*, ed. Richard Sorabji (London: Duckworth, 1987), 215.

31. Cecil J. Schneer, *The Search for Order* (New York: Harper and Brothers, 1960), 47.

32. Schmitt, "Philoponus' Commentary," 213–18.

33. William A. Wallace, *Prelude to Galileo: Essays on Medieval and Sixteenth-Century Sources of Galileo's Thought* (Boston: D. Reidel, 1981), 136, 196–97.

34. Thomas Kuhn, *The Structure of Scientific Revolutions*, 2nd ed. (Chicago: Univ. of Chicago Press, 1970), 119–20.

35. Gary B. Deason, "Reformation Theology and the Mechanistic Conception of Nature," in Lindberg and Numbers, *God and Nature*, 177.
36. Richard S. Westfall, "The Rise of Science and the Decline of Orthodox Christianity: A Study of Kepler, Descartes, and Newton," in Lindberg and Numbers, *God and Nature*, 229–31.
37. See Oscar Cullmann, *Christ and Time* (London: SCM, 1951), 51–60, 211–13.
38. John Dillenberger, *Protestant Thought and Natural Science*, 128–32; Charles Webster, "Puritanism, Separatism, and Science," in Lindberg and Numbers, *God and Nature*, 192–217.
39. See Alfred North Whitehead, *Science and the Modern World* (New York: Macmillan, 1925), chap. 6.
40. David N. Livingstone, *Darwin's Forgotten Defenders: The Encounter between Evangelical Theology and Evolutionary Thought* (Grand Rapids: Eerdmans, 1987).
41. Whitehead, *Science and the Modern World*, chaps. 7–8.

SUGGESTED READING

Barbour, Ian G. *Issues in Science and Religion*. Englewood Cliffs, N.J.: Prentice-Hall, 1966.
Brooke, J. H. *Science and Religion: Some Historical Perspectives*. Cambridge and New York: Cambridge University Press, 1991.
Klaaren, Eugene. *Religious Origins of Modern Science*. Grand Rapids: Eerdmans, 1977.
Livingstone, David N. *Putting Science in Its Place: Geographies of Scientific Knowledge*. Chicago and London: University of Chicago Press, 2003.
McGrath, Alister E. *Science and Religion: An Introduction*. Oxford: Blackwell, 1999.
Russell, Colin A. *Cross-Currents: Interactions between Science and Faith*. Grand Rapids: Eerdmans, 1985.

2 WHAT ARE THE PHILOSOPHICAL IMPLICATIONS OF CHRISTIANITY FOR THE NATURAL SCIENCES?

E. David Cook and Robert C. O'Connor

How do we know what there is?

As human beings, we have to make assumptions when we engage with the world around us. Philosophically these are about ontology (what there is), epistemology (how we know what there is), and communication (how we talk about what there is and our knowing of it). Science assumes that the world makes sense and that human beings can make sense of the world that makes sense. Philosophy says that there is an inherent intelligibility in the nature of things and an inherent intelligence in the nature of people.

The various methods of science proceed on the basis that the world has order and purpose. It is not accidental, nor is it unstable. It is relatively fixed and reliable. These underlying assumptions we often call the laws of nature. Science not only helps us understand the relationships and interactions between different parts of the world, but it can only proceed if we assume such relationships and interactions. Of course, these assumptions must also work in practice. When we assume that the world makes sense and we act on that basis, the results must be what we expect and the power and control over nature real and consistent.

Likewise, we have to rely on our human capacities to know and understand things. This knowledge and understanding develop and change as new information or new insight into old information comes along. But unless our knowledge works in practice, we will not continue to rely on it.

The Christian has a very simple appreciation for these underlying assumptions. God made the world so that it makes sense, and He made human beings so that we can make sense of the world.

Science offers us different levels of explanation and descriptions of what is there. The nature of being can be described in many differing ways—at the subatomic or atomic level or as real objects. For example, we can describe a rock or a chair as an object we can throw or sit on. Or we can describe these objects as particular combinations of atoms—electrons, protons, and neutrons. We can also offer an account in terms of a concatenation of subatomic particles. These different descriptions all describe the same thing—a rock or a chair—but at very different levels and for very different purposes. The world is real and not just a figment or creation of our imagination. Science enables us to know that the world is real and what its nature is. We are able to work with and direct and control our dealings with nature only because science gives us reliable and useful accounts of reality.

What is natural law, and why do we talk about it?

Scientists, philosophers, and theologians all talk about natural law. It is the idea that there is a law in the nature of things and a law in the nature of people. Scientific observations enable us to form hypotheses (reasons why we are experiencing what we find). We test these hypotheses to try to prove them false. This is an interesting method designed because of Cartesian doubt.[1] Descartes suggested that we should try to find what is absolutely certain, what is known by "clear and distinct perception" and "beyond all possible doubt." The method he used to arrive at absolute certainty was to try to doubt everything he knew. If he discovered some knowledge that was beyond all possible doubt, then that was what he really knew to be the case or perceived with clear and distinct perception. Since then, whether in the search for verification,[2] trying to prove that something is true, or falsification,[3] trying to prove that something is false, the final conclusion is that whatever is left after these processes is the case and can be relied on.

Scientists have tended to stress the method of falsification, not to cast real doubt, but rather to arrive at what has to be the case. This knowledge is not absolute but is the best we can do in light of all that we know and is accepted until some better, more reliable knowledge comes along. Human knowledge is always frail and subject to revision. That should make us humble and exceedingly careful in claiming neither too much nor too little. For the practicing scientist, what we know must work in practice and enable us better to relate to and work with the world in all its aspects.

Natural law suggests that there are various regularities in nature that we often describe as cause and effect relationships.[4] We can give general descriptions of these regularities as natural laws that tell us that this is how nature generally operates, that we can rely on this, and that if we discover something that doesn't behave according to these rules, we need to look for an explanation as to why this has happened in this way.

When we talk about natural law in relation to people, we are referring to moral laws that lie at the very heart of what it means to be human. There are certain ways of living that are good for people and certain ways that are harmful for people. If I drink three bottles of whiskey and smoke one hundred cigarettes a day, my body will be affected. Such a way of living is not good for me or any human being. In contrast, following the natural law will allow human beings to flourish.[5] It is easy to see how this fits well with the understanding that God created the world so that there is a basic moral law in nature and in humanity. The moral law in nature is based on the fact that we reap what we sow. Actions have consequences. We experience results from what we do and what we fail to do. Loud shouting in Alpine areas may cause avalanches. Failing to obey explicit warnings and skiing off the piste in Colorado may result in being engulfed in a snowdrift.

The moral law in the nature of people is often associated with the innate knowledge of right and wrong we usually call conscience. Human beings know that killing people is wrong, and that seems to be a universal moral standard. Of course, in war or in violent situations, people are killed, but the very fact that we have to justify such killing by referring to war or violence shows that the general moral law still holds, other things being equal.

Does the world make sense?

Science proceeds on the assumption that the world is rational and makes sense. It also proceeds by assuming that human beings are rational and able to make sense and understand the world and its varying degrees of order. Christians believe that God made the world, and because He is a rational, reasonable God, He imbued the world with that rationality in the very nature of things. In the same way, He gave reason and rational abilities to human beings so we are able to make sense of the world and all that is in it.

Because things do make sense, scientific work can proceed. To properly understand the nature and essence of what we are exploring, we need to be true to the nature of what there is. There is no point in trying to find microscopic realities using a telescope. The nature of the chemical makeup of a rock may not tell us all we need to know about its mechanical and biological capacities.

To be rational is to be conditioned by the nature of the object.[6] The good scientist matches his or her approach to the object in light of what that object is and how it behaves. Rationality is fundamental to science and being human.

Is there such a thing as scientific truth?

Philosophy, like science, is in the business of the search for truth. Science uses empirical methods while philosophy is more a matter of critical reflection on the different methods and the presuppositions behind them. There are different theories of truth, and philosophy has identified three major approaches. The first is the coherence theory of truth, which argues that when a piece of information or new knowledge is discovered, it must fit with what we know already. It literally must cohere. If it doesn't fit in, it doesn't make any sense and is incoherent. The next theory of truth is correspondence.[7] This was formalized by the Empiricist school, which stressed the match between our empirical experience of the world and how we describe that experience. The description should match or correspond with the reality. A good football commentator offers a verbal description that corresponds with what is happening on the field of play. But it is possible to have two different descriptions that are equally coherent and correspond with the realities they describe. How then can we decide between them? Some philosophers suggest that there is a pragmatic test of truth that reduces to which of the theories is more productive in helping humans handle and control the world.

Obviously, human truth is never closed and final. It is always subject to revision and new knowledge. But that does not mean that we cannot rely on what we do know.

Jesus described Himself as "the way and the truth and the life" (John 14:6). In Colossians 1, Paul describes how Jesus is the Lord of creation and the Lord of the church. He is the eternal Logos—principle of order and truth. As scientists pursue truth, Christians believe that the basis of that truth is God Himself and His Son, Jesus. That understanding has underpinned the multitude of Christians who have pursued scientific research and development as part of their Christian mission and service. The good news is that the Creator God is a God who reveals Himself and His nature in the world itself, in and through history, and most of all in the incarnation, life, death, and resurrection of Jesus Christ. The Bible is God's express revelation that helps us understand all that God is and has revealed to humankind.

How does philosophy relate to scientific inquiry?

There has been a good deal of discussion in recent years of the "design inference"—that is, the claim that the inability of natural science to account for certain biological phenomena, like bacteria flagella, provides evidence for the existence of a designer. It is important to note, however, that this inference design depends on how we understand the very nature of scientific inquiry.[8] Still, proponents of intelligent design insist that design should be considered a rival to the scientific theory of evolution and so should have its place in public school classrooms right along with its rival. Clearly, then, whatever philosophical implications commitment to design might carry have a bearing on a social issue that deeply divides our culture. Society in general, and Christians in particular, simply cannot ignore these philosophical controversies as they arise in the practice and teaching of science.

First, proponents of intelligent design insist that the inference is strictly scientific, that is, based on empirical, scientific evidence and proceeding by a kind of scientific assessment of that data.[9] Many scientists, however, reject the inference to design because they believe it goes beyond a strictly scientific analysis of empirical data. That is, the inference to an intelligent agent goes beyond the bounds of proper scientific investigation. If this is so, then no matter how good the argument is for an intelligent design agent, it should not be the subject of scientific study nor gain a hearing in the science classroom. Should we understand science in such a way as to exclude appeal to divine agency, or should the practice of science accommodate research in this area?

Second, according to the design inference, it is precisely in those areas where science fails to account for the specified complexity of some particular entity, structure, or event that scientists might appeal to intelligent agency.[10] Advocates of this argument insist that this is not an argument from ignorance, or what is sometimes called god-of-the-gaps reasoning, precisely because it does not depend on the claim that we simply don't know or cannot tell what caused that phenomenon. Rather, the argument maintains that what we have learned through scientific inquiry shows that natural processes simply do not have the resources to explain it. Based on what we know, nature could not have produced this phenomenon. However, this raises the question of the ability of the scientific method to reveal the workings of nature. Should we be so confident in the findings of science as to suppose that if science hasn't explained some phenomenon, then we cannot account for it by natural means?

Third, a close look at this movement also reveals what looks to be an ambivalent attitude toward the inference to design. In particular, some who endorse design resist the claim that they mean to prove the existence of God. William Dembski even goes so far as to say that there is no intent to establish the existence of a designer of any stripe.[11] Like many theoretical entities in science, design functions as a heuristic device, a way of thinking about the world—as if designed—that will lead scientists into fruitful avenues of research. Although Dembski remains one of the strongest proponents of design, he suggests that we should not take the reference to "a designer" literally, as referring to an actual intelligent agent. But here again, the reader might wonder just how common and how proper it would be to adopt such an attitude toward the theoretical posits of science. Is this ploy simply a way to finesse the question whether, when design proponents speak of design, they mean to refer to God, and so to preserve room for investigating design in the publicly funded scientific laboratory and classroom?

These three areas represent the kinds of philosophical questions confronting Christians who must assess some of the findings of science, particularly those that appear in conflict with their prior religious commitments. First, how should Christians understand the scientific method? How can we determine what is and what is not appropriate to scientific research? Second, how confident can we be in the accuracy and scope of the findings of science? Does the scientific method provide the means for discerning every aspect of the world? Or are there aspects of reality that lie beyond the reach of scientific investigation? Finally, how shall we interpret the findings of science? When we accept a scientific theory, have we thereby committed ourselves to all that theory says about the world in which we live?

These questions provide a glimpse at what we might call the philosophical implications of the natural sciences. The philosophy of science is that discipline that considers these and many more concerns regarding the interpretation of science, both its methods and its findings. And, as is apparent, how we answer these questions will bear very strongly on how we construe the relation between science and Christian belief. Without first answering questions on the nature of scientific method, on the reach of scientific reasoning, or on how to interpret the findings of science, we cannot even begin to address whether science conflicts with the teachings of the Bible, whether it supports it, whether it might make a difference in how we should interpret the Bible, or whether a biblical worldview might make a difference in the outcome of scientific research.

The single most important feature that drives our philosophical inquiry into their methods, their reach, and the status of their findings is the extraordinary success that the sciences have enjoyed in recent years. Because scientific inquiry, unlike other disciplines, provides unimpeachable knowledge of the natural world, we are tempted to think that its methods are distinct and uniquely powerful. Second, because when compared to other disciplines scientific methods have proven so reliable, we are tempted to think that they provide the sole means of discovery. Finally, because scientific findings have so successfully withstood rigorous experimental tests, we are inclined to regard them as most certainly real.

So, with an eye toward comprehending how to understand the methods and findings of science in light of our Christian beliefs, we should ask, first, whether science has a distinctive method for discerning the nature of reality; second, whether there may be alternative means for investigating the world; and finally, what attitude we should adopt toward the theoretical posits of our very best scientific investigations.

What is the scientific method?

Many science textbooks have an opening chapter on the scientific method. It is that procedure about which you have heard ad nauseam since your elementary school days. Science, we are told, begins with pure observations of the world. According to the caricature, these observations are compiled, collated, and compressed, like so much sausage, into the general laws of nature. Initially these laws function as hypotheses. According to these generalizations, under certain conditions we can expect certain structures, powers, forces, causal processes, or mechanisms to produce specific, measurable outcomes. We may observe these outcomes under the right conditions in nature, or as is more likely, we can set up artificial conditions in the laboratory to confirm our results, and the laws from which they have been derived, with absolute care and confidence. This process preserves the objectivity of science.

This is, of course, a very nice story, one bound to generate a sense of awe and confidence in the discipline. Unfortunately, very little of what passes for science outside of the artifice of the high school laboratory matches this description. For instance, take the notion that a good scientific account must generate predictions that can then be checked and confirmed for accuracy. A school of philosophers in the early twentieth century, logical positivism, maintained that science must proceed according to the hypothetical-deductive method.[12] According to the positivists, the methods of science invariably required formulating what we often call the laws of nature, universal generalizations from which, together with a description of the actual natural conditions, we could deduce a specific phenomenon. A proper scientific explanation, then, had this form:

1. A set of general laws: $L_1, L_2, \ldots L_n$
2. Statements of the initial conditions: C_1
3. The data to be explained: E

In fact, Carl Hempel, the leading voice in positivist philosophy of science in the first part of the twentieth century, maintained that the hypothetical-deductive explanations constitute the only legitimate form of scientific explanation. Now, although many explanations in science can be constructed according to this model, particularly in mechanics, this is not true of all. For instance, the great difficulty in formulating evolutionary biology along the lines of general laws from which one might predict specific data was noted early on. The fact that marsupials are found exclusively in Australia cannot be reduced to a deduction from some initial conditions. Even if those early conditions were known with sufficient detail, there is too much indeterminacy in nature to even generate approximate predictions. Now, you might think, so much the worse for evolution, but were you inclined to accept as legitimate some version of the evolutionary account, you would have serious reason to question this construal of scientific explanations.

Indeed, this rather rigorous notion of explanation—one that made science look like formal logic with deductive consequences—came in for a great deal of other criticism. For instance, on a technical note, one might formulate a general law—such as "no men who take birth control pills get pregnant"—which, when combined with known conditions—"John's been taking his sister's pills"—will predict with complete certainty that John will fail to get pregnant. In spite of conforming to this model, somehow we have failed to explain the event.

A rather different problem arises with respect to confirmation. Were there some question as to whether we were on to the right explanation, we might want to test it out. One might wonder, for instance, whether it was in fact the case that the sun rises every morning, a law whose predictions are confirmed in your experience every day of your life—so long as you spend your days in the middle latitudes. If you never happened to venture sufficiently far north at the right time of year, you would have to regard that "law of nature" perfectly well confirmed. Later thinkers sought to address these worries by insisting that such scientific explanations were to be regarded as probabilistic. So long as we couldn't be sure what future experience might suggest, we could assign a probability to such conclusions. Still, the notion that more and more confirming experience would render more and more probable one's scientific account simply ignored the conceptual difficulties of inductive reasoning.

A consensus began to form, then, that however desirable it might be to model scientific explanations after rigorous structure of logic, the efforts failed to capture the reality.[13] Science appeared far too unruly to fall captive to this simple picture. Further problems emerged with, for instance, evidence that failed to confirm a hypothesis. It was observed that, in scientific practice, often that evidence was ignored, shelved for later consideration, simply dismissed, or accommodated by making compensating revision in the original hypothesis. Like the logic of confirmation, the logic of falsification fell prey to the creative whims of the scientific community. Further, the observational basis of science itself was severely challenged by studies that suggested that what we actually observe in our experience results directly from such factors as what we believe we might see, what kinds of things we expect to experience, the categories by which we already carve up experience, and our social or even psychological cast of mind. Observations in gestalt psychology, in particular, undermined the notion of the observational basis for the objectivity of science. Further studies in the history and sociology of science seemed to strengthen the suspicion that the conclusions of science were less the direct product of objective scientific inquiry than the product of largely unseen subjective and social forces over which the scientific community exercises very little control.

Post-positivist philosophy of science

Thus did inquiry into the scientific method meet with some very hard times in the latter years of the twentieth century. Still, the extraordinary predictive and technological success of the sciences demanded that further attention be given to the question of method. Without presuming to give general conditions on scientific reasoning, the most promising line maintained that science proceeds neither by a purely deductive, nor even inductive process, but rather by what we might call an "inference to the best explanation."[14] Inference to the best explanation sees scientific inquiry as largely concerned with positing the existence of some plausible entity, structure, event, power, liability, force, mechanism, and so on, that, were it real and were it operative, would explain the presence of the phenomenon in question. On this construal, the genius of science is found in formulating a natural phenomenon that may or may never be directly observed, in order to understand how or why some other phenomenon took place. Of course, were one to simply ascribe some fantastic capacity to nature, then one could explain anything without difficulty, so the burden remains to posit an explanation superior to its competition. Thus a person infers from the fact that his or her explanation is best that it is more likely than its rival. Now, in judging his or her account best, the person does, as the traditional account of science surmised, seek accounts that predict with some accuracy but also accounts that fully explain the extant data, fit best with what we know already about the natural operations of the world, lead to further discoveries, unify previous bits of knowledge, and are internally coherent, simple, elegant, aesthetically pleasing, and so forth. The more subjective the list, the more pressing the need to spread the responsibility for judging a hypothesis across the whole scientific community. It was recognized that the process would draw upon personal expectations, prejudices, and bias, but the hope remained that the social give-and-take within the scientific community would serve to mitigate these factors. It is the success of scientific inquiry—the result of these very factors—that suggests that this very messy process provides some insight into the nature of the world.

So the question of method leaves us with a rather vague, decidedly messy process of discerning within the community of scientists the explanation that accounts best for the phenomenon in question, accounting for known observations and suggesting new observations, all the while fitting the explanation into our previous understanding of the world. This is what the intelligent design theorists mean by offering intelligent agency to account for these otherwise inexplicable natural phenomena.[15] The postulate of intelligent agency provides the best account, for experience teaches that intelligent agents do introduce design into the natural world, and we know that the design evident in these phenomena is far too complex and specific to these purposes for natural processes or chance to explain. The best explanation, intelligent design theorists maintain, is design. Whether or not we regard this particular kind of explanation as falling within the proper domain of science, it certainly follows the mode of explanation commonly utilized by science.

Does the method of science provide a reliable and comprehensive guide to understanding the world?

Based on our previous comments on scientific reasoning, we may have some reason to doubt whether we should rely fully on the findings of science. Recall that the design inference was based on the inability of science to account for certain phenomena. Yet proponents insist that it is not an argument from ignorance, since, were there natural means by which these phenomena might occur, science would have revealed them to us. Quite to the contrary, our best science maintains that these phenomena could not have occurred by natural means. However, if our brief survey of scientific reasoning is correct, there may be ample reason to question whether the findings of science should carry the weight design theorists apparently grant them.

While science may provide the best explanation for these natural phenomena, we must recognize the significant limitations on our reasoning. First, as is evident in the history of science, scientists can consider only those explanations that happen to occur to them. At most, the best explanation can only be the best among all explanations presently considered. This form of inference is by its very nature vulnerable to the limitations of human imagination. Now this is not to say that scientific posits must be wrong. We may well have hit upon some explanations that accurately portray significant portions of the world. The long-term success of some of the central features of science suggests we have probably gotten something right. Arguably, the central functions of biological development are unlikely to face wholesale revision. Still, we remain fallible. There are real limitations to our ability to discern every feature of our world and to grasp, or even imagine, every process responsible for its development. Indeed, this limitation is nowhere more evident than in a survey of the history of science. Thomas Kuhn's work in the history of science served well to establish the truth: no belief in science is more certain than that scientists make lots and lots of mistakes.[16]

The criteria by which we judge one account superior to its competitors are based on an extensive set of background beliefs. To deem an explanation best because of its natural fit with other phenomena clearly presumes that one's beliefs about those other phenomena is accurate as well. If science seeks a kind of unity whereby every area of investigation draws from other independent sources of knowledge, the ideal will constitute a very tightly woven web of beliefs. This may provide some confidence. It should, however, cause pause, for were every part dependent on some other, an error in one would have a significant ripple effect across the whole.

All this is to say that we should take great care in supposing that science can pronounce with confidence what may not happen. We can claim with some confidence what we think has happened. We haven't found reason yet for a kind of scientific skepticism. Still, insofar as science depends on the imagination of scientific genius and depends for its judgments on such a broad array of beliefs, we may want to be careful not to make too strong of a claim about what nature is incapable of achieving. As such, intelligent design must judge it more likely that these phenomena are the direct result of intelligent agency than that, in spite of our very human limitations, we have exhausted our natural explanatory resources, and all this in spite of the lesson of this history of science.

Can we regard the findings of science as providing us access to the hidden features of reality?

Finally, we come to the point where we can address the status of the findings of science. How should we interpret the claims of science? Where scientific theory mentions a certain entity (say, a "charmed quark") or a certain force or power (like gravity) or a certain mechanism or process (like the Kreb cycle of macro-evolution), the questions remains: "Should we interpret theory as referring to something that actually exists—the real world?" What if there is no way to directly observe that phenomenon? Should we suppose that scientists are referring to actual entities, things that would exist whether or not scientists or scientific theories ever said anything about them at all? Recall again that Dembski sometimes refers to the designer as referring not to a real entity, but rather as simply sketching out a way of going about one's research, anticipating discoveries as if the world were designed.

In many respects, much of what we have said thus far in our analysis supports just this view. Since science so often gets things wrong, and since its findings are dependent on the imaginations and intersubjective judgments of its very human, culturally embedded participants, there would appear to be ample reason to suspect that even the best of our scientific theories may well be mistaken. Is there reason to retain any confidence in scientific investigations at all? As we pointed out earlier, the single most impressive feature of science, that which earns it its exalted status, is its predictive and technological success. The reason we might suppose that science is actually on to something real, existing independently of our theories and not unlike what our theories actually say about it, is the success of our theories in helping us sort out the world.[17]

We mentioned a number of criteria by which scientists do judge their hypotheses, including such features as explanatory success, predictability, fit with other beliefs, internal coherence, fertility, simplicity, elegance, and aesthetic charm. According to tradition, it is insofar as our theories are grounded in empirical data, the evidence of the senses, that we can have confidence that what they tell us about the world accurately reflects that reality. If it looks like a duck, quacks like a duck, and so on, it must be a duck. Furthermore, the more able a theory is to predict— if it is a duck, it will walk like a duck—the more likely it is to be true. So it looks as if explanatory success and predictability provide just the link with the world that should assure us of a right construal. However, we must bear in mind that if science does move forward by affirming just those theories that best explain its data— and it appears that it must—then the supposition that it is a duck may account well for the data at hand, and it may even accurately predict further features yet still be subject to the uncertainties of interpretation. On this construal, even the duck is an imaginative construct, designed to account for our experiences past and future. Being a construct, the suspicion is that we may see a duck only because, being duck season, it is what we want, or need, to see. Can we be so confident that what we see reflects accurately the nature of the world around us?

Such considerations, coupled with the mistakes of science evident in its history, have prompted many to embrace the kind of nonrealism that Dembski espouses for design. There is reason, however, to resist this move. In particular, if a theory proves fertile—that is, if a theory not only makes predictions but leads to observations and fruitful theoretical developments that were simply not anticipated when that theory was first proposed—this may provide some reason for thinking that it actually depicts something of reality. What makes even the observations, much more the theories we construct, suspect is the notion that they are fabricated to serve an interpretive purpose. Prediction alone cannot allay this suspicion if that prediction is of the sort we would expect in just such circumstances. What would speak most powerfully for the reality of the entity posited would be an observation that was unanticipated, even one that was originally thought to conflict, yet that comported well with the interpretation at hand. The best explanation of the ability of the postulate to account for these unanticipated, even supposedly contrary, phenomena would be that it must have gotten something about the world right. This is the argument for realism.

In this respect, maybe Dembski is correct to withhold belief in the reality of the intelligent agent until such time as the research program leads to phenomena that would not otherwise have been expected, but revealed and fully accounted for by design. Until that time, the scientist may well simply consider design a kind of heuristic device, a way of thinking about the world and planning research, rather than as an actual power or force intruding into the natural realm.

How do we relate science and Christian belief?

Where do these philosophical remonstrations leave us in our understanding of the natural sciences? Hopefully they provide a rather more realistic, even if chastened, attitude toward the rational force and the scope of scientific inquiry. There is a process, it seems, by which the sciences can tell us about the workings of the world in which we live. The sciences cannot tell us everything there is to know about the world; still, they speak with some authority about actual natural processes. We must advance scientific findings, however, with a fair bit of humility, recognizing that we are very likely wrong about a good deal and have a great deal yet to learn. Science, as a discipline, provides a means by which to gain insight into a particular domain of reality, that concerning the natural world and its workings. At its best, the sciences provide the best account to date of a limited domain of experience. Insofar as these methods suggest a general strategy for understanding our world in every respect, we must consider the adequacy of the best explanations science provides relative to explanations that draw upon other resources, for instance, those that appeal to intelligent agency. This philosophical analysis of scientific inquiry provides the basis for understanding the dynamics of the challenge to science by design.

From the pre-Socratics to modern times, our worldviews and philosophies of life affect our learning and ways of conducting science. We need to be aware of a possible danger of failing to understand the different bases and methodologies of faith and the sciences. Simply put, flawed science can skew faith and flawed faith can skew science.

Aristotle's philosophy and scientific approach became so closely tied to the development of the Christian faith that when Galileo, Newton, and Copernicus found that the evidence for Aristotelian physics and cosmology was flawed and required a new understanding (known as the Copernican view of the world and Newtonian physics), the church largely opposed and failed to recognize the truth of what was being suggested. The church had become overly dependent on a particular philosophy, and faith itself came under attack as obscurantist. We need to have a sound and proper relationship between our faith and our scientific learning so that each is conducted properly and neither is misused or abused. Partnership is the key and the ground for the integration of what we believe into every aspect of our motivation for and practice of science and every branch of human learning. We must do justice to good science and to the truth of God's wonderful revelation.

QUESTIONS

1. How can Christians properly draw on science to refine our understanding of God?

2. How does philosophy help us understand science and the nature of God and human beings?

3. What does the success of scientific inquiry tell us about how God has designed humans?

4. Does appeal to the existence of God in the Bible explain more than does naturalistic materialism?

NOTES

1. R. Descartes, *A Discourse on Method, Meditations and Principles*, trans. J. Veitch, Everyman's Library (London: S. M. Dent & Sons, 1963).
2. See A. J. Ayer, *Language, Truth and Logic* (New York: Dover, 1946).
3. See K. Popper, *Conjectures and Refutations: The Growth of Scientific Knowledge* (London: Routledge, 1963).
4. K. Rahner, *Encyclopedia of Theology: The Concise Sacramentum Mundi* (New York: Crossroad, 1975).
5. See David Cook, *Dilemmas of Life* (Downers Grove, Ill.: InterVarsity Press, 1990).
6. See T. F. Torrance, *God and Rationality* (London: Oxford Univ. Press, 1971).
7. See "Coherence and Pragmatic Thesis of Faith" in *Encyclopedia of Philosophy*, ed. P. Edward (New York: Macmillan, 1967).
8. A good place to become familiar with the recent work of intelligent design is William A. Dembski, *The Design Revolution: Answering the Toughest Questions about Intelligent Design* (Downers Grove, Ill.: InterVarsity Press, 2004).
9. William A. Dembski, *Intelligent Design: The Bridge between Science and Theology* (Downers Grove, Ill.: InterVarsity Press, 1999), 106–7.
10. Dembski, *Design Revolution*, 27.
11. Ibid., 190.
12. For a helpful overview of this discussion, see Peter Kosso, *Reading the Book of Nature: An Introduction to the Philosophy of Science* (Cambridge: Cambridge Univ. Press, 1992), chap. 3.
13. Thomas S. Kuhn, *The Structure of Scientific Revolutions*, 3rd ed. (Chicago: Univ. of Chicago Press, 1996), provides the classic articulation of many of these worries about the traditional conception of scientific reasoning. Philip Kitcher, *The Advancement of Science: Science without Legend, Objectivity with Illusions* (Oxford: Oxford Univ. Press, 1993), provides a readable summary of much contemporary thinking on these issues.
14. Peter Liption, *Inference to the Best Explanation* (New York: Routledge, 1991).
15. Dembski, *Design Revolution*, 42.
16. Kuhn, *Structure of Scientific Revolutions*, passim.
17. Stathis Psillos, *Scientific Realism: How Science Tracks Truth* (New York: Routledge, 1999).

SUGGESTED READING

Goldstein, Martin, and Inge F. Goldstein. *How We Know: An Exploration of the Scientific Process*. New York: Da Capo Press, 1993.

Kosso, Peter. *Reading the Book of Nature: An Introduction to the Philosophy of Science*. Cambridge: Cambridge University Press, 1992.

Kreeft, Peter. *Back to Virtue*. San Francisco: Ignatius Press, 1992.

Moreland, J. P. *Christianity and the Nature of Science: A Philosophical Investigation*. Grand Rapids: Baker, 1989.

Trigg, Roger. *Rationality and Science: Can Science Explain Everything?* Cambridge: Blackwell, 1993.

WHAT ARE THE THEOLOGICAL IMPLICATIONS FOR NATURAL SCIENCE?

Vincent E. Bacote and Stephen R. Spencer

What is theology?

Theology, etymologically, is words about God or the study of God. Thus any conversation about God is a form of theology. But more specifically, theology is the study of the triune God in relation with human beings and the entire creation. Such study involves some concept of God and His relation to His creation and an investigation of the coherent structure of human knowledge about God. The results of such studies may be presented in various forms—orally, in writing, or in other media.

What are some different kinds of theology?

Christian theology is the study of the Christian God, the triune God, the Father, the Son, and the Spirit.

Biblical theology can be defined in several ways. In one sense, any theology that is faithful to the teachings of the Bible, the Christian Scripture, is biblical theology. A common use of the term would describe a theology that seeks to elaborate the teachings of Scripture by using the distinctive concepts, vocabulary, and emphases of the various units of Scripture, arranged by genres (e.g., prophets, gospels, epistles), historical groupings (e.g., exilic, postexilic, eighth-century prophets), authors (e.g., Mosaic, Pauline, Johannine), by testament (Old Testament theology or New Testament theology), or even the entire biblical corpus (sometimes now called "whole Bible theology"). Some definitions set biblical theology in opposition to any theology that uses church traditions, creeds, confessions, or postcanonical theological writings. This opposition, though quite common in some quarters, is not necessary to biblical theology and is best rejected.

Historical theology studies the teachings and practices of the Christian church (primarily postcanonical), seeking to understand them in their historical and cultural contexts and often to evaluate their fidelity and significance.

Systematic theology, sometimes called *dogmatic theology*, seeks to develop a faithful and thus coherent or integrated understanding of the teachings of Scripture, drawing not only on Scripture itself, but also on historical theology as well as a wide range of other disciplines such as history, philosophy, literature, science, sociology, anthropology, and the arts, among others.

How do theologians "do" theology?

Theologians disagree about the proper theological method(s), but many from a variety of traditions would agree that theology is supremely the interpretation of Scripture as God's written Word, in the context of the church's faithful tradition of teaching, worshiping, and confessing Christ in and to the world. Theology seeks to understand Scripture as God's Word for the church's life of service for Him in contemporary cultures. Thus doing theology is never completed but is an ongoing Spirit-empowered process of Christians hearing and obeying God's Word in the ever-changing historical contexts of the church.

Scripture is God's culminating word about Christ and His redemption of the fallen creation. It is not God's only revelation, however, so it must not be read in isolation from the created order or the history and cultural life of humanity. Moreover, readers must acknowledge others who also have read Scripture. Scripture is the final authority over the church, but no reader of Scripture "between the times" of Christ's comings is a final interpreter of Scripture. Thus all scriptural readings are corrigible, subject to more faithful readings of Scripture, and informed by more faithful studies of the created order, human history, and cultures.

1. REVELATION OF TRUTH/HERMENEUTICS

How can humans know or understand truth?

Humans know because God made them capable of knowing, that is, able to perceive, understand, reason, and communicate. According to the first chapters of Genesis, God spoke to Adam and Eve from the earliest moments of their lives, identifying them and their responsibilities, and they responded. Humans were language users from the beginning of their lives, and the initial language they heard and understood was God speaking to them.

How has God communicated to humans?

God's speech to humans began to disclose His will and thus something of Himself. In addition, God made the world in such a way that it speaks of the One who made it. This perhaps can be inferred from God's repeated approval of what He makes (Gen. 1), but Psalms 8 and 19 clearly teach it. The psalmist describes the creation as "declaring" the glory of God and "proclaiming" the work of His hands. As Psalm 19:3–4 notes, this is equally God's speech, though nonverbal. Elsewhere Scripture records God's self-disclosure by what He says and does on specific occasions in specific places, beyond His daily providential care for and direction of the created order. God's actions in these "special" events (that is, distinctive or nonregular) also communicate something about Him.

Christian theology often classifies these divine self-disclosing communications into two categories: (1) that which is through God's creation, sustenance, and direction of the created order, a disclosure that is regular, repeated, and universal throughout His creation (variously called *general*, *natural*, or *creational revelation*); and (2) that which is not regular, customary, and universal, but rather distinctive in place and time, usually related to the unfolding development of redemption (called *special revelation*). This may be verbal or nonverbal and culminates in the incarnate Son, Jesus of Nazareth.

How do God's modes of communicating to humans relate to each other?

These two modes of God's communication to humans should not be considered alternative or competing sources of knowledge about God, for, from God's speaking in the garden, to His speaking through Moses about the plagues on Egypt, to Jesus' discourses interpreting His sign miracles, Scripture suggests a pattern whereby God's speech interprets God's nonverbal actions. What God says to His imagers guides their understanding of His nonverbal actions.

Can humans reliably know the external world?

Human knowledge may be characterized as a form of *realism* or, more specifically, *critical realism* or *perspectival critical realism*.[1] When used in reference to epistemology (the study of knowledge), realism affirms that humans can know reality beyond themselves, in various measures of accuracy or reliability, with conditions and qualifications. Critical realism (in contrast to "naive realism") acknowledges that humans do not infallibly know reality and thus must beware of believing unquestioningly their experiences. The critical analysis of persons' experiences and their claims to inform them of external reality makes knowledge claims "corrigible," that is, subject to correction. Because humans are always situated in a multitude of ways (for instance, historically, socioculturally, ethnically), human knowledge is "perspectival" rather than universal and inclusive.

What is the role of sense experience in human knowing?

Humans know and understand in many ways. One of the most obvious ways we know and understand is sense experience (or *empirical knowledge*), whether by direct sense experience of what is being studied, through the sensory experience of instruments, or by receiving information from other people. Modern science can be faulted for tending to reduce the legitimate ways of knowing to sensory experience, but empirical knowledge is surely prominent. Note also how often Scripture mentions people seeing, hearing, tasting, touching, or even smelling (note, e.g., the common use of incense in Israel's worship in the tabernacle and temple). Remarkably, John opens his first letter by asserting, "That which was from the beginning, which we have *heard*, which we have *seen with our eyes*, which we have *looked at* and our *hands have touched*—this we proclaim to you concerning the Word of life" (1 John 1:1 TNIV, emphasis added).

What role does reasoning play in knowledge?

Knowledge gained from sense experience is not complete in itself, of course. Reasoning is crucial to knowledge. We make rational judgments about what we see and hear. We can challenge or correct what we receive or infer further premises. Our reasoning is heavily dependent on what we learn through our senses, our primary way of contact and communication with other people as well as with the external world. But by reasoning we are also able to consider what we already know and elaborate on that by inference or even construct thoughts by imagination.

Is community a significant factor in human knowledge?

Learning is profoundly communal. Students learn in classes or study groups. They learn from teachers and from books that communicate the knowledge of previous students of these subjects. Such group or "traditional" ("passed on") learning is essential to education. All learning involves individual effort, but most learning also involves others' efforts, from the earliest days of parental instruction to mature scholarship as members of a research team or department faculty surrounded by libraries and databases.

How important is creativity in knowing?

Creativity and imagination play an essential role in knowing and in teaching others. Problem solving, for instance, often requires creative, imaginative analysis. In the sciences, creativity and imagination also play significant roles in theory formation. Of course, creativity can be reckless or irresponsible, misleading or confusing, and thus requires good judgment. In some disciplines, such as theology, it has often been considered unscholarly. However, for helpfully rephrasing questions, developing fresh approaches to long-standing problems, or applying new insights, students should cultivate skillful, imaginative thinking.

What are the limits of human knowledge?

Some fundamental truths apply in all intellectual activity. Humans are finite, not infinite. Spatially and temporally limited, they are intellectually limited as well. Humans are "fearfully and wonderfully made," but they are made with limits on how they know, what they can know, and how much they can understand. Though humans image God, they are derivative replicas on an infinitely smaller scale. This "downsizing" necessarily results in limitations for the image that do not apply to the original.

Humans are further limited in that they are not in "original condition," but are damaged by sinfulness. Though the effects of sinfulness do not nullify efforts to know, humans are fallible, able to err intellectually, morally, and volitionally. They deceive and are deceived. Mistakes, by misperception, misunderstanding, or erroneous reasoning illustrate such fallibility. Information may be suppressed or distorted, and incorrect conclusions may be drawn from correct information.

How important is intellectual humility?

Humans should always be cautious about their intellectual activities, so the virtue of humility is essential to being good knowers. It is always possible that knowledge claims are wrong at any given point. If not entirely wrong, then perhaps they are wrong in some measure, by omission or overemphasis of some aspect. Claims to know are "corrigible," that is, correctible. Good scholarship, whether in science or any other discipline, should be open to correction from one's own new discoveries, new interpretations, or further analysis or from others.

What is the role of interpretation in knowing?

Acquiring knowledge is sometimes described as though it were like gathering objects. People may imagine that "facts" exist in prepackaged form, waiting to be selected, as if they were picking up seashells on the beach or gathering stones from a field. According to this view, knowledge is accumulating facts, arranging them into larger, more complex structures of truths.

But this seems mistaken in several ways. Gaining knowledge is more complex than merely gathering prefabricated pieces. Knowing also involves making judgments and interpreting or assigning significance. Even "gathering" requires interpreting various objects, events, relationships, information, and statements—is that mushroom safe or poisonous? What kinds of rock are soft or solid? What species of bird looks like that at this season of the year in this location? Does this instrument reading indicate a malfunction or a significant new result? Was a step omitted or incorrectly performed? In these ways and many more, humans continually interpret what is presented to them as potential for knowledge. Rather than being available and ready-made, "facts" may be understood as formulated judgments about the world, the results of interpretive efforts, or conclusions from research.

What is Baconianism, and why is it significant?

"Baconianism" (so-called because it derived from the thought of Francis Bacon [1561–1626]) became widespread in seventeenth- and eighteenth-century Britain and America and endures in popular forms even today. According to this view, scientists (or anyone else who wants to know with care, rigor, and precision) begin by collecting information ("facts"), organizing it into larger patterns, proposing a hypothesis to explain it, and testing the hypothesis against the collected information.[2] It claims to begin from the gathered information alone, putting aside all previous conclusions, letting the facts speak for themselves, and seeking to avoid projecting the scientist's own views on the gathering or analyzing of the information. Popular conceptions of science often consider this (or something like it) "the scientific method."

What is foundationalism, and how is it related to Baconianism?

Baconianism is a version of *foundationalism*, the Western intellectual tradition's dominant conception of knowledge (though with distinctive ancient/medieval and modern versions).[3] Foundationalism envisions human knowledge as two-tiered, a foundation and a superstructure, with each belief in the superstructure supported by one or more of the propositions in the foundation.[4] Foundational beliefs, on the one hand, provide evidence that warrants the beliefs in the superstructure. The propositions in the foundation, on the other hand, are not derived from other beliefs. They are "basic beliefs" and thus may be properly affirmed without the evidential support of other propositions.

With geometry as its paradigm, and thus precision and universal certainty as its goal, *classical foundationalism* designates the traditional, more rigorous way of construing human rationality, including indubitable basic beliefs that are universally acknowledged (or at least universally acknowledgeable).[5] Modern forms of classical foundationalism are committed to "a holistic substructure of logic, language, and method as the absolutely certain and universally accessible grounds of all rationality and knowledge."[6] This forbids idiosyncratic claims about an individual's own basic foundation of knowledge (such as divine revelation), insisting instead on public norms that can be made universal, that is, as measured by the judgment of "any reasonable person."

How does human situatedness affect knowledge? Is all knowledge perspectival?

The mistaken claim that human knowing is disconnected from and unaffected by place, time, and other contextual factors can be called "objectivism." It should be acknowledged, instead, that humans exist in particular historical, geographical, and social relationships as inescapably related beings. This situatedness reflects human creatureliness, or our embodiedness. Made from the earth, as physical beings, humans exist with spatial and temporal particularity, sharing the spatial and temporal limits of the created order. No matter how demanding the schedule, humans can only be in one place at any given time! Personal and social relationships always characterize us in greater or lesser ways, both empowering us and limiting us.

Is human situatedness a fatal flaw?

Such essential human situatedness is not a curse, hindering proper functioning. It does not remove responsible human agency by social, historical, or hermeneutical determinism, and thus it does not threaten the gospel. Because humans are not independent of their historical, cultural contexts, these contexts should be considered essential to human thought, not merely incidental. Moreover, the church, as the body of Christ, is united to its Head, and believers are members of one another, their most significant situatedness.

Can some of the limitations of situatedness be overcome?

Some of the limitations of situatedness can be overcome by learning to appreciate the strengths and weaknesses of other perspectives, other "locations," and learning from them about one's own perspective.[7] Yet even this will fall short of sharing those situations as others experience them. Whether traveling, reading, listening, or broadening themselves in any number of ways, people always do so as themselves, not as others. Such strategies provide significant glimpses of other situated lives, but such enrichment does not remove a person's situatedness. Yet being situated is not bondage or blindness, for situatedness provides perspectives from which to know and act. Faithful perspectives enable a faithful, albeit limited, knowing.

Is certainty essential? Is certainty impossible?

Reluctance to acknowledge this inevitable human contextuality, this sociocultural and historical relativity, contributes to undue concern for certainty and a correlative undue concern to avoid relativism.[8] Unrealistic standards for certainty suggest erroneously that skepticism and relativism are the only alternatives to certainty. Humans should not fear partial and fallible knowing—a perspectivalism. We know with varying reliability and thus with varying confidence. Differing situations require differing degrees of reliability, and we adjust our expectations to the circumstances. Selecting food in a grocery store and preparing to perform brain surgery or launch a space shuttle obviously require differing kinds of knowledge and differing degrees of precision. Interpersonal knowledge differs from repairing machinery. Laboratory research requires a different approach than decisions about a lifelong marital commitment to another person. Each approach is wrong when misplaced.

How does Scripture speak of certainty?

Scripture speaks of assurance for believers and of a form of certainty. For instance, Peter urged the crowd gathered at Pentecost to "be assured" that God had made Jesus both Lord and Christ (Acts 2:36). Later he assured his readers that they had the prophetic word "made more certain" in the transfiguration of Jesus (2 Peter 1:19). But this is not a certainty modeled on geometrical arguments that demands certainty beyond all possibility of doubt and is jeopardized by the presence of any and all doubt. Significantly, such pristine certainty is possible only in abstract, artificial, highly circumscribed arenas such as mathematics and in deductive inferences in logic. Instead, other conceptions of certainty are more appropriate to interpersonal and historical contexts. John Calvin, having defined faith as "firm and *certain* knowledge," insists that faith in this life can and always does coexist with error, unbelief, and doubt without eroding its assurance.[9] Indeed, given modernity's typical geometric construal of certainty, perhaps "assurance," "reliability," and "confidence" may be preferable categories.[10] This also highlights the significance of the Spirit's internal testimony, enabling believers' recognition of the authenticity of the Son of God and the spoken or written Word of God, and also their own identity as authentic children of God.[11]

God's creational design of humans and His abundant communication to them, in a variety of modes, provide for reliable, corrigible, perspectival knowledge of God, other humans, and the vast, intricate, and complex created order. We humans are capable of knowing the truth about God and about His created order. We are also responsible to apply ourselves diligently and critically to that opportunity.

2. BIBLICAL TEXTS, THE CREATOR, AND THE CREATOR'S NATURE

Are there biblical texts that encourage Christians to pursue the discipline of science?

Several biblical texts support and encourage participation in the discipline of science. Genesis 1–2 presents God as intimately involved in forming the creation while assigning function and purpose to Earth. These chapters affirm that God created the world *ex nihilo* (from nothing) and that God is distinct from the creation itself. In contrast to other views in the ancient pagan world, Genesis 1 in particular reveals that the material world and the cosmos are not deities. The universe is a created reality that is separate in identity from God. The act of assigning function and purpose reveals not only that the creation reflects its Creator but also that there is an observable coherence and order to the world that God has made. Furthermore, humans, the crown of God's creation, are made in the divine image and given responsibility for the world; in Genesis 2 this responsibility is not only horticultural but also taxonomical (vv. 15–23).

The nature psalms also speak of the creation in ways that resonate with the aims of the scientific disciplines. Psalm 8 revels in the greatness of God's creation, expressing wonder at the gift of human stewardship over Earth, directly linking worship of God to considered observation of the created order. Psalm 19 states that the cosmos is God's handiwork, constantly revealing God's greatness through the heavens in particular, while Psalms 29, 65, and 104 exult in God's sustenance and maintenance of the world in its being and operations. Readers of these texts are prompted, even compelled, to closely observe the phenomena present in God's work.

Some who consider Christians to be strictly New Testament people might wonder if there is a postresurrection shift in emphasis that directs the Christian's gaze away from a discipline like science. This is a mistaken idea for three reasons. First, there is sufficient continuity between God's purposes in the old and new covenants. The advent of Christ and the emergence of the "church age" do not demand an escape from material reality in any way. This was the error of the Gnostics, who viewed all matter as evil. Second, there are New Testament texts that affirm the splendor of God's creation and his active involvement in it, such as Acts 14 and 17 and Romans 1:18–20. Third, that God became flesh in Christ (John 1:1, 14) reinforces the inherent goodness in the created order. The world that God has made and entrusted to humans remains an appropriate field of inquiry.

Christians believe that the world is fallen. How should we think of God's postfall involvement in this world?

In Genesis 3, things go terribly wrong, and "paradise" is lost. Nevertheless, the biblical witness states and restates that God is the sole creator and sustainer of all things. A creation apologetic is a significant theme throughout the Bible, a central part of which is the statement and demonstration that Yahweh is the one true God and that other gods are disqualified because they are noncreators (e.g., Ps. 115:4–7; Isa. 40:18–20; Jer. 10:1–16). Furthermore, texts such as John 1:1; Romans 11:36; and 2 Peter 3:4–7 affirm God as the creator and sustainer of all things. Two doctrines are also helpful. *Providence* refers to "the act of God by which from moment to moment he preserves and governs all things."[12] In spite of the fallenness of creation, God remains directly and intimately involved in the world he created, moving it forward toward its ultimate God-glorifying purpose. *Common grace* speaks to the reality that the creation is fallen yet good and requires the responsible stewardship of humans. Abraham Kuyper defines this doctrine and its implications well:

> There is a *particular grace* which works Salvation, and also a *common grace* by which God, maintaining the life of the world, relaxes the curse which rests upon it, arrests its process of corruption, and thus allows the untrammelled development of our life in which to glorify Himself as Creator. . . . Thus the church receded in order to be neither more or less than the congregation of believers, and in every department the life of the world was not emancipated from God, but from the dominion of the Church. Thus domestic life regained its independence, trade and commerce realized their strength in liberty, art and science were set free from every ecclesiastical bond and restored to their own inspirations, and man began to understand the subjection of all nature with its hidden forces and treasures to himself as a holy duty, imposed upon him by the original ordinances of Paradise: "Have dominion over them." Henceforth the curse should no longer rest upon the world itself, but upon that which is sinful in it, and instead of monastic flight *from* the world the duty is now emphasized of serving God *in* the world, in every position in life.[13]

In common grace, God through the Holy Spirit preserves the world and enables development. The world remains fallen, as yet unrenewed, but the doctrines of common grace and providence remind us that the Creator remains engaged in the world.

3. CHRISTIANITY AND THE STUDY OF NATURE

Does Christianity provide any rationale for the natural sciences? Does Christianity regard the created order positively or negatively?

Christianity provides a rich, manifold theological rationale for the natural sciences. God repeatedly declared that the results of His creative work were "good." He proclaimed the earth with its variety of vegetation and animals "good" at stages throughout the process of creation and then summarily at the conclusion (Gen. 1:10, 12, 18, 21, 25, 31). These announcements of divine satisfaction indicate God's successful accomplishment of His creative acts. God's approval of the created order invites human labors on behalf of that created order. These labors should include scientific studies.

Such declarations by a good and wise God preclude judging the created order morally inferior and undeserving of human attention. The early church faced the challenge of Gnosticism and Manichaeanism. Though these complex, diverse viewpoints had multiple sources, including Greek philosophies, traditional religions, and some Eastern systems of thought, each denigrated material being and thus the human body and the created order. They considered the material or physical realm to be morally inferior to immaterial or nonphysical being and thus morally harmful for human involvement.

The church recognized these claims as incompatible with Scripture. Early creedal statements such as the Apostles' Creed and the Nicene Creed confessed their belief in "God the Father almighty, maker of heaven and earth." The doctrine of creation entails the goodness of the created order, of physical existence. The Son of God's incarnation and His redemption of the created order underscore the created order's goodness. This redemption includes, most significantly, the resurrection of the body (1 Cor. 15), culminating in the new creation (2 Cor. 5:17; Gal. 6:15), the new heavens and new earth (Isa. 65:17; Rev. 21:1) that will restore, even exceed, the splendor of the first creation (1 Cor. 15:38–57; Rev. 21–22).

What kind of relationship do humans have to the earth?

Because God formed Adam "from the dust of the ground" (Gen. 2:7), humans are integrally earthly. In the poignant words of graveside services, from dust we came and to dust we return at death. Fundamentally related to the earth, humans have every reason to seek to understand that from which they came and in which they so inseparably live. They are part of and depend on the created order (including food, water, and sunlight) to sustain them—though not exhaustively so, for they do not live by bread *alone*. Human existence depends on this realm, which warrants efforts to better understand it.

What responsibility do humans have for the created order, especially the earth?

God's first words to the new man and woman charged them with responsible stewardship of the earth. They were to "fill the earth and subdue" all that was in it (Gen. 1:28), "work it and take care of it" (Gen. 2:15), for God had entrusted the earth and all living things to human care (Ps. 8:6–8). Such an encompassing charge far surpasses the activities of the natural sciences but includes those as well. God's command of creational stewardship warrants the studious investigation of this world.

In the first recorded act of this responsibility, Adam named the animals as God brought them to him (Gen. 2:19–20). Tellingly, whatever Adam named them they were called, indicating that God allowed Adam's decisions to stand without overruling and changing the names. Naming in Scripture, as in most ancient cultures, is more than arbitrary labeling. Names signify character and give meaning. Naming thus involved understanding and interpreting what was named, making the responsibility to provide the enduring names for the animals a significant task.

Humanity's responsibility for creation, such as would appropriately involve scientific research, is displayed in the close relationship between humans and the created order. The creation suffers the effects of human sinfulness and likewise will participate in the joyous freedom of humanity's redemption (Rom. 8:19–22; see also 1 Cor. 15:35–57), even as it shared in Noah's deliverance from the flood (Genesis 6–8). Like the creation of humans from the earth, this displays the intimate relationship between humans and the created order. The creation's condition is so closely tied to humanity's condition that humans should give careful attention to its character and functioning.

Has God commanded compassionate and wise care for animals?

God's covenant with Noah and his descendants included "every living creature that was with you" (Gen. 9:10). As he clothed Adam and Eve in "garments of skin" (Gen. 3:21), God now specified, "Everything that lives and moves will be food for you. Just as I gave you the green plants, I now give you everything" (Gen. 9:3). God's covenant with Moses and Israel at Mount Sinai stipulated how they should live as His people, manifesting His character in their communal life before and with the surrounding nations. The Mosaic covenant includes commands about treatment of animals, including specifying their Sabbath rest along with Israel's (Ex. 20:10) and protecting animals (e.g., Deut. 22:1–4, 6–7; 25:4). The commands for Sabbath and Jubilee years granted rest even to the land. Later passages speak of God's provision for animals (see Ps. 104), call for the righteous to do likewise (Prov. 12:10), and imply that animals are also part of this covenant (Hos. 2:18). These commands illustrate the extent of God's care for what He created, providing another reason for diligent attention to it, including scientific study. God provided his animal creatures to humans for clothing, companionship, and food.

Does God Himself give us a model of attentive, loving care for the created order?

The psalmists often praise God for His work in the created order, not only bringing it into existence, but also displaying His wisdom, goodness, power, love, faithfulness, and generosity (Pss. 8, 19, 104, 139, 148, among others).[14] Recipient of God's care and revelatory of His character, the created order merits study.

How attentive to the created order was Jesus Christ?

Jesus' teaching reflects His extensive attention to the created order. His frequent illustrative use of animals or vegetation required close observation of a wide variety of phenomena. This suggests something of His high evaluation of the created order and suggests that the natural sciences' investigations of the rich diversity and complexity of the creation have messianic precedent.

Among the more memorable of Jesus' teaching references to the created order are His reminders of God the Father's loving care for birds (Matt. 6:26; 10:29–31) and wild flowers (the lilies of the field, Matt. 6:28–30). God's bestowal of His faithful care even on them, so insignificant themselves, grants them worth that should be reflected in ecological responsibility and research efforts. Precisely the relative insignificance of these aspects of the created order makes them powerful examples of God's exhaustive, inclusive care for all that He made. If He cares for the least of His creation, He cares for all of it.

Should the natural sciences consider themselves a stewardship?

Stewardship is a fundamental theme of human involvement with the created order, and it could well characterize Christian scientific activity as well. Humans should engage in science because it is part of their responsibility to care for and develop the created order that has been entrusted to them. Understanding the created order, including detailed investigations of the nature and function of its vast diversity, can aid humans in fulfilling their responsibility.

Should the natural sciences lead their practitioners to worship of God?

Such a stewardship from God, the Creator and Redeemer of all things, should be an issue in worship as well as knowledge. Scripture characterizes knowing in a variety of ways, from bare awareness of information to richer, more complex activities. At its highest, knowledge involves obedience, righteousness, love, and fidelity. Such rich knowing toward God and His handiwork surely should entail the heartfelt worship of this magnificent God, from whom every good gift comes. To understand the wonders of this created order in ever-increasing detail without being moved to humbly adore the Creator is not only willful sin, but also an intellectual failure. Learning about this world that does not result in worship of the providential Creator-God profoundly misunderstands the world. Such worship does not substitute for science, escaping from diligent and rigorous intellectual work, but it is an essential aspect of that intellectual study.

4. Why Have Christianity and Science Sometimes Come into Conflict?

In this form, this question is too ambiguous, failing to distinguish between various versions of natural science. Some forms of science, conceived, for instance, in reductionist, naturalistic ways, surely conflict with classic creedal Christianity's confession of the transcendent and immanent God, creation and providence, humans as imagers of God designed for life with and for God eternally, and redemption by the incarnate Son of God. But Christianity is not at odds with all forms of natural science. Indeed, the biblical teaching that humans were made to serve God by their responsible care and development of the created order provides significant warrant and motivation for natural science. Diverse versions of Christianity must be acknowledged, some with views of God, the world, humans, and salvation that are compatible with more naturalistic forms of natural sciences.

The long and complex relationship of Christian theology and the natural sciences includes failings by both parties. For its part, theology sometimes has misinterpreted those passages of Scripture thought to bear on science, often prematurely establishing, and sometimes incorrectly locating, firm boundaries for orthodoxy. Though geocentric or flat-earth views were less widely held among theologians than is sometimes suggested,[15] some church officials did oppose Copernican discoveries. Among the well-known examples is the claim that the early genealogies in Genesis are complete, entailing that at least relatively precise dates for the early events recorded in Genesis, including the date of creation, can be obtained by compiling these. In this the church failed to note the flexibility of Scripture, overlooking the significance of the different biblical literary genres, for example. In addition, theology sometimes mistook some of Scripture's historical accounts as chronological or took phenomenological language as more precise description. Many Christians, especially among the more conservative, came to regard Darwin's proposals as fundamental challenges to Scripture's authoritative teaching, though by no means did all of them do so.[16]

Theologians sometimes reject scientific corrections of scriptural interpretation. At its best, this is an attempt to protect Scripture's final authority, but it sometimes devalues scientific investigation or denies the significance and authority of creational revelation. Theology at times follows mistaken science against better science. The most famous (or infamous) of these episodes was Galileo's dispute with the Roman Church. Roman Catholic authorities, perhaps understandably but unwisely, followed the counsel of the established Aristotelian scientists against the novel insights of Galileo and other pioneers of the new astronomy.[17] (For more information on historical events, see chapter 1.)

Science has erred as well. Modern science in particular has often, even generally, presumed itself to be the final, if not the sole, source of truth on its subject matter, denying Scripture's authority. Even among those who acknowledge the Bible as Scripture, some scientists have denied, or at least diminished, the relevance of Scripture or theology to their work. From the correct observation that the Bible is not a "scientific textbook," they have sometimes drawn incorrect inferences. The Bible is not given for scientific purposes and does not directly address scientific issues in technical or precise language. It should not be read as a science manual. Yet Scripture's teaching, when touching on the created order, is authoritative. For both theologians and scientists, a crucial issue is how to faithfully understand the teaching of Scripture on the created order, duly acknowledging the Bible's literary genres, the historical and cultural contexts, and the integrity of the scientific investigation of the created order. Much work remains to be done among both disciplines.

The modernity of the natural sciences is evident in its frequent dismissal of earlier, especially ancient, views as primitive or prescientific, not merely in the sense of their historical location, but as an automatic judgment of their unworthiness. This is what C. S. Lewis called "chronological snobbery," assuming that the age and historical setting of those views makes them self-evidently unworthy of serious consideration and making refutation of them unnecessary.

Science long insisted on the pure objectivity of its practitioners and thus of their conclusions. For the past two centuries or more, natural science has considered itself and has been considered by others to be the model of careful, precise, nonpartisan knowing, to which all other disciplines should aspire. In recent decades, research in the history and philosophy of science has challenged this view, though in many quarters of the sciences it continues to reign.

5. Should Christians Be Scientists?

In light of the sometimes adversarial relationship between the Christian community and the scientific guild, is there any way a person of faith can maintain personal integrity and be a scientist? At one level, there is no difference between the pursuit of a career as a research-based scientist (e.g., in fields such as biology, physics, geology, and chemistry) and the pursuit of a science-based career (e.g., a dentist, physician, or veterinarian). Whether the orientation is academic or professional, these activities engage with science. Christians are not discouraged from the pursuit of the health professions, nor should there be discouragement from other forms of scientific engagement. Furthermore, there is no valid theological reason for a Christian to refrain from participating in the scientific enterprise. As mentioned above, the pursuit of science is one way that humans exercise their stewardship responsibility over creation. In addition, far from discouraging a Christian pursuit of science, the doctrines of providence and common grace compel Christians to vigorously pursue the discipline.

What kind of scientist is a Christian to be?

A Christian can pursue any of a variety of scientific avenues. In the various academic specialties, for-profit research careers and health professions, there are diverse ways of practicing science. As long as Christian commitment is not compromised by idolatries of the self or of the creation, the goal for Christians in science is no different from that of any other academic discipline or career. Some may wonder if it is possible to be a "good scientist" if the notion itself involves anti-Christian or anti-scriptural traits. "Good science" is in no way contrary to the Christian faith, at least at the level of observation, measurement, and categorization, for example. The potential for conflict arises in the explanation of data and results. A scientist's prior ideological commitments may frame his or her interpretation of data to the extent that it produces explanations that contradict a Christian view of the world.

This possibility is not itself sufficient reason for Christians to avoid some scientific avenues. It may make engagement in some discussions difficult, but the existence of committed Christian scientists in the numerous scientific avenues is itself evidence that even difficult territory can be survived.

Whose standards for "good science, good scientists" are normative?

In the academic world, each scientific avenue has a range of acceptable standards for "good" scientific practice. Some guilds may include standards or assumptions that challenge core Christian commitments, but the areas of difficulty for Christians come primarily in matters of the interpretation of data, not in matters of experimental procedure.

How does the Christian responsibility to be countercultural bear on Christian scientists' relationship to the non-Christian dominated scientific community and its values?

Scientists' Christian confession may make a difference in the ultimate interpretation of data, especially when "why" explanations are part of the final presentation of research. A difference in values may emerge as scientists navigate their way toward being people of influence in the scientific world, but this would be no different from the consideration of what it is to be Christian in any field (e.g., business, other academic guilds, etc.). A related question would be whether scientists' faith alters their emphasis, character requirements, perspectives, procedures, and goals in science. For example, does the pursuit of science require *methodological naturalism*, in which scientists do not make reference to the existence of supernatural forces or entities? This is an ongoing debate as Christians consider the relationship of theology and science. While many within the scientific guild simply assume methodological naturalism as inherent in true science, many Christian scientists dispute such a claim. Involvement in the scientific world does not require a shift in faith, though it may deepen and broaden one's understanding of God's complex creation.

6. RECONCILIATION AS A CONCEPT APPLIED TO OUR PRACTICE OF SCIENCE

Does the Gospel's message of reconciliation have any meaning for science?

The good news of the Gospel is that as a result of the life, death, and resurrection of Christ, the consequences of sin are in the process of being overturned. Just as sin created a breach between humans and God, humans and other humans, and humans and the created order, the work of Christ in redemption makes possible reconciliation between these three relationships. While it is true that there has not yet been a final reconciliation, there is already a measure of reconciliation that we can see. For example, Christians can now relate to God as His children, Christians can begin relating to each other in ways characterized by love rather than selfishness, and Christians need not regard the world as their adversary. In fact, the world that God is redeeming is reaffirmed as an object of inquiry. Regarding this third reconciled relationship, Romans 8:19–22 presents us with a creation "groaning" for its ultimate eschatological transformation. The "world" still belongs to God and plays a part in the ultimate divine purpose. For scientists and scientific activity, the great significance of reconciliation is that the practice of science as an act of responsible stewardship remains laudable. Christians who participate in the sciences are not giving their time, talents, and energy to a task doomed to futility. The present glimpses of reconciliation ultimately serve to remind us of God's good intentions toward us, and they provide encouragement that scientific activity is included among the tasks that bring glory to God.

QUESTIONS

1. How do natural scientists fulfill the mandate of Colossians 3:1–2 to apply scriptural principles to their work in the natural sciences?

2. What are some of the factors involved in forming natural scientists' interpretive perspectives? How can practitioners of the natural sciences identify them and critically evaluate them?

3. How can scientists manifest and foster in their work the reconciliation brought by Christ and the Gospel?

4. What are additional explanations for the disputes between Christianity and science? What can Christian theologians and Christians who are natural scientists do to prevent such disputes from recurring?

NOTES

1. Millard J. Erickson proposes "perspectival critical realism" in *Truth or Consequences: The Promise and Perils of Postmodernism* (Downers Grove, Ill.: InterVarsity Press, 2001), 264.
2. See, e.g., Theodore Dwight Bozeman, *Protestants in an Age of Science: The Baconian Ideal and Antebellum American Religious Thought* (Chapel Hill: Univ. of North Carolina Press, 1977), 3–31. See also Markku Peltonen, ed., *The Cambridge Companion to Bacon* (Cambridge: Cambridge Univ. Press, 1996), for more on Bacon and his legacy and on the differences between Bacon's own thought and what came to be called "Baconianism." For evangelicals' indebtedness to Baconianism, see George M. Marsden, "The Evangelical Love Affair with Enlightenment Science," in George M. Marsden, ed., *Understanding Fundamentalism and Evangelicalism* (Grand Rapids: Eerdmans, 1991), 122–52.
3. The most accessible introductions to classical foundationalism are Nicholas Wolterstorff, "Introduction" and "Can Belief in God Be Rational If It Has No Foundations?" in *Faith and Rationality: Reason and Belief in God*, ed. Alvin Plantinga and Nicholas Wolterstorff (Notre Dame, Ind.: Univ. of Notre Dame Press, 1983), 1–15 (esp. 1–5) and 135–86; idem, *Reason within the Bounds of Religion Alone* (Grand Rapids: Eerdmans, 1976), 24–58.

4. See O. R. Jones, "Foundationalism," in *The Oxford Companion to Philosophy*, ed. Ted Honderich (New York: Oxford Univ. Press, 1995), 289.

5. This is Alvin Plantinga's use of the term ("Reason and Belief in God," in Plantinga and Wolterstorff, *Faith and Rationality: Reason and Belief in God*, 58–59); cf. Wolterstorff, who uses the phrase for what Plantinga calls "modern foundationalism" (p. 3). Wolterstorff clarifies that classical foundationalism may be (and has been) formulated as a theory of three different things: *rationality*, *knowledge*, and *authentic science (scientia, wissenschaft)* (p. 2). Both he and Plantinga use the term for a theory of rationality (pp. 2, 52).

6. David K. Clark, "Relativism, Fideism, and the Promise of Postliberalism," in *The Nature of Confession: Evangelicals and Postliberals in Conversation* (Downers Grove, Ill.: InterVarsity Press, 1996), 118.

7. See sound advice on this in Erickson, *Truth or Consequences*, 241–42.

8. Perhaps something similar lies behind evangelicals' frequent, but often unqualified, insistence on absolute truth; see, e.g., Douglas Groothuis, *Truth Decay: Defending Christianity against the Challenges of Postmodernism* (Downers Grove, Ill.: InterVarsity Press, 2000): "*Christian truth is absolute in nature*. That means that God's truth is invariant. It is true without exception or exemption. Neither is God's truth relative, shifting, or revisable. The weather may change, but God will not" (p. 69). This should be qualified by acknowledging God's redemptive-historical revelation of His will, embodying some changes in His morally obligatory commands for His people in the course of the long, complex movement from Eden to the new creation. God does not change, but in some respects He changes the manifestation of His character in His revealed will for humans. Note, for instance, the many new obligations instituted at Sinai, or the changes in commands for worship or the laws of purity under the new covenant, or simply the multitude of person- and context-specific commands that seem to require some qualification of "absolute."

9. John Calvin, *Institutes of the Christian Religion*, ed. John C. McNeill, trans. Ford Lewis Battles, Library of Christian Classics (Philadelphia: Westminster, 1960), 3.2.16–17.

10. E.g., Leslie Newbigin, *Proper Confidence: Faith, Doubt, and Certainty in Christian Discipleship* (Grand Rapids: Eerdmans, 1995), and the discussion of confidence and hope in Esther Lightcap Meek, *Longing to Know: The Philosophy of Knowledge for Ordinary People* (Grand Rapids: Brazos, 2003), 81–87.

11. See, e.g., Calvin, *Institutes*, 1.7.4; 1.9.3; 3.2.16–28; 4.8.13; and Herman Bavinck, *The Certainty of Faith*, trans. Harry den Nederlanden (St. Catherine's, Ont.: Paideia, 1980). For recent discussions of these matters, see Nicholas Wolterstorff, "The Assurance of Faith," *Faith and Philosophy* 7, no. 4 (October 1990): 396–417; William J. Abraham, "The Epistemological Significance of the Inner Witness of the Spirit," *Faith and Philosophy* 7, no. 4 (October 1990): 434–50. See also the brief but helpful discussion in William Edgar, *Reasons of the Heart: Recovering Christian Persuasion* (Grand Rapids: Baker, 1996), 107–15. J. I. Packer discusses the witness of the Spirit in a number of writings, perhaps most accessibly in "Inward Witness: The Bible Is Authenticated by the Holy Spirit," *Concise Theology* (Wheaton, Ill.: Tyndale, 1993), 13–15. In general the role of the Spirit is conspicuously absent from many evangelicals' epistemologies or else limited to the application or practice of truth.

12. Herman Bavinck, *In the Beginning: Foundations of Creation Theology*, ed. John Bolt, trans. John Vriend (Grand Rapids: Baker, 1999), 234.

13. Abraham Kuyper, *Calvinism: Six Lectures Delivered in the Theological Seminary at Princeton* (New York: Revell, 1899), 30–31.

14. See, e.g., C. Hassell Bullock, *Encountering the Book of Psalms: A Literary and Theological Introduction* (Grand Rapids: Baker, 2001), 126–31; Hans-Joachim Kraus, *Theology of the Psalms*, trans. Keith Crim (Minneapolis: Augsburg, 1986), 59–65; and Claus Westermann, *The Psalms: Structure, Content, and Message* (Minneapolis: Augsburg, 1980), 90, 92–96.

15. See, e.g., such medieval theologians as the Venerable Bede (*Liber de Natura Rerum*, 9) and Thomas Aquinas (*Summa Theologiae*, 1a, q. 1, a. 1).

16. See David N. Livingstone, *Darwin's Forgotten Defenders* (Grand Rapids: Eerdmans, 1987).

17. Among the many analyses of this celebrated episode, see Pietro Redondi, *Galileo: Heretic*, trans. Raymond Rosenthal (Princeton, N.J.: Princeton Univ. Press, 1987). For a briefer overview, see William R. Shea, "Galileo and the Church," in David C. Lindberg and Ronald L. Numbers, eds., *God and Nature: Historical Essays on the Encounter between Christianity and Science* (Berkeley: Univ. of California Press, 1986), 114–35. Robert S. Westman, "The Copernicans and the Church," in Lindberg and Numbers, *God and Nature* (pp. 76–113), sets the Galileo episode in the context of its immediate antecedents.

SUGGESTED READING

Houston, James M. *I Believe in the Creator*. Grand Rapids: Eerdmans, 1980.

Hummel, Charles E. *The Galileo Connection: Resolving Conflicts between Science and the Bible*. Downers Grove, Ill.: InterVarsity Press, 1986.

Lindberg, David C., and Ronald Numbers, eds. *God and Nature: Historical Essays on the Encounter between Christianity and Science*. Berkeley: University of California Press, 1986.

Livingstone, David N. *Darwin's Forgotten Defenders*. Grand Rapids: Eerdmans, 1987.

Livingstone, David N., D. G. Hart, and Mark A. Noll, eds. *Evangelicals and Science in Historical Perspective*. New York: Oxford University Press, 1999.

Pearcey, Nancy R., and Charles B. Thaxton. *The Soul of Science: Christian Faith and Natural Philosophy*. Wheaton, Ill.: Crossway, 1994.

Warfield, Benjamin B. *Evolution, Science, and Scripture: Selected Writings*. Edited by Mark A. Noll and David N. Livingstone. Grand Rapids: Baker, 2000.

HOW DOES SOCIETY
INTERACT WITH SCIENCE?

Dorothy F. Chappell and E. David Cook

What do the Cold War, dietary supplements, genetic engineering, geriatric medicine, global warming, Ritalin, terrorism, and xenotransplantation have in common? Each of them has something to do with how science is embedded in societies, how science can cross cultural boundaries, and how science impacts the common good. Each example touches on the miraculous and delightful process of discovery, the use of the scientific method, the formulation of policies that help adjudicate the use and regulation of scientific information, the economic relationships intricately entwined with science, and the moral wisdom found in a culture.

Are scientific accomplishments important to all nations and acceptable to all cultural institutions of the world?

Common goals and practice that unite many scientists and their work collectively affect the welfare of humankind globally and individually. Christians and non-Christians work shoulder to shoulder to accomplish goals that diminish human suffering and reveal many mysteries held in creation. There is a relatively broad international understanding among cultures of scientific processes, the benefits they bring, and their effective use.

In addition to the international communities of science, science is often united with and affected by other parts of culture. Noteworthy are the efforts made when nations contribute to development and distribution of products like medicine that alleviate suffering of people at all ages, whether initiated by the agonizing diseases caused by infections, inflammation, genetic predispositions, or natural disasters. The HIV/AIDS crisis is a good example of a disease that requires global attention.[1] Likewise, food production for providing and enhancing nutrition is a major scientific enterprise, and because it is often viewed as being neutral, it easily crosses cultures. Although many aspects of medicine and food production are well accepted by most cultures, some issues do arise in which this is not the case. Some genetically engineered foods, for instance, do not meet particular cultural standards and do not readily pass cultural boundaries. Some recent interesting genetic studies have created cultural discomfort in some tribal cultures.[2] The conflict between genetic researchers at Arizona State University and some Native Americans has taught some scientists who were conducting genetics studies from blood samples "that—in addition to passing scientific peer review—it may be necessary to pass a test of cultural sensitivity."[3]

Government policies are influential in creating and limiting or promoting certain technologies and resources derived through the scientific community. Although divided on other issues, national governments often unite in their efforts to distribute resources to people who are suffering from disasters of various kinds. Economic and political factors contribute to decision making in government and not-for-profit and for-profit organizations as they offer assistance to individuals or populations. Economic factors directly affect the trade of scientific knowledge and products as commodities that many cultures seek. This market is controlled by policies between governments.

Often religious commitment, another cultural factor, influences individuals' sense of responsibility to implement certain humanitarian projects. Studies of global phenomena are important to humans in all cultures, and while they are important to individuals, they also have enormous ramifications for large populations. Global warming, desertification, urbanization, destruction of Earth's atmosphere, pollution of water sources, and changes in the distribution of the rain forests have enormous effects on all of Earth's populations. For Christians, a well-developed theological basis in their respective traditions and practical stewardship are essential.

Are the best products and scientific practice available and acceptable to all cultures?

Technological advances that allow for xenotransplantation, "the hydrogen economy,"[4] immunotherapy, and perilous space travel with landings on the moon and Mars are the stuff of science fiction. Yet the engineers producing the technologies that allow for these remarkable feats have advanced the technology not only for these purposes, but also for other uses that pervade human societies. The assimilation of digital instruments into the United States and other cultures is a direct result of their initial use by the U.S. government and later by NASA in space programs. Digital technology has made an enormous impact on the everyday life of many of the world's populations.

There is great disparity throughout Earth in the distribution of and access to technological advances. The "global vaccination gap" receives regular attention in Christian and non-Christian circles. Adel Mahmoud, president of Merck Vaccines at Merck & Co., Inc., and chair of the Forum on Microbial Threats at the U.S. Institute of Medicine, says that "disease prevention must be placed above political conflict or weapons purchase." He calls for strong leaders to "mobilize local communities and entire nations for the administration of vaccines," and he says "closing this gap will require national and multinational resources and effort."[5]

Joep Lange and Vallop Thaineua point out that control of AIDS, tuberculosis, and malaria is receiving attention from significant organizations that give to resource-poor settings and that many professionals are calling for movement beyond rhetoric and traditional ways of providing therapy for those who are ill. They observe "that some of the 'failed states' which are the hardest-hit with disease are countries in sub-Saharan Africa and they are unable to offer basic health services to the masses." The need is "to increase public-sector health care by motivating and retaining skilled personnel through sufficient remuneration and attractive career prospects."[6] They further address the irony that distribution of drugs to communities should not be a problem since "there is virtually no place in Africa where one cannot get a cold beer or Coca Cola."[7] Their call for greater collaborative efforts and laying aside some economic factors to serve underdeveloped and developed nations are presented as "laudable goals." These goals are to be implemented where international programs can eradicate current diseases with the diligence that has removed smallpox.

In addition to medicine being practiced across international boundaries, other efforts are being made to increase human welfare through conservation of the genetic heritage of plants in seed banks. Science writer Janet Raloff says that Afghanistan, Cambodia, Iraq, Rwanda, and Somalia have made extensive long-term efforts to conserve seeds, thus harboring a genetic bank in seed repositories.[8] Each of these repositories has been a victim of recent wars. Raloff says it is therefore fortunate that some of these important plant seeds were duplicated in other repositories and not damaged. On June 29, 2004, an effective International Treaty on Plant Genetic Resources for Food and Agriculture went into effect, and strong attempts are being made to protect certain plants for human consumption. New rules are being forged, says Raloff, to determine sovereignty over plant genes. Other treaties have been developed, and commercial rights of countries among other considerations remain foremost in some of the debates. The United States has more than twenty gene banks with 450,000 samples of 10,000 plant species. Raloff suggests that this "plant triage" is important to conservation of biodiversity and food and crop production.

The bridging of international culture boundaries also focuses on the issues of human consumption, consumerism, development of energy technologies, water quality, and the development of medical technologies designed to enhance the lives of, rather than heal, humans. The discussions surrounding such enhancements can be read in chapters 9 and 12, which address pharmaceuticals, ethics, and stewardship. The question of how to achieve a "farewell to arms"—an ultimate goal in peacemaking—is one of the most important questions for a Christian to consider relating to the cultural boundaries traversed by science.[9]

The values Christians develop in practicing science transcend culture, and Christians must be very careful to develop humility in their thinking and practice of science among differing cultures. Crises and convenience—responses based on comfort and perceived needs or preferences—demand that Christians respond in love seasoned with reason and extensive knowledge. Compassion can be expressed in the practice of ethics that emerges from the historic faith traditions. Difficult decisions often confront scientists and policy makers, especially when large human populations are affected by those decisions. (For additional reading on these principles, see chapters 3 and 12.)

Is the practice of science isolated from politics, economics, and other aspects of culture?

Like each example cited above, the study of global warming illustrates well how science is intertwined with institutions of culture. Global warming engages many scientific experiments to test conditions on Earth and beyond. These scientific investigations contribute to changes in the atmosphere, aquatic bodies, glaciers, rain forests, and temperatures of land masses and oceans, among others. Even seemingly minute scientific discoveries using the scientific method in research on biotic and abiotic phenomena can contribute to rich insights that depict a very complex picture of how global warming is occurring. This complex portrait of global warming is elucidated through the cooperation and dissemination of data from many teams of scientists. Large databases are created and stored in this process.

However, while scientific data are extremely important to effective decision making influencing global warming, we cannot rely strictly on scientific data in forming policies. Global warming is a phenomenon that affects every culture and the biodiversity of Earth. Embedded in many societies are regulations that help promote or curtail environmental conditions that contribute to global warming. These regulations arise through policy formation, usually at governmental levels, and are initiated by individuals who act on certain moral judgments relating to stewardship and guidelines for use of resources. Some regulations are formed with the interest of an economic community as the highest priority, and these may or may not represent best stewardship practices. Addressing these types of phenomena involving conservation and use of resources often requires international collaboration. The United Nations Conference on Environment and Development (UNCED) held in 1992 (the Rio Summit) is an example of an attempt to gain international cooperation on global environmental issues.[10] We have seen other such attempts of many nations coming together to collaborate in policy making to help regulate global warming. Regardless of the moral bases in such decision making, many scientists, lawyers, policy makers, economic specialists, and ethicists are involved in these conferences. (See chapter 6 for additional information on ethics and biodiversity.)

How does collaboration among scientists and nonscientists help in establishing the proper use of scientific information?

Excellent scientific practice occurs on small and large scales, and scientists from many disciplines around the world contribute to huge international databases. The dissemination of scientists' work occurs through presentations at their professional meetings, peer reviewed publications, entry of data into electronic science library databases, and popular venues of the electronic and print media. Great emphasis is placed on honesty as data are entered and interpreted in the professional science publications and as presentations are made. Within the culture of science, there is great collaboration among professional friends and their science labs, and there is also collaboration among scientists who may not know each other personally but who create models through access to professional databases. Such large models of collaboration often inform judgments and scientific practice relating to the good of humanity.

The development of drugs like Ritalin (a drug occasionally used for treatment of Attention Deficit Disorder and other things) involves knowledge acquired through the work of many scientists over time. In the United States, even though there may be proprietary ownership of that knowledge (in this case, a chemical structure for which a patent is held by a company), the drug must be scrutinized for good and safe use among humans. The development of drugs by scientists is only part of the process that is essential to launching drugs for the good of humanity. An independent scientific collaboration occurs in the United States before drugs are launched for public access. The U.S. Food and Drug Administration (FDA) requires clinical trials of drugs before giving approval for their sale to the population. The scientists who work for the FDA attempt to aid in establishing good practice for the use of drugs, and they also test certain technologies to which humans are exposed, especially in medical procedures.

The events that lead to the FDA clinical trials are significant. Often many papers are published in the refereed scientific journals and show the positive effects of a certain drug compound. However, in many laboratories, negative results may have been demonstrated for the same drugs, and those results have not been published or reported by the scientific community. Because it is harder to publish negative results, these results that could expose certain dangers in administering the drugs may never be seen by scientists and health practitioners. This lack of disclosure results in a biased representation toward the use of the drugs. Likewise, if a bias is held by scientists who hold economic interests in the development of a drug, more public attention may be drawn to the positive effects of the drug than to its deleterious effects.

The FDA has taken steps in requiring that both negative and positive results be exposed by drug developers, but experience has shown that the FDA has limited authority to regulate the testing and dissemination of proprietary results of drug testing by companies. The FDA itself cannot test all of the attributes and claims made by all drug developers, especially to eliminate all potential ill effects of a drug. On the positive side of this issue, some drug developers disclose the positive and negative effects of drugs. Furthermore, the World Health Organization is showing that there is some international interest in developing a registry of drug trials. Another check in the system is that provided by editors of some international journals who question the publication of papers without full disclosure of the positive and negative results of drug trials.

Obvious questions arise relating to quality of drugs, toxicity, and impurities in drugs sold between countries. All research relating to development of legal drugs and chemical substances such as dietary supplements produced for the common good of humans and animal populations, require extensive collaboration among individuals and other entities that represent scientific, political, and economic interests and the common good.

The negotiations that led to the end of the Cold War (a political tension enhanced by buildup of arms between nations; in this case, the build up of arms between the United States and the Soviet Union) are a tremendous example of collaborative efforts used successfully to avert the use of harmful nuclear substances during that time (see the sidebar on the development of the atomic bomb on p. 199). The Cold War was won partially through the use of "soft power," in which scientific and cultural bridges were built to directly save and improve human lives. The world needs soft power and more of it, says Norman P. Neureiter, director of the Center for Science, Technology, and Security Policy of the American Association for the Advancement of Science (AAAS) in Washington, D.C.[11] He cites the remarkable U.S.–Soviet nuclear standoff led by George Kennan, America's most prescient diplomat in the post–World War II period. Kennan argued for an engagement strategy with the Russian people and later lamented the heavy U.S. emphasis on containment in military terms and the relative neglect of available economic, political, psychological, and cultural tools.[12] It is also noteworthy that in the case of keeping the Cold War from becoming hot, a balance of soft power along with firm competitive and financial pressure were important. The modest scientific exchanges on peaceful uses of science called for by Neureiter reveal many niches where Christians can still have a huge impact.

Do science and culture have a marriage of convenience?

The wonderfully complex world where humanity exists is one that values and validates the work of scientists. Some of the strongest influences on humanity are the results of scientific inquiry and technology that emerge from scientific development. Humanity is bombarded with new ideas, new theories, new gadgets, and new expectations—all in some way related to science.

The expansive world of nature is an attractive realm to explore. Scientists are curious and explore the intricate characteristics of nature and formulate theories encompassing systematic behavior about natural entities. They explore the depths of molecular substance and particles in atoms (see chapter 9, "How Does Chemistry Impact Human Society") using nanotechnology (construction of devices from atoms and molecules) and can move to exponential levels of exploration in the depths of space using the Hubble and other telescopes (see chapter 5) to record historical events that occurred eons ago with the light just reaching our solar system. Scientific technological achievements are intricate and mesmerizing, as seen in successfully landing the rovers *Spirit* and *Opportunity* on Mars. More data have been generated disclosing characteristics of Mars than have ever been known.

New technology has made humankind more efficient and freed up more time, but humans have become more involved in their work and have taken on more responsibility. They have lost some of their best qualities of life because of excessive work hours, acceptance of more responsibilities, and the quest to push the frontiers of experience and knowledge. Books like Sir John Templeton's *Is Progress Speeding Up?* and Peter Kreeft's *Back to Virtue* capture some of the dilemmas of progress and some realistic solutions in regard to virtues.[13]

The public is exposed to the "gee whiz" aspects of science through print and electronic media. Some gee whiz aspects of our culture are positive and beneficial while others are harmful and dangerous. Humans are exposed to new pharmaceuticals (see chapter 9, "Are Pharmaceutical Drugs Good or Bad?"), ways to configure genomes, ways to grow food, ways to sustain life, and ways to kill and maim.

Science has emerged in the most recent century and millennium as a major factor in determining the human condition. The effects of science in and on cultures are paradoxical. In fact, during a time when humanity could be very pessimistic, people are in fact, "better fed, better clothed, better housed, and better educated than at any previous time in history."[14] However, great concerns remain that have to do with conservation of resources, development of means to alleviate human suffering, distribution of resources, development and use of weapons, and general care of the environment. The quality of life in some cultures comes at great expense to some in other cultures. Science and culture are tightly interconnected and must face the challenges of any marriage. Good communication, fidelity to truth, commitment to the welfare of others, genuine tolerance, and a gracious civility when promoting and using science, as in a good marriage, bring the best qualities to the influence of science. The partnership of such a complex relationship requires comprehensible painstaking effort and stewardship.

For Christians, the third cord[15] of that successful marriage is the Christian worldview that informs moral dimensions used to influence how science and its products are practiced (see chapters 3 and 12). The Christian worldview facilitates asking some important questions about the practice and use of science, including: What can science contribute to enable peace in our world? What can science contribute to the alleviation of suffering, hunger, and poverty? And who among the scientists and policy makers can make a difference in addressing these problems?

What are the trends in the natural sciences?

The exciting history of science reveals trends that project into the future. Advances in technology, including nanotechnology, that are allowing humans to further scientific exploration at levels unperceived previously, are creating the hope of therapies unknown in human history. The pharmaceutical advances work at a "nano" level, remarkably targeting not only tissues, but also cells, parts of cells, and cell functions. Science writer Alexandra Goho says "the fruits of nanotechnology could transform the food industry."[16]

Alan Leshner, executive publisher of *Science* and CEO of AAAS, in an editorial in the journal says that "new technologies are now driving scientific advances as much as the other way around. These technologies are enabling novel approaches to old questions and are posing brand new ones."[17] He cites techniques such as functional magnetic resonance imaging and positron emission tomography that now enable us to look into the brains of awake, behaving human beings and watch their minds in action. (For further reading, see chapter 6, "What Is the Mind-Brain Problem?") These new technologies "have revolutionized the understanding of such complex issues as mental illness and drug addiction."[18] Xenotransplantation, mentioned in chapter 11, sheds light on another important technique.

Another trend in the natural sciences is the increase in multiple-authored papers from scientists who are working collaboratively and bringing multiple perspectives to their problem solving. In addition, they are bringing interdisciplinary approaches to problem solving, thereby giving broader and deeper, hence more comprehensive, perspectives on how creation functions. Human development, from the fetal state to geriatric years, is best understood using interdisciplinary natural and social science perspectives. Likewise, the complexities of studying Earth's surface, mantle, and core are elucidated by scientists from many disciplines.

In addition to science exploration, the development of technologies requires expertise from interdisciplinary collaboration by engineers, mathematicians, and physicists. Alan Leshner points out that "no field stands alone. Progress in one domain is absolutely dependent on progress in many other disciplines.... Similarly, progress in the information sciences is prerequisite for dealing with the tremendous quantities of new data being generated in genomics, with its huge sequence arrays, or astronomy, with databanks generated from modern radio telescopes."[19] Leshner goes on to forecast a change in the culture of science in "that this interdisciplinarity characterizes so many of today's most exciting works that it may portend the gradual demise of single-discipline science."[20] Leshner calls for a reexamination of organizational structure and funding strategies of both academic institutions and governmental science-supporting agencies and cites some U.S. attempts to focus interdisciplinary teams. This is a trend seen especially in applied sciences and is a large shift for many participants in the science culture.

Increasingly, women and minorities are part of science culture. Evelyn Fox Keller introduced in 1978 the concept of "gender and science" in science literature.[21] Mary Frank Fox indicates that "in the pre–World War II era, women had few employment options in science. Current data show that over 90% of women with doctoral degrees in science and engineering are in the labor force at a given time."[22] The gap is closing between males and females earning doctorates in science and engineering and also between minority and white populations. Because these data shift annually, the reader should access the National Science Foundation website at http://www.nsf.gov/sbe/srs/wmpd/figf–2.htm to determine the latest trends in recipients of doctoral degrees.

More than ever, the practice of science is interacting with and found under the scrutiny of moral and ethical parameters. Although lapses of conduct within the scientific community are what draw public attention, there are larger numbers of scientists who are practicing science within the acceptable and logical realm of the scientific culture. Ethics boards, committees, and institutes help keep scientists in line. They handle such questions about the use of technology as, Are we wise enough to use the technology we have developed? And, Is technology inherently evil? We may be in our greatest moment of history to bring many excellent things from science to improve human life and our planet through agricultural, atmospheric, medical, and other means, but we have the potential to experience the greatest eugenics crisis of all time and inflict our earth systems with the greatest devastation of recent history. (For special discussion on these types of questions, see chapters 6 and 10 on engineering, ethics, and technology.)

The most unexpected and fascinating trend in science may be that documented by Alan Leshner in an editorial in *Science*, where he observes from the Euroscience Open Forum 2004 in Stockholm, Sweden, that "superb science is being carried out in many countries and the scientific enterprise has become truly global in character."[23] Leshner says that the United States is now outpaced by the European Union in the total numbers of papers published, and the share of prizes that have been awarded to U.S. scientists has diminished. He states, "The relationship between science and large segments of the U.S. public and policy communities is eroding and there is a counterproductive overlay of politics, ideology, and religious conviction on the U.S. climate for science." The good news is that "better science is being done around the world." Many cultural entanglements, including trade embargoes, are influencing the U.S. culture of science. The recognition of these cultural conflicts led to the development of the topic "The Nexus: Where Science Meets Society" for the 2005 AAAS Annual Meeting.[24]

How do Christians recognize the effects of science in cultures?

When social scientists are consulted regarding the meaning of culture, they may say that culture is "the more or less integrated systems of ideas, feelings, and values and their associated patterns of behavior and products shared by a group of people who organize and regulate what they think, feel, and do."[25] Hence some of the shared dimensions of culture include the dimensions of the cognition and communication within and about community life. In studying science, students from some cultures may not understand the concept of the microscopic world and have to be taught to trust what they are seeing through the lenses of a microscope. The introduction of a microscopic world affects assumptions and beliefs about reality and how one sees the world. The same could be true in considering the components of atoms, which are not visible to the unaided eye. Care for the elderly is another cultural issue with many prongs.[26] The language and cultural symbols used in scientific and cultural discussions also bear upon the reception of concepts and evaluative judgments that inform cultural boundaries. Moral codes are important to cultures and, in science, are often based in ethical codes. Science pervades many cultures and can shift many cultural practices. The use of cell phones and television by members of Bedouin or African cultures is an amazing sight and, as in more technologically based cultures, have reshaped the way some families use time. The impact of immunization for smallpox and polio has increased population growth and is very obvious on an intercontinental scale. One has to observe cultures and subcultural practices closely over time to accurately determine the impact of science in cultures.

Social science methods used to study culture lend insights and generate empirical and qualitative data to which Christians may respond. God is slowly redeeming parts of His world through His image bearers. Scientific knowledge can be used in these efforts.

Is there a recognized science culture?

In 1959 C. P. Snow published a little book called *The Two Cultures and the Scientific Revolution* that has been endeared by many who are serious about academic cultures. The book suggests that there is a "great gulf"[27] between those who study science and those who do not—affectionately called the "intellectual" and the "literary."[28] Snow saw a great gulf, first, in a lack of communication and, second, between the rich and the poor. This gulf, he said, was created by the scientific revolution—the industrial use of electronics, atomic energy, automation, and so on. He characterized the rich as the United States, Russia, Great Britain, the rest of the Commonwealth, and most of Europe. The rest of the world's population he called "poor."

Snow, trained as a scientist who by vocation became a writer and was in charge of Britain's scientific recruitment, said that in 1959 three menaces stood prominent—the H-bomb, overpopulation, and the gap between the rich and poor. Snow moved socially among the groups he had defined—the intellectual and the literary—and found them "comparable in intelligence, identical in race, not grossly different in social origin and earning about the same incomes."[29] He discovered that they had almost ceased to communicate. He essentially established a set of subculture categories that separated those who practiced the sciences from those who practiced the humanities and arts.

These cultures as defined by Snow still have validity in the twenty-first century. A scientist who talks about a topic like "cell biology and phylogeny of green algae," for instance, finds that this is a conversation stopper, unless that scientist further discusses the beauty of organisms, the cosmopolitan distribution of algae, or algae's significance as a primary producer. Even then there is a slow response and the conversation and nonscientists usually move elsewhere. Likewise, scientists do not frequently enter into conversations about literary criticism, modernity, postmodernity, or related topics of the "other culture." To enter the other culture, one must enter the conversation of that culture.

Snow defined culture in two ways, as "intellectual development (development of the mind) and in an anthropological sense (common attitudes, common standards and patterns of behavior, common approach)."[30] The two cultures defined by Snow fit these definitions. Today we see evidence of the development of subcultures within these cultures. Computer scientists communicate with one another, geneticists talk mostly within their group, theoretical physicists talk mostly with one another, and so the list increases with thousands of subcultures apparent in the culture of science. Similar patterns of communication exist in conversations among nonscientists.

C. P. Snow's lament and theme is important—it is dangerous to have cultures that will not or cannot communicate. Today knowledge is much more accessible than in Snow's lifetime, and people find the amount of knowledge is too vast and that it is impossible to comprehend all of it. People pick and choose to study, read, and discuss those things that are of more interest. Karl Giberson and Donald Yerxa suggest in their book *Species of Origins* that Snow, in the second edition of his book, expressed hope that "some brave humanists will emerge who will make the effort to learn science and then write it in a way that will bridge the two cultures together."[31]

John Brockman wrote in 1995 in *The Third Culture* that "Snow's third culture is here, but incarnated differently than he predicted."[32] Giberson and Yerxa capture well the tone of Brockman's observations. They quote Brockman's assertion that

> the scientific literate humanist has not appeared, but the literate scientist has stepped into the breach and has emerged as the new public intellectual. These third-culture intellectuals have flawless academic pedigrees. They do good science. Some of them are at the forefront of their disciplines, advancing the state of knowledge in their fields. Some have worked with Albert Einstein. . . . they write exceedingly well and one would have to be profoundly disinterested in science not to enjoy their books. The third culture is represented by people like the late Carl Sagan and Gould, Dawkins, Wilson, Daniel C. Dennett (the only non-scientist in the group, but exceptionally well informed), Peter W. Atkins, Weinberg, Dyson, and Francis Crick.[33]

These third culture individuals communicate the nature and content of science as they understand it to the larger culture of science, according to Gilberson and Yerxa. They say that the interesting and important questions are addressed by the third culture writers who hold no traditional views of religion and also speak for the culture of scientists. These popularizers are committed to the proposition that there is no transcendent meaning to the universe or human experience, and this is expressed in several ways. Gilberson and Yerxa say the popularizers have strong convictions that humans shouldn't expect that some things should have a purpose, science has failed to find such a purpose, or they have a fiendish delight in attacking and ridiculing religious beliefs."[34]

Why is this important? The third culture individuals have a large popular audience, and their widespread agnosticism (in contrast to the 40 percent of the scientific community who hold traditional views of religion)[35] is troubling for those who hold religious beliefs. In addition to this, Gilberson and Yerxa say that it should be troubling to the scientific community given the declining importance attached to basic research.[36] The fascination with science has subverted the need to understand the science behind the "controversies like nuclear power, the environment, cloning, genetic engineering, and so on, [and] many ordinary citizens recoil in horror from the bleak worldview that comes through the writings of the third culture."[37]

How does a culture solve disagreements based on differences in its institutions?

The issues raised under the preceding question demonstrate a conflict within the scientific culture. For some insights into the general culture conflicts, we can examine the monumental work of James Davison Hunter. His 1991 book *Culture Wars*, deemed epic by Robert Coles of Harvard, gives constructive analyses on the nature and origins of cultural conflict. Hunter says that the United States has shaped its political discourse in moral terms and even the wars that the nation has engaged in have been portrayed in moralistic terms. The public idealism has been framed in terms of a struggle between good and evil.[38] So even when a view in a culture war is not founded on a religious position, it is actually framed in a "religious" way.

How do we apply this to science? Some of the conflicts in U.S. culture relate to the development of technology that allows humans to explore and participate in the edges of physical existence, whether it be genetic manipulation, life-extending processes, or the impact of human behavior and technology on our environment. Moral distinctives must be brought into the discussions of the use of certain technologies. Scientific studies and developments have an enormous impact on the way people live and how they may extend and/or enhance life.[39] The technologies that are used in abortion, genomic manipulation, in vitro fertilization, food production, and stem-cell research, or that contribute to industry (hence pollutants in the environment), among many others, bring new possibilities to humans in regard to having more control over their lives.

The development and use of the technologies contribute to the conflicts. Increasingly, the popular media and the editors of major scientific journals offer editorial views and articles on issues surrounding usage of technology and the complicated political processes involved in legislating proper use. Embryonic stem-cell research is a science cultural conflict that continues to rage in the United States and across Europe, where patents are being denied because the European Patent Office (EPO) prohibits patents for the industrial or commercial use of human embryos.[40] Ethics opinion pieces are common in science journals.[41] Religious and nonreligious people gather to debate and inform decision making about the use of technology. Many scientific studies give certain individuals or segments of the population an economic advantage. Science affects culture, and culture influences the practice of science in the United States in the ways mentioned early in this chapter.

In James Hunter's own pilgrimage, he wrote another book titled *Before the Shooting Begins*, reflecting his concerns that shooting would begin in these cultural wars in the absence of understanding and tolerance of moral pluralism.[42] This book is another serious academic treatment of American culture and was released almost simultaneously with the climactic event in U.S. culture that began the "shooting," the killing of an abortion doctor in Pensacola, Florida, by a religious person. Clearly this is not a good way to solve the cultural conflict.

The United States and other parts of the world are engaged in cultural wars over euthanasia, homosexuality, use of stem cells, environmental issues, and the use of water and other nonrenewable resources. For some of these issues, there are global consequences of U.S. and other nations' actions, especially as usable water becomes scarcer and other nonrenewable resources recede.

Usually politics influences how scientists practice their skills. Funding that leads to applications of science has produced new ways to construct society. Communication is easy, and the worldwide networks connect remote areas and populations. The global public faces new opportunities for discourse, which will be very important to the future of humanity. Christians have monumental opportunities to influence discourse and bring voices of competence in science, passion for Christian moral values, and humility to these discussions and the practice of science. Most of this work is tedious and requires deep understanding of the cultural institutions at war, humility in bringing warring factions into dialogue, and wisdom to design outcomes that will bring long-lasting and positive effects to the issues being debated.

What role does education have in influencing science in societies?

The culture of science is dynamic, and the influence of education is powerful. Christian students considering a career in the natural sciences may view this as a "calling" and, while enjoying the exploration of their Lord's creation, grow in their walk with the Lord. The entire world depends on science and technology, and the steady stream of students who enter graduate schools and careers in science includes Christians. Some students enjoy studying creation for the sake of knowledge itself, and others have well-defined visions of how science can be applied to help those who are in need and lack food, medical resources, clean water, and other material goods.

The knowledge base of current scientific investigation exceeds that of all previous generations and affords many opportunities for Christians to direct praise to God because their faith affirms their understanding of God's handiwork. "When science is properly conducted, it honors God, and the valid findings of science are wholly consonant with the inspired and authoritative revelation of the Bible."[43]

The study of natural science at the undergraduate level should be punctuated with excellent classroom, laboratory, and field instruction, stimulating seminars, hands-on research and internships, and mentoring of the scientific process of testing hypotheses and theories. Christians can enjoy the intersections created by training in sciences and growth in moral values, and they can have great influence on the economical, ethical, and political dimensions of science.

The joy of discovery is a natural outcome of curiosity, and the appropriate use of technology is a natural outcome of the Christian worldview. Consider the theory and expertise of Enrico Fermi, who experimentally produced the first controlled nuclear chain reaction. The use of that knowledge has established the basis for many good things in medicine and experimental physics, but in the wrong hands can bring devastating circumstances to large portions of the world. The "soft power" of negotiation with rogue nations that are developing nuclear bombs should allay the physical harm to people and devastating effects of nuclear fallout to the land and sea. Christians can serve in the roles of scientists and negotiators. Like this book, a good education in science has to do with answering difficult questions that have to do with God's creation and the care of it. Answering those questions wisely sets and protects the survival agenda for future generations in all societies. The societal implications of science are morally bound, and Christians have a voice in establishing the vision for the welfare of humanity. It is essential that Christians who intellectually engage their faith and the natural sciences continue to be a part of the global response to the Lord's mandate to steward the earth. Can humanity afford not having Christians take part in the science culture?

QUESTIONS

1. What is the relationship between politics, morals, and embryos? Can bioethics rise above politics?

2. Is ignorance of scientific phenomena bliss or tragedy in a cultural sense?

3. Should preserved cultural institutions of certain nations be overruled to protect the common good?

4. What are the true tests of ethical leadership?

5. Can humanity afford not to have Christians influence the practice of science?

NOTES

1. Helen Pilcher, "Snapshot of a Pandemic," *Nature* 430, no. 6996 (July 8, 2004): 134–35; Julie Clayton, "Out of Thailand into Africa," op. cit., 136–37; Helen Pilcher, "Starting to Gel," op. cit., 138–40.
2. "Tribal Culture Versus Genetics," *Nature* 430, no. 6999 (July 29, 2004): 489.
3. Rex Dalton, "When Two Tribes Go to War," *Nature* 430, no. 6990 (July 29, 2004): 500–502.
4. Donald Kennedy, "The Hydrogen Solution," *Science* 305, no. 5686 (August 13, 2004): 917.
5. Adel Mahmoud, "The Global Gap," *Science* 305, no. 5681 (July 9, 2004): 147.
6. Joep M. A. Lange and Vallop Thaineua, "Access for All?" *Science* 304, no. 5679 (June 25, 2004): 1875.

7. Ibid.
8. Janet Raloff, "The Ultimate Crop Insurance," *Science News* 166 (September 2004): 170–72.
9. "No Farewell to Arms?" *Nature* 431, no. 7007 (September 23, 2004): 385.
10. See Fred Van Dyke, *Conservation Biology: Foundations, Concepts, Applications,* for an excellent treatment of the legal foundations of conservation biology (Boston: McGraw-Hill, 2003), 28–55.
11. Norman P. Neureiter, "Talking with North Korea," *Science* 305, no. 5691 (September 17, 2004): 1677.
12. Ibid.
13. John Marks Templeton, *Is Progress Speeding Up?* (Philadelphia: Templeton, 1997); Peter Kreeft, *Back to Virtue* (San Francisco: Ignatius, 1992), 2.
14. Templeton, *Is Progress Speeding Up?* 2.
15. Ecclesiates 4:12.
16. Alexandra Goho, "Hungry for Nano," *Science News* 166, no. 13 (September 25, 2004): 200–201.
17. Alan I. Leshner, "Science the Leading Edge," *Science* 303, no. 5659 (February 6, 2004): 729.
18. Ibid.
19. Ibid.
20. Ibid.
21. Evelyn Fox Keller, "The Origin, History and Politics of the Subject Called 'Gender and Science,'" in *Handbook of Science and Technology Studies,* ed. Sheila Jananoff et al. (Thousand Oaks, Calif.: Sage, 1995), 80–94.
22. Mary Frank Fox, "Women and Scientific Careers," in *Handbook of Science and Technology Studies,* 205–23.
23. Alan I. Leshner, "U.S. Science Dominance Is the Wrong Issue," *Science* 306, no. 5694 (October 8, 2004): 197.
24. "AAAS Annual Meeting—The Nexus: Where Science Meets Society," *Science* 306, no. 5694 (October 8, 2004): cover.
25. Paul G. Hiebert, *Anthropological Insights for Missionaries* (Grand Rapids: Baker, 1985), 30.
26. Donald Kennedy, "Longevity, Quality, and the One-Hoss Shay," *Science* 305, no. 5689 (September 3, 2004): 1369.
27. C. P. Snow, *The Two Cultures and the Scientific Revolution* (Cambridge: Cambridge Univ. Press, 1959), book jacket.
28. Ibid., 43–44.
29. Ibid., 2.
30. Ibid., 10.
31. Karl Giberson and Donald A. Yerxa, *Species of Origins: America's Search for a Creation Story* (New York: Rowman & Littlefield, 2002), 121; C. P. Snow, *The Two Cultures: A Second Look* (Cambridge: Cambridge Univ. Press, 1964).
32. John Brockman, *The Third Culture* (New York: Simon & Schuster, 1996), 18–20.
33. Gilberson and Yerxa, *Species of Origins,* 121.
34. Ibid., 122.
35. Edward J. Larson and Larry Witham, "Scientists and Religion in America," *Scientific American* 281 (September 1999): 89.
36. Gilberson and Yerxa, *Species of Origins,* 122.
37. Ibid.

38. James Davison Hunter, *Culture Wars: The Struggle to Define America* (New York: Basic, 1991), 62.
39. Donald Kennedy, "Just Treat, or Enhance?" *Science* 304, no. 5667 (April 2, 2004): 17.
40. Gretchen Vogel, "Stem Cell Claims Face Legal Hurdles," *Science* 305, no. 5692 (September 24, 2004): 1887.
41. Giuseppe Testa and John Harris, "Ethical Aspects of ES Cell-Derived Gametes," *Science* 305, no. 5691 (September 17, 2004): 1719.
42. James Davison Hunter, *Before the Shooting Begins: Searching for Democracy in America's Culture War* (New York: Simon & Schuster, 1994).
43. "The Natural Sciences at Wheaton College—Understanding Their Significance in Light of Our Educational Mission" (Wheaton College, 2003).

SUGGESTED READING

Kreeft, Peter. *Back to Virtue*. San Francisco: Ignatius, 1992.
Lindberg, David C., and Ronald L. Numbers. *When Science and Christianity Meet*. Chicago: University of Chicago Press, 2003.
Sire, James W. *The Universe Next Door: A Basic Worldview Catalog*. Downers Grove, Ill.: InterVarsity Press, 1997.
Spencer, Aida Besançon, and William David. *The Global God: Multicultural Evangelical Views of God*. Grand Rapids: Baker, 1998.

PART 2

SELECTED NATURAL SCIENCES AND MATHEMATICS

WHAT DO WE LEARN ABOUT THE CREATOR FROM ASTRONOMY AND COSMOLOGY?

Jennifer J. Wiseman

From the beginning of human history, people have looked up to the heavens in wonder and awe. We seem to have an innate sense that by understanding the heavens, we will understand something of our own origins and purpose. Ancient tribes developed myths around constellations in the night sky, imagining that from the arrangements of stars and planets could be gleaned stories of the gods, with all their good and evil deeds and all their battles and heroics. Even today people monitor the motions of the planets and the sign of their birth date as a predictor of their personal future; horoscopes can be read in nearly every newspaper.

The biblical writers also viewed the heavenly bodies as important, but not as gods in themselves. Rather, the heavens were seen to point to the glory of the One who created them—that is, to one, almighty God. In this chapter, we will see what we can learn about God by looking at the magnificence of the universe and discover how science and history are giving us more and more insights. (See plate 1.)

What do the Scriptures tell us about the heavens and their significance?

The very beginning of everything, as recorded in Genesis 1:3–4, was an astronomical event like no other: the appearance of light. "God said, 'Let there be light,' and there was light. God saw that the light was *good*" (emphasis added). The creation account goes on to say that God separated light from darkness and made the sun to "govern" the day (that is, to be the brightest light in the daytime sky) and the moon to likewise "govern" the night. God said that the lights in the sky should serve as signs to mark seasons and days and years. "He also made the stars," says Genesis 1:16, and we will see just how magnificent an ongoing process that is later in this chapter. But from the outset of Scripture, we find that the creation of the heavenly bodies and the light they produce and reflect are foundational to God's creative design. Moving ahead, we find the heavens referred to during times of miracles, such as when celestial motion seemed to pause to allow Joshua and the Israelites more time for battle (Josh. 10:13). We also find the heavens in prophecy. Wise scholars from the East knew of the prophecy of a king of Israel being born when a certain bright star would appear in the eastern sky, and this event led them to find Jesus (Matt. 2:2). And Jesus said there would be signs in the sun, moon, and stars near the end of the age (Luke 21:25).

But most often when the heavens are mentioned in Scripture, it is in the context of *praise* for the great Creator of the universe.

> The heavens declare the glory of God;
>   the skies proclaim the work of his hands.
> Day after day they pour forth speech;
>   night after night they display knowledge.
> There is no speech or language
>   where their voice is not heard.
> Their voice goes out into all the earth,
>   their words to the ends of the world.
>   —Psalm 19:1–4

Still today people of every language and continent can look up to the heavens and see the magnificence that speaks of an awesome Creator. Sadly, for many people in urban and suburban settings around the world, "light pollution" from unshielded city lights and streetlights fills the night sky and drowns out the starlight that would speak to them of the beauty and magnitude of the universe. Many children and adults have never even seen stars. Those of us who live where we can see stars often don't bother to look up as we hurry about our business. And yet contemplation of the heavens, whether as a casual stargazer or a scientific investigator, should stir in us a sense of wonder and humility and praise for the One responsible for the universe.

"Two things continue to fill the mind with ever increasing awe and admiration: the starry heavens and the moral law within."

—Immanuel Kant, *Critique of Pure Reason**

*For a beautiful collection of astronomical images and inspirational quotes, see Michael Reagan, *The Hand of God* (Kansas City: Andrews McMeel), 1999.

How big is the universe?

Measuring the universe is an endeavor that has been ongoing for nearly all of recorded human history. Ancient Greeks, for example, monitored the paths of planets and the sun and moon, and began to mathematically model celestial motion. Eratosthenes (276–195 BC) understood that the earth was round, and he was able to measure its diameter by measuring the angle of sunlight in two Egyptian cities on the same day, with surprising accuracy.[1] Aristarchus (310–230 BC) measured the position of the moon at different phases to estimate from geometry that the sun is twenty times farther from the earth than the moon. By estimating the moon's diameter, the ancient Greeks could then estimate the distance of the sun, getting it right to within a factor of twenty of the current known distance of 93 million miles (150 million kilometers). The model of Ptolemy (c. AD 150) held that the earth was in the center of the universe with all the other heavenly bodies in motion around it. This model worked well for centuries, but in 1543 Copernicus published a model of the universe that placed the sun at the center with all the planets (including the earth) moving around it. Astronomer Galileo Galilei (1564–1642) along with some clergy supported the model, though some church leaders did not. Some found the idea of the earth in motion to be in conflict with their understanding of Scripture (e.g,. "The world is firmly established; it cannot be moved" (Ps. 93:1).[2] Galileo disagreed with this use of Scripture, quoting Cardinal Baronius (1538–1607) for the statement, "The Bible was written to show us how to go to heaven, not how the heavens go." The Copernican model had great implications for the size of the universe, for it implied that the stars were like our sun but just much farther away.

The Copernican model also allowed for the measurement of the *parallax* of nearby stars, to determine their distance. As the earth orbits the sun, the apparent position of a nearby star relative to more distant background stars, as seen from the earth, will appear to vary slightly. Measurements of this variation, or parallax, were achieved in the nineteenth century by Bessel, Struve, and Henderson, and continue to be a useful tool for determining distance to the nearest stars within our own galaxy.

A breakthrough in determining the distance to more distant objects came in 1908, when Henrietta Leavitt, working at the Harvard College Observatory, discovered a fundamental property of a certain type of star, called a Cepheid, which varies periodically in brightness. Leavitt found that the frequency of these variations was directly related to the intrinsic average brightness of the star. Her discovery allowed fellow astronomers to determine the distance of a star cluster by finding a Cepheid star in it, measuring its variation (and therefore its intrinsic brightness), and then comparing that to its apparent dimness caused by its distance. From this the distance to the star cluster could be determined.

> "I do not feel obliged to believe that the same God who has endowed us with sense, reason, and intellect has intended us to forgo their use."
>
> —Galileo

Variable stars were used by Harlow Shapley in 1915 to determine the size of our Milky Way galaxy, now known to be about 150,000 light-years in diameter (a light-year is the distance light travels in one year, nearly 9.5 million million kilometers, or 6 million million miles) and to contain 10 billion stars.

Then in 1923, Edwin Hubble showed, using variable stars, that "spiral nebulae" (fuzzy light swirls) seen with telescopes were too distant to reside in our own galaxy; rather, they were separate distant galaxies of their own. This astonishing realization implied that the universe is indeed enormous, with billions of galaxies each containing billions of stars. Our own galaxy, the Milky Way, is now known to have a "grand spiral" design, with stars and gas orbiting the center of the galaxy in a pattern of spiral arms. Our sun is not in the center of the galaxy, but instead is about two-thirds of the radius of the galaxy out from the center. The nearest neighboring grand-spiral-type galaxy is Andromeda, which is over 2 million light-years away.

To gauge the distance of distant galaxies, individual variable stars won't work because they are too distant to detect. Instead, modern astronomers have found that when certain types of old stars go through a fantastic explosion called a *supernova*, the intrinsic brightness of that supernova can be predicted from basic physical principles. Therefore, by detecting a supernova explosion of a star in a distant galaxy and comparing its observed dimness with its intrinsic brightness, the distance to that galaxy can be determined. We now find galaxies billions of light-years away from our own. This implies that, since the light has taken billions of years to get to us, we are seeing the galaxies as they appeared when the light was emitted billions of years in the past. Astronomy is truly a time machine, allowing us to see galaxies and stars and events like star explosions from different times in cosmic history. (See plate 2.)

Our limited human experience makes it exceedingly difficult for us to comprehend how large the universe is. The moon is about 384,000 kilometers (239,000 miles) away from the earth. When our nearest planetary neighbors, Mars and Venus, are closest to us in their orbits, they are about 54 million and 38 million kilometers away from earth, respectively; that's about 100 times farther than the moon. Earth orbits the sun at a distance of about 150 million kilometers. The most distant planet, Pluto, is 6 billion (or 6 thousand million) kilometers from the sun, on average. The nearest star to the sun, Proxima Centauri, is 4.2 light-years away, or 38,000,000,000,000 kilometers away (at this point you can see why using light-years, rather than kilometers or miles, is a more useful unit of measure!). And as we have already mentioned, our own Milky Way galaxy of stars is 150,000 light-years across, and the nearest neighbor spiral galaxy (Andromeda) is over 2 million light-years away. We see galaxies at distances of several billion light-years and distant radiation telling us that the universe extends over 13 billion light-years. The number of stars is also astounding. With more than 10 billion galaxies and roughly 10 billion stars in each one, that means there are at least 100 billion billion, or 100,000,000,000,000,000,000, stars in the universe! What kind of God would bother to create, care for, and sustain a universe of this magnitude? Pause to reflect on whether your typical view of our Creator-God is consistent with the magnitude of the universe we live in.

What's happening in the universe?

It comes as a surprise to many that our universe is not a static collection of never-changing stars and planets. On the contrary, we live in a universe that is dynamic, varied, and changing. Stars, for example, are not all the same, but differ from each other in color, mass, brightness, temperature, age, and chemical makeup. Most stars are about the same mass as our sun or smaller, but some are over a thousand times more massive. Even the apostle Paul observed that "star differs from star in splendor" (1 Cor. 15:41). Hot stars appear blue, while stars with cooler outer layers appear redder. Stars differ from one another in their chemical makeup, as seen in observations of their detailed light spectra. (See plate 3.)

Modern research has shown us that stars do not stay the same forever, but go through a complete "life cycle" of stages. A star is simply a ball of highly compressed gas, most of which is hydrogen. A star "shines" because of a process of chemical fusion occurring deep in the stellar core. As hydrogen atoms fuse into helium atoms under the conditions of extreme gravitational pressure at the star's core, light photons are released. After thousands of years of interacting with stellar material, a photon of light will finally escape from the star and become what we see as starlight. Stars spend most of their lives steadily fusing hydrogen into helium in their cores, but after they have used up the core hydrogen, they speed toward an end that can be quite spectacular. Lower-mass stars (like our sun) eventually lose their outer layers and become "white dwarfs." A more massive star goes through stages of producing heavier elements like oxygen, silicon, and iron in its fusing core before reaching a massive instability that leads to a giant explosion called a *supernova*. A supernova spreads the elements produced both in the star and during the explosion throughout the surrounding region of space between the stars. From this material, new stars and planets that contain these heavier elements can form. This dynamic process of fusion in stars and dispersal through supernova explosions has allowed the heavy elements needed for life to be available in our modern universe. Thus the stars are really a sensational "factory" for producing the very carbon and oxygen that we depend on for life.[3] In fact, we know of no other physical process in the universe that can generate the elements required for planets and life to be sustained. In our own galaxy, previous generations of stars lived and died, producing the heavier elements that we now enjoy in our subsequent generation star and planet, the sun and planet Earth. When very massive stars explode, they leave behind quizzical remains such as neutron stars (so dense that a teaspoon weighs tons), or black holes (so dense that their gravitational fields will not even allow light to escape).

What about the other end of the stellar life cycle—the "birth" of new stars? Star formation is one of the most beautiful processes in the universe, yet we have only been able to peer into the process within the past few decades, with the advent of infrared and radio telescopes. This is because these "stellar nurseries" are deeply embedded in dense clouds of interstellar gas and dust that block most regular visible light. New stars form when pockets of dense gas within an interstellar gas cloud condense and collapse under their own gravitational pull. If there is enough mass in this gas clump, more surrounding gas will be pulled in by gravity (the pull of gravitational force is proportional to mass), and eventually the pressure at the core of this gas clump will be high enough to cause the hydrogen atoms to fuse into helium atoms, releasing light and—*Voilà!*—we have a new star. We now observe forming stars at every stage, from the youngest "protostars" that are still deeply buried in gas clouds and quickly accreting new material, to adolescent stars that have thick disks of debris still in orbit around them, to "young adult" stars that are now shining brightly enough to clear out the surrounding gas from which the star formed. Since the formation process can take tens of millions of years for a large star and hundreds of millions of years for small stars, we humans cannot observe the birth of a star from beginning to end. But we can take snapshots of entire populations and see many stars at different stages of formation.

The beauty of the process is striking. At early stages of a star's birth, while material is rapidly falling into the star, magnetic fields around the star divert some of the infalling gas into an outflowing "exhaust" valve at the poles of the star. These outflowing jets of gas can reach thousands of light-years into the surrounding space and can even be indicators to astronomers of the infant star at the base.[4] Astronomers are now finding spectacular exhaust jets not only around young stars but also around accreting black holes at the centers of other galaxies. When a massive young star begins to radiate, the energetic light will ionize the surrounding gas cloud from which the star formed, creating beautiful, colorful nebulae. Some interstellar gas clouds such as the Orion nebula are such active stellar nurseries that there are literally thousands of baby stars currently forming, driving jets, and ionizing the cloud in spectacular color.[5] The life cycle of the stars is one example of how God's creative activity is ongoing. Creation is not only a one-time event in the past but also a continuing reality under the dynamic processes that God has put in place to govern the universe. (See plate 4.)

What else is going on in the universe?

Activity is everywhere, from the local, small scale, to the scale of the entire universe. In our own local solar system, we see plate tectonics causing earthquakes on the earth, huge storms in the clouds of Jupiter, and volcanoes on Jupiter's moon Io, to name a few hot spots. In other galaxies, we see ongoing supernova explosions of old stars and occasional "gamma-ray bursts" that, during a brief moment, are the most energetic flash in the sky. On the largest scale, we find that the entire universe is expanding. By observing the frequencies of light from distant galaxies, astronomers can gauge whether that galaxy is moving relative to us. If there is motion, the frequency (i.e., wavelength or color) of the light we observe will be slightly lower than that emitted if the galaxy is moving away from us and slightly higher if it is moving toward us. This frequency shift, called the "Doppler shift," is similar to what we experience with the change in sound pitch when a bus or train comes toward us and then recedes away from us. By careful measurements of distant galaxy Doppler shifts, it is clear that galaxies are moving away from each other—indeed, the universe is expanding. No galaxy is at the "center" of this expansion. Rather, it is like a raisin cake in an oven—each raisin sees all the other raisins moving away from it.

A more accurate description of this expansion is not that the galaxies are rushing outward through space, but rather that the fabric of space itself is expanding and carrying the galaxies along with it. We can mentally extrapolate backward from this expansion and derive a time when the expansion would have begun—this yields an estimate of about 14 billion years ago, which is consistent with other age estimates for the universe. However, the rate of expansion (now believed to be about 70 kilometers per second per megaparsec) has not been constant. At the beginning of the expansion, the high density of material probably would have caused an initial deceleration of the expansion. But one of the most surprising discoveries of the last few years in astronomy has been the detection, by careful study of distant galaxies, of an *acceleration* in the expansion of the universe over most of its history. The physics of gravity would have predicted that the universe would either eventually pull itself back together (in a "Big Crunch") or at least expand more slowly with time. But the discovery of acceleration implies a kind of "dark energy" we do not yet understand that is pushing the universe apart.[6] Indeed, the universe is full of mystery and discovery just waiting for us to investigate. (See plate 5.)

How old is the universe?

Just as the size of the universe is beyond our human comprehension, the scientific evidence gathered in recent decades is showing us that the universe has grown and developed over an enormous, but not infinite, span of time. It appears that God has taken great care in allowing a universe to develop in both beauty and in components that we now need to live. What is some of this evidence? First, there is the expansion of the universe described in the last section. A "rewind" in time of this expansion would allow about 14 billion years of time to reach the current size of the universe. Then there is the light we see from galaxies billions of light-years away. To travel across this great distance, billions of years of time were required, and we see the galaxies as they were when the light was emitted, not as they may be now. Therefore, galaxies we observe that are distant in space (and therefore time) often have different appearances and chemical makeup as compared to nearby galaxies, because galaxies change over time. After several generations of stars have generated heavier elements, the stars and gas in an older galaxy have a different chemical composition than a younger (i.e., more distant) counterpart. And the shapes of galaxies become more well-defined as ordered spheres or beautiful spirals when gravity has had billions of years to pull a galaxy into a regular form. The stars themselves give evidence of age. We now know from basic physical principles how long a star of a certain size can continue to "shine" (i.e., fuse hydrogen into helium at its core). Bigger stars have more internal gravitational pressure and therefore use up their hydrogen "fuel" quicker than small stars do, and therefore smaller stars last longer. By counting the fraction and types of younger and older stars in a star cluster, astronomers can then gauge the age of that cluster. Globular star clusters in our own galaxy, the Milky Way, indicate a galaxy age of at least 10 billion years, which is consistent with independent radiometric measurements of our earth and moon that give an age of about 4.6 billion years for our solar system, which formed within the galaxy.

How do these age estimates square with a biblical understanding of time? Some Christians believe that the "days" mentioned in the creation account of Genesis are to be interpreted as literal, twenty-four-hour periods. This, combined with counting the number of human generations described in the Bible, would indicate that the universe can be only a few thousand years old. Some argue that God created the light from distant galaxies already in transit toward us, so that with only a few thousand years of world history, we could still have evidence of distant stars. An almighty God could certainly do this. The problem with this view is that the light we receive from distant galaxies tells us of events and activity there, like supernova explosions and galaxy collisions from billions of years ago. While God could create light "in transit" that indicates activity that didn't really happen, it is not generally seen as in keeping with His character. God seems to delight in us using our senses (and thus our science) to discover what He has done. Some posit the idea that perhaps the speed of light is not constant but has changed drastically over time, allowing us to see objects at great distances with less time available. But light speed is a fundamental physical component of many other physical laws. Such a large change over time would show up in changes to the basic processes of physics and chemistry we would observe in distant galaxies, and no such changes are evident.

Other Christians throughout history have believed that the "days" of Genesis were not necessarily meant to be interpreted as twenty-four-hour sun-divided days (particularly since the sun and moon were not created until the fourth "day"). These include Irenaeus, second-century bishop of Caesarea; Origen, third-century apologist; Basil, fourth-century bishop of Caesarea; and Thomas Aquinas, thirteenth-century theologian. This view was also held by first-century Jewish writers Philo and Josephus, as well as some modern-day theologians and literary scholars.[7] While Scripture can answer the "who" and "why" questions of creation, God has given us our scientific curiosity to investigate some of the "how" and "how long" questions of what He has done.

One thing most Christians do agree on is that the universe as we know it has not always been here—and this is confirmed by modern science. Indeed, the evidence for a "beginning" to the universe is overwhelming. While some scientists in the middle of the twentieth century preferred a universe without a beginning, most scientists now agree that the universe we live in began in a fantastic burst termed in modern times the "Big Bang." The expansion of the universe supports this conclusion. And recent discoveries of NASA's Wilkinson microwave anisotropy probe confirm the presence of background radiation still detectable from an initial big bang 13.7 billion years ago. These detections also show slight spatial variations in the temperature of the subsequent initial background of space that would eventually lead to sites for galaxy and star formation as the universe cooled.[8]

We may speculate about the possibilities that there are other universes we will never even detect. It is clear from our observations, though, that the universe we know is one that is dynamic, changing, and awe-inspiring. (See plate 6.)

Is there life on other planets?

One of the most exciting discoveries of the last few years is the presence of planets around stars other than our sun. Throughout history humans have wondered if our planets are the only ones; now we know they are not. In fact, more than one hundred planets outside our solar system have been detected to date, not by direct imaging but by precise measurement of the "wobble" induced by the gravitational tug of planets in orbit around them. So far the only planets we have the capability to detect are those that are large gas-giant planets, like Jupiter, instead of small rocky planets where life as we know it could exist.[9] But telescopes are being developed that should be able to detect and study Earth-like planets around other stars, if they exist, and to determine if conditions needed to sustain life are present there. We would also then search for any signature of by-products from living systems in the planet's atmosphere and environment. How exciting if we detect evidence for life elsewhere in the universe.

It should not surprise us if life exists on other planets. We find that life thrives in even the unlikeliest places on earth, such as in chemically "toxic" pools in Yellowstone Park or at the bottom of highly pressurized, dark thermal vents at the bottom of the ocean. If God has been able to create exotic life forms on earth, why not elsewhere? Unfortunately, Scripture is silent on the issue.

The new sciences of "astrobiology" and "exobiology" are studying just the kinds of conditions in other worlds that might be able to sustain life. In 2004 the Mars exploration rovers discovered evidence of past pools of water on Mars.[10] Water is essential for life as we know it, and therefore simple life-forms could possibly have been sustained on Mars in the past. What about intelligent life—life-forms that can communicate with us, or with God? Currently an ambitious program, the Search for Extra-Terrestrial Intelligence (SETI), "listens" for distinct radio waves from space that would have been produced by an intelligent civilization trying to make contact.[11] So far, no such signal has been detected, but those who listen have great patience. There is reason to believe that with such an enormous universe and countless planets around other stars, God may be interacting with life-forms we can only dream about.[12] God can relate to (and redeem if necessary) anyone or anything in all creation. There is also reason to speculate that we on earth may in fact be the only life-forms advanced enough to relate to God (and even rebel). While there may be countless stars and galaxies and even planets, the conditions we require for sustained intelligent life on earth are quite unique—it is possible that for reasons we cannot fathom, the whole universe may sustain life on only one tiny planet: ours. With God, however, wonders never cease—so continual searching and investigation will lead to blessing and wisdom about what—or even who—is out there with us in the universe.

If the universe is so incomprehensibly immense in space and time, does that make me insignificant?

The human life span is insignificant on the scale of the history of the universe. And we have already seen how our earth and solar system are not in any significant place in our galaxy, which itself is only one of 10 billion galaxies. We are indeed insignificant if we gauge significance by our location and prominence. However, we are significant because God has chosen us to be so—indeed, Scripture teaches us that we are eternal beings. Just as the Israelites were "chosen" people, not because of anything they had done but because of God's love and desire, so we are infinitely significant. We are so significant that the Creator of the universe knows the number of hairs on our heads and came to experience life on earth with us, dying and living yet again for us.

We are not the first to muse about our seeming insignificance relative to the immensity of the heavens. David the psalmist wrote:

> O LORD, our Lord,
> how majestic is your name in all the earth! . . .
>
> When I consider your heavens,
> the work of your fingers,
> the moon and the stars,
> which you have set in place,
> what is man that you are mindful of him,
> the son of man that you care for him?
> [Yet] you made him a little lower than the heavenly beings
> and crowned him with glory and honor.
>
> —Psalm 8:1, 3–5

What do the heavens tell us about God?

Jeremiah the prophet prayed, "Ah, Sovereign LORD, you have made the heavens and the earth by your great power and outstretched arm. Nothing is too hard for you" (Jer. 32:17).

The magnitude and magnificence of the heavens point to a very *powerful* and *creative* God. As scientific study reveals distances, numbers, and ages for the elements of our universe that are too unfathomably large for our human minds to comprehend, our recognition of the power and vastness of God should likewise grow. The splendor of stars, planets, and galaxies, and indeed the mathematical magnificence of the forces of nature tell us that God is a lover of *beauty* and that we, created in God's image, can recognize it. The heavens tell also of God's *faithfulness*. The physical laws that govern the universe are reliable predictors of how the physical world operates. Indeed, science itself relies on an unshakable faith in the reliability of physical law, such that, for example, the law of gravity is measurable in a repeatable fashion everywhere, and time proceeds forward discernibly to allow cause and effect. Even the fundamental uncertainties that are an intrinsic part of quantum mechanics are quantifiable in a predictable fashion. What, then, gives the universe and the laws that govern it such stability, giving us the ability to scientifically study and understand it? The Bible teaches that God both created and sustains the universe through His Son, Jesus Christ (Heb. 1:2–3). The order and beauty of the physical laws that allow scientific comprehension of the universe are evidence of God's faithfulness in sustaining it.

According to the psalmist, study of the heavens should tell us not only about God's *power* and *glory* but also something about God's *righteousness*, which is a more challenging attribute to derive from astronomical study. The psalmist writes, "The heavens proclaim his righteousness, and all the peoples see his glory" (Ps. 97:6).

As you reflect on this chapter, can you think of ways our scientific discoveries in astronomy reveal God's righteousness and glory?

> "For astronomy is not only pleasant, but also useful to be known; it cannot be denied that this art unfolds the admirable wisdom of God."
>
> —John Calvin (1509–64), theologian and Reformer

QUESTIONS

1. Does scientific analysis and explanation of a process in the universe diminish (or enhance) its beauty?

2. How can a growing awareness of the development and majesty of the universe shape your understanding of God and your relationship with God?

3. If life were to be discovered elsewhere, how would your faith be affected?

NOTES

1. For a more detailed discussion of historical and current astronomy from a Christian perspective, see Deborah Haarsma and Jennifer Wiseman, "An Evolving Cosmos," in *Perspectives on an Evolving Creation*, ed. Keith Miller (Grand Rapids: Eerdmans, 2003), 97–119, from which much of this summary is drawn.
2. The Galileo controversy is a fascinating and complex interplay of science, religion, authority, and personality conflict, and it is often erroneously oversimplified. For excellent detailed accounts from a Christian perspective, see Charles E. Hummel, *The Galileo Connection* (Downers Grove, Ill.: InterVarsity Press, 1986), and Owen Gingerich, *The Great Copernicus Chase* (Cambridge: Cambridge Univ. Press, 1992).
3. A. A. Goodman, "Recycling in the Universe," *Sky & Telescope* (November 2000): 44–53.
4. T. P. Ray, "Fountains of Youth: Early Days in the Life of a Star," *Scientific American* 283(2) (August 2000): 42–47.
5. J. Reston, Jr., "Orion: Where Stars Are Born," *National Geographic* (December 1995): 90–101.
6. C. J. Hogan, R. P. Kirshner, and N. B. Suntzeff, "Surveying Spacetime with Supernovae," *Scientific American* 280(1) (January 1999): 46–51; L. M. Krauss, "Cosmological Anti-Gravity," op. cit., 52–59.
7. Fred Heeren, *Show Me God: What the Message from Space Is Telling Us about God* (Wheeling, Ill.: Daystar, 1997).
8. C. L. Bennett et al., "First-Year Wilkinson Microwave Anisotropy Probe Observations: Maps and Basic Results," *Astrophysical Journal Supplement* 148, no. 1 (September 2003): 1–27.
9. Current planet search results can be found at the *California and Carnegie Planet Search* website, http://exoplanets.org.

10. Highlights of the discoveries of the Mars exploration rovers can be found on the Internet at http://marsrovers.jpl.nasa.gov/home/. See Sarah Graham, "Mars Rover Reveals Red Planet's 'Soaking Wet' Past," *Scientific American.com*, March 3, 2004, http://www.sciam.com.
11. Heeren, *Show Me God,* 50–51.
12. J. Tartar and C. Chyba, "Is There Life Elsewhere in the Universe?" *Scientific American* 281(6) (December 1999): 118–23.

SUGGESTED READING

Danielson, Dennis. *The Book of the Cosmos: Imagining the Universe from Heraclitus to Hawking.* New York: Perseus, 2000.

Gingerich, Owen. *The Great Copernicus Chase.* Cambridge: Cambridge University Press, 1992.

Hummel, Charles E. *The Galileo Connection: Resolving Conflicts between Science and the Bible.* Downers Grove, Ill.: InterVarsity Press, 1986.

Jeeves, Malcolm A., and R. J. Berry. *Science, Life, and Christian Belief.* Leicester: Apollos (InterVarsity Press), 1998.

Polkinghorne, John. *Belief in God in an Age of Science.* New Haven, Conn.: Yale University Press, 1998.

Ross, Hugh. *The Creator and the Cosmos: How the Latest Scientific Discoveries of the Century Reveal God.* Colorado Springs: NavPress, 1995.

CRUCIAL QUESTIONS AT THE INTERFACE OF CHRISTIAN FAITH AND BIOLOGICAL SCIENCE

The living world offers an extraordinary assortment of subjects for study through use of the scientific method. The phenomenon of life is something only fully comprehended by the Creator. As His intellectual stewards, we grasp knowledge about life only partially, and we know that our Creator is the only author of life. We have great pleasure in examining living things and undertaking experimental approaches to study structure and function in all aspects of biological organization and complexity. Sometimes in our problem solving, we copy God's designs in nature because His design cannot be improved.

There are many topics in the biological sciences on which we could have written—beautiful organisms living on the ocean floor, flowering plant distribution, genetic expression, infectious disease organisms and cycles, large mammals and the diseases they carry, or the ecological effects of grazing. But this chapter presents a greater understanding of some of the complexities and principles that scientists in the biological sciences face as they grapple with issues at the intersection of the Christian faith and biology.

This chapter deals briefly with five complex concepts and questions concerning species extinction, bioengineering, mind-brain interactions, wellness, and human origins.

Why Should We Care about the Extinction of Species?

Raymond J. Lewis

> The earth is the LORD's, and everything in it,
> the world, and all who live in it.
> —PSALM 24:1

God's good earth is filled with an amazing array of living organisms. Scientists estimate there are 5 to 10 million species on this planet,[1] living in diverse habitats such as coral reefs, deep sea hydrothermal vents, prairie grasslands, tropical rain forests, hot deserts, and frozen tundra, to name just a few. The flourishing diversity of life on earth is a witness of God's creative work, wisdom, and care. These species are not independent groups of like organisms, but interdependent living organisms that live and interact in diverse ways in ecosystems. Predators, such as wolves, depend on their prey, such as rabbits and other animals. Herbivores, such as these rabbits, depend on the plants they eat, while plants thrive on the nutrients released by both kinds of animals. This web of interdependence involves all living organisms, forming a complex network of interactions that results in the flourishing of life on this planet. Each creature depends on other creatures for its livelihood while each creature provides for the needs of other creatures. The great number of species present results in a very complex set of interactions.[2] Out of this complexity, scientists working in this area conclude that maintaining the diversity of life is necessary for maintaining both the functioning and stability of ecosystems.[3] Is the diversity of life being diminished?

Are species going extinct at an accelerated rate?

From the plight of the passenger pigeon, which went extinct when the last one died in the Cincinnati Zoo in 1914, to the current efforts made to protect species in danger of going extinct, it is apparent that more and more species of God's creatures are disappearing. The rising wave of species extinctions has become so evident to some scientists that a new field of biology was birthed to study and maintain biodiversity: conservation biology.[4] The extinction of species is listed as one of seven degradations of creation that is occurring because of the actions of humanity.[5] Yet, there are those who claim that the extinction crisis is exaggerated.[6] The fact that some extinctions have occurred is not at issue. The question is whether the rate of extinction is accelerated due to human activity.

Scientists have observed and described about 1.5 million species of the 5 to 10 million species estimated to exist at present.[7] The fact that we only know a minority of the species on this planet means that we may not even realize what we are currently losing. However, scientists have made careful estimates based on what is known. If we look at the fossil record, it is apparent that some extinction has always occurred at a background rate, estimated to be one extinction per year for every 1 to 10 million species present.[8] Thus we might expect to see between one and ten species per year going extinct. A further examination of the fossil record reveals five mass extinction events, with much higher rates of extinction resulting in a loss of a significant percentage of species. The most recent mass extinction occurred about 65 million years ago, with the dinosaurs being among the species that were lost. Each of these mass extinction events is assumed to be due to the result of environmental changes. Those at the end of the Permian and Cretaceous periods are thought to be the result of the impacts of asteroids, which would have thrown massive amounts of debris into the atmosphere, blocking sunlight and cooling temperatures.[9] Is the current rate of extinction closer to the estimated background rate, or is it more similar to a mass extinction event?

The number of known extinctions is documented by the International Union for Conservation of Nature and Natural Resources (IUCN) 2003 Red List, which lists

680 species of animals and 82 species of plants that are known to have gone extinct between AD 1500 and the present.[10] While this estimate is similar to the background rate, it is based on the assumption that we can accurately determine the number of species lost from this planet, when we do not even know most of the species on this planet. In addition, it is difficult for species to be listed as extinct, because they must not have been observed for fifty years in order to be considered extinct.[11] A different conclusion is drawn if we use the Red List data to determine extinction rates in conspicuous organisms. Among vertebrate animals, 330 have been recorded to be extinct out of about 45,000 species, or about .75 percent. The rates are higher among mammals (1.7 percent, 78 extinct out of 4,500 species) and birds (1.5 percent, 132 out of 9,000). If one percent of species on earth have gone extinct in the past 500 years, there may already have been 50,000 to 100,000 extinctions, averaging 100 to 200 per year, which is well above the background rate.

However, conservation biologists estimate that the current rates of extinction are much higher than this. E. O. Wilson, applying principles of island biogeography to current trends in habitat degradation, estimates that 17,000 species per year are being lost from tropical rain forests alone.[12] Similar estimates of extinctions due to environmental degradation range from .6 to 30 percent of the world's species disappearing over a decade.[13] If the most conservative estimate, .6 percent per decade, is combined with a conservative estimate of the number of species on earth, 5 million, then 3,000 species are going extinct each year. God's creation is being depleted of its fullness well above the background rate. (See plate 8.)

Is extinction a natural process?

Given the extensive history of extinction of species recorded in the fossil record, one might ask whether extinctions are merely a result of natural processes. While past mass extinction events appear to be the result of natural global catastrophes, the causes of the current wave of extinctions can be traced to human activity. The magnitude of human activity has been summarized as human domination of the planet.[14]

Human domination has resulted in species extinction through a variety of means.[15] The most important is habitat destruction, such as when tropical forest or prairie grassland is converted to farmland or when a forest is cut down for its timber, eradicating the original species. Habitats may also be modified by fragmentation, resulting in habitat patches with reduced populations that may go extinct locally. Habitat degradation can occur via the introduction of toxic chemicals into the air, water, or soil of an ecosystem. Global climate change can have effects that are even more profound, as the warming climate changes the nature of the ecosystem more rapidly than the composition of organisms in those ecosystems can adjust. The introduction of exotic species into habitats has changed the ecological dynamics in many ecosystems and can result in the extinction of native species via competition, parasitism, predation, or disease. This has been particularly evident in isolated ecosystems, such as on islands. Overexploitation of species has been the cause of extinction for some species, such as the dodo bird and Steller's sea cow, each of which was extinguished a few decades after its discovery by humans. Human-caused extinctions are not merely the result of amoral natural processes, but due to the actions of humans who possess moral agency, and thus moral responsibility.

What can and should be done to preserve species?

A scientific description of the extent and causes of extinction is necessary to determine appropriate action. While there can be little question that we are experiencing accelerated rates of extinction, a precise understanding of the extent of the problem remains elusive. The fact that we know only about a fraction of the living organisms on this planet emphasizes the need for a deeper scientific understanding of biodiversity, including describing the many species that have yet to be discovered. These many unknown species may be necessary components for the functioning of entire ecosystems, just as Aldo Leopold expressed: "Who but a fool would discard seemingly useless parts? To keep every cog and wheel is the first precaution of intelligent tinkering."[16] Keeping the parts is necessary but may not be sufficient to preserve these functioning ecosystems. We must better understand how ecosystems function and how our activities impact the environment so we can intelligently choose to act in such a way as to preserve it.

Successful action in "keeping the parts" will require us to work together in implementing appropriate policies based on a scientific understanding of the problems. Legislation such as the Endangered Species Act is an example of a potentially effective corporate response because it is based on science. Through this act, individual species that are in danger of extinction are listed as endangered or threatened, depending on the degree of risk. The habitats of listed species are to be preserved or restored, thus addressing the effects of habitat destruction, which appears to be the main cause of extinction. By protecting these habitats, additional species beyond the target species also gain protection. The effectiveness of this act is hampered by the slow process of appropriately listing species and then developing recovery plans. This potentially effective policy action, informed by science, needs to be supported by the populace.

We are the only species on earth capable of noticing and mourning the loss of another species. As moral agents, we have the capacity to do right or wrong. Reasons for choosing to protect species, and the environment, may be based on our desire to see human existence continue (*anthropocentrism*), on our wish to see individual organisms flourish (*biocentrism*), or on our realization that the entire system of life is good and worthy of protecting (*ecocentrism*). Christians have the most compelling reasons for protecting species. Since God is the Creator of all there is, the creation belongs to God and God values it. Human rebellion against God resulted in death, and this has affected the entire creation (Rom. 8:20–22). Christ came to redeem humans and reconcile all things to Himself (Col. 1:18–20). Thus a first step for Christians is to realize God's role in creating, sustaining, and reconciling all things, and that reconciliation reaches beyond humankind to encompass all of creation.

A second step is to understand our place and responsibility in creation. God created humans in His image, making us a part of this creation while setting us apart for good works. Before the fall, humans were given dominion over the rest of creation and the responsibility to care for the garden (Gen. 1:26; 2:15). Human responsibility may be understood as a stewardship in which God entrusts care of the creation to us.[17] As stewards, we are to serve God and the creation for which we have responsibility.

As good stewards, we ought to be transformed people who display the virtues of a godly character. Steven Bouma-Prediger has described fourteen ecological virtues derived from the contexts of biblical revelation and our place in this groaning creation.[18] Virtues combine attitude and action, since "our conduct forms our character."[19] Actions of creation care will flow from our lives as we show love, benevolence, respect, receptivity, frugality, hope, and wisdom, among other virtues, in all things.

QUESTIONS

1. Do living organisms have intrinsic value, and if so, can they be considered as moral subjects? Why?

2. How do we resolve conflict between preserving species and honoring human rights?

NOTES

1. See Robert M. May, "How Many Species Inhabit the Earth?" *Scientific American* 267 (October 1992): 42–48, for a discussion of this topic, with estimates of species numbers ranging from 3 million to 120 million.
2. M. Loreau, S. Naeem, P. Inchausti, J. Bengtsson, J. P. Grime, A. Hector, D. U. Hooper, M. A. Huston, D. Raffaelli, B. Schmid, D. Tilman, D. A. Wardle, "Biodiversity and Ecosystem Functioning: Current Knowledge and Future Challenges" *Science* 294 (2001): 804–9.
3. Loreau et al., "Biodiversity and Ecosystem Functioning," 808.
4. See, e.g., Fred Van Dyke, *Conservation Biology: Foundations, Concepts, Applications* (New York: McGraw-Hill, 2003).
5. "Declaration on the Care of Creation" sponsored by the Evangelical Environmental Network, reprinted in R. J. Berry, ed., *The Care of Creation: Focusing Concern and Action* (Leicester: Inter-Varsity Press, 2000), 18–22.
6. For opposing viewpoints, see Brenda Stalcup, ed., *Endangered Species: Opposing Viewpoints* (San Diego: Greenhaven, 1996), or Helen Cothran, ed., *Endangered Species: Opposing Viewpoints* (San Diego: Greenhaven, 2001). An opposing religious declaration can be found in Michael B. Barkey, ed., *Environmental Stewardship in the Judeo-Christian Tradition: Jewish, Catholic, and Protestant Wisdom on*

the Environment (Washington, D.C.: Interfaith Council for Environmental Steward-ship, and Grand Rapids: Acton Institute for the Study of Religion and Liberty, 2000).

7. Robert M. May, "How Many Species Inhabit the Earth?" *Scientific American* 267 (October 1992): 42.

8. David M. Raup, "Diversity Crises in the Geological Past," in Edward O. Wilson and Frances M. Peter, eds., *BioDiversity* (Washington, D.C.: National Academy, 1988), 54.

9. Luann Becker, Robert J. Poreda, Andrew G. Hunt, Theodore E. Bunch, and Michael Rampino, "Impact Event at the Permian-Triassic Boundary: Evidence from Extrater-restrial Noble Gases in Fullerenes," *Science* 291 (2001): 1530–33. Luis W. Alvarez, Walter Alvarez, Frank Asaro, and Helen V. Michel, "Extraterrestrial Cause for the Cretaceous-Tertiary Extinction," *Science* 208 (1980): 1095–1108.

10. International Union for Conservation of Nature and Natural Resources, 2003 IUCN Red List of Threatened Species, June 12, 2004, www.redlist.org.

11. IUCN follows the criteria of the Committee on Recently Extinct Organisms; see "New Criteria for Analyzing Recent Extinctions," http://creo.amnh.org/goals2.html.

12. E. O. Wilson, "The Current State of Biodiversity," in Wilson and Peter, *BioDiversity*, 3–18.

13. Nigel E. Stork, "Measuring Global Biodiversity and Its Decline," in Marjorie L. Reaka-Kudla, Don E. Wilson, and Edward O. Wilson, eds., *Biodiversity II: Under-standing and Protecting Our Biological Resources* (Washington, D.C.: Joseph Henry, 1997), 41–68.

14. Peter M. Vitousek, Harold A. Mooney, Jane Lubchenco, and Jerry M. Melillo, "Human Domination of Earth's Ecosystems," *Science* 494 (1997): 494–99.

15. A fuller description of these causes can be found in Richard B. Primack, *Essentials of Conservation Biology*, 3rd ed. (Sunderland, Mass.: Sinauer Associates, 2002).

16. Aldo Leopold, *A Sand County Almanac with Essays on Conservation from Round River* (New York: Ballantine, 1966), 190.

17. Loren Wilkinson, ed., *Earthkeeping in the Nineties: Stewardship of Creation* (Grand Rapids: Eerdmans, 1991), 275–325.

18. Steven Bouma-Prediger, *For the Beauty of the Earth: A Christian Vision for Creation Care* (Grand Rapids: Baker, 2001), 137–60.

19. Ibid., 139.

SUGGESTED READING

Berry, R. J., ed. *The Care of Creation: Focusing Concern and Action*. Leicester: Inter-Varsity Press, 2000.

Bouma-Prediger, Steven. *For the Beauty of the Earth: A Christian Vision for Creation Care*. Grand Rapids: Baker, 2001.

Van Dyke, Fred. *Conservation Biology: Foundations, Concepts, Applications*. New York: WCB/McGraw-Hill, 2003.

Wilson, E. O. *The Diversity of Life*. Cambridge: Harvard University Press, 1992.

Wilson, E. O., and Frances M. Peter, eds. *BioDiversity*. Washington, D.C.: National Acad-emy, 1988.

What Are the Limits in Bioengineering?

E. David Cook

Medical schools today are exploring replacing the traditional medical curriculum of anatomy, physiology, and biochemistry with one based on genetics. Before long the whole human genome will be mapped in an extraordinary task of cooperation by scientists across the world.[20] This mapping project is not just for the sake of gaining genetic information, but is a first step toward the cure of horrific, disabling diseases, for it provides insight into the links between genes, disease, and predispositions. The information gained opens the door to genetic manipulation, replacement, and enhancement.

What is normality?

Scientists have been concerned to find genetic abnormality and the link between particular diseases and certain genes. They have been concentrating on the negative side of such genetic links rather than examining the possible positive benefits from so-called genetic abnormalities. We know that certain racial groups suffer from sickle-cell anemia. While that can cause terrible disease in children as well as early death, the very same gene provides the vast majority of those who carry it with a natural immunity from malaria. There is a fear that we might get rid of what we currently regard as a "bad" gene, only to find that we have lost some as yet unknown benefits and deprived the world of a basically "good" gene.

Behind all such genetic information lies a disparity in how humans see and interpret scientific data. The link of genetics to diseases has tended to define what is regarded as normal. There is a problem in that no one's genetic complement is perfect with 100 percent good genes. Everyone is affected by their parents and grandparents, and no one has control over his or her genetic inheritance. Humans who are unfortunate enough to develop the diseases that lead to, or play a key factor in, ill health are not responsible for such a handicap in life. Unfortunately, the media play upon society's tendencies to be riddled with gender and racial discrimination where there are dangers in the advances of genetic science that may lead to the kind of genetic discrimination so well displayed in the movie *Gattica* and the kind of terrifying world pictured in Aldous Huxley's novel *Brave New World*.

What humans count as normal and abnormal often seems more a function of what is felt at certain comfort levels and what is normalized in terms of oneself and seems to be just like "me." It is vital that we learn to see beyond the disease or handicap and to appreciate and value the person, for he or she is created in God's image, and that gives the ultimate value to every member of humanity.

Who owns and controls genetic information?

One dispute that has arisen as our genetic understanding has grown is over the ownership of genetic information. The European approach stresses that genetic information belongs to the whole of humankind and should be available for any and every scientist to use and work with. Some American geneticists stress the cost of genetic research and development and the need for the information discovered to belong to those who discovered and first published it. A more nuanced view suggests that the information in general belongs to all of us, but the applications and various uses of that information belong to those who have developed and patented them.

What is perhaps even of more concern is whether genetic information about a particular person should be accessible to others, such as insurance companies, employers, or governments.[21] A problem lies in that most of us do not realize the significance of our genetic information. We do not realize that it indicates whether we are carrying a gene that could potentially lead to the development of a disease.

Some human diseases are *monogenetic*—if humans have the gene, they will develop the disease. Others are *multifactorial*—whether they develop the disease depends not on their genetic makeup and susceptibility, but rather on their environment and, in general, on lifestyle and exercise. Even when people have a monogenetic disease, the tests and results do not indicate the timetable for the occurrence of the disease or how seriously the person will suffer from it. Time of onset and severity depend on many other factors than simply the genes themselves.

Genetic information belongs to each individual and to parents in the case of children. But if a person were to apply for a job or for health or life insurance, that information would be highly useful to employers and insurance companies. It is possible that if an insurance provider knew that someone would develop a particular disease by the time he or she was forty, they would not supply life or health insurance, and an employer might not offer a job. Such genetic discrimination would inevitably mean that some people would become unemployable and uninsurable. At best, insurance companies might provide coverage but on a limited and costly basis. Likewise, employers might not offer certain jobs, yet others may be seen as very suitable for carriers of harmful genes.

Privacy rights lie at the heart of who controls and owns our genetic information, but scientists need to explain the significance of genetic information and what it actually means and does not mean so that people can make appropriate decisions about whether and when to reveal that information to others.

How far should we go in genetic manipulation?

Genetic discovery has created the opportunity for manipulating genes, replacing genes, and enhancing certain qualities both in humans and in plants and animals.

At one level, farming and animal husbandry have long been in the business of genetic selection and breeding. Plants, bushes, and trees have been grafted and genetically changed by bioengineering. Now we use genetic selection at the simple level of choosing the gender of our children or the more complex level of manipulating the structure that leads to muscular dystrophy or designing plants that are resistant to certain insects. Cloning is an acceptable practice for animals, like Dolly the famous sheep.[22] Some groups have even claimed that they have cloned humans. Cloning parts of human genetic material leads to replication of cells in tissues such as skin and other organs. Still much debate is occurring over the efficacy, safety, and wisdom of further steps in that direction as well.

Christians are particularly concerned about the use and discarding of human embryos in areas like stem-cell research, in which particular parts of the body can be cloned from stem cells that are forced to develop in controlled settings.[23] The source of such stem cells, especially when they are derived from embryonic life rather than from adults or from umbilical cord material, raises fundamental questions about the status of the embryo and how science is conducted, controlled, and limited by science, government, or the public.

Modern medicine deserves applause for its accomplishments in preventing disease or curing humans suffering from disease and enduring lives of pain. Care must be taken to be honest and assess the real motives at work. The desire to eliminate and ease pain may be good, but commercial moneymaking or winning the Nobel Prize for Science as the sole aim of genetic engineering gives a very different flavor to how we regard such scientific work. What actually is involved in the manipulation or replacement of genetic material and the work done to establish the validity of the research and the application should be morally assessed.

The principles at stake, such as the integrity of the individual and the uniqueness of the material must be clear. Similarly, concerns regarding the consequences and application of genetic work must be addressed. Will the genetic manipulation lead to a slippery slope, or can we honestly draw moral and legal lines to protect humanity and our environment? Christians tend to be very realistic about human nature, and they stress concern about the effects of introducing any step that devalues life and is based simply on the idea that the end justifies any and every means.[24] Rather, some means may be so evil in themselves that these are lines that ought not to be crossed. There is no technological imperative that suggests that simply because we have the capacity to do something, we ought to do it. Humans may have knowledge of how to destroy the world by nuclear holocaust, but that certainly does not imply that it ought to be done.

The safety of genetic manipulation in plants, animals, or human beings should register highly among our concerns. Much of genetic and bioengineering work has been hyped and the promises exaggerated.[25] This is in part to develop funding when raising money for research is very hard and when the pressure to produce, publish, and develop new technologies is great. There is an inevitable gap between what can be done in the lab today and when that technology will become a genuine treatment option, if indeed it ever does. Science is not a steady forward process but is about steps forward and backward, successes and failures. There are few absolute guarantees in scientific research and development.

Perhaps the key moral principle to be applied to bioengineering is whether we are seeking to put right something that has gone wrong in the same way that medicine seeks to restore the natural function of a person's body. The concern should not be merely to enhance particular functions or qualities. For example, producing a generation of superathletes who can break the three-minute mile and leap eight feet without a pole and twenty feet with one ought not to be the focus of modern science, especially medical science in a world where too many continue to die of malnutrition, famine, and preventable disease.

Science only happens in a context. Our context is finely balanced between a world of traditional values where the individual and his or her dignity, worth, and value are crucial and a world where efficiency and material success are the driving principles. Christianity holds firmly and absolutely to God's law and His standards embodied in Jesus and His teaching. Science is based on values. The only question, then, is which values will be that basis?[26] Christianity offers values to guide humanity through the use of the contemporary developments in genetics and other sciences.

QUESTIONS

1. Are bioengineers in danger of "playing God"?

2. How do we understand and define what is normal?

3. What limits should be set to using genetic manipulation for enhancement?

4. What effects would enhancing humans have in terms of sports, education, work, life expectancy, and relationships?

NOTES

20. F. S. Collins and K. Jegalian, "Human Genome Project," *Encyclopedia of Public Health*, ed. L. Breslow, L. W. Green, W. Keck, J. Last, and M. McGinnis (Woodbridge, Conn.: Macmillan Reference, 2002).

21. E. David Cook, "Genetics at the British Insurance Industry," *Journal of Medical Ethics* 25, no. 2 (April 1999): 157–62.

22. Ian Wilmot, Keith Campbell, and Colin Judge, *The Second Creation: Dolly at the Age of Biological Control* (New York: Farrar, Straus & Giroux, 2000).

23. Henk Jochemsen, ed., *Human Stem Cells* (Lindenborn Institute, Centre for Medical Ethics, Ede, The Netherlands, and the Business Centre of Jerusalem, Israel).

24. E. David Cook, *Dilemmas of Life* (Downers Grove, Ill.: InterVarsity Press, 1990).

25. See the discussion on the Third Culture in chapter 4.

26. See Jacob Bronowski, *Science and Human Values* (New York: Harper & Row, 1965).

SUGGESTED READING

Colson, C. W., and N. M. Des Cameron. *Human Dignity in the Biotech Century*. Downers Grove, Ill.: InterVarsity Press, 2004.

Jochemsen, Henk, ed. *Human Stem Cells*. Lindenbook Institute, Centre for Medical Ethics, Ede, The Netherlands, and the Business Centre of Jerusalem, Israel.

Kass, Leon, ed. *Being Human*. New York: W. W. Norton, 2004.

Kilner, J., C. Ben Mitchell, and D. Taylor. *Does God Need Our Help? Cloning, Assisted Suicide and Other Challenges in Bioethics*. Wheaton, Ill.: Tyndale House, 2003.

What Is the Mind-Brain Problem?

William M. Struthers

The question about the relationship between our private mental experience and the physical states of our brains is often referred to as the "mind-body problem." It may initially appear that the mind-body problem is not really a question, but a description of a state of affairs. The problem is rooted in the fact that our mental experience appears to be a qualitatively different sort of substance and maintains different properties than the stuff of brain matter. What is the nature of the mind, and how is our mind related to the body? Is the mind nonphysical (i.e., supernatural)? Does it leave the body after we die? Is it an epiphenomenal by-product of millions of neurons firing in sequence? Does the mind exert its will over the body to control it? Philosophers, theologians, and physicians across the centuries have offered a variety of pictures and opinions on how our private, subjective experience is (or is not) related to the functioning of our bodies.[27]

In the fourth century BC, Aristotle maintained that the mind was in the heart. Hippocrates placed it in the brain, and during the second century, Galen placed it in the fluid filled ventricles of the brain. Rene Descartes pinpointed the pineal gland as the seat of the soul in the later part of the seventeenth century. Each of these philosophers and physicians maintained a view of mind that was Hellenic and dualistic in nature. There were two worlds, and the mind was in the nonmaterial, the body in the material.

Over the past 150 years, brain scientists have accumulated a substantial amount of data, ranging from case studies of individuals suffering from brain damage, to drug treatments for mental disorders, and to the recent brain-imaging technologies

One of the more famous cases in the history of brain science is that of Phineas Gage. In 1848 this unassuming railroad worker from New England was involved in an accident that would dramatically change his life and give us a surprising view into the mind-brain problem. Gage had the misfortune of being too near to an explosion that sent a tamping iron through the front of his brain. Prior to this accident, Gage possessed a pleasant disposition and was a moral and temperate man. After the accident, however, his behavior became increasingly erratic and his aspirations, moral outlook, and personality were dramatically altered. After his death, his autopsy revealed that the tamping iron had passed through the frontal lobe of his brain. By passing through the frontal part of the brain, the regions involved in keeping him alive were spared. The frontal lobe is responsible for higher order cognitive processing, and the damage to this area is clearly seen in Gage's inability to make long-term plans and make moral decisions. While Gage's case provides a graphic example of the interrelatedness of the mind and brain, similar medical disorders and head trauma combined with scientific research have been pieced together so predictions about cognitive and behavioral deficits can be made after brain damage. (See plate 9.)

to pinpoint the specific brain regions for mental phenomena (see sidebar for the famous case of Phineas Gage). These findings have led many scientists, philosophers, and theologians to reevaluate the fundamental questions of human nature and psychological experience toward a view of the mind that is more rooted in the biology of the brain. Mind and brain are not different types of "stuff," but are different aspects of the same thing. The mind is the brain looking upon itself.

"Does my soul leave my body when I die?"

For several centuries theologians, philosophers, and physicians have debated what it is about us that makes us so unique. In the Judeo-Christian tradition, special emphasis is given to (1) *imago Dei* (image of God, (2) the Hebrew word *nephesh* (commonly translated "soul"), and (3) the Greek word *psyche* (also translated "soul"). While considerable hermeneutical energy has gone into determining what these terms mean within the context of Scripture, it is apparent that many in Western Christian traditions embrace a dualistic view (see the sidebar "Philosophical Positions on the Nature of Mind," p. 122). The unique conscious experience that we have is not that of individual brain cells firing, but is of a qualitatively different sort. The stream of consciousness, the internal "Cartesian theater"—where we view the world around us from within as when an audience member watches a play—and the subjective nature of conscious experience seem to support a soul in a body, or a "ghost in the machine." The challenge for this dualistic view is that it must examine whether the view that the human identity resides in the soul and

---

But it is the soul, the great soul, of man, that does especially bear God's image. The soul is a spirit, an intelligent immortal spirit, an influencing active spirit, herein resembling God, the Father of Spirits, and the soul of the world. The spirit of man is the candle of the Lord. The soul of man, considered in its three noble faculties, understanding, will and active power, is perhaps the brightest, clearest looking-glass in nature, wherein to see God."*

How do we interpret the Genesis passages regarding *imago Dei*? Is it a nonphysical soul or a mental property? What is the biological basis of sin? Can I really be blamed for something if my brain made me do it? The Christian in brain sciences working on these brain-mind-soul questions generally has a number of options (although each option has many different manifestations). The naturalistic worldview, which sets the ontological agenda for nearly all of the natural sciences, works within a deterministic and materialistic mind-set. The epistemological tools are those of the scientific method, and they dictate what counts as data and how it is to be analyzed. It is remarkably difficult for many Christians to hold strongly to these assumptions, as their ontological understanding of the world may include a spiritual (nonphysical) realm and their value of Scripture and theological epistemology may be in sharp contrast with the naturalistic worldview.

---

*Matthew Henry, *Matthew Henry's Commentary on the Whole Bible*, vol. 1 (Iowa Falls, Iowa: World Bible Publishers), 10 [on Gen. 1:27].

leaves the body after death is biblically based, theologically necessary, or historically accurate. Some Christians, however, point to the findings of the brain sciences, which "tighten the link" between the brain and mind and offer an alternative.[28]

How may Christians understand the discoveries of the brain sciences?

Even the most passive observer of the evening news cannot help but be aware that recent advances in brain imaging and genetics have dramatically altered how we view ourselves. Use of brain-imaging technologies to monitor neural activity and explore the functionality of the brain has led toward localization of neural activity for simple sensory tasks, ethical decision making, mathematical calculations, and even mystical experiences. The possibility of a "God spot" in the brain might suggest that religious experience is nothing more than the activation of a specific brain resin.[29] Interestingly, it has long been reported that some epileptics experience a mystical experience just prior to the onset of their seizures. For Christians these findings challenge our view of how we are made. Can we trust that when we feel the presence of God it is truly His presence?

As we consider an increasingly biological, genetic, and deterministic view of human nature, we may begin to wonder how many important theological factors are interpreted. The trends in the neurosciences point toward a convergence of human cognitive processes and neural activity. Christian theologians and scientists of faith have suggested that the classic dualistic account of human souls is not biblical, philosophically sound, theologically necessary, or biologically possible. Instead, a monistic view moves us from *having* souls to *being* souls.

Perhaps the best known version of this option within Christianity is referred to as non-reductive physicalism (NRP).[30] NRP maintains that there exists an "irreducible intrinsic interdependence" between mental phenomena and their underlying neural correlates. We do not have "souls," but we are "souls." We are made of only one type of stuff—physical—but our psychological experience emerges out of our brains, yet cannot be reduced to neurons. In addition, these mental events have causal properties that, in turn, alter the brain. These downward streams of causation, however, are still poorly understood and may just be a repositioning of the "mind-body problem." How can a subjective mental state have any real causal properties? It is still, at its core, a network of neurons. In what realm does the private world exist to exert its will on the brain?

If morality is a function of the brain, do we really have control over our actions and are we really morally accountable?

It would not be unfair for the Christian to argue that brain sciences (and their naturalistic assumptions) have painted a picture of humanity that dooms (or alternately exalts) us to the cognitive and behavioral fates of our genes. There is limited room for either our mind or soul to save (or wreck) us.[31] The Christian doctrines of sin, redemption, and the saving power of Jesus' death on the cross have little

PHILOSOPHICAL POSITIONS ON THE NATURE OF MIND

Eliminative materialism. There are no mental states, only brain states. All mental life can be reduced to the firing of neurons.

Dual-aspect monism. Mind and body are not different substances; they are two aspects of the same thing viewed from the mental and physical perspectives.

Functionalism. The defining features of any mental state are the causal relations it has with the physical stimuli (inputs), other mental states (information processing), and/or bodily behavior (outputs).

Substance dualism. We are made of two types of substances: substance extended in time and space (*res extensa*)—the body; and a thinking substance (*res cogitans*)—the mind/soul.

Nonreductive physicalism. A monistic view that holds that humans are only one substance—a physical body. Mental events are brain events that depend on lower-level brain

potency if we can't really be accountable for anything. We may think, "My genes and neurons made me do it, but I am really a *soul* held captive by those things." For the unitary theorist, moral agency is a function of complex modulation of action loops. These loops are amplified by the capacity for language and the increased cortical resources humans have.[32] From within these nested neural feedback loops, we have the moral agent who is responsible and accountable. If this is the case, then our moral agency, responsibility, and culpability reside within these complex neural loops. Moral decisions are neural events (albeit exceedingly complex ones). It is here that most NRP theorists find themselves in a bit of a bind. The notion of being embedded in our bodies, our mental capacities ultimately physical in nature, appears to entail a form of physical determinism and, in turn, a sort of moral relativism. As such, any behavior's moral status must refer to a cultural or evolutionary standard. Cultural standards are man-made, and evolutionary standards are selected by either natural selection or group selection. In either case, cultural and evolutionary standards act as arbitrary rules for moral codes of conduct. The morality of any behavior is ultimately determined by its ability to aid in survival and procreation, not its agreement with an objective, transcendent moral standard given by God.

A major concern for Christians includes arriving at a view of the mind-body problem in which individuals are not held morally accountable for their actions. This is an unacceptable conclusion for many theists, and a return to the dualistic view of mind offers an easy out. The nonphysical soul exerts its will on the body and is held morally accountable.

How does the Holy Spirit direct us toward a Christlike mind?

Where does the Holy Spirit come into our lives? How does the Spirit have the freedom to act in us if only through the physical? For the Christian, the work of the

Holy Spirit is either a supernatural process beyond the scope of science (dualist) or God working through the physical world in a hands-on manner. Ontological dualists appeal to these questions as scriptural defeaters for a monist/physicalist theological anthropology.[33] The Holy Spirit shapes our minds in the spiritual (nonphysical) realm and is not limited to physical laws or amenable to direct scientific investigation. The Christian dualist is therefore left with the philosophical problem of how these two substances interact, a vast amount of neuroscientific data, and a Holy Spirit who is limited to the supernatural realm. Moral accountability of the soul is kept, but the mind is now off limits for scientists because the mind is a priori a nonphysical substance. And the mind-body problem will remain a mystery beyond the limits and tools of neuroscience.

On the other hand, a Christian monist theory (i.e., NRP) opens the possibility of investigating the mind but denies a classically spiritual nature of the Holy Spirit. If the mind is a part of the physical world, it is fair game for the scientist. Additionally, the Holy Spirit acts through the workings of the physical realm. While many philosophers and theologians have a relatively naive understanding of neurons, it may be argued that they have an overly supernatural view bordering on a "magical" belief in the working of the Holy Spirit leading to a Gnostic view of the body that degrades the physical body and elevates the nonphysical mind or soul. The Christian monist holds out that as we understand our biological nature, we will begin to appreciate the neurocircuitry of linguistic processing (reading and hearing of Scripture) and semantic organization (insight into and meditation on God's laws) as the neural substrates through which the Holy Spirit works to minister to us and develop a Christlike mind/brain.

QUESTIONS

1. How does current research in the neurosciences affect the way we interpret the Old Testament passages regarding *imago Dei*? Humans?

2. Can we be held morally accountable for our actions (or inactions) if our genetics or brain chemistry are the primary factor(s) in determining our behavior?

3. What effect does nonreductive physicalism's conceding of the immaterial soul have on eschatology?

NOTES

27. Colin McGinn, "Can We Solve the Mind-Body Problem?" *Mind* 98 (1989): 349–66; David Chalmers, *The Conscious Mind* (Oxford: Oxford Univ. Press, 1996); and Daniel Dennett, *Consciousness Explained* (Boston: Little, Brown and Co., 1991).
28. David G. Myers and Malcolm A. Jeeves, *Psychology through the Eyes of Faith*, rev. and updated ed. (San Francisco: HarperCollins, 2003).
29. McGinn, "Can We Solve the Mind-Body Problem?"; Chalmers, *The Conscious Mind*; Dennett, *Consciousness Explained*; Andrew Newberg, Eugene D'Aquili, and Vince

Rause, *Why God Won't Go Away* (New York: Ballantine, 2001); Eugene D'Aquili and Andrew Newberg, *The Mystical Mind*: *Probing the Biology of Religious Experience, Theology and the Sciences* (Minneapolis: Fortress Press, 1999); and Matthew Alper, *The "God" Part of the Brain*: *A Scientific Interpretation of Human Spirituality and God* (New York: Rogue, 2001).

30. Malcolm Jeeves, *Human Nature at the Millennium* (Grand Rapids: Baker, 1997); Warren Brown, Nancey Murphy, and H. Newton Malony, eds., *Whatever Happened to the Soul?* (Minneapolis: Fortress Press, 1998); Caroline Walker Bynum, *The Resurrection of the Body* (New York: Columbia Univ. Press, 1995); Malcolm A. Jeeves, ed., *From Cells to Souls—and Beyond* (Grand Rapids: Eerdmans, 2004); *Body, Soul, and Life Everlasting*: *Biblical Anthropology and the Monism-Dualism Debate* (Grand Rapids: Eerdmans, 1989).

31. Richard Dawkins, *A Devil's Chaplain* (New York: Houghton Mifflin, 2003); Gregory R Peterson, *Minding God* (Minneapolis: Augsburg Fortress, 2003).

32. M. Donald, "The Neurobiology of Human Consciousness: An Evolutionary Approach," *Neuropsychologia* 33, no. 9 (1995): 1087–1102.

33. Caroline Walker Bynum, *The Resurrection of the Body* (New York: Columbia Univ. Press, 1995); John W. Cooper, *Body, Soul & Life Everlasting* (Grand Rapids: Eerdmans, 1989).

SUGGESTED READING

Block, Ned, Owen Flanagan, and Güven Güzeldere, eds. *The Nature of Consciousness.* Cambridge, Mass.: MIT Press, 1997.

Damasio, Antonio. *Looking for Spinoza.* Orlando: Harcourt, 2003.

Fleischman. John. *Phineas Gage: A Gruesome but True Story about Brain Science.* Boston: Houghton Mifflin, 2002.

Konner, Melvin. *The Tangled Wing.* 2nd ed. New York: Henry Holt, 2003.

Is Wellness a Human Body Stewardship Issue?

Peter H. Walters

The long-standing definition of health was "the absence of disease."[34] For centuries infectious diseases were the number one cause of death in most developing countries.[35] The devastation caused by rampant disease is evident from the following examples. Procopius, the court historian to Emperor Justinian I in 541, describes an epidemic in Constantinople as follows: "the whole human race came near to being annihilated."[36] In less than a year, approximately 200,000 people, 40 percent of the city's population, had lost their lives. Eight centuries later, the black death swept through Europe, eliminating about one-third of the population.

As medicine developed, vaccinations were produced and became widely available. By the mid-1950s, infectious diseases such as influenza and pneumonia had largely been eradicated in developing countries. No longer were infectious diseases the number one killer. But health and humanitarian organizations were no longer satisfied with the elimination of disease. The World Health Organization redefined health as "not merely the absence of disease but a state of complete physical, mental, and social well-being."[37]

Two major emphases in the World Health Organization's redefinition of health paved the way for the modern wellness movement. The first was the expansion of health care beyond the treatment of pathology. Rather than focusing exclusively on sickness and disease, health professions began to speak of adequacy and sufficiency. Some even dared to think about maximization and optimization. The second major emphasis was that health was no longer limited to one's physiology. Individuals with strong bodies but troubled minds were no longer deemed healthy. An organization that pioneered this expanded approach was the Young Men's Christian Association (YMCA). Their motto, "The improvement of the spiritual, mental, social and physical condition of young men," recognized the need for multidimensional maturity.[38]

Two terms emerged that best capture this expanded view of health: *holistic health* and *wellness*. Though the terms are new, the concepts of multidimensional growth and fullness have a long heritage in Christian tradition. Scriptures record that Jesus developed in mind, body, spirit, and social depth and that He was concerned with human suffering and its effect in every aspect of life (Luke 2:52; John 8:2–10; Matt. 25:31–46). Christ was actively involved in physical restoration, emotional and mental healing, restoring financial responsibility, and participating in deeply loving relationships. He demonstrated a desire for complete redemption.

In addition to the breadth of his reach, Christ challenged His followers to go beyond even the highest standards of moral conduct outlined in previous Scripture (Matt. 5:1–7:29). He told His followers that their righteousness should exceed that of the spiritually elite. This was the way to the kingdom of God (Matt. 5:20). He also told his followers that He had come to give them not adequate life but abundant life (John 10:10). The Bread and Water of Life would be sustenance and satisfaction for the deepest longings of humanity (John 4:1–15; 6:30–58).

Wellness is fullness in all aspects of our humanity. It is being a person who reaches beyond "the absence of disease" to a state of richness in every facet of his or her being.

Are there substantial differences in the way Christians and non-Christians view wellness?

Young and old, rich and poor, male and female, secular and spiritual—we all want health and well-being. Sweeping generalities like this tend to blur our vision of underlying concepts and worldviews that in reality have much greater disparity than similarity. There is disparity between a secular and distinctly Christian view of wellness.

Here are some of the leading cover stories advertised on two of the most popular health and fitness magazines currently in circulation:[39]

30 Days to the Body of Your Dreams
Six Weight-Loss Tips to Keep It Off
Wake Up More Beautiful
Your Sexiest Hips and Thighs
The Best Facials for Your Skin Type
Get Your Ultimate Body

These captions reveal that gaining and possessing an attractive body are of supreme value. Beyond reducing our exposure to disease, increasing physiological capacities, or enjoying competitive and restorative leisure, data suggests that one of the strongest reasons for exercise is enhanced physical appearance.[40]

Less obvious, but just as consistent, are the underlying motives for smooth skin, abs of steel, and a shapely physique. These highly publicized attributes bestow an increased sense of confidence and self worth, the ability to attract attention and recognition from the opposite sex, and a life conducted with greater poise and power. The bottom line is that it is all about you—your self-concept, your self-worth, your physical appeal, your power.

Both societal values and the rationale for pursuing them stand in stark contrast to a Christian ethos. Though Scripture often celebrates aesthetic beauty, when compared to inward virtue, outward attractiveness pales in comparison. The apostle Peter wrote to wives: "Your beauty should not be an external one. . . . Instead, it should be the inner disposition of the heart, consisting of the imperishable quality of a gentle and quiet spirit, which is of great value in the sight of God" (1 Peter 3:3–4 ISV).

Though there are noteworthy differences with regard to the emphasis of external attractiveness, the most striking disparity emerges over purpose. Christ's followers are exhorted to reject the concept of self-glory and power in pursuit of a higher and nobler vision of service to Christ and His kingdom. "Didn't you realize that your body is a sacred place, the place of the Holy Spirit? Don't you see that you can't live however you please, squandering what God paid such a high price for? The physical part of you is not some piece of property belonging to the spiritual part of you. God owns the whole works. So let people see God in and through your body" (1 Cor. 6:19–20 Message).

The societal view of wellness, which emphasizes beauty and brawn for the sake of personal satisfaction, is inconsistent with biblical truth. God's perspective of internal health and spiritual maturity has eternal significance. It reveals His glory on earth to build up His kingdom.

What is the future of wellness as a discipline?

In many regards, the future is bright. The leading cause of death in the United States, heart disease, is declining. Smoking, a lifestyle habit that contributes to more premature deaths than any other single behavior is lessening. Many research scientists believe that it is not a matter of "if" a cure for AIDS and cancer will be discovered but merely a matter of "when." Changes like these have precipitated increases in life expectancy for all Americans. Currently children born in America are expected to live 77.2 years.[41] At no time in American history has the number been higher.

Other facets of wellness have been shining as well. Despite brief periods of recession, Americans have benefited from substantial economic growth. Although a handful of countries have a higher per capita income than America, most economists believe that because per capita income is generally based on a narrow range of goods and services when all things are considered, U.S. citizens enjoy the highest standard of living anywhere in the world.[42] The breadth and depth of knowledge are also escalating at unprecedented rates. A recent review reported there were more than 30,000 books in print on the topic of weight management alone. The percentage of U.S. adults with four or more years of college education more than doubled from 1970 to 1991.[43]

Based on our history, many Americans are quite optimistic about the future. One such person is historian and futurist Robert Naisbitt, who writes, "The idea of progress holds that mankind has advanced in the past ... is advancing, and will continue to advance through the foreseeable future."[44] If such trends continue, by the next century the average person may live to be over one hundred years of age, make over $100,000 a year, and be at least a college graduate.

While all seems quite well at first glance, there are deeper issues that suggest an internal decomposition. Though living longer than ever before, the Centers for Disease Control reports that the average American can expect almost twelve years of sickness, disease, and dysfunction throughout life.[45] The National Opinion Research Center (NORC), which has measured feelings of well-being among the population since 1957, reports that despite a more than doubling of yearly income, the number of Americans who describe themselves as "very happy" has declined.[46] The National Institute of Mental Health reports a tenfold increase in the number of Americans suffering from depression[47] within the past five decades. During the same time, the rate of divorce, acts of violence, sexual misconduct, and frequency of litigation have all significantly increased. Nobel Prize winner Aleksandr Solzhenitsyn was one of many who saw the dangers of a society bent on gaining more power, money, and success: "All this endless progress turned out to be an insane, ill-considered, furious dash into a blind alley."[48] We have focused on economic, technological, and educational growth to the detriment of our spiritual and emotional selves.

So what does the twenty-first century have in store for wellness and health professionals? According to the Bureau of Labor Statistics and the Occupational Outlook Handbook, health-care professions will be the third-largest job growth market in the foreseeable future.[49] We need young men and women committed to the task of teaching wellness from the inside out. We need wellness that proclaims forgiveness and love to those bound in prisons of hate and selfishness, purpose to those lost in a sea of meaninglessness, and spiritual insight to those blinded by external measures of success.

QUESTIONS

1. Are balanced living and high achievement somewhat mutually exclusive?

2. As we strive and press toward becoming all that God created us to be, how can we also fully embrace contentment?

3. Why is it that material prosperity, educational enrichment, and expanded personal options have not yielded increased life satisfaction and happiness?

4. What is the Christian view of beauty in a culture obsessed with body image and appearance?

NOTES

34. Jerrold S. Greenberg, George B. Dintiman, and Barbee M. Oakes, *Physical Fitness and Wellness*, 3rd ed. (Needham Heights, Mass.: Allyn and Bacon, 2004), 7.

35. Sandra Alters and Wendy Schiff, *Essential Concepts for Healthy Living*, 3rd ed. (Sudbury, Mass.: Jones & Bartlett, 2003), 4–5.

36. Christopher King, *Chasing the Plague through the Centuries* (Philadelphia: Institute for Scientific Information, 1997).

37. Alters and Schiff, *Essential Concepts for Healthy Living*, 2.

38. Pamela Bayless, *YMCA at 150: A History of the YMCA of Greater New York 1852–2002* (New York: Fordham Univ. Press, 2002).

39. Barbara Harris, *Shape Magazine* (March 2003), cover; Joe Weider, *Muscle and Fitness* (February 2004), cover.

40. Robert Weinberg and Daniel Gould, *Foundations of Sport and Exercise Psychology*, 3rd ed. (Champaign, Ill.: Human Kinetics, 2003), 401–427; Bess Marcus and LeighAnn Forsyth, *Motivating People to Be Physically Active* (Champaign, Ill.: Human Kinetics, 2003), 4–23.

41. *United States Health* (Washington, D.C., National Center for Health Statistics, 2003); http://www.cdc.gov/nchs/fastats/ifcpc.htm, accessed March 5, 2005.

42. Michael Watts, *The Literary Book of Economics: Including Readings from Literature and Drama on Economic Concepts, Issues, and Themes* (Wilmington, Del.: Intercollegiate Studies Institute, 2003).

43. *Population with More Than Four Years of College Education* (Washington, D.C.: U.S. Census Bureau, 2003); http://www.census.gov/prod/2004pubs/p20–550.pdf, accessed March 5, 2005.

44. John Naisbitt, *Megatrends: Ten New Directions Transforming Our Lives* (New York: Warner, 1982).

45. *Aging and Morbidity* (Washington, D.C.: Centers for Disease Control, 2003); http.//www.cdc.gov/nchs/data/hvs/hvs99.pdf, accessed March 5, 2005.

46. Randi Glatzer, "The Happiness Prescription," *American Health* 18, no. 9 (1999): 18.

47. *U.S. Mental Health Disorders* (Washington, D.C.: National Institutes of Mental Health, 2000); http://www.nimh.nih.gov.

48. Harry Schwartz, "Solzhenitsyn without Stereotype," *Saturday Review World* 1, no. 16 (1974): 24.
49. *Occupational Outlook* (Washington, D.C.: Bureau of Labor Statistics, 2004); http://www.bls.gov/oco.

SUGGESTED READING

Brand, Paul, and Philip Yancey. *Fearfully and Wonderfully Made*. Grand Rapids: Zondervan, 1987.
Ibid. *In His Image*. Grand Rapids: Zondervan, 1987.
Cooper, Kenneth H. *The Aerobics Program for Total Well-Being: Exercise, Diet, Emotional Balance*. New York: Bantam, 1991.
Nieman, David C. *Exercise Testing and Prescription: A Health-Related Approach*. Boston: McGraw-Hill, 2003.
Seligman, Martin E. *Authentic Happiness*. New York: Free Press, 2002.
Sharkey, Brain. *Fitness and Health*. 5th ed. Champaign, Ill.: Human Kinetics, 2002.

How Do Scientific Views on Human Origins Relate to the Bible?

Dean E. Arnold

According to the Bible, humans have a dual nature. They are made in the image of God but corrupted by sin.[50] Unfortunately, operationalizing these qualities in a way that they can be identified and investigated in the artifacts of the prehistoric record is difficult. Nevertheless, of these two qualities, the image of God has the most potential for empirical study because it suggests that humans have significant qualitative differences in cognition and behavior from nonhuman animals. So what is the meaning of image of God in tangible terms that relate to the actual data of human origins? At least two issues must be examined: the nature of humans and their differences from the rest of the living world. While humans are animals and share many similarities with the higher primates (e.g., the chimpanzees and gorillas), both anthropology and the Bible affirm that human anatomy is not as important as human cognition and behavior. Because we are animals but are not *merely* animals, the paleontological record of humanlike fossils is not as useful for understanding human origins as the archaeological record of cultural beginnings.

What is a scientific view of humans?

Biologically, humans are hominids.[51] Being hominids means that humans are upright walkers[52] with a series of associated features in the pelvis and skull. They also have generalized teeth that are not used as tools to obtain food. Hominids thus do not rely on their anatomy to adapt to their environment. On the contrary, their large brain relative to body size permits an adaptation that is behavioral rather than biological. In modern humans, this adaptation is exclusively learned rather than innate and is based on the massive use of symbols that are predominantly, but not exclusively, vocal in nature. Anthropologists call this phenomenon "culture," and it permits a wide variety of behavioral adaptations to diverse environments around the world. Therefore, culture, not anatomy, makes possible a life that we recognize as human.

How do the human beginnings in the Bible relate to the fossil record?

Great differences exist between the scientific record of the ancient human past and popular readings of the Bible. One great difference is the implied date of the beginning of humans in Genesis and the great antiquity of hominids. The Genesis text says that Adam's son Cain was a "tiller of the ground" and his son Abel was "keeper of sheep" (Gen. 4:2 KJV). Does this mean that Cain and Abel used domesticated plants and animals and thus relied on agriculture for subsistence? The earliest evidence of agriculture occurs about 8000 BC. Elsewhere, such as the New World, the genetic changes required to produce domesticated plants and animals required about 2,000 to 3,000 years. So, if Adam was the first agriculturalist, he probably lived about 10,000 BC. Anatomically modern humans, however, date back at least 100,000 years, and the earliest hominids (although not "human" in a modern sense) may occur as early as seven million years ago (e.g., *Sahelanthropos tchadensis*).

The time gap between virtually any kind of ancient hominid and what might be agriculture in the biblical account thus creates a problem for the serious student of the Bible. The biblical doctrine of the unity of the human species that affirms that all human beings alive today share the dual nature of humans because all humans are descended from the first couple, Adam and Eve, is critical.

One way to help fix the time of the first biblical humans is to examine the characteristics of Adam and Eve after creation. The Bible says that Adam and Eve talked with one another and with God and that Adam named the animals. Further, they were charged with the responsibility of taking care of the garden and had a position of control over it in a way unlike the animals. Moreover, the language of Adam and Eve had all of the characteristics of human language: creativity (Adam named the animals) and the ability to communicate information not present to the senses that permitted human minds to transcend the limits of space, time, and the concrete through the massive use of symbols.[53] These qualities, foundational to what is commonly regarded as the "spiritual" or the "soul," permit humans to transcend their own anatomy (unlike animals) and to create a new social and material world that enables them to adapt to an incredible diversity of social and environmental circumstances. These characteristics are consonant with what anthropologists call "culture."

All modern humans have this capacity, and since all normal humans can learn any culture, Christian anthropologists believe that the image of God in humans is (at least partly although not entirely) what gives them the human capacity for culture.[54] There is at least some evidence that this capacity is biologically based. For instance, studies of the anatomical structure and organization of the brain have demonstrated that specific parts of the brain are responsible for human language (Broca's area and Wernicke's area[55]) and for moral and social consciousness (the frontal lobes).[56] Furthermore, evidence exists for a gene (known as FOXP2) for language,[57] and there appears to be an anatomical basis for self-consciousness, a moral sense, and a feeling of free will[58] (the option to choose as Adam did).

What is one of the scientific views of human origins?

The most enduring (nonreligious) scientific explanation for the origin of humanity postulates a series of evolving populations among which the forces of natural selection were operating. Early hominids, it is said, were descended from nonhominid, arboreal ancestors that came down from the trees during a dry period when a gallery forest was developing from a wet, heavily forested environment. Natural selection favored upright posture and bipedal locomotion because it gave these creatures greater height to see approaching predators over the grass. Since some early hominids had anatomical characteristics that indicated both bipedal and arboreal adaptations (e.g., *Australopithecus afarensis*), they presumably retreated periodically into the trees to escape predators. As hominids spent more time on the ground, they began making rudimentary stone tools called "choppers." This change in manual dexterity gave them a selective advantage over other creatures. The growth of brain size followed, for tool-making hominids were increasingly competitive and adaptive. Eventually human culture was favored, and modern humans emerged both anatomically and culturally no later than 35,000 BC.

Although informed speculation, this explanation is an attempt to account for the data of the fossil record. Early hominids of more than 4 million years ago, for example, had a brain size very similar to chimpanzees and gorillas (the modern anthropoids). Brain size grew slightly in the australopithecines that lived about 1 to 4 million years ago. By the time of the beginning of the genus *Homo* (about 2 million years ago), brain size had increased to a size almost 25 percent larger than the brain size of the australopithecines. Simple chopper tools also appeared at this time. By 1 million years ago, the brain size of *Homo erectus* and *Homo egaster* had doubled from that of the earliest hominids and then grew another 50 percent to that of anatomically modern humans (*Homo sapiens*) that began as early as 100,000 years ago.

How do we integrate a scientific view with a view that takes the Bible seriously?

Some would argue that a view of human origins that takes the Bible seriously is incommensurable, but not necessarily contradictory, with materialistic explanations. God is the first or ultimate cause, while evolution is the instrumental or immediate cause. At this level of integration, God used evolution to create humans and it is a complementary, but not a competing, explanation for their origin. This position (one kind of theistic evolution) has a kind of simplicity that recognizes both the limitations of scientific explanations (they are not religious) and religious explanations (which it is presumed are not materialistic or scientific) and their complementarity.

Consequently, one of the simplest ways of integrating science and the Bible is to say simply that "God did it!" God is not only the Creator of the universe, but also its Sustainer. The physical processes that humans see are the result of a God-created system set in motion and sustained by the power of God. This position thus sees evolution as the materialistic explanation for processes by which God brought the world into being and directed it with His power. Similarly, this position argues that humans were the result of the evolutionary process by which they were made in God's image.[59] Since *Adam* means "man" or "humanity," this position argues that Adam is a metaphor for the entire human race and that the story of Adam and Eve is a result of God's intent through the biblical writers to anthropomorphize the evolution of the population of modern humans from previously existing hominids.

While this viewpoint may seem the simplest kind of integration of the Bible and the data of anthropology, a deeper examination of the biblical text and its relationship to Christian doctrine creates some problems. Beyond the obvious first question of whether we have warrant to remove the entire historical character of the early chapters of Genesis, a number of serious theological questions emerge regarding our understanding of the origins and nature of humankind. First, we can look at the population of the first humans. In evolutionary theory, the interbreeding population is the unit of evolution while the biblical text implies that the first humans were an interbreeding couple.[60] The text indicates that humans did not come into being with the same kind of process responsible for the rest of creation. Rather, the act by which humans were created was unique in the created order and was different from those acts that produced the remainder of the universe described earlier in Genesis. Further, the text implies that the creation of humans was a direct intervention by God in the creative process. Consequently, while the divine creative process for the rest of nature is more general, the text affirms a unique, divine intervention in that process with the creation of humans. This intervention resulted in an unusual creature, one that uniquely had the stamp of divine qualities, the image of God.[61]

More directly, the biblical text further suggests that Adam was a real historical person rather than a metaphor[62] for humanity. This interpretation is substantiated by the apostle Paul, who refers to Adam as an analogy with Christ.[63] Because Christ is a historical person, Adam is also a historical person. Because Adam was morally responsible for his act of disobedience, Christ was morally responsible for His act of obedience.[64] The fate of humanity thus rests on the choices of Adam and Christ.

The Genesis account of Adam's choice in the garden teaches that humans are morally responsible agents and are capable of choice. The first humans abrogated this responsibility by their historical choice of going their own way and disobeying God. Because all humans are descended biologically and spiritually from an ancestor who made that choice, all humans bear consequences of that choice just as the historical couple did. The Bible thus puts the responsibility for sin on individual humans who continually choose to disobey God. This understanding of the theological issues intertwined here makes problematic any understanding of Adam and Eve as merely metaphorical and therefore nonhistorical.

How do we affirm the historicity of Adam and an evolutionary explanation for the data of fossil hominids?

One way out of the dilemma of the nature of the first population is to argue that God caused a body to evolve and placed His divine image[65] in the bodies of a historical couple that He selected out of a preexisting evolving population. In this form of theistic evolution, the infusion of the divine image was separate from the biological evolution of the human body and brain. Indeed, bipedalism, brain size, and skull morphology became modern well before the development of cognitive and symbolic capacities of modern humans began in the Upper Paleolithic Period in Europe (about 35,000 BC; see plate 10).

The divine image, however, is not just some mystical quality, infused into an animal at some remote point in the past, but rather it has biological foundations that give it a physical basis. Certainly, it had antecedents before the Upper Paleolithic Period (about 35,000 BC), but how did such a change in cognition, creativity, and adaptation appear so suddenly[66] when premodern hominids were around for millions of years?

All explanations that add God's image to a preexisting body also require a philosophical dualism that directly contradicts the biblical view of the unity of the human person (crudely, an implantation of a soul into an evolved hominid body). Such a view is theologically unsound. The physical, psychological, and spiritual aspects of the human are not separate, but uniquely integrated. The transcendent spiritual dimension of a person is an integral part of being human, not separate from the body. Humans thus began as the result of the direct action of the divine that produced an integrated person with physical, biological, emotional, cognitive, and spiritual dimensions. From where do we deduce support for this argument?

First, the early portion of Genesis teaches that humans live in a moral universe in which the physical is intertwined with the spiritual and that the divine and human choices had, and continue to have, physical repercussions. God created the world with His Word, and He proclaimed a moral judgment that the world was "good." His image bearer, and the entirety of God's creation, however, was corrupted by the choices of the first humans so that these choices had, and continue to have, physical as well as spiritual implications.

Further, the text indicates that the unique creative act of Spirit ("God") that produced the first human had physical dimensions. Man was created from the dust of the ground (Gen. 3:19) and was not just created as a "mental" or "spiritual" being. Similarly, the creation of Eve resulted in a physical but sexually dimorphous and genotypic female clone of the person created in the image of God.[67]

Second, there were physical repercussions of Adam's choice. Adam and his descendants would have to work "by the sweat of [their] brow" (Gen. 3:19), and women would bear children in pain (v. 16). Further, they were physically banished from the garden because of their disobedience (v. 23).

Third, the last Adam was the ultimate God-man (Jesus Christ) and was a spiritual and physical entity. God became tangible. The Word became flesh (John 1:14). God's Spirit was not placed in the flesh, but rather the incarnation was a unified physical expression of fullness of Spirit (God). Christ was conceived by the Holy Spirit (spirit) but born of a virgin (physical) (Matt. 1:18–25). His death had physical and spiritual dimensions. His resurrection was physical as well as spiritual (Luke 24:15–49).[68]

Fourth, Scripture repeatedly affirms that human actions are the result of thoughts. The New Testament describes this unity using the metaphor of fruit (Luke 6:43–45; Gal. 5:22–25). Behavioral "fruit" reveals the nature of our mental commitment and betrays the nature of the human "spirit" (John 15:1–16). The inner life is so connected to behavior that our actions reveal the character of our inner life.

Fifth, humans are called to live in light of the incarnation (Phil. 2). The incarnation affirms the value and importance of the physical world because God became tangible. Just as God incarnate had a redeeming effect on the physical and social world, so humans made in His image and imbued with His Spirit should have a redeeming effect on that world. The physical and spiritual world are tied together.

Sixth, the separation of body and spirit at death is unnatural because after death the bodies and spirits of humans will be reunited at the resurrection (1 Cor. 15:12–26; 1 Thess. 4:15–17).[69]

This unity of the human person thus suggests that the origin of modern humans was not the result of a body separately created from an intangible divinely infused "soul," but rather that both began from a single direct act whereby body and soul, mind and body were knit together in a single creative act at a point in time.

How does this view of human origins fit the fossil record?

We have already explored the seeming conflicts between the anthropological record and the popularly understood Genesis creation account, as well as the difficulties with explaining away these tensions. Is there any way to respect and embrace both the scientific data and a serious commitment to biblical authority?

Biologically speaking, modern humans (*Homo sapiens*) began anywhere from 200,000 to 100,000 BC, but modern human cognition, language, and religion[70] began no later than 35,000 BC. This cognitive and behavioral change was remarkable not only for the development of a great variety of types and styles of tools, but also because the first art, associated with an explosion of creativity, also developed during this time. Furthermore, modern humans expanded to all parts of the world and propagated the entire earth in less than 30,000 years. This rapid expansion is remarkable[71] since the australopithecines were present for millions of years but never migrated out of Africa. Previous members of the genus *Homo* required hundreds of thousands of years to migrate into all parts of Europe and Asia.

The relatively sudden appearance of a new and unique kind of cognition and behavior[72] in the Upper Paleolithic Period (without clear local antecedents in many cases) supports a Christian view of the uniqueness of modern humans and their relatively "sudden" appearance. The evidence to support such explanations, however, is very controversial among anthropologists.[73] Some scholars, largely biological anthropologists (and the textbooks written by them)[74] understandably focus more on the biological data and see more continuity than discontinuity between the modern humans of the Upper Paleolithic Period and their predecessors. Other scholars, largely Paleolithic archaeologists who work with the cultural materials, see great discontinuity between the Upper Paleolithic and the cultural remains of the earlier Middle Paleolithic.[75] From the analyses of these remains, the cognitive and mental capabilities of modern *Homo sapiens* of the Upper Paleolithic are different from their predecessors, the Neanderthals,[76] although the cultural capabilities of the Neanderthals remain controversial.[77]

Since the cognitive and cultural capability of modern humans began as much as 30,000 years earlier than agriculture as implied by some interpretations of Genesis, is there a scientifically defensible date for a historical Adam? Was the creation of humans a spiritual infusion of the image of God in a preexisting biologically and cognitively modern mind and body, rather than a physical/cognitive/spiritual one? Can the intellectual and cultural capabilities of humans that developed tens of thousands of years ago be separated from the implied date of the biblical Adam at 10,000 BC?

One problem with a date of 10,000 BC for Adam is that modern humans lived in the Americas before this time.[78] The date of the first migration is unknown and estimates are controversial, but most New World archaeologists would argue that humans were probably in the New World by 20,000 BC. Mitochondrial DNA studies of modern New World Native American populations indicate that they may be as much as 46,650 to 23,535 years old.[79] The earliest archaeological evidence of occupation comes from central Chile and dates to more than 12,000 years ago.[80] Movement deep into South America probably required thousands of years because migration must have been slow. For all intents and purposes, humans were already in the New World long before the evidence suggesting the initiation of agriculture existed in the Old World.

One logical (but unacceptable) way to reconcile the above dates for the presence of humans in the New World before agriculture in the Old World (at 10,000 BC) would be to deny that the indigenous populations of the New World are the descendants of Adam. Such a resolution is both scientifically and theologically unacceptable, however. A "late" dating of Adam to 10,000 BC would violate the biblical doctrine of the unity of humanity. Do the Native Americans Indians of the New World have the image of God? Are they corrupted by sin? The theological answer to these questions must be yes. If so, we are driven to an earlier date for the creation of Adam, one before 10,000 BC and no later than the Upper Paleolithic at 35,000 BC when the cultural capability of modern humans first began. Such a "pushing back" of the date for the creation of the first truly human couple seems scientifically possible, since they probably were not all agriculturalists. In any event, a "late" Adam of 10,000 BC violates the biblical doctrine of the unity of humanity.

Relating a scientific view of human origins with a view that takes the Bible seriously is fraught with difficulties. There are no ultimate answers without raising issues of integration to a level that places authority in our minds rather than faith in the God who created humans in His image. There are no final answers to be advanced with greater certainty about exactly what the Scriptures or science say that seems merited under the circumstances. It would seem better to speak tentatively and then live in faith in the resulting tension. Having said that, however, Christian faith and scientific knowledge of human origins are not incompatible. (See plate 10.)

QUESTIONS

1. If humans are made in the image of God, then how can we think about that image in a tangible way in light of the archaeological record of human beginnings?

2. How necessary is it for a Christian to believe in a historical individual that is responsible for the choice of bringing evil into the world?

3. Does a divine infusion of the image of God in an existing hominid require a dualistic view of the human person?

4. Given the fact that the biblical genealogies contain deletions and additions and vary according to the purpose of the author, are they elastic enough to include an Adam that lived at 35,000 BC?

NOTES

50. This sin resulted when the first humans chose to disobey God. This choice has affected all of the natural world and accounts for the presence of evil in the world personally and structurally.

51. The biological grouping to which humans belong is called *hominidae* and is commonly referred to as the "hominids." Anatomically defined as having habitually upright posture and bipedal locomotion (walking on two legs), hominids have a number of characteristics in the skull, pelvis, and teeth that distinguish them from the other primates. Hominids include the genera *Ardipithecus* (extinct), *Australopithecus* (extinct), and *Homo* (the genus to which modern humans belong), while the living anthropoids consist of the chimpanzee, the orangutan, and the gorilla. Modern humans belong to one species (*Homo sapiens*). That is the only species of hominids alive today.

52. Anthropologists describe this characteristic as upright posture with bipedal locomotion.

53. The number of these symbols is limited (usually between twenty and sixty) for each language, and their sequences bear no inherent relationship to the phenomenon to which they refer. Rather, the relationship of sounds of language to their meaning is set by social tradition.

54. James O. Buswell III, "Anthropology and the Nature of Man," *Journal of the Evangelical Theological Society* 13 (Fall 1970): 219–27.

55. Wernicke's area "appears to be responsible for the content and comprehension of speech [and] is connected by a nerve bundle called the *arcuate fasciculus* to Broca's area, which influences the areas of the brain that control the muscles of the lips, jaw, tongue, soft palate, and vocal cords during speech" (Roger Lewin, *Human Evolution: An Illustrated Introduction*, 4th ed. [Oxford: Blackwell Science, 1999], 195).

56. Frederick L. Coolidge and Thomas Wynn, "Executive Functions of the Frontal Lobes and the Evolutionary Ascendancy of *Homo sapiens*," *Cambridge Archaeological Journal* 11 (2001): 255–60.

57. Nicholas Wade, "Language Gene Is Traced to Emergence of Humans," *New York Times*, August 15, 2002 (late ed.), A18.

58. Sandra Blakelee, "Humanity? Maybe It's in the Wiring," *New York Times*, December 9, 2003, K1, 4.

59. This explanation of the development of all of life was in many ways anticipated by fifth-century Augustine, one of the great saints of the Christian faith. He argued that God directed the unfolding of life long before science, Darwin, Huxley, or "creation science." See Davis A. Young, "The Contemporary Relevance of Augustine's View of Creation," *Perspectives on Science and Christian Faith* 40, no. 1 (1988): 42–45.

60. This problem has existed for a long time because of the unknown source of Cain's wife. The first couple likely had other offspring, and brother-sister marriage is likely, but it is rare among the populations of the world and then found only among certain royal families. In some cases, the sibling pair may have been the offspring of polygynous unions, in which case the couple shared only half their genetic information. With previously existing hominids, however, the problem of Cain's wife disappears.

61. These qualities make humans the most divine animals on earth and thus form the theological basis of proper Christian attitudes toward different individuals, races, and cultures. Humans are thus worthy of respect because they bear the image of God, the Creator of the universe. At the same time, individual humans and their cultures (and the attitudes toward them) are in need of redemption and transformation, because while humans bear the image of God, they bear the consequences of their sinfulness because they have inherited this characteristic biologically and spiritually from Adam. This explains human evil both individually and structurally and accounts for humans' propensity to see things in their own way at the expense of other human beings.

62. Some theologians try to avoid this problem by arguing that Adam was a "federal" ancestor (a kind of metaphorical spiritual ancestor) for humanity rather than a biological one. While this may avoid the problems of the historicity of an "Adamic" ancestor for humans, it does not explain why both the human capacity for culture and human evil appear to be inherited biologically. Theologically speaking, both the image of God and sin appear to be passed down together in human beings because all humans are in need of redemption.

63. Rom. 5:12, 16–19; 1 Cor. 15:21–22, 45.

64. Rom. 5:16–19.

65. Although it may be tempting to separate the physical creation from the dust of the ground from the imputation of life itself (breathing into humans the breath of life as in Gen. 2:6), such a separation implies a dualism and separation of body and

mind/spirit that reflects early Christian heresies such as Manicheanism that have their roots in ancient Greek philosophy. These views have deeply affected contemporary American culture and contemporary Christianity. See Mark Noll, *The Scandal of the Evangelical Mind* (Grand Rapids: Eerdmans, 1994), 52–56.

On the contrary, by affirming the holistic origin of humans, Christians affirm their commitment to the significance of the whole person, intellectually, spiritually, and physically—not just the spirit, but also the mind and the body. This holistic nature of the human person has implications for education, politics, evangelism, and missions.

66. When I say "suddenly," I do not mean instantaneously. Rather, I use the word relatively in contrast to what occurred previously in the 1,965,000 years of hominid "cultural" evolution.

67. Another option for interpretation is to argue that God caused a mutation that resulted in Adam, but getting Eve from that mutation is more problematic.

68. In these verses, Jesus walked with two individuals to Emmaus, and they failed to distinguish Him from any other human being (v. 16). After explaining the meaning of His own death, they invited Him inside. He broke bread with them and they recognized Him, and then He disappeared (vv. 30–31). Later He showed His disciples the scars on His hands and feet from the crucifixion, asked them to touch His wounds (vv. 39–40), and ate fish (v. 42). Then He elucidated the meaning of His death (vv. 44–48) and told His followers to wait for the power of the Holy Spirit (v. 49). Finally, after leading them to Bethany, He disappeared and was carried up to heaven (v. 51).

69. Note that 1 Corinthians 15:26 boldly declares that the last enemy to be defeated is death itself.

70. In a stimulating book synthesizing the mass of information concerning religion in the Upper Paleolithic, archaeologist D. Bruce Dickenson says: "The material patterns in the archaeological record, together with the formal interpretations of those patterns conforms with the expectations of two hypotheses. First, religion in Franco-Cantabria during the Upper Paleolithic period was a) based upon a complex intellectual and theological order and b) was ultimately experiential in inspiration. Second, two profound natural phenomena—a) perceived cyclicality in the passage of time and b) the dialectic of human sexuality, especially the periodicity and fecundity of women—were generalized into universal principles or 'grand analogies' that formed the basis of speculation and thought about nature, humankind, the universe, and reality" (D. Bruce Dickenson, *The Dawn of Belief: Religion in the Upper Paleolithic of Southwestern Europe* [Tucson: Univ. of Arizona Press, 1990], 215).

71. This position assumes a common origin for all hominids and all modern humans (what is known in anthropological circles as the "out of Africa" hypothesis). The alternative explanation, "the multiregional theory," which postulates that modern humans in different parts of the world evolved from different ancestral populations, is not consonant with a biblical view of humanity. Presently, the "out of Africa" hypothesis appears to be the dominant explanation and has the support of studies of mitochondrial DNA that show a common origin for humanity in a single female about 200,000 years ago (the hypothetical mitochondrial "Eve").

72. These data are focused on Western Europe because it has been the center of the most research. The culture that is mentioned here is called the Aurignacian (see plate 10), and it was very different from that which preceded it. Some scholars place the origin of the Aurignacian culture in central Asia in Afghanistan. The archaeological picture of the Upper Paleolithic is much more complex than this because the Neanderthals were still living in the region of the people of the Aurignacian and they modified their

tools to a type of tools called the Châtelperronian, which appeared to copy some of the features of the Upper Paleolithic tool types. Sometimes modern humans and Neanderthals occupied the same caves successively, as indicated by interstratification of the Aurignacian and Châtelperronian tool types. These issues remain controversial among Paleolithic archaeologists. Some of the most recent information on these points can be found in the Proceedings of the Symposium 6.1 of the 14th Congress of the International Union of Prehistoric and Protohistoric Sciences (USIPP). See Joao Zilhao and Francesco D'Errico, eds., *The Chronology of the Aurignacian and of the Transitional Technocomplexes: Dating, Statigraphies, Cultural Implications*, Trabalhos de Arqueologia 33 (Lisbon: Instituto Portugues de Arqueologia, 2003).

73. See Christopher S. Henshilwood and Curtis W. Marean, "The Origin of Modern Human Behavior: Critique of the Models and Their Test Implications," *Current Anthropology* 44, no. 3 (2003): 627–51.

74. Textbooks about the hominid fossil record are usually written by biological anthropologists because there is so much more biological evidence for fossil humans than cultural evidence. The chopper tools of early *Homo* were eventually replaced by the hand axes of *Homo egaster*, although chopper tools continued to be used in Asia by *Homo erectus*. It is not until the time of the Neanderthals and the Mousterian tool complex associated with them that the cultural evidence gets interesting. With the arrival of the Aurignacian tool complex (presumably used by *Homo sapiens*), culture changed from the preceding Mousterian tools although the Neanderthals did apparently copy some of the techniques to make Châtelperronian tools (see plate 10).

75. This discontinuity is seen in Western Europe where most of the research in the Paleolithic has occurred. The Upper Paleolithic is intrusive and appears to have been brought by migrants from Western Asia. The beginning of the first culture of the Upper Paleolithic, the Aurignacian, appears to have its origin in Afghanistan (see Zilhao and D'Errico, *Chronology of the Aurignacian and of the Transitional Technocomplexes*).

76. Frederick L. Coolidge and Thomas Wynn, "Executive Functions of the Frontal Lobes and the Evolutionary Ascendancy of *Homo sapiens*," *Cambridge Archaeological Journal* 11, no. 2 (2001): 255–60; Michael S. Bisson, "Interview with a Neanderthal: An Experimental Approach for Reconstructing Scraper Production Rules, and their Implications for Imposed Form in Middle Paleolithic Tools," *Cambridge Archaeological Journal* 1, no. 2 (2001): 147–63; S. Mithen, *The Prehistory of Mind* (London: Thames and Hudson, 1994).

77. Michael Balter, "Dressed for Success: Neanderthal Culture Wins Respect," *Science* 306, no. 5653 (October 1, 2004): 40–41.

78. Attention was first drawn to this problem by Christian anthropologist James O. Buswell III in 1967. See James O. Buswell III, "Adam and Neolithic Man," *Eternity* 18, no. 2 (1967): 29–30, 48–50.

79. Theodore G. Shurr, "Mitochondrial DNA and the Peopling of the New World," *American Scientist* 88 (2000): 251.

80. This is the youngest Carbon-14 date from Monte Verde in Chile and includes one standard deviation, but ten of the twelve C-14 dates that Dillehay lists for this site, however, range from a mean (without the standard deviation) of 11,790 years BP to 12,780 BP. One isolated date is 33,370 years +/–530 BP and the other is 13,565 +/– 250 BP (Thomas D. Dillehay, *The Settlement of America: A New Prehistory* [New York: Basic, 2000], 303). Dillehay also lists twenty-six pages of C-14 dates from the New World mentioned in his book and many of these occur 10,000 years ago or more (pp. 295–321).

SUGGESTED READING

Most of the Christians who write about this subject are nonanthropologists writing outside of their areas of expertise. There are very few Christian anthropologists, but below are some who have tackled this subject in the past.

Arnold, Dean E. "Who Was Adam? Fossil Humans from a Christian Perspective." *Pascal Center Notebook* 2, no. 4 (1992).

Buswell, James O., III. "Anthropology and the Nature of Man." *Journal of the Evangelical Theological Society* 13, pt. 4 (1967).

Hurd, James P., "Hominids in the Garden?" In *The Evolving Creation,* ed. Keith Miller. Grand Rapids: Eerdmans, 2003, 208–31.

Wilcox, David L. "Recent Evidences for a Late-Date Adam (AMH@100,000 BP)." *Perspectives on Science and Christian Faith* 56, no. 1 (2004): 49–54.

Wilson, Donald R. "A Different Way of Looking at Genesis 2." *Pascal Center Notebook* 2, no. 2–3 (Fall 1991–Winter 1992): 1–4.

Although not written by an anthropologist, the following article is a thoughtful approach to the subject.

Young, Davis A. "The Antiquity and Unity of the Human Race Revisited." *Christian Scholar's Review* 33, no. 4 (1981): 239–41.

Although not written from a Christian perspective, the following is an important summary of some of the positions described in this article but seen from a secular perspective.

Scott, Eugenie C. "Anti-evolution and Creationism in the United States." *Annual Review of Anthropology* 26 (1997): 263–69.

CRUCIAL QUESTIONS AT THE INTERFACE OF CHRISTIAN FAITH AND EARTH SCIENCES

Earth, the third planet from the sun, maintains an intricate balance between all the phenomena that sustain the planet. The Earth sciences engage scientists who study the physical features of Earth. Oceanographers study the oceans, meteorologists study the atmosphere, especially the weather, geologists study the matter in solid celestial bodies (in this case, earth), and environmental scientists study and protect the terrestrial and aquatic environments. It is essential that Earth scientists engage in interdisciplinary approaches from the natural sciences, social sciences, and theology to scrutinize the characteristics of Earth. The cadre of people who study and steward humanity's home planet require broad and specific discussions about all aspects of Earth. They include social scientists, theologians, and ethicists, to name a few. This is well illustrated in the topics the editors have selected for discussion.

Natural disasters present many issues for Christians to analyze and respond to. Many scientists have been stirred in knowing the dynamics of the forces that interact with the surfaces and core of Earth. Some of those phenomena result in natural disasters. The environmental sciences have an underlying paradigm of "care" or "stewardship" for Christians and secularists. The care of Earth is often conducted by a wide variety of people united by strong desires to maintain or restore this beautiful planet God calls "good."

What Is God's Purpose for Natural Disasters?

Stephen O. Moshier

What is God's purpose for natural disasters?

Earthquakes, volcanic eruptions, hurricanes, tornados; these catastrophes inspire great fear in people living near a fault line, in the mountains, along coasts, or even in the heartland. Along the mangrove-lined shores of North Sumatra, a peaceful day-after-Christmas 2004 was suddenly interrupted by the violent jerk of an earthquake of historical proportions, followed by the crushing surge of tsunami waves across the beach and inland to horrified villagers. The terror reached far across the Indian Ocean, north and east to the coast of Thailand and west to India, Sir Lanka, and the Maldives.

Is there any place on earth where we are safe from violent acts of nature? Natural disasters, including significant events in the Bible, have influenced the course of history. Hollywood knows the power of catastrophes to draw spectators. People have their own stories to tell of personal encounters with natural disasters. They may talk about God's protection in a dangerous situation, but they may also question why God would have allowed such a terrible thing to happen.

Confusion is common in the church over God's involvement in nature and His purposes for natural disasters since biblical times. Erwin Lutzer, pastor of Moody Church in Chicago, wrote of a group of ministers in California who gathered for prayer after a major earthquake. They agreed that God was not responsible for the damage and deaths because Earth is in a fallen state and prone to "natural evils." However, one of the ministers thanked God in prayer that the earthquake happened in the early morning before people were out of their homes.[1] Newspapers reported that other Christian leaders were convinced that God had brought particular destruction to a neighborhood where pornographic movies were produced. Contradictory perspectives are revealed in these responses to the earthquake. Is God responsible for natural disasters? Are violent acts of nature an expression of God's wrath or His glory? Are natural hazards the result of original sin? Do these "natural evils" reflect "cosmic evil" and associated demonic activity that affects Earth and its people? Careful consideration of Christian theology and modern science can lead to a more satisfying and logical understanding of God's purpose for natural disasters.

What causes natural disasters?

Scientists recognize that natural processes on earth, including violent activities, result from interactions between *earth systems*: the solid earth represented by the *geosphere*, all the liquid water and ice on earth represented by the *hydrosphere*, all the components in air by the *atmosphere*, and all life by the *ecosphere*. Figure 7.1 (p. 143) shows that most natural hazards are produced by interactions between multiple systems. Catastrophic natural activity results from the sudden release of excessive concentrations of energy derived from the sun, earth's interior, or gravity, returning the systems involved to equilibrium conditions.

Do humans play a role in natural disasters?

The very description of violent natural processes as "natural disasters" may be an oxymoron. Consider hurricane danger. Most of the population of the world lives in coastal regions. There is no evidence that hurricane frequency has increased along the Atlantic and Gulf coasts, yet as populations doubled there each decade of the twentieth century, the cost of property loss increased at a greater rate. The potential for *natural* hazards in these regions has not changed, but the frequency of *disasters* has surely risen with population growth. Fortunately, advances in weather forecasting have reduced human casualties from U.S. hurricanes, but that is not the case in underdeveloped regions such as Bangladesh. Affluent North Americans may

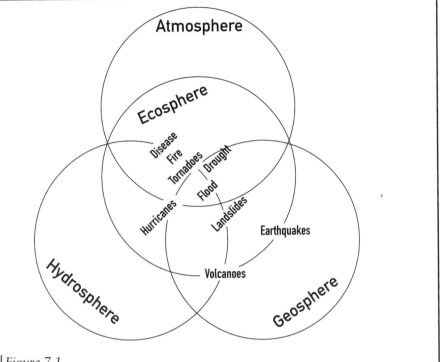

Figure 7.1.

Each circle in the diagram represents one of four Earth Systems: Geosphere (the solid earth), Hydrosphere (water in the hydrologic cycle), Atmosphere (air related to weather and climate), and Ecosphere (life). Almost every earth process involves an interaction between two or more of these systems, so the diagram shows overlapping circles. Selected natural disasters are placed on the diagram to represent their associations with particular earth systems.

choose an ocean view, but occupants of the impoverished coastal regions of Bangladesh have little choice where they live.

Geologist-author Simon Winchester recounted in a bestselling book the impact of tsunami on the Indonesian islands and beyond following the violent 1883 eruption of Krakatoa volcano.[2] Winchester repeated a warning scientists have known all along, that such a disaster could be repeated in the same region. Now, after the loss of nearly 300,000 lives in a few terrifying minutes of December 26, 2004, regional and world leaders must explain why the available technology for detecting tsunami had not been implemented for the benefit of populations along the affected coasts.

Wildfires also illustrate this point. Recent wildfire *disasters* are the result of previous *unnatural* management of forests. The policy of the U.S. Forest Service for much of the past century was to suppress all natural and human-caused fires. The idea was to preserve public lands for recreation and logging and to protect the growing human population in forested regions. Increased tree density in the forests actually led to more severe wildfires that have devastated forests and communities in recent years. Ecologists have learned that fire is an essential process of forest and grassland ecology, responsible for frequent revitalization of the soil and flora. Now it is proper management to allow natural fires to burn or to ignite "prescribed burns" to restore forests to more natural conditions.[3] Yet people in the forest continue to expect their lives and property to be protected from the threat of fire.

One solution to the problem of natural disasters is for people to avoid living in hazardous regions, but that is not a practical or even desirable solution. Trying to control nature is more often futile and usually extremely expensive. Flood control and coastline stabilization are two examples of engineering approaches that can have some short-term benefits but more often than not introduce unexpected negative consequences to the environment or give communities a false sense of security.[4] In *The Control of Nature*, John McPhee recounts the experiences of communities and nations struggling to live with the threats of lava flows, mud slides, and regional flooding.[5] The best practice is to use the knowledge we have of earth processes and ecology and employ the technology available to build safe structures, in the safest places possible, with minimal impact on the environment.

Are there any benefits from natural disasters?

The new "fire ecology" is but one example of science revealing the importance and necessity of extreme natural processes for a planet that supports life as we know it. Other scientists have pointed out that Earth is uniquely endowed, some would say designed, to support life and human culture.[6] Extreme nature is no less important than tame nature in this respect, even in the maintenance of biodiversity on our planet.

Geologist Keith Miller summarized some of the positive impacts of natural disasters:

> Earthquakes and volcanic eruptions are part of the dynamic processes driven by the release of Earth's internal heat by which the Earth's crust is continually created and destroyed. Landslides, avalanches, and mud slides are mechanisms by which the weathered materials of the Earth's surface are transported by the forces of gravity eventually to be deposited and become incorporated into the rock cycle. Intense storms, and the flooding rains and high winds they contain, are consequences of atmospheric circulation driven by differences in the amount of solar radiation received and absorbed at the Earth's surface and by the effects of the Earth's rotation. Flooding rivers also supply nutrient-rich sediment to their floodplains and carry sediment to delta wetlands, preserving them against the effects of subsidence.[7]

Were natural disasters intended in God's original plan for creation?

Some Christians hold the view that the natural order with all its dangers was not characteristic of the original creation. Rather, violent natural processes are the inevitable result of original sin and God's curse on the ground. Most scientists find that difficult to accept. There is no evidence from astronomy that physical processes (as described by "natural laws") have changed since the very first moments of creation. There is no evidence from geology (and paleontology) that earth systems behaved any differently before human history. A world that worked in any other way would have to be supernaturally manipulated or sustained by means different from how God appears to superintend creation today. God never reveals in Scripture that He acts any differently in creation, or that natural processes in creation are substantially different before or after the historic fall event. Paul wrote, "For since the creation of the world God's invisible qualities—his eternal power and divine nature—have been clearly seen, being understood from what has been made, so that men are without excuse" (Rom. 1:20). This declaration would be nonsense if God's activity in creation, or the functions of created nature that reflect His dangerous and powerful divine nature, changed at some point in history since the very beginning.[8]

Does the "goodness" of creation pronounced by God in Genesis 1 imply that natural disasters did not happen on earth before the fall? The concept of good creation in Genesis is not about physical or moral perfection, as represented by the Greek word *kalos*. Good creation in Genesis is about God's personal gratification or aesthetic satisfaction over His completed work, represented by the Hebrew word *tob*.[9] God did curse the ground after the fall (Gen. 3:17), but He did not say that it was no longer good. Scripture only reports that the ground will produce thorns and thistles. Yet Paul declares that creation stands in need of redemption from its subjection to frustration (futility), "not by its own choice but by the will of the one who subjected it, in hope that the creation itself will be liberated from its bondage to decay" (Rom. 8:19–20). Furthermore, "the whole creation has been groaning as in the pains of childbirth right up to the present time" (v. 22). Physicist David Snoke points out that a better translation of "right up to the present time" would be "all the way up to the present time," meaning from the beginning up until now.[10] If creation's "groaning" and "bondage to decay" can rightly be associated with natural disasters (and that is not a certain case to be made), then it appears that God in His wisdom made it that way for a purpose. This view of creation is consistent with the physical nature of the universe as understood from a scientific perspective.[11]

The idea that natural disasters are the expression of "natural evil" in this world finds its fullest expression in the theology of Eastern Orthodox Christianity. The perversion of good creation follows the angelic rebellion against God led by Satan. Thus God did not create the evils in nature. Most evangelical theologians are uncomfortable attributing such creative power to demonic presence in the world. For example, Satan must secure God's permission to "control nature" in order to test Job. In 1 Kings 18 we find that the pagan god Baal (representing Satan) is unable to ignite even a simple fire before the prophet Elijah.

Is God responsible for natural disasters?

The Bible describes a creator God who is in control of every aspect of His creation. Psalm 104 tells of God's sovereign power over the weather, hydrologic cycle, food web, ecology, agriculture, volcanoes, and earthquakes. All of these processes can be understood scientifically as resulting from natural causal chains of events. The Bible reveals that the primary mover, the initiator of the first cause, is God, who upholds the universe by the power of His word (Heb. 1: 3).[12] In the Old Testament book of Jonah, God causes a storm at sea to achieve His means of getting Jonah's attention. In the New Testament book of Mark, Jesus calms a storm at sea to achieve His means of getting his apostles' attention! Not surprisingly, natural disasters in the Bible are used by God either to reveal some aspect of His character or to accomplish specific purposes in redemptive history. "When disaster comes to a city, has not the LORD caused it?" (Amos 3:6). "I bring prosperity and create disaster; I, the LORD, do all these things" (Isa. 45:7).[13]

If God has any control over nature, by virtue of His creative power, He must have control of natural disasters.

As latter-day bystanders to biblical history, we may understand why God sent His enemies plagues, floods, storms, and geological catastrophes. It is more difficult to know if God continues to use natural disasters in a wrathful or corrective way in our times. It is probably wise not to judge God's motives for any particular disaster, because His actions promote an agenda that transcends our lives and even physical creation. There is no promise in Scripture that either the righteous or unrighteous (in the sight of God) will be spared the tragedy that can result from nature's violence. It is often in the midst of danger that God's presence is most strongly felt.

> God is our refuge and strength,
>   an ever-present help in trouble.
> Therefore we will not fear, though the earth give way
>   and the mountains fall into the heart of the sea,
> though its waters roar and foam
>   and the mountains quake with their surging.

—Psalm 46:1–3

QUESTIONS

1. How does the question of God's role in natural disasters relate to the more general issues of God's involvement in nature and free will in creation?

2. Do you think that science contributes anything to answering the question of God's role in natural disasters?

3. How would the world be different if there were no extreme natural processes like volcanoes, floods, wildfires, or earthquakes?

NOTES

1. Erwin Lutzer, *Ten Lies about God and How You May Already Be Deceived* (Nashville: W Publishing Group, 2000), 99.

2. Simon Winchester, *Krakatoa: The Day the World Exploded, August 27, 1883* (New York: HarperCollins, 2003).

3. Seth R. Reice, *The Silver Lining: The Benefits of Natural Disasters* (Princeton, N.J.: Princeton Univ. Press, 2001).

4. Keith B. Miller, "Natural Hazards: Challenges to the Creation Mandate of Dominion?" *Perspectives on Science and Christian Faith* 53, no. 3 (2001): 184–87.

5. John McPhee, *The Control of Nature* (New York: Farrar, Straus & Giroux, 1989).

6. For a secular perspective on the uniqueness of Earth, read Peter Douglas Ward and Donald Brownlee, *Rare Earth: Why Complex Life Is Uncommon in the Universe* (New York: Copernicus, 2000). Information on the view that the uniqueness of Earth reflects an intelligent designer can be found on apologist Hugh Ross's website, http://www.reasons.org.

7. Miller, "Natural Hazards," 184–87.

8. David Snoke, "Why Were Dangerous Animals Created?" *Perspectives on Science and Christian Faith* 56, no. 2 (2004): 116–25.

9. K. A. Kitchen, "Good," in *The New Bible Dictionary*, 2nd ed. (Wheaton, Ill.: Tyndale House, 1982), 433.

10. Snoke, "Why Were Dangerous Animals Created?" 116–25.

11. The biblical testimony of creation should be understood from the mind-set of the ancient Hebrews, who first received it. We must translate their words in a way that preserves their meaning but without the additional meanings that moderns would bring to those words. The Hebrew word *'eres* is generally translated as earth. We immediately think of a planet in orbit around the sun. *'Eres* can imply the known extent of the physical world or simply mean land or soil. See K. A. Kitchen, "Earth," in *The New Bible Dictionary*, 293. When we read in Genesis 3:5 that God had not sent rain on the earth until He formed man, it need not be interpreted to mean that no rain had fallen previously anywhere on the planet. The same verse also says that shrubs and plants had not appeared until that moment, yet in Genesis 1:11–12 we read that plants are created on day three of the creation week.

12. John C. Collins, *The God of Miracles: An Exegetical Examination of God's Action in the World* (Wheaton, Ill.: Crossway, 2000). Collins provides an exceptionally thorough exploration of the theology of how God works in the world, covering different approaches that fall within Christian biblical faith and some approaches that do not.

13. The word "disaster" in this verse was chosen for the New International Version over the use of "evil" in the King James Version. In the context of the verse, evil would refer to so called "natural evil" but not human sin.

SUGGESTED READING

Collins, John C. *The God of Miracles: An Exegetical Examination of God's Action in the World.* Wheaton, Ill.: Crossway, 2000.

Lutzer, Erwin. *Ten Lies about God and How You May Already Be Deceived.* Nashville: W Publishing Group, 2000.

McPhee, John. *The Control of Nature.* New York: Farrar, Straus & Giroux, 1989.

Miller, Keith B. "Natural Hazards: Challenges to the Creation Mandate of Dominion?" *Perspectives on Science and Christian Faith* 53, no. 3 (2001): 184–87.

Snoke, David. "Why Were Dangerous Animals Created?" *Perspectives on Science and Christian Faith* 56, no. 2 (2004): 116–25.

Why Should Christians Be Interested in Geology?

Ralph Stearley

For students of the Bible, God's pleasure in creating our world is blatant. God's pleasure in creation is often linked to biblical descriptions of Earth's inherent majesty. For example, the closing chapters of the book of Job contain detailed descriptions of Earth and its life, aspects typically termed "natural history," provided by God Himself speaking out of the wind. Job had bitterly complained to God for good reason: God had permitted several disasters to befall him, including the loss of all his children. However, when faced with this catalog of creation, Job is overawed by the magnificence of God's handiwork and humbles himself:

> I know that you can do all things;
>   no plan of yours can be thwarted. . . .
> Surely I spoke of things I did not understand,
>   things too wonderful for me to know.
>
> —Job 42:2–3

The biblical wisdom literature also supports the notion that there is a fundamental goodness attached to the activity of disciplined study of the creation. People like Solomon and David analyze and interpret Earth and its creatures with obvious delight. This necessitates attention to clues that yield their secrets only to those able to invest considerable effort: "It is the glory of God to conceal a matter; to search out a matter is the glory of kings" (Prov. 25:2). Solomon, the author of this passage, is privileged with the provision of time and ability to indulge his search for hidden things—evidently things that God, in His timetable and according to His pleasure, makes clear.

Christians, persuaded by these two considerations—the magnificence of God's handiwork (see plate 11) and His encouragement of its study—have a profound rationale for the study of Earth. A third consideration also is present: God's initial mandate to humankind to tend the earth, presented in the opening chapters of Genesis. This mandate permits rational exploitation of earthly resources, such as soil qualities, fresh water supplies, mineral products for construction, and fossil fuels. It comes as no surprise that, because of sin, humans are capable of abusing and do abuse all these, leading to damage or destruction of natural systems. To be able to fulfill our God-given cultural task requires knowledge of the behavior of Earth systems and the costs and benefits of utilization of Earth's resources.

God may call particular persons to special pleasure in the study of His world or to particular motivation to work at considerate tending of this planet, but all people—especially Christians—should manifest delight in examining this world and showing concern for good stewardship in managing its finite resources.

How does the solid earth function?

The interior rocky planets, including Earth, are zoned by density into three primary layers: a dense core formed of metal alloys (typically, iron-nickel alloys), a mantle of silicate rocks that are highly compressed at depth, and a crust of relatively uncompressed silicate rocks.[14] The relative sizes of the three zones differ among the "terrestrial" planets (Earth's moon, because of its large size, is usually counted as a planetary body). Mercury, for example, has a huge core relative to its planetary radius, while Earth's moon has a very tiny core. Evidence for this internal zonation comes from studies of planetary gravitation, from exacting measurements of wobbling behavior of planets around their axes, and from seismic studies accomplished by many instruments on Earth and by seismic stations set up on Earth's moon and on Mars. Layering by density does not stop at the solid surface. Earth keeps a substantial liquid water ocean, and Earth, Venus, and Mars possess gaseous atmospheres as well.

Energy is supplied to Earth's surface from two primary sources: solar radiation and internal heat. While the internal heat supply is the lesser of these sources, it is extremely important for understanding the behavior of the solid Earth. Earth's internal heat derives from two sources: (1) the residual heat left over from Earth's initial formation, mostly still residing in its metallic core; and (2) heat produced from the decay of radioactive elements in Earth's mantle. Collectively, these sources provide around 4×10^{13} watts of energy to Earth's surface.[15] One is not too far off the mark to think of Earth as a giant "lightbulb" rated at 4×10^{13} watts. The heat is not delivered to the surface uniformly; some areas are warmer than others.

This heat is passed to Earth's surface by way of large convective movements within the rocky mantle. In today's high-tech world, the slow creep of hot mantle rock can actually be discerned through subtle differences in the speed of seismic waves as they are recorded by thousands of seismometers at the surface, in a fashion similar to that of instruments that can monitor the motions of an unborn fetus in its mother's womb. We can now image these slow motions of Earth's mantle, motions that were inferred on the basis of physical principles only a few decades ago.

We can also now monitor the actual motions of large regional blocks of Earth's surface as these respond to the convective motions of the hot mantle. The surface is divided into approximately seven large and a dozen or so smaller segments, which behave as "rafts" on the underlying plastic mantle. The rafts consist of crustal material, which is between 10 and 70 kilometers thick, and the uppermost layer of mantle, around another 50 kilometers of rock, which is plated to the bottom of the crust as though glued to it. The large regional segments are thus termed "lithospheric plates," the lithosphere being this solid laminate crust/uppermost mantle. The science of plate motions, their causes, and resultant deformation of Earth's surface is termed *plate tectonics*.

These lithospheric plates can relate to one another in only three possible fashions: (1) a plate moves away from its neighbor, (2) a plate slides by its neighbor (typically sticking and creeping), or (3) a plate converges on its neighbor. At junctions where plates move apart, a large rift will form, with volcanism supplying new crust. This type of new igneous crust is derived directly from molten mantle material and is termed *basaltic*. The rift zones are elevated, due to high regional heat flow and thermal expansion of the rock, to form the massive mid-ocean ridges, which collectively are the largest single geographic feature on Earth. At junctions where two plates converge, one must yield to the other and be forced to fold back into Earth's mantle, a process termed *subduction*. As this plate is forced downward, a portion of it melts, and magma is supplied to a chain of volcanoes marking the zone of subduction. The fold is also diagnosable by a linear-arcuate trench. These trenches are the lowest topographic features on Earth; all occur below the surface of the global ocean. The magma formed at subduction zones differs chemically from basalt and gives rise to a different suite of volcanoes, the *andesitic* ones, named for the Andes Mountains. In general, the andesitic volcanoes are much more hazardous to humans. Included among their number are Mount St. Helens and its neighbors in the Pacific Northwest; most Japanese volcanoes, the notorious Indonesian volcanoes like Krakatoa, and Mount Vesuvius in southern Italy.

Many geological subdisciplines address the effects of plate tectonics. *Earthquake seismologists* detect and analyze motions along great cracks within Earth's crust, termed faults. *Structural geologists* map deformed rock terrains and analyze the directions and magnitudes of the forces that produce these deformations. *Tectonicists* analyze the broadscale motions of lithospheric plates and explain the history of continents and ocean basins. *Volcanologists* focus on volcano origin, magma chemistry, surface structure, and hazard estimation. These scientific disciplines are legitimate fields of study for Christian students for reasons of intrinsic fascination or by way of practical service in the evaluation and prediction of hazards resulting from ongoing plate motions.

How do Earth's surface processes function?

Earth's solid surface is framed by way of plate geometries and motions, as well as by volcanism. However, it is dramatically modified by gravity and by engines fired by solar energy. Earth's mean solar input is about 240 watts/m^2.[16] When summed over the entire planet, this energy is about 4000 times the energy delivered by internal heat sources. Surface processes that depend on this energy provide a varied and interesting landscape, a hydrologic cycle, and chemical cycles that foster life.

Earth is of sufficient size for its gravity to retain an atmosphere. In turn, the pressure of the atmosphere permits water to remain in the liquid state on Earth's surface. (For an example of an alternative scenario, look to our neighboring planet Mars: Mars hosts an atmosphere about 1/100 the pressure of Earth's, which will not permit water to exist as a liquid.) Both these fluids respond to the radiative input from the sun and act to redistribute this energy from warmer regions (i.e., low latitudes) to cooler regions (high latitudes). This heat redistribution system results in large-scale circulation patterns in Earth's atmosphere and global ocean.

Liquid water is a solvent of great potency. It destroys rocks easily by geologic standards and puts elements like potassium, calcium, and phosphorus into solution. Elements necessary for the production of organic compounds like carbohydrates, lipids, structural proteins, and enzymes are readily transmitted through the air and water; complex geochemical cycles move these elements between living organisms and the large reservoirs we know as the global ocean and the atmosphere. *Biogeochemists* study these complex cycles.

Surficial processes also give us our soils and landforms. *Geomorphology* is the subdiscipline of the Earth sciences that studies processes acting at Earth's surface that transform the face of the land. The discipline is inherently aesthetic, addressing diverse, dramatic landforms that cannot remain static. The processes that influence the landscape include the ongoing translation of the surface resulting from plate tectonics, deformations caused by converging and diverging plates, the downward motion of rocks and debris caused by gravity, and the erosion and transfer of Earth's materials by wind, liquid water, and ice.

The Christian who believes that God created Earth to be beautiful might easily praise His creative work by examining the instruments by which the Creator runs the planetary surface: running water, flowing wind, and slowly grinding ice. Avenues for practical service open up in the careful assessment of precious surface resources, like productive soils; and in assessments of construction sites and practices.

Is Earth a creation of great antiquity?

Since the sixteenth century, geologists have examined and pondered rocks revealed in uplifted regions, in deep mines, and in cores drilled into the subsurface. The crustal rocks are not homogenous, nor are they arranged at random. Rather, they exhibit structure and pattern. The early geologists came to the realization that rocks are spatially placed in a layered relation, and these horizontal layers, analogous to the layers in a cake, were formed sequentially.[17]

Scientific study of these layers, which were eventually christened *strata*, is the discipline of *stratigraphy*. Some stratigraphers focus on the fossil content of sedimentary rocks and are thus termed *biostratigraphers*. Others focus on the texture and chemistry of the layers themselves and are termed *lithostratigraphers*. In recent years, seismic technology has become refined to the point where detailed three-dimensional views of crustal rocks can be formed primarily on the basis of seismic data; practitioners of this style of stratigraphy are termed *seismic stratigraphers*. The science of stratigraphy undergirds all attempts to sample the subsurface for resources, like oil and gas deposits. For example, a modern offshore drilling rig typically costs a billion dollars or more and is operated at a cost of several hundred thousand dollars per day. If hydrocarbon exploration companies operated only on guesswork, they would be bankrupt within a month.

Around 1800 a small group of stratigraphers realized that fossils—the remains of former living creatures—were located within the strata in an order. Certain fossils were found only in lower (earlier) strata, while others were found only in upper (later) strata. The fossils were thus recognized as handy tools for the correlation of strata from one region with strata from a neighboring region. A new generation of working biostratigraphers refined this technique, identifying and classifying thousands of fossils. The order was found to be global in scope. Operating a generation prior to Darwin, many of these early workers assumed that the orderly history of life that these remains demonstrated was due to providential oversight of the history of Earth.[18]

Where tectonic plates converge, the strata are compressed and deformed. The layers that were originally horizontal may be uplifted, bent, or fractured. This compression can be charted and measured in uplifted mountain zones. (See plate 11.) It is not difficult to analyze this internal structure into a series of sequential events involving the deposition of strata, interruptions of deposition, deformation of prior stratigraphic sequences, and erosion. Each region of Earth's surface contains its own local sequence that can be linked into neighboring regions. Ultimately, a global history of events can be deciphered.

However, the sequence of strata and deformational events thus far deciphered only yields a narrative without a calendar. A timepiece independent of this narrative is necessary if dates are to be attached to the history. Early in the twentieth century, the first generation of physicists who attempted to understand the structure of the atom realized that some varieties of elements, termed isotopes, were inherently unstable and decayed at constant rates. Because the decay rates were constant, these isotopes thus behaved like natural clocks. Methods for computing chronologies of rocks, employing these minute clocks, were initially worked out by Ernest Rutherford and Frederick Soddy (both of whom would win the Nobel Prize for chemistry for their work on the structure of the atom); and later by R. J. Strut, Bertram Boltwood, Arthur Holmes, and Alfred Nier.[19] The methods have been expanded to encompass a variety of techniques that can be used to cross-check one another. A time scale for Earth's history, extending back some 4.5 billion years has been refined. Meteorites and rocks brought back from the surface of the moon have been thus dated as well. These chronologies link with the early history of Earth and help elucidate the conditions under which Earth was formed.[20]

Many Christians have been taught that "secular" science is opposed to the knowledge of God. Conversely, many scientists have been educated in an atmosphere that presumes that a "modern" empirical viewpoint has no place for a creator God. Historians and sociologists of science have demonstrated that this warfare metaphor is not the only model for the relationship between science and faith, and may in fact be only a contemporary misunderstanding.[21] However, the notion that there exists a conflict over doctrines of origins remains a commonplace.

The early chapters of Genesis describe the design and function of Earth and its life as the intentional creation of a good God. This intention is expressed as a sequence of creative decrees, resulting in an atmosphere, a global ocean, a heterogeneous landscape, and their population by a vast diversity of living creatures.

Genesis 1 presents the basic outline of Earth's creation. It is formulated as occurring in seven days. However, geologic discoveries during the past few centuries have convinced most observers that Earth is an object of great antiquity. Does a conflict exist between our observations and biblical teaching?

The textual clues surrounding the sense of the "days" intended in Genesis 1 indicate, first, that the words describe literal (i.e., twenty-four-hour) days. However, we must remind ourselves that some biblical passages use literal language for nonliteral purposes. In particular, God is often described by means of literal terms invoking human appearances or types of activity. For example, Scripture speaks of God's "face" and "hands" and of God employing Earth as a "footstool," etc. Such expressions are termed *anthropomorphisms*. Christians do not feel compelled to believe that God, who is a spirit, has literal hands or literally stretches out his legs to rest his literal feet upon an earthly stool.[22] In this view, the "days" of Genesis are plainly *God's days* and are only crudely comparable to human days in the same way that God's "hands" only functionally parallel human hands.

Moreoer, many biblical passages use ordinary language descriptions of natural events. The sun is said to rise and fall; Joshua commands the sun to stand still in the sky. The book of Job has many more examples.

> "Who shut up the sea behind doors
>   when it burst forth from the womb,
> when I made the clouds its garment
>   and wrapped it in thick darkness,
> when I fixed limits for it
>   and set its doors and bars in place,
> when I said, 'This far you may come and no farther,
>   here is where your proud waves halt'?"—Job 38:8–11

God speaks directly to Job here. Does this passage, employing literal language for "doors and bars," require the Christian to believe that if one travels to the coast he or she will see gates of some sort at the end of the land? It is doubtful that God worries that one's vacation to the beach will destroy his or her faith. Rather, that personal experience of sand and surf enhances one's understanding of the nature of coastlines and illuminates the biblical passage quoted above. Our investigations into the details of the fashioning of Earth through time are no different from the example derived here from Job.

The terse descriptions of creative fiats in Genesis 1 can thus be understood as schematics for the formation of a planet.[23] Moreover, this particular planet is designed to teem with life. Verse 20, for example, begins, "And God said, 'Let the water teem with living creatures.'"

As in all sciences, our gain in empirical understanding merely fleshes out the details of the workings and history of creation. The Christian may gratefully study the history of Earth, knowing that this history gives praise to its Author.

How does Earth function as an abode for life?

Scripture in many places indicates that our home world was designed with the intent to support organic life, and to enable that life to flourish (e.g., "Let the water teem with living creatures," Gen. 1:20). Isaiah 45:18 states, for example:

> For this is what the LORD says—
> he who created the heavens,
> he is God;
> he who fashioned and made the earth,
> he founded it;
> he did not create it to be empty,
> but formed it to be inhabited.

How may the study of Earth illuminate our creaturely understanding of its life-promoting organization and construction?

Comparison of Earth with other planets, an enterprise that began during the past century, has only served to amplify our understanding of how well-engineered our world is for life.[24] Factors promoting organic life include such items as Earth's distance from the sun and the radiative output of the sun; the shape of Earth's orbit; Earth's size and bulk chemistry; Earth's internal heat engine and resulting plate tectonics; the presence of a substantial ocean; an atmosphere of sufficient pressure to retain water in the liquid state on Earth's surface; and the complex interaction of all of these to provide ample routes for geochemical cycles that promote life. Within our local solar system, Earth is unique in these qualities, a fact that was dramatically illustrated when the first photographs of Earth from space were released. (See plate 12.)

The Christian student who is sufficiently impressed with this truly amazing organization might wish to devote some effort to the study of Earth's integrated systems. As a case in point, the discipline of *oceanography* includes, in part, examination of the interrelationships of Earth's heat distribution and atmospheric motions with ocean currents. Deep currents, in turn, provide oxygen to the abyssal biota, while upwelling currents return nutrients such as nitrogen and silicon to the upper waters where photosynthesis can operate. How is this system engineered, and how might humans affect this for the benefit or detriment of oceanic life? Other planetary features that are commonly studied as dynamic systems include river basins, lakes, estuaries, permafrost regions, and drylands.

Other avenues for investigation open up in the reconstruction of the history of life on Earth. How was Earth populated with diverse creatures through time? There is a universal fascination with Earth's ancient life-forms. These ancient creatures, like our existing ones, were often elegant or bizarre and give cause for praise to the Creator. The Christian *paleontologist* thus has a powerful incentive to study these long-gone biotas.

How have living creatures affected the physical environment of the planet? As new taxa have been added to the inventory of life, these have undeniably altered planet-wide ecosystems. While the biosphere has certainly become more diverse through the ages, has it also become more robust? One recent philosophical approach, termed the *Gaia hypothesis*, holds that life-forms (chiefly microbial life) control our planet's atmospheric composition and ultimately the global climate. A strong form of this theory stresses that life, in effect, controls Earth so as to maximize organic productivity and habitability. Is this reasonable? This strong Gaian viewpoint is amenable to co-option by pantheistic theologies.[25] A Trinitarian Christian response to this pantheism should be framed, emphasizing supernatural design of Earth features and processes. (For more on this topic, see chapter 3.)

How can the Earth sciences help us fulfill our role as stewards?

A comprehensive and biblical theology of stewardship, beyond the scope of this chapter, conclusively demonstrates that God is concerned that His people exhibit respect and care for the world and its resources.

To fulfill a careful stewardship role, organized and principled knowledge must be obtained. Culturally useful Earth objects or products do not occur at random; they are framed according to the logic of Earth function. Often such products result from processes that require large amounts of time and cannot be renewed, at least in terms of human life span or even the span of whole cultures. For example, aquifers in western Kansas that accumulated potable water over the span of millennia are being depleted over the span of decades. In many cases, this will inevitably result in a shift in agricultural practices on the high plains of the United States.

For millennia, management of water supply has been a crucial aspect of human culture. It has been a significant factor in the rise of civilizations, to the extent that much cultural theory has been devoted to understanding the rise and fall of "hydraulic civilizations" like those of Egypt or Mesopotamia.[26] Fresh water will remain a critical resource in many parts of the world for the foreseeable future.[27] Regions of water scarcity should not be visualized as cliché pictures of third-world deserts. Areas of perennial scarcity also include portions of the southwestern United States and northern China.

High-quality agricultural soils are among our most underappreciated systems undergirding regional cultural prosperity and our global agroeconomic system. Good soils are not universal. They are generated over time through a concatenation of climate, parent rock, and vegetation; and they must be carefully husbanded to permit centuries of high productivity. Yet abuse of soil resources is commonplace. In North America conversion of quality agricultural land to urban use is occurring at a staggering rate.[28] Other global forms of soil abuse include erosion resulting from overgrazing and salinization through intensive irrigation.

Our present industrial civilization requires large amounts of purified metallic resources. The appropriate ores, like soils, are not universal. Location, evaluation, and development of ore resources requires extensive training in geology and geochemistry. Mining and processing of ores is a rough business and can result in extensive scarring of the landscape and pollution by heavy metals, acid mine run-off, and/or release of acid-forming sulfur gases from smelters. A considerate exploitation of mineral resources that minimizes human danger and damage to ecological systems also requires extensive training in geology and geochemistry.

We live in a culture glutted on accessible transportation and reliable winter heating and summer cooling provided by fossil fuels. If the price of gasoline at the pump jumps, complaints abound. But most persons have no understanding of the geology of fossil fuel resources that undergirds our efforts to discover and exploit these. We are also reluctant to face the fact that these resources are limited and should not be squandered.

A biblical model for our role as stewards of Earth and its creatures requires an attitude of responsibility and accountability to our Creator. Responsibility, in turn, requires knowledge. Presently Earth is blemished with the wrecks of past abuses that need to be remedied; future abuse needs tempering. At the same time, millions of fellow humans, created in the image of God, lack basic cultural commodities. There is abundant scope here for focused, God-honoring efforts to develop and conserve Earth's resources for the benefit of the many.

How is Earth a revelation of its Creator?

We live on a planet that periodically exerts a power over humans, often perceived as violent. The earth shakes; volcanoes erupt; hurricanes engulf coastal communities (see chapter 7, "What Is God's Purpose for Natural Disasters?"). But all these are symptomatic of a planet that functions, a planet invested with engines. These engines maintain processes that in turn permit life to exist. If God allows the time, our Earth will eventually "wind down," and life will diminish with it.

The same power of the planet, operating through its engines over time, has stocked Earth with materials that promote life and provide the ingredients for culture. Humans need to learn gratitude for these processes and gratitude for the long time over which they have acted.

We need to learn to respect natural systems for the engineered structures that they are. Natural systems can be modified and exploited, but always at some cost. Often the costs are passed forward to another generation.

Earth exhibits an aesthetic dimension that to many directly proclaims the oversight of a Creator. (See plates 11 and 12.) Our increasing knowledge of its functions should only serve to increase our praise of this Creator. The life of the Christian earth scientist thus can be one of ever-increasing knowledge of the goodness of the triune God.

QUESTIONS

1. How has Earth's formation and subsequent history provided a very different world from its near neighbors in space—one extremely favorable for population by innumerable life-forms?

2. How should Christians respond to the myriad life-forms that have affected Earth's climate and surface conditions?

3. How may Christians cultivate a sense of awe and gratitude to the almighty God for His guidance and provision to the Earth and its creatures over the ages?

NOTES

14. D. L. Anderson, *Theory of the Earth* (London: Blackwell Scientific, 1989), chaps. 1–4.

15. K. Lodders and B. Fegley Jr. *The Planetary Scientist's Companion* (Oxford: Oxford Univ. Press, 1998), 128.

16. J. Lean, "The Sun's Variable Radiation and Its Relevance for Earth," *Annual Review of Astronomy and Astrophysics* 35 (1997): 33–67.

17. C. C. Albritton Jr., *The Abyss of Time: Changing Conceptions of the Earth's Antiquity after the Sixteenth Century* (Mineola, N.Y.: Dover, 1980); G. Gohau, *A History of Geology*, trans. A. V. Carozzi and M. Carozzi (New Brunswick, N.J.: Rutgers Univ. Press, 1990); S. Winchester, *The Map That Changed the World: William Smith and the Birth of Modern Geology* (New York: HarperCollins, 2001); and A. C. Cutler, *The Seashell on the Mountaintop* (New York: Dutton, 2003).

18. M. J. S. Rudwick, *The Meaning of Fossils*, 2nd ed. (Chicago: Univ. of Chicago Press, 1985).

19. G. B. Dalrymple, *The Age of the Earth* (Stanford, Calif.: Stanford Univ. Press, 1991), chap. 2; and S. G. Brush, *Transmuted Past: The Age of the Earth and the Evolution of the Elements from Lyell to Patterson* (Cambridge: Cambridge Univ. Press, 1996), 66–85.

20. H. E. Newsom and J. H. Jones, *Origin of the Earth* (New York: Oxford Univ. Press, 1990); R. M. Canup and K. Righter, *Origin of the Earth and Moon* (Tucson: Univ. of Arizona Press, 2000).

21. E. A. Burtt, *The Metaphysical Foundations of Modern Science*, rev. ed. (New York: Doubleday, 1954); R. Hooykaas, *Religion and the Rise of Modern Science* (Grand Rapids: Eerdmans, 1972); M. J. S. Rudwick, *The Meaning of Fossils*, 2nd ed. (Chicago: Univ. of Chicago Press, 1985); D. Lindberg and R. Numbers, eds., *God and Nature: Historical Essays on the Encounter between Christianity and Science* (Berkeley: Univ. of California Press, 1986); D. N. Livingstone, *Darwin's Forgotten Defenders: The Encounter between Evangelical Theology and Evolutionary Thought* (Grand Rapids and Edinburgh: Eerdmans and Scottish Academic Press, 1987); and J. H. Brooke, *Science and Religion in Historical Perspective* (Cambridge: Cambridge Univ. Press, 1991).

22. C. J. Collins, "How Old Is the Earth?" *Presbyterian* 20 (1994): 109–30.

23. D. Stoner, *A New Look at an Old Earth: Resolving the Conflict between the Bible and Science* (Eugene, Ore.: Harvest House, 1997).

24. L. J. Henderson, *The Fitness of the Environment* (New York: Macmillan, 1913); W. S. Broecker, *How to Build a Habitable Planet* (Palisades, N.Y.: Eldigio Press, 1985);

N. Horowitz, *To Utopia and Back: The Search for Life in the Solar System* (New York: W. H. Freeman, 1986), chap. 4; Colin A. Russell, *The Earth, Humanity, and God: The Templeton Lectures, 1993* (London: UCL Press, 1994); S. R. Taylor, *Destiny or Chance: Our Solar System and Its Place in the Cosmos* (Cambridge: Cambridge Univ. Press, 1998); P. D. Ward and D. Brownlee, *Rare Earth: Why Complex Life Is Uncommon in the Universe* (New York: Copernicus, 2000); L. J. Rothschild and A. M. Lister, eds., *Evolution on Planet Earth: The Impact of the Physical Environment* (London: Academic Press, 2003); and G. Gonzalez and J. Richards, *The Privileged Planet* (Washington, D.C.: Regnery, 2004).

25. R. Radford Ruether, *Gaia and God: An Ecofeminist Theology of Earth Healing* (San Francisco: Harper, 1992).

26. D. Worster, *Rivers of Empire: Water, Aridity and the Growth of the American West* (Oxford: Oxford Univ. Press, 1985), chap. 2.

27. S. Postel, *Pillar of Sand: Can the Irrigation Miracle Last?* (New York: W. W. Norton, 1999); and P. Gleick, *The World's Water, 2002–2003: The Biennial Report on Freshwater Resources* (Washington, D.C.: Island, 2002).

28. C. DeWitt, "Introduction: Seven Degradations of Creation," in *The Environment and the Christian: What Can We Learn from the New Testament?* ed. C. B. DeWitt (Grand Rapids: Baker, 1991), 13–23.

SUGGESTED READING

Gonzalez, G., and J. Richards. *The Privileged Planet*. Washington, D.C.: Regnery, 2004.

Russell, Colin A. *The Earth, Humanity, and God—The Templeton Lectures, 1993*. London: UCL Press, 1994.

Young, Davis A. *Christianity and the Age of the Earth*. Grand Rapids: Zondervan, 1982.

Environmental Stewardship: What Are the Roles for Science and Faith?

Randy Van Dragt and James A. Clark

During the *Apollo* flights to the moon in the late 1960s, Earth's human inhabitants were offered an unprecedented series of pictures of their home planet from the perspective of space.[29] The first color photograph, taken by astronaut William Anders as the *Apollo 8* spacecraft emerged from the dark side of the moon, shows the sphere of Earth partially obscured by its own shadow, blue and green with grand swirls of white, hanging between the featureless blackness of space and the barren landscape of the lunar surface. In that photo we can see, through the astronaut's eyes, the true dimension of that wonderful earthly environment that makes life possible for what today are more than 6 billion humans and innumerable other organisms belonging to several million species. That photo has motivated many to ask in a new way an old and fundamental question: Where are we, and what is this place that sustains both humanity and the many other creatures that live here with us? (Many other photos of Earth have been taken from space; see, e.g., plate 13.)

A short answer to this question is that we are on a planet of modest size near a sun of modest size in an average galaxy in a very large universe. Despite its many average qualities, however, our planet possesses unique properties that nurture life; among these are abundant water, a protective atmosphere with adequate oxygen, an active magnetic field to deflect solar emissions, and a distance from our sun that provides generous energy and moderate temperatures. These features come together most critically on the surface of the planet in a thin layer of water, earth, and atmosphere that we call the *biosphere*. The biosphere provides the needed environment for humans and other organisms to flourish. Study of the structure and function of the biosphere is at the center of environmental science. The goals of environmental science are to better understand the physical, chemical, and biological processes that maintain Earth's environment and to understand how human activities affect those processes.[30] In recent years, the findings of environmental scientists have raised troubling questions about how the expanding human population is affecting the long-term welfare of Earth's environment.[31] Addressing these questions requires not only ongoing scientific investigation but also an evaluation of our earthly situation from a faith perspective. It is our Christian faith that can uniquely address such questions as, To whom does this earth belong? What is the place of humanity on Earth? and How can we live here in a manner that is sustainable?

Where are we?

This question produces various answers, depending on who is responding to it. The environmental scientist might evoke the analogy of a spaceship and paint a picture similar to that seen from the moon, of living creatures hurtling through space protected by Earth's atmosphere and sustained by multiple intricate systems to which the physical, chemical, and biological processes of Earth contribute. A theologically astute Christian, while not contradicting the scientist, might expand the answer by noting that the biosphere is more than just an effective means of preserving life in space. Earth and its systems function as an expression of the Creator's providential care for His creatures. Furthermore, the structure and function of creation testify to its human passengers of the design, power, and care of the Creator. To use a different and ancient analogy, the creation is also a dynamic book that is intended to turn us humans to its author, the creator God. If we stay with the scientist's spaceship analogy, we might ask, "How does this thing work?" What has science taught us about the environmental systems of this planet?[32]

How does this thing work?

The sheltering and life-nurturing environment of the planet is the product of interactions between two major components of the biosphere. The first is the nonliving, or abiotic, component that includes the atmosphere, the water covering 72 percent of the planet, the geological substance and structure of Earth's surface, and incoming sunlight. The second is the living, or biotic, component comprising all the living creatures that populate Earth. Together these diverse and complex components of the biosphere create life-support systems that have remained remarkably stable for long periods of time.

What is the abiotic context?

The planet God chose for humans as home is one that requires cycles to maintain, renew, and continue life. The most important ones are clearly and succinctly described in Ecclesiastes 1:5–7. The sun, continuing on its daily and annual course, causes the wind to mix and redistribute heat, effectively moderating temperature extremes throughout the planet. In addition winds transport water vapor over the

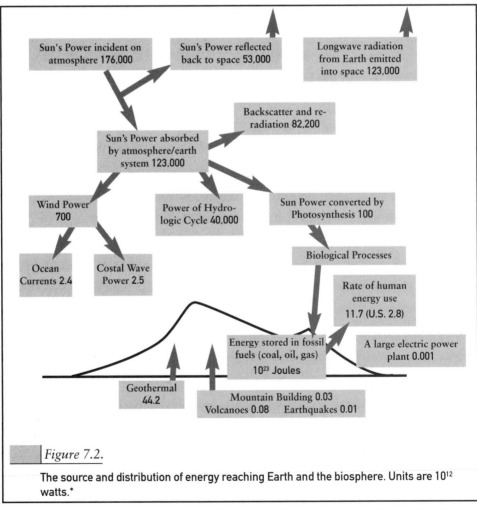

Figure 7.2.

The source and distribution of energy reaching Earth and the biosphere. Units are 10^{12} watts.*

* Arthur L. Bloom, *Geomorphology: A Systematic Analysis of Late Cenozoic Land Forms,* 3rd ed. (Englewood Cliffs, N.J.: Prentice-Hall, 1998).

PLATE 1. *SPIRAL GALAXY NGC 4414.* This beautiful galaxy of several billion stars has a spiral form similar to our own Milky Way galaxy. The starlight blends together; the spiral arms contain massive clouds of dust and gas where new stars form.

Courtesy NASA and The Hubble Heritage Team
(Space Telescope Science Institute [STScI]/AURA)

PLATE 2. *THE ULTRADEEP FIELD OF THE HUBBLE SPACE TELESCOPE*. This image was obtained by pointing the telescope at a small, relatively "empty" direction of space for many days, collecting light from some of the faintest, most distant objects in the universe. The resulting image is truly astounding: each patch of light is a galaxy of thousands of stars, and there are at least 10,000 galaxies in the image. Note the many colors and shapes, such as spirals and spheres. Distance measurements show that some of these galaxies are billions of light-years away; the light we now see from them was emitted much closer in time to the beginning of the universe.

Courtesy NASA, ESA, S. Beckwith,
and the UDF Team

PLATE 3. *SAGITTARIUS STAR CLOUD.* This star field near the center of our own galaxy shows the beauty and variety of star colors and brightness, like a collection of glittering gems. Blue stars are generally hotter than our sun, and red stars are cooler.

Courtesy NASA and The Hubble Heritage Team (STScI/AURA)

PLATE 4. *THE ORION NEBULA.* Thousands of stars are forming in this dense cloud of interstellar gas and dust. Large newly formed stars radiate light back into the surrounding cloud from which they formed, ionizing the gas and creating a colorful display.

Courtesy C. R. O'Dell and S. K. Wong
(Rice University), NASA

Jupiter's
Great Red Spot

Hubble
Heritage

PRC99-29 • Hubble Space Telescope WFPC2 • Hubble Heritage Team (AURA/STScI/NASA)

PLATE 5. *THE GAS PLANET JUPITER.* Jupiter's giant red spot is a swirling storm in Jupiter's atmosphere that is larger than planet Earth, with winds of 270 miles per hour. Subsequent images (insets) taken over a period of seven years show the storm changing in shape, size, and color.

Courtesy Hubble Heritage Team
(NASA/STScI/AURA)

PLATE 6. *SPIRAL GALAXIES*. These two spiral galaxies are undergoing a close encounter. As the galaxies pass closely by each other, tidal forces fling out stars and gas into long streamers. In the very distant universe, we see more galaxies interacting with one another; the universe was smaller billions of years ago when the light we now see was emitted from these galaxies.

Courtesy NASA and the Hubble Heritage Team (NASA/STScI/AURA)

PLATE 7. *HUBBLE SPACE TELESCOPE.* The extraordinary Hubble Space Telescope, launched in 1990, has provided beautiful images of the universe never seen before with other telescopes. The unique technology was named for Edwin P. Hubble, famed American astronomer. The telescope orbits at 600 kilometers above the Earth and completes an orbit every 97 minutes.

Courtesy NASA/STScI/AUR0A

PLATE 8. *BLACK-FOOTED FERRET AND DELHI SANDS FLOWER-LOVING FLY.*
The black-footed ferret and the Delhi Sands flower-loving fly are two examples of endangered species in the United States. Populations of the black-footed ferret were decimated by the destruction of prairie dog towns, on which they depend for food, and by the introduction of feline distemper. The last-known black-footed ferrets died in the 1970s in South Dakota. However, they were rediscovered in 1981 on a ranch in Wyoming. Since then they have been reintroduced to several localities to reestablish local populations.

The Delhi Sands fly is the first fly to be protected under the provisions of the Endangered Species Act. Its habitat is limited to the fine Delhi series sands of Southern California, most of which has been developed for other uses. Its continued existence is imperiled by the demands for further development of land in this area.

Courtesy U.S. Fish and Wildlife Service,
LuRay Parker (ferrets);
B. "Moose" Peterson (fly)

PLATE 9. *PHINEAS GAGE.* *Science* magazine cover from 1994 featuring Phineas Gage.

From H. Damasio et al., "The Return of Phineas Gage:
Clues about the Brain from a Famous Patient,"
Science 264:1102-1105 (1994).
Department of Neurology and Image
Analysis Facility, University of Iowa

PLATE 10. *UPPER PALEOLITHIC CAVE.* View of an excavated portion of La Grotte Walou à Forêt in the Province of Liège, Belgium. This cave was surveyed and excavated between 1984 and 1990 and from 1996 to 2000 by Belgian archaeologists. Eight meters of cultural deposit occurred in this cave with identifiable tool complexes beginning with the Mousterian tools during the Middle Paleolithic Period (seen at the bottom of the photo) around 40,000 BC. They were associated with a Neanderthal tooth. The top of the deposit lies at the top of the photo. Part of a column of unexcavated strata was left for comparison (left side of photo). Above the Mousterian level, the Aurignacian complex occurs at 29,000 BC; and above that the Gravettian complex occurs between 25,860 and 22,800 BC; finally, the Magdalenian at 13,030 BC. Stratigraphy is complex because the detritus slopes down from each level in front of the cave. Levels above that were associated with the Mesolithic and Neolithic complexes that were not dated. (Data summarized from editeurs Camille Bellaire, Joelle Moulin, and Anne Cahen Delhaye, "Guide de Sites Préhistoriques et Protohistoriques de Wallonie," *Bulletin de la Fédération des Archéoloques de Wallonie* (Namur, Belgium), Numéro Spécial [2001]: 22–23.) The strings are attached to the steel superstructure to locate the depth and spatial extent of the stratigraphy and artifacts precisely during the excavation. This same scenario of carefully excavated stratigraphy of Paleolithic sites (and the excavated sequence above) occurs scores of times across Western Europe.

Photo by Dean E. Arnold

PLATE 11. *MOUNT COOK.* The lovely Southern Alps flaunt extensive glaciers and snow-fields. Mount Cook, the highest mountain in New Zealand, has three summits. Sir Edmund Hillary first climbed Mount Cook with an impressive team of climbers.

Photo by Dorothy F. Chappell

PLATE 12. *EARTH FROM SPACE.*

Courtesy NASA http://eol.jsc.nasa.gov/sseop/images/
EFS/lowres/AS17/AS17-148-22727.jpg

PLATE 13. *APOLLO 8* EARTHRISE FROM MOON.

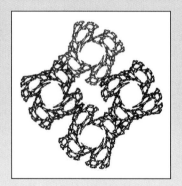
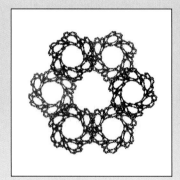
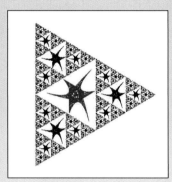

CHAPTER 8

PLATE 14. *FRACTALS*. The study of some chaotic phenomena requires the iteration of an enormous number of points through many repetitive cycles of an iteration process. Results of such experiments are usually summarized by plotting graphs of the long-term behaviors of each point. Frequently the graphs exhibit beautiful symmetries and structures that give clues to important underlying features of the iteration process itself. To produce each graph shown on this page, author Terence Perciante wrote a compuer program that iterated a minimum of 200,000 points through systems of two or more simple linear mappings.

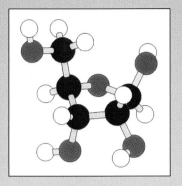 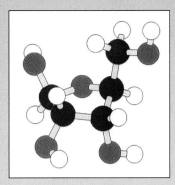

CHAPTER 9

PLATE 15. *RIGHT- AND LEFT-HANDED MOLECULES.* The molecule represented on the left is D-ribose, the form of sugar that is incorporated into RNA. The molecule on the right is L-ribose, which looks exactly like what D-ribose would look like in a mirror, similar to the relationship between right and left hands. Only D-ribose can be used in RNA.

Courtesy Larry Funck

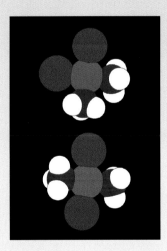

PLATE 16. *CIS-PLATIN MOLECULE.* The drug shown at the top is called cis-platin and was the first drug used in chemotherapy (its full name is cis-diamminedichloroplatinum [II]). The mauve central atom is a platinum atom. Cis-platin's anti-tumor action was accidentally discovered during unrelated research of platinum compounds.

The chemical shown at the bottom, which differs only in the spatial arrangement of the green chlorine atoms, has no anti-tumor properties.

Courtesy Peter Walhout

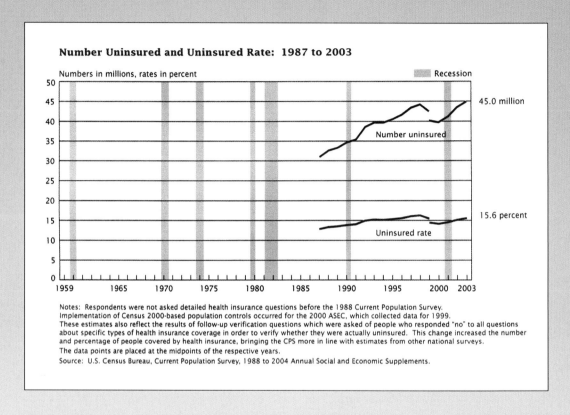

CHAPTER 11

Number Uninsured and Uninsured Rate: 1987 to 2003

Numbers in millions, rates in percent — Recession

45.0 million

15.6 percent

Number uninsured

Uninsured rate

Notes: Respondents were not asked detailed health insurance questions before the 1988 Current Population Survey.
Implementation of Census 2000-based population controls occurred for the 2000 ASEC, which collected data for 1999.
These estimates also reflect the results of follow-up verification questions which were asked of people who responded "no" to all questions about specific types of health insurance coverage in order to verify whether they were actually uninsured. This change increased the number and percentage of people covered by health insurance, bringing the CPS more in line with estimates from other national surveys.
The data points are placed at the midpoints of the respective years.
Source: U.S. Census Bureau, Current Population Survey, 1988 to 2004 Annual Social and Economic Supplements.

PLATE 17. *U.S. CENSUS BUREAU DATA SHOWING THE NUMBER OF UNINSURED AND UNINSURED RATE.*

U.S. Census Bureau—Income, Poverty and Health
Insurance Coverage in the United States 2003

surface and in large part control location and amount of precipitation. Surface water and groundwater inexorably move toward the sea, but the sea is never filled, as the writer of Ecclesiastes states, because evaporation returns that water to the atmosphere and the cycle repeats. In similar fashion important biogeochemical cycles circulate carbon, nitrogen, sulfur, phosphorus, oxygen, and other elements essential for life.[33] Although generations of humankind pass away, the cycles are meant to endure. Energy, gases, liquids, solids, and ions are swirling about Earth in a dance that is expertly choreographed by God but nevertheless complex. The rhythm is different for every process, but the chorus repeats unceasingly. A single misstep can have unexpected consequences throughout the entire production.

The sun's energy is the ultimate power source for all of these cycles except for the contributions made by geological mountain-building processes. This energy is distributed throughout Earth in a manner summarized in figure 7.2. There we see that much of the available energy fuels the hydrologic cycle, with only a small fraction of that energy powering the very important process of photosynthesis. Some of the sun's energy, converted by photosynthesis and incorporated into plants buried in the earth, is the source of the fossil fuels (coal, oil, natural gas) that power much of modern society. At the present rate of human energy consumption (11.7×10^{12} watts) the total stored fossil fuel energy (approximately 10^{23} joules), much of it coal, will be consumed in only 270 years. U.S. oil production peaked more than thirty years ago, and most geologists claim that global oil production will peak within the next ten years.[34] It seems inevitable, if present energy consumption patterns are to be maintained, that society will need to move toward sustainable sources of energy, such as wind or solar, or develop safe means to employ nuclear technologies, especially fusion energy.

The atmosphere is extremely thin, with at least 80 percent of the gases within ten miles of Earth's surface. This distance is less than the average commute to work, yet this thin layer of gas is essential for life. It is now possible for the quantity of man-made effluent to contaminate the atmosphere. In 1952 London, England, was shocked as pollutants from coal-burning heaters built up to dangerous levels in the city. Over a four-day period more than 4,000 deaths were attributable to the pollution and more than 8,000 more resulted later from complications,[35] more deaths than London sustained during the fifty-seven-day London blitz of World War II. The London case was localized in extent, but the atmosphere is readily mixed, and any effluent will transgress borders of nations and even continents. Coal-burning power plants have introduced sulfur into the atmosphere that ultimately precipitates as acid rain, and studies of air trapped in polar ice cores show that carbon dioxide levels have increased dramatically during the twentieth century through voracious burning of fossil fuels. During much of the past millennium, atmospheric CO_2 levels were around 280 parts per million, but during the last two centuries the concentration has risen, at an accelerating rate, to 370 parts per million.[36] Although these CO_2 concentrations have no known physiological effects upon humankind, the ability of carbon dioxide molecules to absorb long-wave radiation emitted to space from Earth could cause the climate to change with unknown consequences.

Rain or snow ultimately replenishes our rivers, lakes, and groundwater. Water, tainted by salts or contaminants and therefore unfit for human consumption or agriculture, is naturally distilled during evaporation and condensed as pure life-giving water. Yet many regions have a very short supply of this water. More than 18 percent of the world's human population has insufficient water, and 40 percent lack sanitation necessary to maintain even the most basic health standards.[37] In developing countries, 80 percent of illness is directly attributable to water-related diseases that are largely preventable. Although earth systems were designed by God to purify groundwater through filtering and microbe activity, there is a limit that has often been exceeded, and many manmade chemical contaminants are not readily broken down into harmless materials by natural processes. When irrigation waters, necessary for increased crop production for a growing world population, are extracted from the ground, the water table will drop if inflow to the groundwater reservoir is less than the extraction rate. Even in a region such as Chicago, blessed with huge quantities of freshwater, water level in municipal wells used for many years dropped 900 feet.[38] The need for water is growing with adverse repercussions not only in health and agriculture but also in politics and civil unrest.

What is the biotic connection?

Interacting with, and in many cases driving, the cycles of the abiotic sector are all of Earth's living creatures, the biotic community. Earth is populated by millions of species of organisms, and each species makes its living through unique sets of interactions with the abiotic world and with other creatures. Among the most important functions living organisms contribute to the biosphere are energy capture and the uptake and cycling of nutrients. Particularly crucial to these processes are plants.

Plants are the bridge for the transfer of matter and energy between the abiotic and biotic realms. In photosynthesis plants trap sunlight and use the light energy to produce carbohydrates from carbon dioxide and water. From those carbohydrates, often combined with other elements from the environment like nitrogen or phosphorus, plants produce new plant tissue, or biomass, as they grow or produce seeds. This generation of new plant tissues is a process known as primary production, and the continuing production of new biomass by plants is the fundamental source of nutrients and energy for most other organisms. Whether consumed directly by animals or decomposed by bacteria and fungi, it is plant biomass that supplies matter and energy in a form other creatures can use. In addition to being primary producers, plants contribute to the environment in other important ways. As a by-product of photosynthesis, plants produce the oxygen that constitutes 21 percent of Earth's atmosphere. On land, plants help to capture and retain water. They also build up soil and slow erosion, condition the air moving over them, and provide physical structure to the environment that countless other creatures exploit. To support much of the life we know, healthy plant communities are essential.

Wherever the abiotic and biotic sectors interact in a local unit—perhaps as a marsh, grassland, or forest—that unit is known as an ecosystem. Together Earth's many and diverse ecosystems produce global processes that support the biosphere and provide its inhabitants with essential goods and services. Those processes include the storage and cycling of water, biological productivity, biogeochemical cycling and storage of nutrients, decomposition, and the maintenance of life's diversity of species.[39] From a human perspective, when these processes function well both locally and globally, they produce a steady supply of necessary goods and services. While we recognize these products as beneficial to human welfare on Earth, most are essential for other organisms as well.

WHAT YOUR LOCAL ECOSYSTEMS DO FOR YOU

The basic ecological processes of the local ecosystem, and indeed of the biosphere as a whole, supply us with many essential goods and services that are supplied largely without our being aware of them.*

GOODS
- Food and water
- Construction materials
- Energy for domestic and industrial use
- Medicines
- Wild genes for maintaining domestic plants and animals
- Tourism and recreation

(See "'Man Eats Planet! Two-fifths Already Gone'" sidebar on page 169 for a measure of our appetite for plant production alone.)

SERVICES
- Maintaining hydrological cycles
- Cleansing water and air
- Maintaining the gaseous composition of the atmosphere
- Regulating climate
- Pollinating crops and other important plants
- Generating and maintaining soils
- Storing and cycling essential nutrients
- Absorbing and detoxifying pollutants
- Providing beauty, resources for education and research, and spiritual inspiration

*Adapted from Norman Christensen, "The Report of the Ecological Society of America Committee on the Scientific Basis for Ecosystem Management," *Ecological Applications* 6, no. 3 (July 1996): 667.

Where are we really?

From a biblical perspective, the question of where we are is not fully answered until we include the idea that Earth with its processes is God's creation and an expression of divine provision for all of life. In providing for His creatures, God has designed a match between life and its environment so close that neither element can be fully defined without the other. The writer of Genesis 1 used this complementarity between creature and environment to structure one account of creation. In that account, God forms land and soil and then populates the land with plants, animals, and humans. He separates water from land and calls on the waters to teem with schools of fish. He creates the atmosphere above both land and sea and there too places creatures specially adapted to the aerial environment. In each context, the Creator matches creatures to that portion of the environment that is uniquely their own and in which they can flourish. To know where we really are, we must see ourselves as embedded in the Creator's work.

More specific reference to God's provision for His creatures through creation's cycles is found in Psalm 104. There, for example, a product of the hydrologic cycle, a mountain stream fed by springs and rain, is depicted as the Creator's direct provision for donkeys, streamside vegetation, birds, and human crops. Through the productivity of well-watered soil, God provides for human needs. In the wild food web of the desert, God provides food for the lion. On this earth, creation and providence are woven together both as a natural expression of the Creator's care and as a testimony to His powerful presence in the world. As the poet of Psalm 104 puts it, we are caught up in the great garment that clothes the Creator and testifies to His glory and majesty (v. 1). Through that testimony God calls on us to recognize Him and to seek Him out (Rom. 1:20).

How do all these other creatures fit in?

In reading the testimony of creation, it seems safe to conclude that Earth's Creator has a profound love of diversity. God has so tended and cared for life on earth that the globe is now filled with a wide array of species. Environmental biologists refer to the diversity of species as biological diversity, or biodiversity, and Earth's biodiversity is truly something to wonder at. Over the last three hundred years, biologists have officially named approximately 1.75 million species.[40] Of these more than half are insects and nearly 20 percent are plants.[41] The number of known species is likely only a fraction of all the species on earth today. Many biologists put the total number at between 5 and 10 million species.[42]

How does biodiversity help maintain the biosphere? In every ecosystem, different groups of organisms contribute vital elements of ecosystem function. Bacteria and fungi play key roles in decomposition and the cycling of nutrients between biotic and abiotic reservoirs. Fungi also help plants to absorb nutrients and water from the soil. Plants trap energy and nutrients that other organisms, including ourselves, need to live, and in many ecosystems they give physical structure to the environment. Animals pollinate flowers, disseminate seeds, regulate the flow of nutrients and energy in ecosystems, and much more. From ecosystem to ecosystem, the particular species performing these functions varies, but in every case, they are tied together in unique ways, and the welfare of one species is inevitably linked to the welfare of the others. Humans draw on the wild diversity of Earth directly for food and medicine, and from that diversity, we have also derived our domesticated plants and animals. Even in an agricultural environment dominated by domesticated creatures, wild diversity is significant because it harbors the genetic diversity needed to maintain and adapt domesticated organisms. Agricultural landscapes that harbor high biodiversity are also more productive.[43]

Given all the life-forms God has created, we do well to consider whether species, or individual organisms, have more than purely practical value. One question Christians have asked is whether as objects of God's creation species have intrinsic value, a value that lies in something other than the functions they perform or the ways humans can use them.[44] The Bible does not set out specifically to teach us the value of species, but it does offer insights that suggest nonhuman species have their own value in the eyes of their Creator. Consider the following:

- In Genesis 1 when God creates, He declares the works of His hand "good." In this God clearly places a value on what He has made, including life in all its many forms.
- In Genesis 1 God specifically blesses the creatures He has made. We are familiar with the "be fruitful and increase in number" blessing of Adam and Eve in Genesis 1:28, but we often overlook the fact that the same blessing is given to the creatures that God made to fill the seas and the air (Gen. 1:22).
- At the end of the account of Noah's flood, God makes a covenant with His creation (Gen. 9:8–16), the sign of which is the rainbow. It is noteworthy that the covenant is not just with Noah and his descendants but includes all the creatures who rode out the flood in the ark and their descendants.
- In his Sermon on the Mount, Jesus encourages His followers not to worry about how their physical needs will be met (Matt. 6:25–34). What is the basis of this exhortation? Jesus points his disciples to God's particular care for the sparrows flying above them and the field lilies at their feet. In effect he says that if God so lavishes His care on these His humbler creatures, how much more is He likely to take care of you?
- In Romans 8:19 Paul tells us that all of creation is looking forward to the salvation of God's people, for therein the creation itself will be relieved of the curse to which it was subjected through the fall of humankind. Personal salvation in Christ eventually translates to the redemption and restoration of all creation. This bears out God's redemptive intent expressed in John 3:16, where Jesus says, "For God so loved the cosmos [all that He had made] that he gave His only Son. . . ."

These passages and others imply two things about the diversity of creatures with which we share this world. First, though they may be directly valuable to humankind as resources or indirectly valuable for their ecological functions, God values, delights in, and cares for these creatures for their own sakes. Second, the providential, life-giving systems of this planet were intended not only to support humankind but also to allow the full diversity of life to flourish. As we assess our place in this world, we must consider that God intends for us to share it with the rest of His creatures.

How are humans affecting Earth's systems?

Until quite recently, Earth's human population was small and major population centers were relatively few and isolated. As such, the human population had almost no impact on planetary processes. In the last few hundred years, however, growth in the human population has accelerated dramatically; the last century alone has seen an increase from 2 billion to more than 6 billion people. In addition, technology and commerce have raised the standard of living for much of that population. The combined effect is that the growing human population is now having clear impacts on the global environment.[45]

Environmental biologist Peter Vitousek and a team of coworkers have identified a series of related impacts that, like falling dominoes, lead from a rapidly expanding human population pursuing higher levels of consumption to some very significant impacts on the biosphere.[46] At the first level, increases in population and per capita consumption predictably generate increased agricultural and forestry output to produce food and raw materials, expanded industrial output to provide manufactured goods, accelerated global commerce to move raw materials and manufactured goods, and for the reasonably affluent, ever more recreational use of environmental resources.

These activities, in turn, erode the resource systems on which all life depends, and they collectively produce broader impacts that reduce the ability of ecosystems to sustainably produce essential goods and services. Vitousek and his team categorize these secondary impacts in the following way:

- *Land transformation.* Land conversion from wild to domesticated ecosystems is increasing, and both wild and domesticated ecosystems are being used more intensively. One aspect of intensification is the widespread use of agricultural chemicals to increase yields; another is the more intensive grazing of marginally productive lands leading to desertification in many areas of the globe.
- *Alteration of biogeochemical cycles.* Human activities are changing fundamental biological and geological cycles. For example, the need for greater crop productivity leads us to use fertilizers to such an extent that the total of industrially produced nitrogen injected into the environment now exceeds all the nitrogen fixed by natural processes.[47] Excess nitrogen contaminates water supplies and may pose a serious health risk for humans and other organisms.

- *Additions and losses of species.* Diverse human activities, such as introduction of exotic species like the lamprey into the Great Lakes, have led to losses of species, like the lake trout, in native ecosystems.
- *Climate change.* As mentioned above, human activities at the scale they are occurring today are now thought to be changing Earth's climate, the full effects of which would affect the biosphere in ways that we cannot fully anticipate.
- *Loss of biodiversity.* Perhaps most disconcerting is that human population growth and increased resource consumption are accelerating the loss of biological diversity as lands are converted from native ecosystems to human use.

Current population models estimate that the human population will level off sometime around 2050 at between 9 and 10 billion individuals.[48] To meet the demands of this increase, we will see more land converted for agriculture, industry, and urban development and greater intensification of farming, grazing, and forestry operations. As human impacts spread, we will also see deterioration in the ability of both wild and converted ecosystems to meet the demands of the human population, let alone populations of other organisms. Finally, wild populations of many organisms with which we share this planet will be driven to unsustainably low population levels. In some cases, this will mean that these species are no longer available for use by humans. In others, it means eventual species extinction.

WHERE HAVE ALL THE BUTTERFLIES GONE?

It is well known that a substantial number of Earth's animal species are in decline and many have become extinct in the recent past. Bird declines have been particularly well documented,[*] and the rates of loss among birds have generally been taken as a measure of loss rates among other animal groups as well. A team of British investigators recently tested whether bird declines in fact correlate well with declines in another well studied group of animals—butterflies.[†] Comparing range changes in British butterflies over a twenty-year period to similar observations for British birds, the researchers found that butterfly populations were declining at a much higher rate than those of the birds. Among the birds, 54 percent showed shrinking distributions over the study period while 71 percent of native butterfly species disappeared from some or all of their previous range. If these results hold for other regions of the world and other groups of animals, and the authors of the study present evidence that they do, then anticipated rates of population and species extinctions based on birds alone underestimate the losses. If this is the case, we are moving toward a major extinction event—the sixth in the known history of earth—at a faster rate than previously predicted.

[*]For a survey of worldwide data, see Howard Youth, "Watching the Birds Disappear," *State of the World Report* (New York: W. W. Norton, 2003), 14–37. Two sources provide a good survey for North American birds: Scott Widensaul, *Living on the Wind: Across the Hemisphere with Migratory Birds* (New York: North Pointe Press, 1999), and Robert Askins, *Restoring North America's Birds* (New Haven, Conn.: Yale Univ. Press, 2000).

[†]J. Thomas, M. Telfer, D. Roy, C. Preston, J. Greenwood, J. Asher, R. Fox, R. Clarke, and J. Lawton, "Comparative Losses of British Butterflies, Birds, and Plants and the Global Extinction Crisis," *Science* 303, no. 5665 (March 19, 2004): 1879–81.

Can humans continue to exploit the resources of Earth?

For a very long time, Earth's life-support systems have sustained a broad diversity of species at population levels ranging from rare to abundant. As the preceding discussion indicates, the human population is in many ways compromising the ability of the biosphere to sustain life in its historic numbers and diversity.

To get an idea of how human impacts come together to affect sustainable use of a major resource, consider the taking of wild ocean fish as a human food source. An existing fish population or stock (a stock is a particular species caught in a particular area) can produce a more or less fixed amount of new fish for harvest each year. To borrow a financial analogy, the base population of fish represents the capital that annually generates a certain amount of interest—new fish—that can be caught for food. As long as our consumption of fish does not exceed the annual production, the production base remains intact and our harvest is sustainable; that is, we are living within the income of the system. If human need or market forces increase demand beyond this annual production, however, the harvest begins to deplete the base population, using up some of the capital on which production is based and thereby reducing production in subsequent years. Declines of this sort are occurring today throughout the world's oceans. According to estimates by the United Nations Food and Agriculture Organization, eleven of the world's fifteen most important fisheries are being heavily exploited, are in decline, or are effectively exhausted.[49] Furthermore, fish declines are hastened where industrial fishing destroys ocean floor habitats, where coastal waters receive polluted runoff from nearby land surfaces, and where coastal ecosystems are lost to development.

What does it mean for the human population to live sustainably?

Sustainable resource use is a much debated concept, but at its core lies the idea that our demands on Earth's systems (food, fiber, clean water, energy, etc.) should not exceed the capacity of those systems to generate resources or to process wastes. If for each renewable resource we were to stay within present limits of Earth's annual production, future generations should have the same access to ecosystem goods and services the present generation has. But what if sustainability includes not only humans but also the welfare of other species? If the needs of the full spectrum of God's creatures are to be met and all species maintained at sustainable levels, then as the human population grows, the per-person demand on Earth's system must decrease. Our present claim on the most fundamental of resources, plant production, requires more than 40 percent of what Earth has to give (see sidebar next page), and what flows to us is diverted from other species with resource requirements like our own. If the human population grows another 50 percent until it stabilizes in 2050, the decline and loss of other creatures—the reverse of the divine blessing in Genesis 1—is inevitable.

How can we achieve a sustainable human presence in the world that meets human needs yet allows conservation of other species?

In helping us understand how the world works, science makes a valuable contribution to moving human societies toward sustainable living, but is scientific understanding enough? In 1980 the International Union for the Conservation of Nature and Natural Resources (IUCN) proposed a statement of eleven principles to guide human societies toward sustainable lifestyles consistent with the conservation of biodiversity.[50] Of those principles, only three are derived from scientific findings such as those presented in this chapter. The others make social and economic (e.g., "Sustainability is the basic principle of all social and economic development"), political (e.g., "The present generation should limit its consumption of nonrenewable resources"), and moral assertions (e.g., "All species have an inherent right to exist") that address the social framework needed for sustainable living and the motivation to adopt a sustainable lifestyle. None of these principles is overtly religious, none recognizes Earth as God's creation or the embodiment of His

"MAN EATS PLANET! TWO-FIFTHS ALREADY GONE!"

With the words "Man eats planet! Two-fifths already gone!" ecologist Stuart Pimm begins a summary of humanity's present impact on global plant production.* The impacts come in two forms: actual use of plant materials by humans and their domesticated animals or potential production lost to land conversion or ecosystem degradation. Here is Pimm's final tally sheet:

Earth's Potential Plant Production	141 billion tons
HUMAN USE AND OTHER IMPACTS	
Production losses to land conversion for cities, roads, industry, etc.	3 billion tons
Cropland production	26 billion tons
Forest production	14 billion tons
Grazing livestock	17 billion tons
Total Human Use of Earth's Annual Plant Production	60 billion tons

By Pimm's calculations, humans command 42 percent of Earth's annual plant production either through direct consumption or through losses to other human activities. If this proportion of global plant production goes to meet the needs of Earth's present 6.2 billion human inhabitants, how much more will be needed when the human population reaches 9 to 10 billion people, as it is expected to do by 2050?

*Stuart Pimm, *The World according to Pimm: A Scientist Audits the Earth* (New York: McGraw-Hill, 2001), 99–107.

providence. Yet they collectively recognize that to live within the capacities of the biosphere, we need more than scientific knowledge. We need a proper recognition of our place in the world, and we need to embrace the value of the others here with us, both human and nonhuman.

For the Christian, it is Scripture that reveals the value God places on both humans and nonhumans and the provision He makes for all those He has created. Scripture also has some powerful things to say about our place in God's world and our role in caring for it.

What is the place of humans in the world?

When God created Adam and placed him in the garden (i.e., the biosphere), He provided good food that He permitted Adam to eat (Gen. 2:16). We are clearly created to be consumers, and the creation is available to us for that purpose. In addition to permitting consumption of garden produce, God also required that Adam *tend* and *keep* the garden (v. 15). The garden did not belong to Adam, but it was available for him to use with the added God-given responsibility that he care for it. The care envisioned by the Hebrew words used in Genesis 2:15 would cause the garden to flourish and all the functions of the garden to reach their fullest richness and complexity. However, God also placed a limit on Adam's consumption habits, and when he transgressed that limit, the relationship between Adam and God and between Adam and the garden was estranged. Being aware of this, we should recognize that our consumption patterns may be contrary to the welfare of creation. Then we must acknowledge that our place is not only to consume what is in the creation but also to care for the creation in the same way that a steward manages and watches over the property owned by an employer. (See also chapter 3.)

As both Scripture and science teach us, we are clearly a part of this world, as dependent on its healthy function as any other creature. But we are also set apart from the rest of creation because of our status as image bearers of God and the sanctification of the Holy Spirit (1 Cor. 6:11). In addition we are given special responsibilities not delegated to any other creatures. As alluded to in Genesis 2:15, those responsibilities are awesome. We are commissioned to maintain the healthy function of God's garden and to work for its flourishing. We are thus called to be stewards of what God has made and cares for. If we take this call seriously, we must then ask how we will live out our role as Earth's stewards.

How then shall we live?

Because humans have become a dominant force in Earth's biosphere, the human population and its interactions with global systems are necessarily at the heart of environmental science. As such, environmental science raises substantial challenges to contemporary societies with respect to the demands they make on the biosphere through their economic aspirations, lifestyles, and direct treatment of Earth's environment. Scripture places these challenges in larger perspective. Earth is God's world, and its systems are both a loving provision for all His creatures and a testimony to His power and care. Humans are among the creatures provided for, but they also carry the unique charge of caring for the larger creation on God's behalf. Behind humankind's historical and contemporary relations with the world is the blight of sin, a curse mercifully and graciously addressed by God in the sacrifice and resurrection of Christ. Redeemed Christians must ask, "In the light of what we know from science and Scripture, how then shall we live?"

As others have suggested,[51] there are three essential components to a Christian's stewardship response. First, we must come to understand better the biosphere and how it functions. No longer can we mindlessly treat the biosphere as a limitless source of goods and services and a limitless sink for the physical, chemical, and biological abuses we dish out as individuals and societies. As we learn more of how the biosphere works, we will also come to appreciate in greater detail our individual and corporate impacts on the world and discover ways we can reduce or mitigate these impacts.

Second, we must come to appreciate that Earth and its creatures have intrinsic moral value, and because of this, in our role as stewards we live with ethical responsibilities toward the Creator and His world. Our Creator's intent expressed in Genesis 2:15 is that we humans work to maintain the creation and preserve it. Where through greed or ignorance we have failed in this, we must repent and find other ways to live. To do this in today's world, we must first find ways to keep from being co-opted by cultural pressures to maintain the status quo. This is often best done in the company of like-minded Christians.

Finally, we must commit to acting on what we know. As Jesus told his disciples, the test of our love for Him is whether we follow His commands and those of His Father (John 14:15). If we understand the concern of the Creator for His creation and we know the Christ who is not only the world's redeemer but the One by whom and for whom the world was created (Col. 1:16), our life of faithful response will reflect a concern for all of creation. And in that life no detail will escape care-filled attention; not our cars, our homes, our recreation and entertainment, our sense of what it takes to be fulfilled in this world. Every aspect of a life under the lordship of the creator Christ is open for review and revision with regard to its impacts on creation.

QUESTIONS

1. Because both abiotic and biotic earth processes seem to be highly interrelated, accomplished space scientist James Lovelock promoted the notion that Earth as a whole is, in some sense, like a living organism. He called this "organism" Gaia after the Greek goddess of the earth. How do his ideas, or the misuse of them, lead to conflicts with the Christian faith?

2. Most people agree that it is good to preserve wild areas and to avoid polluting the environment. Problems arise when, inevitably, the formation of preserves requires eviction of occupants of the land, or when pollution controls result in economic hardship and loss of jobs. As a Christian, how would you address these issues?

3. When the topic of endangered species is raised today, especially in Christian circles, a commonly asked question is "Isn't it more important to spend our resources saving people than saving an obscure species?" What do you think? Christian environmentalist-author Calvin DeWitt suggests that if we are inclined to reply yes to this rhetorical question, we should consider the story of Noah (Gen. 6–9) and ask if God would also agree.

4. In Colossians 1:20, Paul tells us that through Christ God is reconciling all things to himself, and in 2 Corinthians 5:18, he informs us that we, in Christ, are given the ministry of reconciliation. Describe how through sin our relations with the rest of creation have become broken, and suggest some ways that you can minister to bring reconciliation in those relations.

NOTES

29. Jim Wilson, ed., "Earthrise on Christmas Day," NASA Multimedia, Image of the Day Gallery, September 16, 2004, www.nasa.gov/multimedia/imagegallery/image_feature_102.html.

30. Richard Wright, *Environmental Science: Toward a Sustainable Future*, 9th ed. (New York: Simon & Schuster, 2005); and Daniel Botkin and Edward Keller, *Environmental Science: Earth as a Living Planet*, 4th ed. (New York: John Wiley & Sons, 2003).

31. Paul Harrison and Fred Pearce, *AAAS Atlas of Population and Environment* (Berkeley: Univ. of California Press, 2001).

32. See Wright, *Environmental Science*, or Botkin and Keller, *Environmental Science*.

33. Fred Mackenzie, *Our Changing Planet: An Introduction to Earth System Science and Global Environmental Change* (Upper Saddle River, N.J.: Prentice Hall, 1998), 155–79.

34. Kenneth Deffeyes, *Hubbert's Peak: The Impending World Oil Shortage* (Princeton, N.J.: Princeton Univ. Press, 2003), 208.

35. Devra Davis, *When Smoke Ran Like Water* (New York: Basic, 2002), 316.

36. J. Barnola, M. Anklin, J. Porcheron, D. Raynaud, J. Schwander, and B. Stauffer, "CO_2 Evolution during the Last Millennium as Recorded by Antarctic and Greenland Ice," *Tellus Series B: Chemical and Physical Meteorology* 47 (1995): 264–72. D. D. Keeling and T. P. Whorf, "Atmospheric CO_2 Records from Sites in the SIO Air Sampling Network," in *Trends: A Compendium of Data on Global Change, Carbon Dioxide Information Analysis Center* (Oak Ridge: Oak Ridge National Laboratory, 1990).

37. *Water for People, Water for Life: UN World Water Development Report* (New York: Berghahn Books, 2003), 36.

38. H. L. Young, D. I. Siegel, R. J. Mandle, and A. L. Kontis, "Northern Midwest Regional Aquifer System Study," in R. J. Sun, ed., *Regional Aquifer-System Analysis Program of the U.S. Geological Survey—Summary of Projects, 1978–84*, U.S. Geological Survey Circular 1002 (1986), 72–87.

39. Norman Christensen, "The Report of the Ecological Society of America Committee on the Scientific Basis for Ecosystem Management," *Ecological Applications* 6, no. 3 (July 1996): 665–99.

40. Wright, *Environmental Science*, 274.

41. Ibid., 274–75.

42. Ibid., 275. See also endnote 1 in chap. 6.

43. Nicholas Jordan, "Sustaining Production with Biodiversity," in *The Farm as Natural Habitat: Reconnecting Food Systems with Ecosystems* (Washington, D.C.: Island, 2002), 155–68.

44. Fred Van Dyke, David Mahan, Joseph Sheldon, and Raymond Brand, *Redeeming Creation: The Biblical Basis for Environmental Stewardship* (Downers Grove, Ill.: InterVarsity Press, 1996), 46–54.

45. G. Tyler Miller Jr., *Environmental Science: Working with the Earth*, 8th ed. (Pacific Grove, Calif.: Brooks/Cole, 2001), 6–22.

46. Peter Vitousek, Harold Mooney, Jane Lubchenco, and Jerry Melillo, "Human Dominated Ecosystems," *Science* 277, no. 5325 (July 25, 1997): 494–99.

47. David Tilman, ed., "Human Alteration of the Global Nitrogen Cycle: Causes and Consequences," *Issues in Ecology* 1 (Spring 1997): 1–15. *Issues in Ecology* is a series of position papers published by the Ecological Society of America.

48. Miller, *Environmental Science*, 6–7.

49. Ibid., 402.

50. Botkin and Keller, *Environmental Science*, 127–28.

51. Van Dyke et al., *Redeeming Creation*, 162–83.

SUGGESTED READING

Bouma-Prediger, Steven. *For the Beauty of the Earth: A Christian Vision for Creation Care.* Grand Rapids: Baker, 2001.

DeWitt, Calvin. *Earthwise: A Biblical Response to Environmental Issues.* Grand Rapids: CRC Publications, 1994.

DeWitt, Calvin, ed. *The Environment and the Christian: What Can We Learn from the New Testament?* Grand Rapids: Baker, 1991.

Houghton, John. *Global Warming: The Complete Briefing.* 2nd ed. Cambridge: Cambridge University Press, 2000.

Schaeffer, Francis A. *Pollution and the Death of Man.* 1970. Reprint, Wheaton, Ill.: Crossway, 1992.

Wilkinson, Loren, Peter DeVos, Calvin DeWitt, Eugene Dykema, and Vernon Ehlers. *Earthkeeping in the Nineties: Stewardship of Creation.* Rev. ed. Grand Rapids: Eerdmans, 1991.

Young, Richard A. *Healing the Earth: A Theocentric Perspective on Environmental Problems and Their Solutions.* Nashville: Broadman and Holman, 1994.

8 CRUCIAL QUESTIONS AT THE INTERFACE OF CHRISTIAN FAITH, MATHEMATICAL SCIENCES, AND COMPUTER SCIENCE

The ancient and modern history of mathematics and the recent history of computer science is replete with professionals who have enjoyed their work. Careful historical study reveals that some scholars have modeled Newton's laws and characterized geometrical properties of the pyramids in the context of mathematics. Plotting the orbits of moons around planets or the paths of planets in the solar system requires good understanding of mathematics. Administering medicinal substances and planning one's household budget requires the most basic understanding of mathematics. Humans have undertaken remarkable modeling feats using mathematics, and even though much is known in mathematics, there are unanswered questions. To some of these are attached tremendous financial prizes. The sport of solving rigorous mathematics problems is not undertaken by the fainthearted.

Using mathematics as a foundation and following the overwhelming human desire to calculate and arrange large amounts of data, scientists have developed remarkable machines and technology that can do many things faster and with greater expediency than humans. These computers help orchestrate travel to the moon and scan groceries with a single swipe and direct your means of transport. Many Christians embark on careers in computer sciences and engage the important questions arising from the advent of developments in computer technology.

Some of the creativity and logic of mathematicians and computer scientists is demonstrated below.

Whose Idea Was Mathematics?

Terence H. Perciante

The feared multiheaded hydra of Greek mythology not only grew two heads in place of any severed one, but the stench of its breath could kill a person. To some quantitatively challenged individuals, mathematics raises its heads with such a computational stench in daily activities, commerce, and careers that even simple arithmetic becomes a feared hydra.

In contrast, for another group of people, mathematics possesses a power that enables them to flourish where others fail. What privileged mathematical weapons does this latter group wield? Have they learned a special way of thinking? Have they mastered some set of advanced skills? Is it possible that they know how to wed theory to application better than most of us? What exceptional features of mathematics allow such people to develop miraculous mathematical advances or potent applications?

Some incredible recent mathematical successes may give some clues to the source of individual mathematical effectiveness.

Can order emerge from chaos?

The development of calculus during the 1660s effectively provided tools for understanding smooth and essentially unbroken behaviors. From innumerable problems involving force, work, and energy to methods for modeling instantaneous change, the calculus laid a foundation for the industrial revolution and the subsequent mechanistic age. Unfortunately, successful application of the algorithms of the calculus required that studied phenomena had to proceed in an essentially smooth and unbroken fashion. When phenomena exhibited breaks or abrupt state changes, the methods of the calculus lost their usefulness. In short, despite the effectiveness of the calculus for representing many phenomena, mathematical models for turbulent processes, violent behaviors, or erratic variations remained elusive.

During the latter half of the 1900s, experimental and theoretical researchers alike conducted a host of inquiries into (1) erratic population variations present in certain biological systems, (2) turbulent fluid dynamics, and (3) unpredictable mathematical iteration behaviors. Although some of these inquiries were of an applied and experimental nature, others were more purely theoretical. Investigations of this latter type included studies performed during the 1970s by Mitchell Feigenbaum[1] into the behavior of points repeatedly iterated through a given class of functions. Although these mathematical "logistic" functions modeled a number of specific biological population behaviors, Feigenbaum's interest focused on points at which the numerical iteration patterns changed. Using a programmable calculator that would be considered primitive by today's standards, Feigenbaum discovered that the ratio of distances between successive pattern changes converged to a constant.

By 1986 the implications of this immense observation not only won the Wolf Prize in Physics for Feigenbaum (the second most prestigious prize after the Nobel), but it also made possible the prediction of when certain repetitive patterns would transition into chaos. Remarkably, during the last twenty-five years, both pure and applied mathematical studies have demonstrated that virtually all turbulent systems exhibit the same typical underlying features that are common to many if not all chaotic phenomena. Moreover, profound complexity quite often emerges from surprisingly simple repetitive processes.

Can old problems produce new mathematics?

In the history of mathematics, only a few problems have gained universal repute and celebrity status. A conclusive demonstration of the independence of Euclid's paral-

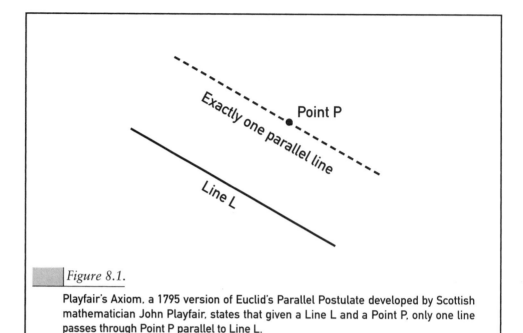

Figure 8.1.

Playfair's Axiom, a 1795 version of Euclid's Parallel Postulate developed by Scottish mathematician John Playfair, states that given a Line L and a Point P, only one line passes through Point P parallel to Line L.

lel postulate (approximately 300 BC) required more than 2,100 years. This landmark result concluded centuries of investigation and failed attempts, but from these inquiries emerged altogether new geometries.

About 350 years ago, Pierre de Fermat single-handedly elevated another ancient problem to international notoriety by a note he wrote in the margin of a Latin translation of Diophantus's *Arithmetica* (approximately 250 BC). Pre-Christian mathematicians from Greek, Egyptian, and a number of other distinct ancient cultures knew examples of the following sort:

> The perfect square 25 is the sum of two other perfect squares.
> The perfect square 169 is the sum of two other perfect squares.

Although many other examples exist for perfect squares, try finding even one perfect cube that is equal to the sum of two other cubed integers. You can't, and you will similarly fail to find solutions for higher powers! The problem demanded a proof for the conjecture that in fact no integral, nonzero solutions would ever be found for equations of the form

for exponents n > 2.

Incredibly, just before Fermat's death in 1665, he wrote a tantalizingly brief note in which he affirmed, "I have discovered a marvelous proof to this theorem that this margin is too narrow to contain." Despite Fermat's claimed proof that solutions to the equation did not exist beyond squared numbers, try as they might, no others could conclusively prove that solutions would never be found, until 1994. Then, after a lifetime of attempts to construct such a proof, the meticulous and intensely theoretical work of British mathematician Andrew Wiles finally culminated in a successful demonstration of the elusive proof. The argument required 150 pages of painstaking deduction and seven years of single-minded concentration while he served as a mathematics professor at Princeton University in New Jersey.

Does science really own mathematics?

Although the motivation and work of both Mitchell Feigenbaum and Andrew Wiles were deeply mathematical, the efforts of Feigenbaum involved computational experimentation in a way that implicitly connected his numerical experiments to empirical scientific investigations. In contrast, the profound deductive work of Wiles emerged from issues central to the number theoretic core of pure mathematics. Ten years after the remarkable success of Wiles, the proof still does not remotely suggest any apparent potential for applications beyond mathematics.

In this context, any presumed relationship between mathematics and science is tenuous at best. The methods of mathematics differ from those of science. Mathematics traffics in a world of ideas and logical structures; science explores a more material world. Nonetheless, despite these distinctives that place mathematics in a different domain than that of science, the miracle of mathematics is the remarkable applicability of its theoretical results to other domains of knowing. This astonishing

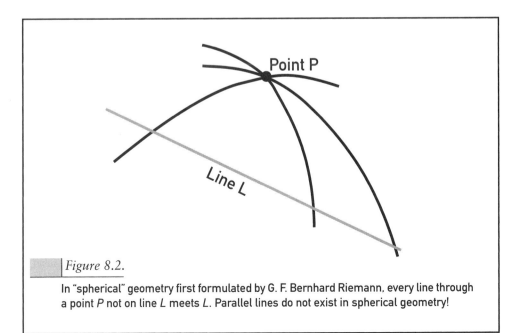

Figure 8.2.

In "spherical" geometry first formulated by G. F. Bernhard Riemann, every line through a point *P* not on line *L* meets *L*. Parallel lines do not exist in spherical geometry!

utility of mathematics even follows from formal mathematical investigations like that of Andrew Wiles, which was not empirically motivated and did not convey any initial promise for some "practical" outcome in another discipline. The history of mathematics repeatedly teaches us that amazing applications usually follow rather quickly from some of the most esoteric mathematical machinations. For example, the non-Euclidean geometry investigated by Riemann during 1854 would eventually provide the mathematical setting for Einstein's 1916 general theory of relativity.[2]

The extraordinarily productive dialogue that exists between mathematics and science, indeed between mathematics and many disciplines beyond science, may issue from certain intrinsic features of human thought and linguistic expression. If language provides one medium for expressing the results of cognition, then the highly technical language and precise symbolic/graphical expressions of mathematics summarize and convey important quantitative ideas, relationships, structures, and methods. Mathematics has repeatedly served as the mode of expression for analytical or quantitative investigations. As a language, it facilitates cognition and analysis in domains that are distinct from mathematics but that depend on it for their codification. Moreover, to the extent that mathematics consists of whole systems of axioms, definitions, and deductive structures, other disciplines embrace these models for the sake of prediction. For both codification and prediction, mathematics becomes the indispensable container wherein analysis proceeds and where forecasts find their precise linguistic statement. Mathematics is the language of science.

Are mathematical results true?

Despite the miraculous applicability of mathematics, the arbiter of mathematical quality is not the extent to which some particular result can be effectively applied. While applicability is a source of wonderment, appreciation, and something to be celebrated when a result facilitates progress in another discipline, applicability hardly adjudicates the quality of the result itself. Mathematical quality depends on the correctness of the deductive argument, the consistency of the result with the assumptions from which it was derived. Mathematicians don't ask if their work is "true." Rather, they insist on elegant derivation and absolute deductive consistency with the assumptions.

Is mathematics true? The meaning of mathematical truth continues to be an open question, and it often promotes rather virulent discussions among philosophers of mathematics. Discussions usually focus on two central issues: (1) In what sense, if any, is mathematics true, and (2) What is the nature of mathematical objects? Among people of faith, these two prior issues frequently give way to an issue of origin. Does mathematics exist in a completed a priori sense that is independent of human thought, or does mathematics emerge, a result of human assumptions and thoughtful deduction?

Belief in the Creator makes the meaning of truth in mathematics all the thornier. God is truth. He is not only true to Himself, but He is the absolute reference point for all that is. In this respect, Christians commonly assert that "all truth is God's truth." Moreover, under His sovereign control, all things exist and continue their course in perfect harmony. Believers tend to affirm an eternal consistency in all aspects of God's creation. Although human behavior, and to some extent the fabric of creation itself, has been afflicted by sin, it is difficult to identify a sense in which mathematics has been so impaired. To the contrary, mathematics seems to possess a kind of spiritual neutrality. After all, the miraculous power of mathematics for modeling scientific processes even points to the consistency of mathematics with a presumed God-ordained and God-sustained order within His creation. Being referenced to God in this way suggests that mathematical results are true.

Is mathematics impaired by logical fallibilities?

During the 1700s, Guillermo Saccheri, a Jesuit priest, raised the centuries-old confidence in the truth of mathematics to religious proportions. Saccheri sought to demonstrate that the parallel postulate of Euclidean geometry was necessarily true and that any negation of it would lead to contradictions.

Figure 8.3.

To some people, the meaning of truth and the nature of mathematical objects seem inconsequential. They argue that math works. Correct manipulation of mathematical operations and techniques provides reliable answers in all practical settings. In mathematics right is right and wrong is wrong. In fact, such an argument is itself as wrong as wrong can be. During the early 1900s, antinomies arose within core mathematical disciplines of set theory and logic that pointed to serious internal difficulties. Universally accepted axioms, rules of logic, and definitions should not have produced contradictions, but they did! Moreover, during 1931 Czech-born mathematician Kurt Gödel

Probably the most famous of the set-theoretical paradoxes, Paradox 2 was formulated by Bertrand Russell in 1901.*

*Source: http://www-history.mcs. st-andrews.ac.uk/ history/ PictDisplay/Russell.html.

showed that within a rigidly logical system such as Russell and Whitehead had developed for arithmetic, propositions can be formulated that are undecidable or undemonstrable within the axioms of the system. That is, within the system, there exist certain clear-cut statements that can neither be proved or disproved. Hence one cannot, using the usual methods, be certain that the axioms of arithmetic will not lead to contradictions. . . . It appears to foredoom hope of mathematical certitude through use of the obvious methods. Perhaps doomed also, as a result, is the ideal of science— to devise a set of axioms from which all phenomena of the external world can be deduced.[3]

The assumed reliability of carefully performed mathematics was leading to contradictions, and Gödel added insult to injury by showing that solutions to some well-posed mathematical problems could not even be solved within mathematics itself. What was the source of such disconcerting difficulties? Were the methods of deduction flawed? Were mathematical definitions poorly framed? Some logicians sought to ban proofs by contradiction. They suggested, for example, that proving the falsity of a statement's negation did not imply the truth of the original statement. Maybe the original statement is neither true nor false.

Perhaps the following two paradoxes will convey the depth of the dilemmas.

Paradox 1.   This sentence is false.

(a) If the sentence is true, then by its own assertion it must be false.
(b) If the sentence is false, then the statement it makes is correct and the sentence is true.

Paradox 2.   Define a set containing each and every set that fails to contain itself.

Suppose such a set exists.

(a) If it contains itself, then it shouldn't, since the proposed set contains only those sets that fail to contain themselves.
(b) If it fails to contain itself, then it should, since it is required by definition to contain every set that fails to contain itself.

Do the inherent contradictions derive from a failure of logic or perhaps from imperfect definitions? Maybe the dichotomies between truth and falsity or the existence versus the nonexistence of a particular kind of set are artificial and not the only possibilities. Maybe human thought is limited and more impaired than we imagined after all!

On the one hand, mathematics is miraculously applicable. On the other hand, virulent flaws afflict the foundational methods of the discipline. Profound applicability and pernicious fallibility should not so easily coexist. If a hydra exists within mathematics, then simultaneous applicability and foundational fallibility may form two of its heads. In view of these foundational troubles that bring turbulence to mathematical waters, one might again inquire after the special power possessed by those who succeed within such a discipline.

Is mathematics the most creative of the arts?

The practice of the successful mathematician's craft seems to be more that of an artist than that of a technician. To be sure, such people tend to be extremely proficient mathematically, and that at very deep levels. But their creativity, their informed mathematical sense, and their application of mathematical tools and insights is marked more by the traits of an artist than those of a robotic human calculator. They thrive in a maze of problems, and the results they produce reflect the extraordinary elegance, clarity, and power of a sculpted artifact.

The derivation, the conclusion, and the eventual application all speak to the intrinsic beauty of the mathematician's work. Herein is art indeed! The mathematician's medium for expression can be found at the confluence of foundational issues, theoretical axiomatic/deductive systems, and applications begging for solution. Opportunities for exploration and research, investigation and experimentation spill from the historical stream, and the river of problems seems to be ever expanding, never running dry. The endless possibilities for creative mathematical activity only await the talented creativity of clever analytical minds devoted to the mathematician's art.

If unsolved problems provide the lifeblood of mathematics, then any forecast of the impending death of the discipline is premature. Problems internal to mathematics arise in number theory, graph theory, knot theory, and probability theory. They emerge from the need for effective models for summarizing scientific and social phenomena or for predicting possible behaviors. Hard questions flow from the interfaces of mathematics with modern computing. Challenging problems pervade every branch of mathematical theory and every imaginable application. More than ever, the discipline is dynamic and charged with potential.

Which came first, mathematics or the Maker?

That mathematicians find their discipline to be one that evokes a sense of awe and inspiration should carry little surprise. The art of mathematics, its linguistic power for precise thought, its uncommon applicability, and its culturally transcendent universality all seem to elevate the discipline to a celestial status. Had the abstract objects of mathematics already been created by God and then subsequently discovered by humankind, a provision of Him for us that follows from His common grace? Or perhaps the artful abstractions of mathematics are freely created by humans who, in their making, are allowed by the Maker to especially reflect His own image and creative propensity. Even more problematic is the possibility that mathematical objects have an independent and necessary existence quite apart from the mind of God and apart from those of His creatures. The notion of ten is, after all, the notion of ten, an idea that has a kind of a priori necessity that means the same amount irrespective of its pronunciation in another language or its representation in a different numeration system.

> Abstract objects raise a dilemma for the Christian. It is fundamental to Christianity that God is the creator of everything (other than God, of course). Intuitively, however, abstract

THREE UNSOLVED PROBLEMS

Does every obtuse triangle admit a periodic orbit for the path of a billiard ball?*
Does there exist a rectangular box all of whose edges and diagonals are integers?†
Are there an infinite number of twin primes (pairs of prime numbers that differ by 2)?‡

*Hallard T. Croft, Kenneth J. Falconer, and Richard K. Guy, *Unsolved Problems in Geometry* (New York: Springer Verlag, 1991), 16.

†Stanley C. Ogilvy, *Tomorrow's Math: Unsolved Problems for the Amateur* (New York: Oxford Univ. Press, 1972), 120.

‡Waclaw Sierpinski, *A Selection of Problems in the Theory of Numbers* (New York: Pergamon, 1994), 30–31.

objects—many of them, anyway—seem to be, like God, eternal. For instance, it is hard to imagine what it could mean for concepts like one, two, and three not to exist. That is, it seems impossible to conceive of a point at which God brought them into being, and hence it is difficult to think of them as created.[4]

On the one hand, to assert that God did not create "ten" demotes Him from His position as maker of everything. On the other hand, to argue that God made "ten," affirms that He made it without free choice, because the value of ten is absolute, necessary, and immutable. Such an assertion denies the freedom of God to do whatever He chooses.

Who is the author of mathematics? What truth value does it have? How can one explain its miraculous applicability? Does the linguistic nature of mathematics suggest that it is a concomitant of human thought? How can logical contradictions be banished? To some, so many questions would be disheartening, but not to genuine mathematical thinkers! Thank God, the doors of the discipline are still wide open, and it invites our participation at all levels.

"For we know in part, . . . we see but a poor reflection" (1 Cor. 13:9, 12).

QUESTIONS

1. Who authors mathematics? Do theorems originate with the mathematicians who prove them, or do original mathematics and authorship really belong to God who created and designed the human writer in the first place? If God is the author of mathematics, then is He also the author of this article about mathematics?

2. If "all truth is God's truth," is there any sense in which mathematical truth is absolute and certain?

3. Euclidean geometry and Riemannian geometry, though contradictory to each other, have both achieved significant and wide application. Can both of these geometries be simultaneously true, or if only one is true, which one is the true geometry?

NOTES

1. M. J. Feigenbaum, "Universal Behavior in Nonlinear Systems," *Physica D* 7, nos. 1–3 (1983): 16–39.
2. R. Osserman, "Mathematics with a Moral," *The Chronicle Review* 40, no. 33 (April 23, 2004).
3. Carl Boyer and Uta Merzbach, *A History of Mathematics* (New York: John Wiley & Sons, 1989), 685.
4. Russell W. Howell and W. James Bradley, *Mathematics in a Postmodern Age* (Grand Rapids: Eerdmans, 2001), 69.

SUGGESTED READING

Gleick, James. *Chaos: Making a New Science*. New York: Viking, 1987.

Howell, Russell W., and W. James Bradley, eds. *Mathematics in a Postmodern Age: A Christian Perspective*. Grand Rapids: Eerdmans, 2001.

Kline, Morris. *Mathematics in Western Culture*. New York: Oxford University Press, 1980.

How Is God's Creativity Manifested in Computer Science?

Thomas VanDrunen

One evening at Cambridge's Analytical Society, a cranky scientist named Charles Babbage sat at a desk with his head sprawled over a table of logarithms, frustrated by the rampant inaccuracy of such tables and the tedium of checking the calculations by hand.

"What are you dreaming about, Babbage?" asked a fellow society member.

"These tables," whined Babbage. "Could not the calculations just be executed by steam?"[5]

This frustration gave Babbage the impetus to spend his life designing and building a machine that would do calculations automatically with gears and cranks. Not only would this be immune from human inaccuracy (if the machine was designed right, of course), but also it would free humans from painstaking and dull work.

The automation of repetitive tasks is an important strain in the development of human civilization. Why not also automate mathematics? And if mathematics, why not the plethora of uses to which computers are put today, or are expected to be put tomorrow? The computer, then, begun as machine to execute calculations, has become our chief tool for all kinds of automation.

Can a machine perform logic?

Logic is part of everyday language with the construction of relationships among facts or conditions with logical indicators like *and*, *or*, *not*, and *if*. "If the book is damaged or if the due date is past and the book has not been renewed, a fine is charged." To answer the question, "Will a fine be charged on this book?" one must supply the answers to the contingent questions—"Is it damaged?" "Is the due date past?" "Has it been renewed?"—and evaluate the statement by applying rules of logic. Could a machine be built to do logic?

Let us try to build such a machine out of water pipes and gates that respond to water pressure. A pipe will stand for a statement, and water will flow in the pipe if its statement is true; no flow will stand for false. Assume three types of gates are available to us:

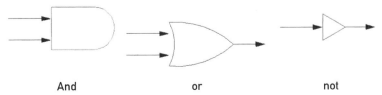

And   or   not

The **and** gate works like a door, and only the combined water pressure from both incoming pipes is strong enough to open it. Therefore, if both pipes are flowing, the door opens, and water comes out of the gate; if neither or only one pipe is flowing, nothing comes out. In this way, it models the logical use of the conjunction *and*, since the truth of a statement using *and* depends on both of its underlying statements being true. The **or** gate, however, has no door—the water flows out if water is flowing in either or both incoming pipes, just as a statement tying two other statements with the conjunction *or* is true even if only one of its underlying statements is true. The **not** gate is trickier. Imagine it like a faucet that is usually producing water but also has a switch to turn it off; water pressure from the incoming pipe will activate the switch and stop the flow.

Now these gates and pipes can comprise a machine to determine if a book will carry a fine, given that source faucets are turned on depending on whether the book was damaged, past due, or renewed. Water will flow out of the machine if there will be a fine.

Can a pipe and gate machine do math?

Consider arithmetic on binary numbers, where instead of marking digits 0 through 9 in columns representing powers of 10, we use only the digits 0 and 1 in columns representing powers of two (1 means 1×2^0 or 1; 10 means 1×2^1 or 2; 100 means 1×2^2 or 4; etc.). Single-digit binary numbers use this addition table:

+	0	1
0	0	1
1	1	10

If pipes having a flow or not can stand for *true* or *false*, why not let them represent 1 and 0, and arrange the pipes and gates to work like the addition table? One problem is that 1 + 1 = 10; how can the pipes represent 10? To handle this, let each pipe represent one digit, and have two pipes coming out of the machine. These two output pipes could represent up to four different answers (although only three are possible for adding two digits): 00, 01, 10, and 11; in decimal, the numbers 0 through 3.

The extra pipe is called *carry* because it would be the digit carried to the next column in the addition of multidigit binary numbers. Attach many of these together, and you have a pipe machine that computes binary arithmetic. Do this with electronic circuitry instead of water pipes, and you have the foundation of a computer.

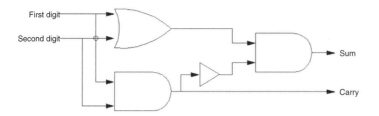

Can a machine remember information?

A computer is a machine that can receive input, store information based on its input, and produce output revealing something of its stored information. Our water-pipe machine modeled input and output with the pipes flowing into the machine and those flowing out, respectively. It did not easily demonstrate how a machine has any sort of memory. Parking meters accept input—in this case, coins—and display an output, the time allotted for parking, based on the input. In this case, the machine's memory is the position of the needle. Assume this meter accounts for time in fifteen-minute blocks (another form of "input")—every five cents adds a block of time, and every fifteen minutes the needle goes back one block.

This simple rule does not fully describe the meter, because the meter can record only a fixed set of times, say, from zero up to two hours. Any money added after two hours has been bought is wasted, and the needle will not regress into negative time after reaching zero. This is because the meter's counting capacity is finite. There are exactly nine states this meter can be in, standing for 0, 15, 30, 45, 60, 75, 90, 105, and 120 minutes. Machines like this are called *finite state machines*. They have a set of states, a set of input tokens that they accept, and a set of rules stipulating how tokens effect transitions among states. The meter's behavior is captured by a graph where the nine states are locations in the graph (labeled by the number of minutes remaining in the meter) and arrows (labeled by the types of token—5 cents, 10 cents, 25 cents, or 15 minutes) show how the machine changes states. Note that sometimes a certain input will not induce a state change—like adding more money when the two-hour maximum has already been reached.

A finite state machine is a model of computation. It is severely limited in that it does not have infinite capacity, but as long as you know the maximum size of the problem ahead of time, there is nothing computable that you cannot compute with a finite state machine. There are more powerful models that each involve some structure to store an infinite amount of information, and these are often

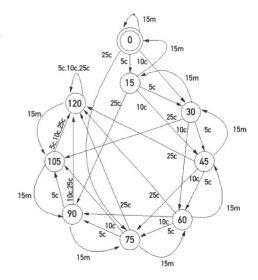

more useful for describing modern computers with their massive capacity. It is humbling, however, to realize that even the computer on your desk is at its core a finite state machine. The computer on which this chapter was written has about 1.3×10^9 bytes of storage if you add up the hard drive, memory, and a few other pieces that contribute to its state. With eight binary digits to a byte, that comes to 1.04×10^{10} memory positions that could be one or zero. Hence it has $2^{1.04 \times 10^{10}}$ states. While that seems a lot, it cannot compute and remember all the digits of π.

Note that under this model, a desk lamp is a legitimate computer: it has an input device (the switch), an output device (the bulb), and two states (on and off).

Can a machine remember instructions?

In 1805 a French factory worker named Joseph Jacquard designed an attachment to a textile loom that used a set of cards in which a weaver could encode a pattern for a rug or another textile. The cards had holes to specify where hooks could emerge to pull the parallel threads under the passing perpendicular thread. The loom worked by itself, simply taking instructions from cards like a player piano from its roll.[6]

The Jacquard loom not only revolutionized the textile industry, it also changed the course of computer science. The water-pipe machine, the binary adder, and the parking meter could perform only the computations that are built into them. To make the water-pipe machine evaluate a different logical statement, you must rearrange the pipes. If the similarities between these machines and real computers are still hard to believe, perhaps you are bothered by the absence of *software*. For your computer at home, you can purchase applications (or write them yourself) that seem to extend the capabilities of the machine. The cards in the loom demonstrate that the operations desired of the machine need not be impressed upon the machine's design, but instead can be communicated in the input and stored in the state. The computers you are used to must accept instructions and data in their input, and they must automate not only the execution of the instructions, but also their interpretation.

A computer programming language is also a model of computation, a way of expressing what a machine does. You already know plenty of specialized languages in addition to natural, human languages, like notation to express mathematical formulas. Specifying languages for telling a computer how to compute allows for great flowering of creativity, because for every model of computation, new forms of expression are defined that demonstrate that model.

What are the limitations of computer science?

A traveling salesman wants to know the shortest routes from his home base to various cities in his area. Some pairs of cities are not directly connected by a road but require stops at other cities, so there are several possible routes between them. How can one find the best route?

First, assume the "distance" from the home base to itself is zero, but the distances to all other cities is unknown, and our initial safe estimate is that the distance is infinite. Then look at all the cities to which the home city has a direct road. One can improve the estimate of the shortest distance to those cities by changing them to be the length of that direct road. From then on, consider each city, each time picking the remaining city with the smallest distance to process next, and treating it as the home city was treated: compute the distance of the route from the home city to all of the current one's adjacent cities by adding its own distance to the distance of the direct roads. If any of those distances is smaller than the estimate for those adjacent cities up to that point, then it is a shorter route than previously known. In the end, the routes left are those with the shortest distances from home to all of the cities. The length of time it takes to compute this is based on the number of cities to be considered. If there are n cities, then each city requires the inspection of up to $n - 1$ adjacent cities, so the time it takes to compute would grow with the number of cities at a rate no greater than n^2.

What are the limitations of computation?

Designing algorithms like the one above and evaluating their efficiency by comparing computation time with the size of the data is an important part of computer science. It not only weeds out good algorithms from the bad, it also helps identify impossible problems. Suppose the salesman wants to know the shortest tour of all the cities—a single route that hits every one. Enumerating every possible tour and picking the shortest would take time proportional to n factorial. Does that make a difference? Suppose the time in milliseconds to compute the first algorithm on a certain computer really could be computed exactly by n^2 and the second by n. If there are 30 cities, a computer finds the shortest paths in 900 milliseconds, less than a second. The second algorithm would take 2.65×10^{32} milliseconds, or 8.62×10^{18} millennia.

Can an algorithm be found for the second problem that brings it in range with the first? Researchers suspect not, but it has never been proven that no such algorithm could exist. Stubborn problems like this are what drive human curiosity, but they can also be humbling reminders of human limitations. Christians can bring a perspective to a field like computer science, remembering that it is God who allows for progress of human knowledge and He who also restricts it. Just as humans are limited, so are the machines they build. There are some mysteries that will never be fathomed; there are some problems that computers will never solve.

What are the limitations of benefit?

As computers have made their way into society, they have elicited both rank suspicion and utopian excitement. Some note that much early development in computers was pushed by militaries (to compute artillery trajectories or predict the behavior of atomic weapons), but consider how much the early spread of the gospel was helped by the Roman Empire's well-built roads, set in place to move their armies quickly. Those who trumpet the Internet's ability to bring the world together should wonder if this is not another attempt to rebuild the Tower of Babel. God's common grace allows human development; that same grace halts it when it advances evil. The computer is nothing more than a tool. It can be used for good or evil. It does not cancel out human incompetence, but multiplies it. It helps us not to make fewer mistakes, but to make them faster.

An American astronomer who visited China in the early 1980s was amazed to find a serious researcher processing astronomical data using only tables and abacuses. Determined to "show him the right way to analyze data," the American went to his portable computer and in two days produced a program that in one minute performed the computation his Chinese colleague had spent five months doing by hand. However, when they compared the results, they noticed slight differences—and the figures computed by hand were right.[7]

"He hadn't spent his summer doing rote mechanical calculations," Clifford Stoll recounts. "Instead, he'd developed a complex method for analyzing the data that took into account the accuracy of different observers. . . . His results, literally crafted by hand, showed his meticulous care. Moreover, they were right. . . . Having a computer, I had naturally cast the problem as simple data analysis. The calculations weren't the hard part. . . . The real challenge was understanding the data and finding a good way to use it."[8]

There are important questions to be asked about the effect computers have on society. The ease of access to information has spurred reflection of copyright laws and ethics. The online community provides anonymity that emboldens people to sin, for example, in obtaining pornography. A computerized society isolates those who lack access or skills. Some of these questions may be better addressed by those who study other fields, but computer scientists who understand the effects of their research will make a difference in their work and witness.

What does the existence of computers say about human creativity?

Is the designing of computing machinery an activity of a certain realm of logical thinking that has close parallels to other fields? John Montgomery has pointed out how many of the first to experiment with computing machinery were also intently involved with Christian apologetics.[9] Fredrick Brooks finds joy in the craft of programming because "the programmer, like the poet, works only slightly removed from pure thought-stuff. . . . Few media of creation are so flexible . . . so readily capable of realizing grand conceptual structures."[10] Nevertheless, computers raise questions about the uniqueness of human creativity. The suggestion that machines that could legitimately be called creative and intelligent can be built and programmed is disturbing, but since the early days of computer science, some people have been predicting just such machines.[11]

What about categorizing computer science? Does it really deserve the name *science*? Its experimental side is undeniably different from that of other branches: testing the speed of a new microprocessor is experimenting with something humans built, not something discovered in nature; experiments testing which user interfaces human subjects prefer seem more cognate with psychology. The study of algorithms has the feel of a branch of mathematics; the construction of machines sounds like it fits better among engineering disciplines. In many ways, computer science is a craft, but it is more than a craft. It is a stage for exploring mysteries of the universe that computing power can tame, from astronomy to genetics; it is a handmaiden to the sciences and other fields of learning; and it is a field ripe with questions that appeal to human curiosity.

One computer science graduate student took classes in ancient Greek as a diversion. A humanities major in the class asked him about his research. "Are there really any more things to discover about computers?" she asked. Computer science as a field is only 75 years old; the instructor in that class had gotten a Ph.D. in a field that had been studied for 2,500 years. If there is a field that will not run out of interesting questions any time soon, it is computer science.

QUESTIONS

1. Do computers provide more power to certain segments of society?

2. In what ways does the Internet bring people together, and in what ways does it isolate people?

3. Could a computer compose poetry or music?

4. What are ways people give instructions to various sorts of machines?

5. Should computer programming be used to develop games that inspire people to develop Christian moral character?

NOTES

5. A harmonization of two accounts given in Herman H. Goldstine, *The Computer from Pascal to von Neumann* (Princeton, N.J.: Princeton Univ. Press, 1972), 11.
6. Ibid., 20.
7. Clifford Stoll, *Silicon Snake Oil* (New York: Doubleday, 1995), 28.
8. Ibid., 29.
9. John Warwick Montgomery, "Computer Origins and the Defense of the Faith," *Perspectives on Science and Christian Faith* 56, no. 3 (2004): 189–203.
10. Frederick P. Brooks Jr., *The Mythical Man-Month* (Boston: Addison-Wesley, 1995), 7.
11. See, e.g., Alan Turing, "Computing Machinery and Intelligence," *Mind* 59 (1950): 433–60.

SUGGESTED READING

Brooks, Frederick P., Jr. *The Mythical Man-Month*. Boston: Addison-Wesley, 1995.
Harel, David. *Computers, Ltd*. Oxford: Oxford University Press, 2000.
Hofstadter, Douglas. *Gödel, Escher, Bach: An Eternal Golden Braid*. New York: Basic Books, 1999.

CRUCIAL QUESTIONS AT THE INTERFACE OF CHRISTIAN FAITH AND THE PHYSICAL SCIENCES

A. How Does Christianity Influence How to Think about Physics?

The exciting field of physics, the most fundamental science, has pushed the frontiers of understanding our universe to the depths of knowledge about the structure of atoms and elemental particles, to other interesting topics involving the laws and theories of how the cosmos works. The laws of thermodynamics—wherein one studies the relationship of heat and work or laws of gravity—stir one's imagination when studied carefully and applied to phenomena that may be earthbound or nonearthbound. Many phenomena studied in nuclear physics have far-reaching applications, and some of the technologies developed from this knowledge may be applied to improve human health. Classical physics and modern physics engage marvelous creativity and imagination. Students will be captivated by the exploration of the nature of curved space, dark matter and dark energy, or redshift. For Christians, many questions arise at the intersection of physics and their faith.

This section of the book will introduce you to some concepts of classical physics and modern physics and will address some of the ultimate questions that have intrigued scientists who are Christians.

What Are Matter and Energy at the Most Fundamental Level?

Loren Haarsma

God created humans with a strong sense of curiosity. What are stars made of? Why is the sky blue? What causes the wind, rainbows, and lightning? Physics has succeeded in answering these questions and others like them by investigating more fundamental questions: What is the basic material of the universe? How does this basic material combine to form all the different kinds of matter? What principles determine how objects move and interact? Physics pursues basic questions about matter, energy, and motion. The goal is to understand as many things about nature as possible in terms of a few fundamental, universal laws.

Nature is complex, but careful observation reveals patterns. Stars move on predictable paths. Tides rise and fall regularly. Thrown objects move on predictable trajectories. When scientists observe such predictable phenomena, they construct "models." Scientific models reduce complex situations into simpler forms that are easier to understand and predict. Models are kept simple when possible, expanded when necessary. For example, a baseball's trajectory can be approximately predicted assuming constant gravity and no air resistance. For more accurate predictions, physicists can add to the model air resistance, the shape of the baseball (that it is not perfectly spherical), air turbulence, and other tiny effects.

The words *model* and *theory* inspire humility. They are a reminder that scientific understanding is imperfect. However, scientists are constantly testing their models. Successful models gain credibility; unsuccessful models are modified or discarded. In this way, scientific understanding of nature gradually changes and improves.[1]

How do objects move?

Some of the earliest successes in physics came in understanding the motion of everyday objects. The most fundamental discoveries of Galileo Galilei and Sir Isaac Newton[2] can be summarized as follows.

1. An object with no force acting on it moves at a constant velocity in a straight line.
2. A force acting on an object causes it to accelerate proportional to the force and inversely proportional to the object's mass.[3]
3. When two objects interact, they exert forces on each other equal in magnitude and opposite in direction.
4. All free-falling objects near the earth's surface, regardless of mass, experience the same constant downward acceleration (neglecting air resistance).

These "laws" form the basis of classical mechanics. Physicists still use them to understand and predict motion in a wide variety of circumstances. The second and the fourth laws are now considered only approximations. They are reasonably accurate for everyday objects moving at everyday speeds; however, for tiny particles or for high speeds, they are replaced by quantum mechanics and relativity. The first and third laws have not been overturned by any subsequent discovery. They are still considered fundamental laws of nature.

Newton also discovered his law of universal gravitational attraction. This, combined with the first three laws listed above, explains not only the fourth law, but also the orbital motions of stars, moons, and planets. Before Newton, heavenly bodies and earthly objects were considered different realms—perhaps governed by entirely different laws. Newton showed that the same laws cover both realms.

Newton's discovery beautifully illustrates another theme in physics: unification. Physicists endeavor to explain phenomena that appear very different (in this case, falling apples and orbiting planets) with a single, fundamental set of laws that are universal in scope.

Physicists believe that all matter and motion in the universe obey certain "fundamental laws of nature." They are laws in the sense that there are no known exceptions. They are fundamental in that they seem to be at the foundation of all natural processes. From a Christian perspective, it appears that when God created the universe, part of that creative work involved designing and establishing the fundamental laws of nature.

What is energy?

Classical mechanics led to the discovery of three other laws: conservation of momentum, conservation of angular momentum, and conservation of energy. Momentum and angular momentum are determined simply by an object's mass, velocity, and motion around some axis. Energy is a more difficult concept because energy can take many forms. To mention just a few, kinetic energy is associated with motion, heat energy is associated with temperature, and chemical energy is associated with each type of substance.

Momentum can transfer from one object to another, but the total momentum remains constant when nothing external is acting on the objects. Energy can be transformed from one type to another, but the total remains unchanged. These *conservation laws* appear to be fundamental laws of nature, true about the tiniest particles and the largest galaxies and at every level in between.

Is the future determined by the laws of physics?

To the delight of some people and the dismay of others, the discoveries of physics are usually written in the language of mathematics. Much of the success of physics, especially its ability to make predictions, comes from quantifying concepts such as energy using mathematics. For example, the laws of motion and gravity expressed in mathematical equations allow scientists to launch a spacecraft from Earth on just the right trajectory so that several years later it meets Saturn, more than a billion kilometers away.

The laws of classical mechanics are "deterministic." If you precisely know an object's mass, position, velocity, and all the forces acting on it, you can mathematically predict precisely what it will do at every future moment. If all matter moves

ARE THE LAWS OF NATURE THE SAME EVERYWHERE?

Each type of atom and each type of molecule absorbs and emits electromagnetic waves at a unique set of frequencies—each has a sort of electromagnetic "fingerprint." Astronomers have discovered that light (and radio waves and X-rays) from distant galaxies contains the same absorption and emission frequencies as are made by atoms and molecules on earth. This tells scientists that even the most distant objects in the visible universe are made from the same particles, obeying the same fundamental laws of nature, as are here on earth. Since the light from distant galaxies has traveled for a very long time to reach us, this also tells scientists that the fundamental laws of nature have not changed for as far back in time as can be measured.

according to deterministic laws, then *is it the case that every future natural event is completely determined by the laws of nature?* In the decades following Newton's discoveries, it seemed to many people that this philosophy of determinism might be true. Pierre Laplace, another brilliant scientist and mathematician, wrote:

> Given for one instant an intelligence which could comprehend all the forces [laws of nature] by which nature is animated and the respective situation of the beings who compose it [the position and velocity of everything in the universe]—an intelligence sufficiently vast to submit these data to analysis, it would embrace in the same formula the movements of the greatest bodies of the universe and those of the lightest atom; for it, nothing would be uncertain, and the future—as the past—would be present before its eyes.[4]

Even though humans cannot do the necessary measurements and calculations in practice, the question remains whether or not it is possible in principle. Human limitations do not apply to God. If these calculations are possible in principle, then is the future absolutely determined already? Human bodies and brains are composed of matter. Whenever you move or think, nerve cells in your body fire electrical signals. Nerve cells presumably obey the laws of nature. If the motion of all matter is determined by the laws of nature, does this mean that all the future actions of your body and your brain are determined? Does this suggest that free will is an illusion?

Does God govern, or do natural laws govern?

The philosophy of Deism proposes that God created the universe, its initial conditions, and its laws of nature and now simply lets it run on its own without interacting with it. Deism is unacceptable to Christians, but some Christians since the time of Newton have adopted an "occasional interventionist" model. In this model, God usually allows the universe to run on its own according to the laws of nature but occasionally intervenes by superseding those laws.

While the occasional interventionist picture might be philosophically attractive, Scripture paints a different picture. Scripture implies that the universe continues to exist and behave in an orderly fashion only because of God's continual sustaining action. Consider Psalm 104:19–21:

> The moon marks off the seasons,
>   And the sun knows when to go down.
> You bring darkness, it becomes night,
>   And all the beasts of the forest prowl.
> The lions roar for their prey
>   And seek their food from God.

Note the parallel levels of description in the passage. The sun goes down (natural event); God brings night (divine action). Lions hunt prey (natural event); they seek their food from God (divine providence). If something happens "naturally," God is still in charge. The Psalms are filled with praise to God for times in Israel's history when God performed miracles. The psalmist also insists that God is equally in charge of natural events.[5]

From a biblical perspective, it is incorrect to say that natural laws "govern." God created natural laws and typically governs creation through those laws.[6] God can supersede their ordinary functioning, but most of the time God chooses to work in consistent ways through those laws. The regularity of God's governance allows humans to do science.

Of what is matter made?

Around the beginning of the twentieth century, scientists discovered that matter was composed of *atoms*. Atoms are too small to see with ordinary microscopes. There are about a hundred chemically different types of atoms, and they combine in different arrangements to make millions of types of molecules.[7] Molecules combine to form all varieties of gases, liquids, and solids. Atoms and molecules exert attractive and repulsive forces on their neighbors. They are constantly in motion, colliding with and bouncing off each other.[8] In chemical reactions, atoms rearrange themselves to form different molecules.

The atomic model of matter connects physics to chemistry and helps explain many phenomena. Solids stretch and compress because spacing between the atoms increases and decreases. Solids fracture when attractive forces between neighboring atoms are overcome. Honey is viscous because of strong attractive forces between the molecules. Air pressure is caused by atoms continually bouncing off each other. Submerged objects feel a buoyant force because of unequal pressure on their top and bottom sides. Sound consists of traveling waves of higher and lower pressure. Temperature is a measure of how fast the atoms are randomly moving about. This is just a small sample of what can be explained and mathematically modeled with an atomic model of matter.

What is entropy, and is it a bad thing?

Imagine watching a movie of sixteen billiard balls moving and colliding randomly. Assuming no friction to slow the balls, you wouldn't be able to tell if the movie was running forward or backward. But if the movie ever showed the fifteen numbered balls meeting in a triangular shape at rest at one spot on the table, with the cue ball moving rapidly away, you would strongly suspect the movie was running backward. When objects interact, things tend to move from orderly to disorderly states, not the reverse.

Kinetic energy of a large object is orderly—all the atoms of the object have the same time-averaged velocity. Heat energy is disorderly; it consists of random atomic motion within the object. Orderly energy often converts spontaneously into disorderly heat energy (e.g., through friction) but not the reverse. *Entropy* is a mathematical measure of the disorder of matter and energy.[9] Orderly energy can be used to decrease entropy in limited places—for example, you can use food energy to neatly arrange billiard balls—but this process still increases the total entropy of the universe as a whole.

The second law of thermodynamics says that the entropy of the universe is always increasing. How can creation be good if disorder is always increasing? The everyday meaning of disorder is not the same thing as the scientific concept of entropy. Entropy is an inevitable result of large numbers of particles interacting with each other. When a flower's scent diffuses outward so that the surrounding area is perfumed and bees find the blossom, entropy increases. When ice melts, when winds blow and rains fall, entropy increases. Living organisms eat food with chemical energy, thereby decreasing entropy inside themselves while increasing the entropy of the surrounding environment. The second law of thermodynamics is an integral part of all the wonderful natural processes in this creation.

How do atoms interact, and what is light?

In the eighteenth and nineteenth centuries, scientists developed a mathematical understanding of electric and magnetic forces.[10] In the nineteenth and early twentieth centuries, scientists discovered that all atoms are made of arrangements of three kinds of particles: protons, neutrons, and electrons.[11] Protons and electrons have electric charges. Electric charges create electric fields. Moving electric charges create magnetic fields. Electric and magnetic fields, in turn, exert forces on charged particles. These electromagnetic forces are what hold atoms and molecules together and determine how they interact with each other.

Understanding electromagnetism also allows scientists to create many technologies. Some materials are electric conductors. They allow some electrons to move from atom to neighboring atom with very little resistance. Changing magnetic fields (e.g., from rotating magnets) can create electric currents in wires. Electric currents can exert forces on magnets (e.g., in electric motors). By combining these technologies, engineers

WHAT IS THE "HEAT DEATH" OF THE UNIVERSE?

The universe started in a low-entropy state. The universe might eventually collapse due to gravity or spread thin due to "dark energy." Even if neither of those events occurs, eventually all the energy in the universe will be converted into disorderly forms. Stars have enough nuclear fuel to burn for billions of years, but if the laws of nature keep operating the way they currently do, eventually all stars will burn out and no more will form. Hot parts of the universe will cool until everything is at the same temperature. No more meaningful change will be able to happen. Life will become impossible. Some call this the "heat death" of the universe.

Is the predicted heat death of the universe a theological problem? If this universe is all there is, it would seem to be a problem. But Scripture teaches that this creation in its present form is not meant to be eternal. The second law of thermodynamics shows that this universe is finite in time—just like all of God's creatures. But God has promised a new creation beyond this life and this universe.

can take kinetic energy from falling water or rising steam in a power plant, use it to rotate magnets near some wires, and thus convert it into electrical energy, transmit that over wires, and transform it back into mechanical energy doing useful work hundreds of miles away. All devices that are plugged in or that run on batteries are made possible by the ability to mathematically model electromagnetic forces. New electromagnetic technologies are still being invented. The possibilities for these technologies are built into the laws of nature. God gave humans the ability to understand and to invent, thus enabling better stewardship of creation.

James Maxwell discovered that light is electromagnetic waves.[12] Light is part of a spectrum that includes radio waves, microwaves, and X-rays. Studying how electromagnetic waves interact with matter has led to many more technologies, including eyeglasses, microscopes, telescopes, cameras, radio broadcasters and receivers, microwave ovens, lasers, radar, X-ray cameras, and magnetic resonance imagers.

How fast can objects move?

If light obeyed classical mechanics, its speed should depend on the speed of the object emitting the light.[13] But Maxwell's discoveries imply that all light should move through space at the same speed regardless of the light source's velocity. Albert Einstein confronted this contradiction and developed the special theory of relativity. He hypothesized that Maxwell was correct about light and that the laws of nature are the same in every inertial frame of reference.[14] This has some surprising consequences: mass itself is a form of potential energy. Objects cannot move faster than the speed of light. In an inertial reference frame that is moving relative to you, clocks will seem to run slower, distances will seem to be shorter, and masses of objects will seem greater. But an observer in that reference frame will consider himself or herself to be stationary and your frame to be the moving one.

Einstein extended this work to include accelerating frames of reference and gravitational fields. In his general theory of relativity, gravity can be pictured as warping the geometry of space and time. Astronomers use general relativity to calculate the long-term, large-scale behavior of the entire universe and to understand extremely massive objects like black holes.

While some predictions of special and general relativity are surprising, they are supported by many experiments. In the "everyday" situations of ordinary gravitational fields and ordinary velocities, relativity makes nearly identical mathematical predictions as the older classical mechanics. Einstein's discoveries thus incorporate, rather than overthrow, Newton's earlier discoveries.

What are particles?

Classical mechanics, electromagnetism, and relativity all model particles as points—like spheres shrunk infinitely small—with precisely definable positions and velocities at every moment in time. However, if these theories were correct and complete, all atoms should convert their potential energy into radiation, and physically collapse, in a fraction of a second! In the early twentieth century, physicists confronted this, and other problems with earlier theories, and developed a new theory.[15]

"Quantum mechanics" models electrons, protons, and neutrons with equations similar to equations used to describe waves. Just as waves are spread out in space, quantum mechanics models an electron in an atom, for example, as being spread over the whole volume of the atom. If one measures the electron's position, one can get a precise answer as if the electron were pointlike; however, so long as one doesn't measure its precise position, the electron behaves like a wave spread over the entire atom. This mixed behavior is called "wave-particle duality."

Another surprise is that a particle in a precisely defined "quantum state" does not have a precisely defined position and velocity. Measuring one property of a particle can change its quantum state so that its other properties become less precisely defined.[16] In classical mechanics, when a particle moves from one location to another, it moves along a single well-defined path. One interpretation of quantum mechanics is that, when a particle moves from one location to another, it travels like a spreading wave moving along *all possible* paths simultaneously.

Quantum mechanics is counterintuitive in many ways, only some of which have been described here, but has been supported by thousands of experiments. It correctly predicts that atoms are stable and that atoms absorb and emit light only at certain frequencies. It also correctly predicts many other properties of matter not predicted by earlier theories. While quantum mechanics differs radically from classical mechanics in the realm of tiny particles, it makes the same predictions as classical mechanics regarding the behavior of everyday objects composed of many atoms. Thus it also incorporates earlier theories.

Does God "play dice" with the universe?

Unlike classical mechanics, quantum mechanics is not entirely deterministic. There is an element of randomness in the behavior of every particle. Quantum mechanics can precisely predict *on average* when a million radioactive atoms will decay. However, the exact time when any one *particular* radioactive atom will decay is unpredictable. Some people find this indeterminism in quantum mechanics to be not simply unexpected, but unacceptable. Einstein—expressing his opinion that the fundamental laws of nature ought to be deterministic—once said, "God does not play dice with the universe."[17] Some physicists are trying to revise or reinterpret quantum mechanics in ways that render it as deterministic as classical mechanics. But most physicists interpret quantum mechanics as implying that some events in nature really are fundamentally unpredictable.[18]

When people say that some event happened "by chance," they may mean that it had no cause and no purpose. This, however, is a philosophical and theological judgment, not a scientific one. In science the term *chance* is a statement about predictability. When the concept of chance is used strictly scientifically, it means simply this: scientists could not completely predict the final state of a system based on their knowledge of earlier states. In quantum mechanics, some unpredictability is built into the mathematical formalism of the theory. While classical mechanics is deterministic, if a system is sufficiently complex—sometimes called a "chaotic" system—the final state can still be unpredictable in practice. Some common examples of chaotic systems include throwing dice and predicting the weather. Biologists and doctors also use the word *chance* this way when talking about genetic mutations or the probability that a disease will recur.

What does the Bible say about apparently random events?

Proverbs 16:33 says, "The lot is cast into the lap, but its every decision is from the LORD." Biblical writers proclaimed God as sovereign over random events such as casting lots and over events that are now described scientifically using probabilities (e.g., the weather). Some Christian writers have suggested that indeterminism, built into the laws of nature, allows God to interact with creation without superseding natural laws by sometimes selecting the outcomes of scientifically unpredictable events to achieve particular outcomes. An analogy might be helpful: A scientist has designed a computer simulation of leaves falling off a tree. For most leaves, the timing and trajectory of the fall are selected randomly by the computer. However, this scientist can control her program to cause any one particular leaf to fall at a particular time and a particular place. Observers cannot tell which leaves, if any, are specifically controlled by the scientist and which are not.[19]

Other Christians have suggested that God might have created indeterminism in the laws of nature to give the created world a bit of freedom to explore a range of possibilities.[20] For an analogy, consider how some computer programmers use "genetic algorithms." Some mathematical functions, when creatively displayed, make beautiful pictures. An artist could permit a computer program randomly to change one variable, then another, allowing the computer to explore a range of possibilities. Thus a process combining both deterministic and random elements could generate a whole series of beautiful pictures.

Are protons, neutrons, and electrons really fundamental particles?

In the twentieth century, physicists looked deeper into atoms and found more surprises. Protons and neutrons bunch together in the tiny nucleus at the center of each atom. Protons electrically repel each other, so there must be another, stronger attractive force holding the nucleus together. Physicists call it the strong nuclear force. Experiments show that, while electrons seem to be fundamental particles, protons and neutrons are not. Each proton and each neutron is composed of three particles called "quarks."[21] The strong nuclear force holds each quark triplet together to form protons and neutrons, and it holds protons and neutrons together in the nucleus.

When a large nucleus splits apart, nuclear fission occurs. When small nuclei merge, nuclear fusion occurs. The strong nuclear force is stronger than electromagnetism, so the amount of energy converted in nuclear fission and fusion events is far greater than in chemical reactions. Stars, including our sun, are powered by nuclear fusion. Scientists have successfully built power plants that run on nuclear fission, and they are trying to invent power plants that run on nuclear fusion—potentially environmentally cleaner than nuclear fission. On the destructive side, scientists have invented bombs that use both fission and fusion.

Radioactivity refers to several different processes whereby a nucleus emits a particle.[22] Physicists have discovered that some forms of radioactivity are governed by yet another fundamental force: the weak nuclear force. This force is involved whenever one type of particle changes into other types. While studying this force, scientists discovered another fundamental particle—the neutrino. Neutrinos have no electric charge and rarely interact with other particles.

How many fundamental forces and particles are there?

In the late 1920s, Paul Dirac discovered a way to unify special relativity and quantum mechanics. His theory predicted the existence of something that had not yet been seen but was discovered several years later: antimatter. Antimatter is a picturesque name given to particles that have the same mass and the opposite electric charge as ordinary matter particles. When a particle of matter meets its antimatter counterpart, the particles disappear and 100 percent of their mass is converted into other forms of energy. Physicists have discovered many more matter particles. The

THE ATOMIC BOMB

The atomic bomb resulted from a massive research effort during World War II. It was based on discoveries during the previous fifty years and was motivated by concern that Germany might develop an atomic weapon first. Work on the atomic bomb was the largest research and development effort up to that time and became the model for large postwar projects such as the space program. The $2 billion wartime effort was coordinated by the U.S. Army under the Manhattan Project and involved a large group of American, British, and European-refugee scientists at several universities and in secret locations.

Germany was defeated before a successful detonation occurred, but the use of the atomic bomb did hasten the surrender of Japan without requiring an invasion. Approximately 100,000 people died at Hiroshima and about 50,000 more died at Nagasaki, plus several thousand more from cancer and other problems caused by radioactive fallout. As tragic as this was, War Department estimates predicted that an invasion of the Japanese mainland could have caused up to a half million American casualties, plus as many as 2 million Japanese casualties.

The morality of stockpiling and using nuclear weapons has been debated for several decades. Unfortunately, development of the atomic bomb contributed to the postwar arms race and all the unforeseen problems associated with nuclear waste products. It also led to the development of nuclear-power reactors, nuclear medicine, and other peacetime technologies.

—Joseph Spradley

electron, the neutrino, and the up and down quarks appear stable, but each one of these has two heavier, unstable counterparts.[23] Many physicists expect that there are still other particles that have not yet been discovered, either because they are too difficult to produce or because they barely interact with ordinary matter.

Physicists speak of four distinct fundamental forces of nature: gravity, electromagnetism, and the strong and weak nuclear forces. In the latter half of the twentieth century, physicists combined Dirac's theory with electromagnetism and both nuclear forces into a unified mathematical formalism called *quantum field theory*. However, the best model for gravity—general relativity—has not yet been unified mathematically with quantum field theory.

What is the scientific consensus on the "fundamental questions"?

The best models of modern physics can be summarized as follows.

What is the basic material of the universe? Just three particles—the electron, the up quark, and the down quark—combine to make nearly all ordinary matter. Other particles exist, but aren't components of ordinary materials on the earth.

How does this basic material combine to form all the different kinds of matter? Quarks combine to form protons and neutrons. These combine with electrons to form atoms. Atoms combine to form molecules, which in turn combine to form all ordinary matter.

What determines how objects move and interact? Particles exert four kinds of forces on each other. General relativity describes gravity. Quantum field theory describes electromagnetism and both nuclear forces and describes how all particles respond to those forces. (For everyday situations, these theories simplify to classical mechanics.)

Physicists endeavor to understand everything else in nature—such as the properties of atoms and molecules; the behavior of solids, liquids, and gases; the characteristics of thunder and lightning, heat, energy, vibrations, light, electricity, magnetism, ocean currents, wind and climate, sunlight and starlight, blue sky, and white clouds; and the motion of planets, stars, and galaxies—as particular outworkings of those few fundamental, universal laws.

How can physicists agree about the universe but disagree about God?

How is it possible that scientists can hold very different philosophical and religious worldviews from each other yet reach consensus on scientific questions? What are the fundamental philosophical beliefs that underlie the practice of science? Historians and philosophers have written entire books to answer these questions, but these four points very briefly summarize some of the basic philosophical beliefs.[24] (1) It is possible for humans to understand nature, at least in part. (2) Nature operates with regular, repeatable, universal patterns. (3) Scientists should test their theories with observations and experiments. (4) A systematic study of nature is a worthwhile activity.

Those are philosophical beliefs that come from outside of science. They may seem obviously true today, but they were not widely believed throughout most of human history. Many ancient cultures held some of them but not others. Several historians of science have argued that the founders of the scientific revolution held this combination of philosophical beliefs, at least in part, because they held biblical views about God and nature.[25] For example, the four beliefs listed above can be supported by Christian theological beliefs: (1) Humans are made in God's image. (2) Nature is not filled with capricious gods or nature spirits, but is ruled by one God in a faithful and consistent manner. (3) God was free to create as He wished; humans are limited and fallen, so their theories about creation can be incorrect and should be tested. (4) God commissions humans to study and have stewardship over creation.

Christian theology can motivate the philosophical beliefs that underlie the scientific method. When Christians employ the scientific method, they are not acting "as if God doesn't exist." They are acting like nature is governed by the God of the Bible, who made an orderly world and governs it in an orderly fashion.

This doesn't mean that Christians are the only ones who can do science. The philosophical beliefs that underlie science (such as the four listed above) are compatible with many, though not all, worldviews. Simply by agreeing that those underlying philosophical beliefs are true, scientists of different worldviews can work together and reach consensus on scientific questions, even if they disagree on philosophical and religious levels about why those underlying beliefs are true.

Has physics found the most fundamental theory?

Just as classical mechanics is an approximation for the deeper theories of general relativity and quantum field theory, physicists have several reasons for believing that these two theories are themselves only approximations for a more fundamental theory that they have not yet figured out. First, these two theories make contradictory predictions about the behavior of tiny particles in intense gravitational fields.[26] Second, these two theories don't explain why there are so many different kinds of particles, or why those particles have the masses that they do, or why the four "fundamental" forces have the strengths that they do. Third, astronomers have discovered evidence that the universe contains a lot of matter and energy that do not fit our current theories. They are called "dark matter" and "dark energy" because they do not interact with light. They were detected only because of their influence on the large-scale motions of stars and galaxies.

Physicists hope to construct a single fundamental "theory of everything" that will, in a few elegant mathematical equations, explain these mysteries and unify all the known particles and forces.[27] Many physicists think that a final unified theory of everything is both possible and nearly achieved. However, physicists have also learned from the history of science that nature is always turning up new surprises.

Why does our universe have the particular laws of nature that it does? Could there be other universes operating according to different laws? These are ongoing questions at the forefront of research. One intriguing recent discovery is the so-called anthropic principle—the laws of nature in our universe appear to be finely tuned for life to exist.[28]

If physics discovers those fundamental laws, does that explain everything?

Discovering fundamental laws of nature is only one task of physics. A far greater task is applying that knowledge to understanding the universe's vast array of natural processes and to developing new technologies.

Physics builds understanding from the "bottom up." It starts by understanding single particles or simple systems and adds layers of complexity as necessary. *Causation* also is modeled from the bottom up. The behavior of complex systems is modeled as being reducible to the sum of behaviors of its constituent particles. Is the behavior of even human bodies and brains reducible to the sum of behaviors of their constituent particles? If so, then it is difficult to understand how our brains could give rise to such "higher order" experiences as consciousness and free will.

One possible clue is that in many complex systems, there are higher-order organizing principles that at least appear to exert some "top-down" causation on their constituent particles. For example, the molecules of the earth's atmosphere organize into global convection patterns. At a more complex level, living cells control the movement of molecules through their membranes as they eat and excrete, react to the external environment, and sometimes repair themselves or reproduce themselves. At an even more complex level, animals and humans evaluate information and make decisions about how to move their bodies.

Top-down causation principles are not thought to be overriding bottom-up causation principles, but augmenting them. Complex systems are not completely predictable, and quantum mechanics is indeterministic. Perhaps bottom-up causation principles, such as conservation of energy, only constrain complex systems to a certain *range* of behaviors; top-down causation principles might "select" which particular outcome within that allowed range actually occurs.

Can complex systems ultimately be reduced to bottom-up causation, or are there some top-down organizing principles that cannot simply be reduced to the laws of physics acting on constituent particles? What is the ultimate connection between the fundamental laws of nature and the human experience of consciousness and free will? These are some of the greatest outstanding research questions. Scientists and philosophers, Christian and non-Christian alike, continue to study them.[29]

Can knowledge of the laws of nature allow scientists to determine the history of the universe?

Although scientists do controlled experiments whenever possible, a great deal of science is "observational science." Astronomy, meteorology, ecology, and other sciences use clever measuring devices, careful observations, and calculations to understand things that are too far away, too big, or too complex to control experimentally. Experimental sciences provide discoveries that help observational sciences construct better models. Observational sciences frequently make discoveries that are later supported by experiments.

"Historical sciences" are extensions of observational sciences, because any study of the present behavior of a system depends on inferences about its history. Cosmology, geology, paleontology, and evolutionary biology attempt to reconstruct the history of the universe in general and the earth in particular. Information from historical sciences provides direct evidence that the fundamental laws of nature have not changed for as far back in time as can be observed. This allows scientists to build models of the history of the universe, then test those models with careful observations of the evidence left behind from past events. Advances in experimental and observational sciences allow historical sciences to make increasingly detailed and predictive models. Historical sciences often develop hypotheses and make predictions that are later supported by observation and experiment. By pursuing all of these areas at once, scientific knowledge about the history of the universe keeps improving.

Where is God in science?

Science makes progress by asking questions about the natural world (What is lightning? How are stars formed?) and attempting to find explanations in terms of known natural laws (or sometimes in terms of newly hypothesized laws that are compatible with well-established laws). God's consistency in governing creation motivates this search. But what about miracles, which might appear like an interruption in ordinary natural processes? Should Christians search for, and expect to find, scientific evidence for miracles? Or, when they do science, should they always look for explanations exclusively in terms of natural laws? These questions have been around since the time of Newton.

Newton discovered that the motions of planets could be explained by a few simple equations. It's easy to solve Newton's equations when there are only two gravitationally attracting objects (e.g., the sun and one planet). They stay in stable orbits around each other. It's usually impossible to solve Newton's equations exactly when there are three or more objects (e.g., our solar system with several planets plus many moons and smaller objects). Each time one planet's motion brings it close to another, they perturb each others' orbits. Over time these perturbations can cause one or more orbits to become unstable. Are the planetary orbits in our solar system stable? Newton struggled with this question and did not come to a definite conclusion, but he made some mathematical approximations and concluded that some planetary orbits probably would become unstable after a few hundred years. This would seem to create a problem, because humans have observed consistent planetary orbits for thousands of years. One proposal to get around this problem is that God occasionally (every few decades or centuries) sends a comet through the solar system—a comet with just the right mass and just the right trajectory so that its gravitational attraction "corrects" the planetary orbits and keeps them stable for another few centuries.

A generation after Newton, Laplace found better approximate solutions to Newton's equations. Laplace showed that planetary orbits in our solar system really are stable for much longer periods of time—stable without the need for God to perform the occasional correction. What if Laplace's results had come out differently and Newton's hunch had been correct? What if God made the solar system in such a way that planetary orbits are unstable, requiring a careful correction every few centuries. Would Christians consider that a good thing or a bad thing? The traditional answer of Christian theology is that God could have created the solar system however He wished. Humans cannot tell God which way is better or worse. Yet most Christians would have to admit having a preference. On the one hand, planetary orbits that remain stable without intervention sound like a better design. On the other hand, the timely arrival of comets with *exactly* the right mass and trajectory to correct unstable orbits would provide a powerful scientific argument for God's existence and providential intervention.

The question of planetary orbits is settled. Laplace was correct. Orbits are stable over long periods of time. Other questions remain. How rare is planet Earth as a suitable home for life? How did life on Earth begin? Are there other universes besides our own? Are there scientific arguments for God's existence and intervention—evidence for miracles—within the answers to these questions? Each person approaches these questions with personal hopes and biases for how they will ultimately be answered. Christians don't even all agree on what those biases should be. Perhaps the best way to minimize the impact of these biases is, first, to be aware

WHAT IS THE "ANTHROPIC PRINCIPLE"?

If the masses of particles or the strengths of fundamental forces were a few percent different from what they are measured to be, life as we know it could not exist. It seems like the laws of nature are "fine-tuned" for us to exist. The "weak anthropic principle" avoids reading any purpose into this, asserting that it is simply the case that if the laws of nature weren't fine-tuned, then we wouldn't be around to see it. The "strong anthropic principle" asserts that this fine-tuning is so remarkable that there must be an explanation. One popular theory is that there are many different universes—produced all at once or continually being produced by a mechanistic process—each with a different set of fundamental laws. Our universe is just a rare one suitable for life. There may be scientific reasons for proposing multiple universes, but the hypothesized process generating those universes might also need to be fine-tuned. The fine-tuning of the laws of nature fits well with the Christian belief that this universe was designed and created for God's purposes. Some Christians also claim that this fine-tuning should be used as scientific evidence for the existence of a creator.[*]

[*]E.g., Hugh Ross, *The Creator and the Cosmos: How the Latest Scientific Discoveries of the Century Reveal God* (Colorado Springs: NavPress, 1993).

that everyone has them and, second, to remember that God is just as sovereign over natural laws and natural processes as He is sovereign over miraculous breaks in natural processes.

When scientists discover a new scientific explanation, God is not excluded. Instead, His governance is illuminated. When science fails to explain an event in terms of known natural laws, it might indicate that God miraculously superseded natural laws during that event—but not necessarily. It might also mean that God brought about that event by some unknown natural laws or processes that scientists might yet discover.[30] Every time scientists solve a new puzzle, they are not taking territory away from God's control. Rather, they are learning more about how God typically governs His creation. Every time Christians learn a new scientific truth about God's creation and the gifts He gave it, they should be prompted all the more to worship the Creator.

QUESTIONS

1. Which seems more compatible with a biblical picture of God's governance: a universe where the laws of nature are entirely deterministic, or one where the laws are a mixture of deterministic and indeterministic?

2. Does God's sovereignty over creation also allow creation to have some randomness and freedom to explore its potentiality?

3. What would be the implications if scientists discovered evidence for life on other planets in other solar systems?

4. What would be the implications if scientists discovered evidence for the existence of other universes operating according to different laws of nature?

5. Can the behavior of the human brain, with its experiences of consciousness and free will, ultimately be understood the way physicists try to understand everything—from the "bottom up" in terms of the behavior of its constituent particles—or is this reductionistic approach ultimately doomed to fail (or at best, only partially succeed) when tackling something so complex as the brain?

NOTES

1. Many introductory physics textbooks discuss the interplay between theories and experiments in building scientific models. One helpful description is chapter 1 of Edwin R. Jones and Richard L. Childers, *Contemporary College Physics*, 3rd ed. (New York: McGraw-Hill, 2001).

2. As is always the case in science, they built on the work of earlier scientists, and other scientists who came after them built on their work. Nevertheless, Galileo and Newton have earned the greatest share of credit for these discoveries. One reason they are

given so much credit is that some of these discoveries flatly contradict some earlier models of motion proposed by Aristotle and other ancient philosophers. The first three "laws" listed are commonly called "Newton's Laws of Motion." The fourth law listed was discovered by Galileo several decades before Newton.

3. Experience with automobiles provides a general understanding of acceleration. The technical definition of acceleration is the *rate of change of velocity*. For example, an object that accelerates uniformly from a velocity of 4 meters per second to a velocity of 10 meters per second in 2 seconds has an acceleration of 3 meters per second per second.

4. P. S. Laplace, *A Philosophical Essay on Probabilities*, trans. F. W. Truscott and F. L. Emory (New York: Dover, 1951).

5. With a modern scientific understanding of natural laws, neuroscientist Donald MacKay described the biblical picture this way: "The continuing existence of our world is not something to be taken for granted. Rather, it hangs moment by moment on the continuance of the upholding word of power of its creator" (Donald MacKay, *The Open Mind and Other Essays* [Leicester: Inter-Varsity Press, 1988], 23).

6. There are at least two different ways for understanding the ontological status of natural laws, both of which are within the tradition of Christian orthodoxy. One view: God prescriptively determines the activity of all material objects from moment to moment. Natural laws are formulas that merely describe the regularity with which God normally acts. Breaks in natural laws are instances in which God acts, for particular reasons, in ways that are different from the regular patterns of God's governance. A second view: God has gifted His creation and everything in it with certain creaturely capacities. These capacities are designed to interact with one another in regular fashions that we call natural laws. They do not operate independently of God but are dependent on God for their continued existence. God can interact with his creation through these creaturely capacities within the uncertainty and flexibility of the systems (e.g., such as in quantum or "chaotic" systems) or through acts of radical reorganization. Both of these views have proponents among scientists who are Christians, and both views agree that miracles can occur. The relative merits of and the differences between these views are interesting questions but will not be pursued any further in this chapter.

7. Consult a Periodic Table of Elements, found in any chemistry textbook, for a complete list of atoms and their properties. Since about 1990, it has become possible to see single atoms. Physicists can use electric and magnetic fields to trap a single atom in a metal and glass vacuum chamber and shine an intense laser on the atom, allowing one literally to see the atom via photons of light scattering from it.

8. Even in solids, atoms are constantly moving and bouncing around "in place"—analogous to students fidgeting at their desks but not leaving their assigned place. Strong mutually attractive forces keep the atoms from moving around each other. In liquids the attractive forces keep atoms close enough to touch one another, but the atoms are free to move around one another and change places; this allows liquids to flow. In gases, atoms are relatively far apart—with literally nothing (just empty space) between them—and interact mostly by bouncing off each other.

9. The mathematical formulas for quantifying entropy can be found in any textbook on thermodynamics.

10. Some of the most famous contributions were by Benjamin Franklin, Hans Oersted, Charles Coulomb, Karl Friedrich Gauss, André Ampère, Jean Baptiste Biot, Felix Savart, Michael Faraday, and James Clerk Maxwell, although other scientists also contributed.

11. Hydrogen atoms have one proton; one electron; and zero, one, or two neutrons. Helium atoms have two protons, two electrons, and one or two neutrons. For details on all the atoms, consult a Periodic Table of Elements.

12. A time-changing electric field creates a time-changing magnetic field, which in turn creates a time-changing electric field, etc. In this way, an oscillating electric charge creates oscillating electric and magnetic fields that self-propagate outward like a wave, analogous to ripples in a pond spreading outward from where a stone was dropped in.

13. E.g., in classical mechanics, if you stand on a platform moving 30 kilometers per hour and throw a rock forward at 50 kilometers per hour relative to yourself, the rock moves 80 kilometers per hour relative to the ground.

14. An "inertial" frame of reference is one that moves at a constant velocity—not accelerating. According to Einstein, any experiment performed in one inertial reference frame will have exactly the same result in any other inertial reference frame. The theory of relativity is sometimes caricatured as saying that one frame of reference—or one person's point of view—is as good as any other. It would be more accurate to say that the theory of relativity shows that the fundamental laws of nature are the same for everyone, regardless of a person's frame of reference. Most college-level introductory physics textbooks include chapters on the theory of relativity.

15. Some of the most famous contributions were by Max Planck, Albert Einstein, A. H. Compton, Niels Bohr, Enrico Fermi, Louis deBroglie, Erwin Schrödinger, Lise Meitner, Werner Heisenberg, and Wolfgang Pauli.

16. E.g., when the electron of a hydrogen atom is in a quantum state with a precise energy, it does not have a precisely defined velocity. If one measures its velocity, the measurement changes the state of the electron so that now it no longer has a precisely defined energy.

17. This quotation is variously referenced. Einstein probably said or wrote versions of it more than once. One particular reference: Albert Einstein, "Letter to Max Born, 4 December 1926," in *Einstein und Born Briefwechsel* (Edition Erbrich, 1969), 130.

18. There is a variety of philosophical interpretations of quantum mechanics. Many textbooks on quantum mechanics include some discussion of these competing interpretations and their relative merits.

19. For more reading on this topic, see Donald MacKay, *Science, Chance, and Providence* (Oxford: Oxford Univ. Press, 1978); and Robert John Russell, Nancey Murphy, and Arthur R. Peacocke, eds., *Chaos and Complexity: Scientific Perspectives on Divine Action* (Rome: Vatican Observatory Publications, 1996).

20. For more reading on this topic, see John Polkinghorne, *Science and Providence: God's Interaction with the World* (Boston: New Science Library, 1989); Russell et al., *Chaos and Complexity*.

21. During the last few decades, physicists have been somewhat playful when naming newly discovered particles. Protons consist of two "up" quarks and one "down" quark, while neutrons consist of one "up" and two "down" quarks.

22. Some of the earliest and most famous discoveries were made by Henri Becquerel, Marie Curie, and Pierre Curie.

23. The electron's two heavier counterparts are the muon and the tauon. The four heavier quarks are called *strange*, *charm*, *bottom*, and *top*. The neutrino's counterparts are the mu-neutrino and tau-neutrino, which may not technically be unstable, but there is evidence that the different neutrino types can change into each other.

24. This short list is, of course, a simplification. These ideas are discussed at greater length in Loren Haarsma, "Does Science Exclude God?" in Keith B. Miller, ed., *Perspectives on an Evolving Creation* (Grand Rapids: Eerdmans, 2003).

25. E.g., R. Hooykaas, *Religion and the Rise of Modern Science* (Edinburgh: Scottish Academic Press and Chatto & Windus, 1972).

26. Performing an experiment to test the conditions where these two theories make contradictory predictions is, alas, beyond physicists' technical capabilities for now.

27. Physicists are currently working on several possible theories, which may result in accomplishing this unification. The most famous, and perhaps most promising, of these is called "string theory." Brian Green has written an informative and readable book on string theory titled *The Elegant Universe: Superstrings, Hidden Dimensions, and the Quest for the Ultimate Theory* (New York: W. W. Norton, 1999).

28. There are many recent books on this topic. Two of the most popular are Timothy Ferris, *The Whole Shebang: A State of the Universe Report* (New York: Simon & Schuster, 1998), and Martin Rees, *Just Six Numbers: The Deep Forces That Shape the Universe* (New York: Basic, 2001).

29. Two Christians who have written about this are John Polkinghorne, *Science and Providence: God's Interaction with the World* (Boston: Shambhala, 1989), and Malcolm Jeeves, *Mind Fields: Reflections on the Science of Mind and Brain* (Grand Rapids: Baker, 1993). The terms "bottom-up" and "top-down" causation are used by these authors as well as others. Some Christian theologians are now suggesting that indeterminacy in bottom-up causation allows yet another means for God to interact with the world. Two examples are Polkinghorne, *Science and Providence*, and Russell et al., *Chaos and Complexity*.

30. "Unknown natural law" is just one of several possible explanations for events that are otherwise unexplainable in terms of known natural laws. More possibilities are discussed in Haarsma, "Does Science Exclude God?"

SUGGESTED READING

Ferris, Timothy. *The Whole Shebang: A State of the Universe Report*. New York: Simon & Schuster, 1998.

Green, Brian. *The Elegant Universe: Superstrings, Hidden Dimensions, and the Quest for the Ultimate Theory*. New York: W. W. Norton, 1999.

MacKay, Donald. *The Open Mind and other Essays*. Leicester: Inter-Varsity Press, 1988.

Ibid. *Science, Chance, and Providence*. Oxford: Oxford University Press, 1978.

Miller, Keith, ed. *Perspectives on an Evolving Creation*. Grand Rapids: Eerdmans, 2003.

Polkinghorne, John. *Science and Providence: God's Interaction with the World*. Boston: New Science Library, 1989.

Russell, R. J., Nancey Murphy, and A. R. Peacocke, eds. *Chaos and Complexity: Scientific Perspectives on Divine Action*. Vatican City: Vatican Observatory Publications, 1996.

B. How Does Christianity Influence How to Think about Chemistry?

Scientists who explore the world of chemistry open the dynamic realm of the study of the components, properties, reactions, and structure of matter. It is a fascinating world and includes the interactions of chemicals and their impact on human societies. An outstanding comprehension of chemistry is essential to understand the chemistry of life exhibited by the living organisms that inhabit the earth and its atmosphere. Extraordinary technology has been developed to help scientists learn more about biochemistry and inorganic, organic, physical, and analytical chemistry. Students who are interested in chemistry learn to use very sophisticated technology to answer questions at molecular levels. Among them are organic chemists who study substances that have carbon components. They open the world of organic syntheses and interactions. Biochemists are interested in the chemistry of living organisms, and inorganic chemists focus on the properties of substances that lack carbon. Physical and analytical chemists target the physical properties and analysis of chemical systems. These represent only a few types of chemistry Christians may be called to practice.

To illustrate some interfaces of chemistry with Christian faith, we have selected topics in chemistry where these intersections are apparent and significant. Among those are the age-old questions humans have asked about the creation of life, the impact of chemistry on human society, the nature of pharmaceutical drugs, and the chemistry of life.

The Creation of Life: Charting When, Where, and How?

Larry L. Funck

When did life begin? How did it originate? And where did it come into existence? These are important questions for scientists, but especially so for thinking Christians who are engaged in the work of science. As believers, such scientists can confidently assert that God is the source of all life. And with the psalmist, Christians in science can faithfully acknowledge that God "knit me together in my mother's womb" (Ps. 139:13). Just as God has been intimately involved in the origin of each person who has ever lived, so He was involved in the origin of life itself. The intriguing question for the scientist in each case is "How did He do it?"

Modern science is capable of answering questions about the origin of an individual human life with ever-increasing detail. We know that humans come into being through the union of a male sperm and a female ovum. From that first cell, through multiple divisions, a viable fetus emerges that ultimately—if born naturally—descends the birth canal of its mother. Scientists can even describe human development at the molecular level in terms of the combination of DNA molecules and their expression in the formation of the various cellular components that determine physical makeup. True, numerous unanswered fundamental questions remain, many about the specifics of human development. However, as scientific research continues, increasingly these complex and interrelated mysteries are being unraveled. Clearly, descriptions of one's physical origin in terms of biology and chemistry do not negate the prior description in terms of God's creative activity. In fact, the intricate mechanisms involved in the development of the human fetus, as revealed by modern science, can become a source of wonder and even worship.

The key scientific questions about the origin of life, including when, where, and how, will be addressed. Likewise, the implications of current scientific answers for the person of faith will then be raised. But before these matters can be addressed, we must consider some important terms and definitions.

How do we distinguish an entity that is alive from ordinary, nonliving matter?

What is life? Perhaps surprisingly, this is not an easy question to answer. Scientists are not totally in agreement in their responses. One possible approach is to describe what a living thing ought to be able to do to be qualified as being alive. First of all, living things should have the capacity to reproduce themselves, in other words, the ability of *self-replication*. All biological specimens that can multiply—or in biblical terms "replenish the earth"—can be considered to be alive.[31] Can the same thing be said about life at its origin?

A second capacity that is a generally accepted characteristic of living systems is the ability to use energy to carry out various life-sustaining processes. In terms of human life, the scope of these life-sustaining processes is extensive, ranging from mobility to thinking. Humans derive the energy to carry out these processes from the chemical energy stored in the food that they eat. In contrast, for a simple one-celled organism, neither mobility nor thinking may be necessary; nevertheless, energy is still required to keep the cell operating at the molecular level. The maintenance of various chemical functions, including such things as the manufacturing of cellular components (e.g., cell walls) requires the continuous supply of energy. The sources of energy for organisms are as varied as the organisms themselves. In fact, organisms can be categorized according to their energy sources. *Autotrophs* are organisms that produce energy themselves; they include both *chemotrophs*, which derive their energy from inorganic compounds, and *phototrophs*, which derive their energy from light via photosynthesis. By contrast, *heterotrophs* derive their energy from the consumption of other living things, including representatives ranging from bacteria to human beings. Regardless of the source of energy, the ability of an organism to use energy is a critical characteristic of a living system.

Most scientists agree, then, that living organisms share two basic traits: they are self-replicating and energy-consuming systems. But when and how these organisms first emerged are matters of great debate within the scientific community.

When did life first appear on the earth?

The question of when life first appeared on earth is an important one for those involved in origin-of-life science. Current thinking points toward a very ancient origin of the simplest life-forms, single-celled organisms. The evidence consists of two types, fossil and chemical. For example, some of the oldest rocks extant on the earth show fossilized evidence of microorganisms inside of them. The best preserved among these fossils occur in rocks found in the Pilbara region of northwestern Australia.[32] Eleven different types of microorganisms have been identified among these fossils in rocks dated at roughly 3.5 billion years. The fossilized, single-celled organisms found in these rocks resemble modern species of cyanobacteria.

There is also chemical evidence that suggests the presence of life even earlier. In particular, for the process of photosynthesis, light energy is used by living organisms to produce sugar from carbon dioxide and water. Carbon atoms in natural carbon occur mainly in two forms that differ in mass, known as carbon-12 and carbon-13. The process of photosynthesis results in a higher fraction of carbon-12 being incorporated into the sugar than exists in the carbon dioxide. The sugar is said to be enriched by the carbon-12. When the sugar molecules later decompose, leaving behind carbon, the carbon remains enriched in carbon-12. This enrichment is believed to be a telltale sign in fossils that the carbon had a biological origin. In fact, some examples of carbon-12 enriched carbon have been found in rocks dated at around 3.8 billion years ago.

Both the fossil and the chemical evidence point to a very early beginning for life, although these claims are not without controversy.[33] Based on studies of lunar craters, it is believed that the earth, like the moon, was under heavy bombardment by large meteors until around 3.8 billion years ago and would have been a very hot and inhospitable place for life to begin. Thus the current evidence tentatively suggests that life made its first terrestrial appearance shortly after the earth cooled down from its hot, molten, primordial state. Certainly the earth at that time was far different from the relatively quiescent planet that we know today.

Where on earth did life begin?

The question of where life started has long intrigued scientists. For example, Charles Darwin, in a letter to a friend, wrote about the possibility of the right conditions existing for life's start "in some warm little pond." Later scientists hypothesized about the presence of a "primordial soup" of organic molecules, in which life might have started. Many scientists now think that the more likely locus for the origin of life occurred deep in a primordial sea at or near rifts in the ocean floor. The rifts are known as "thermal vents," since they function much like underwater volcanoes, constantly spewing hot lava.

The reasons for the belief in this location as the starting point of life are several. First is the fact that the most ancient forms of microorganisms (whose ancient character is based on studies of their genetic material) thrive under these extreme conditions. These *extremophiles*—translated as "lovers of extremes"—have been found in hot springs, as well as deep within the earth. Second, the early earth would not have had a protective ozone layer in its atmosphere, since its oxygen content was very low. Consequently, surface life would have had difficulty surviving not only the intense bombardment of ultraviolet light from the sun, against which ozone protects, but also the last stages of bombardment of meteors referred to above. Therefore, it is thought that the first living systems may have arisen in the rock bed on the ocean floor, protected from these bombardments and provided with the right chemical composition, rich in minerals, believed to be necessary to initiate the chemical reactions required to get life going. Furthermore, this deep-sea location would have been close to an energy source, the thermal vents, which would have been necessary for life's start.

The foregoing theoretical proposal for the location of life's origin is admittedly highly speculative, and at this time, there is essentially no conclusive evidence to support a specific location for life's starting point. All proposals for the location of life origins, including the currently popular deep-sea proposal, are necessarily provisional, since fossilized remnants of the first cells most certainly do not exist. The disputed, very old fossils (referred to earlier) are actually quite advanced forms of life. All of this speculation, then, illustrates a common problem for origin of life science in addressing the various questions that arise. There is essentially no record of what the first, very primitive life-forms were like. Thus scientists engaged in research of the origin of life are left with virtually no options other than provisional attempts to deduce possible mechanisms for life's origins.

Generally, how does chemistry factor into the processes involved in origin of life science?

A primary aspect of the question about life's origins is chemical in nature. The starting materials for making life are presumably simple compounds, such as CO_2, H_2O, NH_3, and perhaps CH_4, plus inorganic minerals containing the elements iron, sulfur, and phosphorus. One of the goals of the origin of life scientist is to explain how chemical processes can turn these simple substances into the simplest possible form of life. But what exactly is meant by the "simplest possible form of life," as the scientist intends it?

The simplest forms of life known to exist today are small, one-celled organisms that are actually quite complex. They contain three important types of components, each of which is much larger and more complicated than the simple molecules mentioned earlier. First, there is the cell membrane that encloses the cell. It is mostly composed of large molecules made of chains of carbon atoms connected to hydrogen atoms. The chains have a negatively charged end containing phosphorus and oxygen atoms in a grouping known as phosphate. Next, within the cell membrane are the other two principal types of molecules that must be present for the cell to function.

Nucleic acids, so called because they were first found inside the nuclei of cells, are also chainlike molecules. The nucleic acids store the information that instructs the cell how to make the parts of the cell that it needs to continue functioning and to divide when that becomes necessary. The chains are made of sugars and phosphate groups with molecular projections (known as bases) made of carbon, nitrogen, and hydrogen, extending perpendicular to the chain. And finally, there are the proteins, the "workhorses" of the cell. They make sure that the right chemical reactions take place and that they happen rapidly enough. Again, these are chainlike molecules, with pieces of the chains known as *amino acids*. The backbone of the chain contains carbon and nitrogen atoms. Each amino acid has a "side group" with a different molecular structure containing carbon, hydrogen and, perhaps, oxygen, nitrogen, and sulfur atoms. For the purposes of this text, it is not appropriate to explore these structures in any great detail. Rather, it should suffice to note that all of these molecules are far larger and much more complicated than CO_2, H_2O, or NH_3, for example. Furthermore, there is not just one type of protein molecule per cell. The simplest known cells around today contain DNA with instructions for at least 250 different proteins and various forms of the other nucleic acid, RNA. These various proteins and nucleic acids appear to provide the minimal complexity necessary for the sustenance and reproduction of the simplest cells known today.

Clearly, the molecular components of a living cell prove to be more complex than the starting materials. A primary task of origin of life scientists is to propose tenable chemical schemes for the synthesis of complex, molecular, cellular components under conditions that existed on the primitive earth. Unfortunately, since the location of life's beginnings is unknown, the conditions for these chemical reactions seem very uncertain. Did life's important molecules form in the atmosphere or in the seas? Were mineral catalysts available, and, if so, what were they? Furthermore, the conditions required for the synthesis of one of the biological compounds may not be compatible with the conditions required for others. Thus it is necessary to speculate that the substances formed in separate places and were then brought together to react or interact.

What have chemistry experiments in origin of life science shown?

Undoubtedly the most famous attempt at simulation of origin of life via chemistry was the Miller-Urey experiment performed in 1953. Stanley Miller, a graduate student of the Nobel laureate Harold Urey, successfully synthesized several amino acids under conditions that, at the time, were believed to correspond to a primitive earth atmosphere. Specifically, the mix of gases that Miller used was "highly reducing," meaning that its content of hydrogen atoms was much greater than that of oxygen atoms. The result of the experiment was the discovery that amino acids could be obtained under these conditions, and it led to great excitement within the scientific community. However, that excitement was quickly tempered by the realization that amino acids are only the building blocks of proteins; in other words, only the bricks themselves, so to speak, had been manufactured, not the buildings (i.e., the proteins), which were yet to be constructed. The excitement from the experiment was further tempered when geologists began to call into question the highly reducing conditions that Miller had assumed. It is now believed by many scientists that the atmosphere of the earth, at the time life first emerged, contained more oxygen and less hydrogen than Miller and Urey assumed, conditions that would likely result in a much smaller production of amino acids.

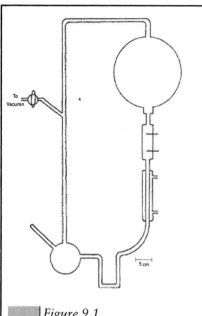

Figure 9.1.

The Miller apparatus used for synthesizing amino acids.*

*Stanley L. Miller. "A Production of Amino Acids under Possible Primitive Earth Conditions." *Science* 117. no. 3046 (15 May 1953): 528.

Regardless of the actual validity of the Miller-Urey experiment, it did stimulate numerous other similar attempts at synthesis of life's molecules under presumed prebiotic conditions. Many of the other molecules that are classified as essential for the larger molecules, such as the sugar ribose or the organic bases used in RNA and DNA, have been successfully synthesized in chemical laboratories. In spite of these successes, however, there remains lingering doubt about the artificial or inappropriate nature of the experimental reaction conditions chosen.[34] Chemists set up their reactions with the choice of solvent and concentrations of reactants, along with the inclusion of catalysts, to maximize yield of products. Strictly speaking, origin of life scientists should not be afforded this freedom of supposed conditions, since their task is to demonstrate how life could have begun under primordial conditions, not the idealized conditions of the present-day chemical laboratory.

What are some of the implications of the "isomer problem" in origin of life chemistry?

Even when the building blocks of life have been synthesized under arguably appropriate simulation conditions, frequently there remains what may be termed the "isomer problem." Isomers are different forms of molecules that contain exactly the same atoms. They differ based on how the atoms are connected and/or how the atoms are spatially arranged, relative to each other. For example, the sugar that is incorporated into RNA is known as D-ribose, a so-called aldopentose (*pent-* means "five," i.e., five carbons) with the formula $C_5H_{10}O_5$. The commonly used approaches at synthesis of pentoses from simple molecules, such as formaldehyde, CH_2O, can lead to at least eight different possible products, only one of which is the molecule that occurs in living systems. Origin of life scientists remain puzzled by the question of how or why only D-ribose occurs in nucleic acids.

The *D* in D-ribose raises another aspect of the isomer problem. It stands for dextro, which means that D-ribose is a "right-handed" molecule. L-ribose, which has an equal likelihood of being formed, is the mirror-image isomer of D-ribose, much like your left hand is the mirror image of your right hand. Similarly, in the case of amino acids, only "left-handed" isomers, the so-called L-amino acids, occur in protein molecules. When amino acids are formed in simulation experiments, such as the Miller-Urey one, both left- and right-handed isomers are formed in equal concentrations. How and why only the one-isomeric form of sugars and of amino acids were formed and used to make life's big molecules remains one of the unanswered questions of origin of life science. (See plate 15.)

What are some other problematic questions involving origin of life chemistry?

As difficult as the synthesis of life's building blocks is, it is neither the only nor the most difficult of problems in origin of life chemistry. How to get from the building blocks to the larger molecules, the nucleic acids and the proteins, is a major question. In terms of energy, the formation of these larger molecules from the smaller building blocks is like going uphill; that is, energy must somehow be supplied. In virtually every case, the reactions to form the larger molecules can be accomplished through evaporation of the water in which the reactants are dissolved. Unfortunately, when the water is put back into the mix, as it must be for living systems to function, the reverse reaction tends to occur. In other words, the protein and nucleic acid molecules are susceptible to breakup by water.

Another important question for origin of life scientists involves that of priority among the three major cellular components. Were proteins formed before nucleic acids or vice versa, and when did encapsulation (formation of the cell membrane) take place? These are crucial and very thorny questions for several reasons. All modern cell membranes necessarily contain protein molecules to act as channels, allowing substances to get in and out of the cell. Thus if encapsulation took place before these proteins were available, it is difficult to imagine how the cell could function. In the simplest modern cell, nucleic acids cannot perform their function without the aid of proteins, and proteins cannot be formed without the blueprint for their construction stored in the DNA; how life could occur without both present is hard to imagine. Yet the likelihood of both types of molecules simultaneously appearing in the same physical context is essentially zero.

A possible way out of this latter quandary involves the proposal that the first life-forms consisted of RNA only, with or without encapsulation. This suggestion is popularly known as the "RNA world" hypothesis.[35] RNA is another kind of nucleic acid that is like DNA in that it stores information. RNA is used in the translation of the DNA messages into protein. About twenty years ago, certain forms of RNA were found to have catalytic capabilities analogous to that of proteins. These catalytic RNAs were given the name *ribozymes*. Their discovery gave the RNA world proposal a considerable boost. For the origin of life scientist, ribozymes represented a kind of dual-purpose molecule that could both store information and catalyze chemical reactions, thereby performing the functions of both DNA and proteins.

Since the discovery of ribozymes, research exploring the possibilities of RNA–based life has been intense on a number of fronts. A primary question for the RNA world that continues to plague its supporters involves the difficulty of synthesizing RNA from its building blocks. RNA is an exceptionally fragile molecule and difficult to make and retain, even under the best of conditions. Explaining how it could first form, then survive, and ultimately prosper in the rough and tumble of the primitive earth is a considerable challenge for the origin of life scientist.

The questions raised about the chemistry involved in the origin of life are challenging. Scientists began to address them seriously about fifty years ago and have given more intense attention to them only over the last thirty years. Significant advances have been made, but there remain huge holes in our understanding.[36] The gap between the starting materials and modern "simple" cells is enormous. Leaping this gap is comparable to going from the south rim to the north rim of the Grand Canyon without the aid of a helicopter. As Sir Fred Hoyle, a famous British physicist, has described, the single-step formation of a cell from inorganic starting materials is analogous to the assembly of a 747 in a junkyard during a tornado. Clearly, such "spontaneous generation" is out of the question. Most origin of life scientists believe that the chemical gap can be spanned in small increments; nevertheless, the difficulty is in determining how. But even if origin of life scientists were somehow able to solve all of the chemical problems enumerated above, an issue would still remain that many scientists view as even more fundamental.

What is "information content," and how does it relate to origin of life science?

Previously, a definition of *life* was put forward, but the arrangement of words in that definition might be challenged by some scientists for leaving out an important trait. According to Leslie Orgel, one of the pioneers of origin of life science, "information content" is a critical component of all living things.[37] What is it? Information content is that which must be replicated for the entity in question to be classified as living. How this information came into being is, therefore, a crucial question for the origin of life scientist.

Chemistry is a reductionistic science. In other words, chemists attempt to understand how reactions occur on the basis of the component parts of the molecules, the atoms as well as the electrons and protons of which the atoms are composed. In doing this, chemists draw upon the similarly reductionistic science of physics. The problem is that the question of how biological information came into existence is essentially a higher-level question, not answerable in terms of reductionistic sciences like chemistry and physics.

As mentioned earlier, biological information is stored in the genetic material of the cell, in molecules known as DNA. These DNA molecules contain all the instructions that the cell follows in maintaining and reproducing itself. A bacterium such as *E. coli* has a distinctive shape and behavior because its DNA provides instructions for the production of proteins and RNA molecules that generate the chemical reactions that in turn cause the various structures and behavior-linked processes to occur. But such an explanation, again, proceeds according to the dictates of chemistry. Prior to the questions involving chemistry, we must ask how the information content came to be present in the DNA in the first place.

DNA stores the information about how to make proteins using a kind of chemical alphabet. There are only four letters in DNA's alphabet, corresponding to four different organic bases that can be attached to the DNA backbone. Different arrangements of these four letters, in groups of three, result in different amino acids being inserted in the construction of proteins, all in a complicated process involving both

RNA and proteins. The important thing to understand is that the information stored in DNA works in a manner analogous to the way information is stored in language. The information in the sentence that you are now reading is related to the order of the letters and spaces that make up the sentence. In a similar fashion, the information that is stored in DNA results from the sequence of the organic bases along the DNA chain. For example, a given person's DNA contained the instructions to make the molecules that led to having blue eyes (or for that matter, brown or green). These instructions were spelled out in a specific gene (a large DNA molecule) that directed the appropriate protein molecules to be made to create a particular eye color. Similarly, the DNA of the bacterium *E. coli* dictates that its shape should be rodlike, using essentially the same alphabet that is used by human DNA for creating an eye-color message.

The question of the origin of information is viewed by many as being the most crucial in origin of life science. Manfred Eigen, a prominent origin of life theorist, says, "Our task is to find an algorithm, a natural law that leads to the origin of information."[38] This question is so important that a million-dollar prize is currently being offered by The Origin of Life Foundation to the first scientist to make a significant contribution in answer to it.[39]

How does "specified complexity" factor into information content?

In order for a sentence on a page or for a message in DNA to contain information, both must have the property of *specified complexity*. What does it mean to be specifically complex? To answer this question, consider the following contrasting meanings of key words. *Complexity* is the opposite of *simplicity*. *Specific* is the opposite of *random*. The following examples of strings of letters illustrate something significant about the concept of specified complexity:

1. THE END THE END THE END THE END
2. GTNSSTIE CCIESAHSN SETME A EONAN
3. THIS SENTENCE CONTAINS A MESSAGE

Line 1 is not random, but it is simple. It contains little information. Line 2 is complex, but it is also random. It contains no information. Line 3 is complex, but it is not random. Instead, the sequence of letters and spaces, which are the same ones that occur randomly in 2, is highly specific. This combination of specificity and complexity yields a meaningful sentence, in other words, something that contains information. The information stored in DNA is specifically complex in a manner analogous to the sentence in line 3. How did the information get into DNA? The responses of origin of life theorists to this question have been very different.

The fundamental issue, with regard to the origin of information, involves the question of whether it can be spontaneously generated from a chaotic medium. Most origin of life scientists trust that it can. They believe that all that is needed is an initially fortuitous generation of a self-replicating system. Such a system would, by definition, contain information that could be transmitted to the next generation in the self-replication process. The prime candidate to be this information-containing, self-replicating entity in the RNA world hypothesis is an RNA molecule that could catalyze its own replication. It is postulated that RNA with this capacity might have formed in a "primordial soup." To date, no laboratory has succeeded in artificially producing such a so-called "naked gene" capable of its own reproduction all by itself.

What do critics of a self-replicating "naked" RNA assert?

Not everyone in the origin of life field believes that such a self-replicating "naked" RNA, (so-called because it lacks any of the accompanying machinery of protein catalysts) represents a viable option for life's start. Stuart Kauffman, for instance, argues that even if researchers succeed in producing an RNA molecule that can catalyze its own reproduction, that would not constitute a truly living system, nor would it constitute evidence for the validity of the RNA world hypothesis. Kauffman contends that a simple RNA self-replicator could not evolve into more advanced forms, but rather would be subject to what Leslie Orgel terms a "runaway error catastrophe." In Kauffman's words, "the molecular system would tend to mutate itself and its progeny faster than natural selection could rectify the errors, and all information in the molecular system would degrade. The system would destroy itself."[40]

Kauffman expresses a further concern, contending that a naked gene would not be able to carry out the other important processes required for its own sustenance. Perhaps, and most important, it would lack the means for deriving the energy from its surroundings that is necessary to drive the chemical reactions involved in its sustenance and reproduction. Kauffman postulates instead that life got its start as a collection of encapsulated autocatalytic polymers. Polymers is another word for long molecular chains, such as proteins or nucleic acids. Autocatalytic means that the collection of polymers is capable of causing its own production by mutual catalysis. Kauffman claims that once such an organized system reaches a certain stage, life simply happens.

> As the complexity of a collection of polymer catalysts increases, a critical complexity threshold is reached. Beyond this threshold, the probability that a subsystem of polymers exists in which formation of each member is catalyzed by other members of the subsystem becomes very high. Such sets of polymers are autocatalytic and reproduce collectively. Thus the new view I shall propose is disarmingly simple. Life is an expected, collectively self-organized property of catalytic polymers.[41]

As might be anticipated, Kauffman is not without his critics. A primary concern arises from the paucity of experimental confirmation for his hypothesis, which remains largely only theory, based on computer models. Physicist Paul Davies raises an additional, more fundamental question. Davies contends that life involves more than "self-organization." According to Davies, "life is in fact *specified*—i.e., genetically directed—organization. Living things are instructed by the genetic software encoded in their DNA (or RNA)."[42] In other words, in Davies' view, Kauffman has failed to account for the origin of the complex specified information, the possession of which is a fundamental requirement for something to be classified as living.

Criticism of Kauffman's ideas has also come from William Dembski, the primary proponent of intelligent design. Dembski argues that complex specified information (CSI) cannot arise out of chaos. He contends that scientific laws are inadequate to explain the origin of information and that the search for an information-producing law or algorithm that Manfred Eigen called for is fundamentally a hopeless one. Dembski claims that scientific laws cannot produce complex specified information because "laws are deterministic and thus cannot yield contingency, without which there can be no information."[43] Similarly, he contends that algorithms simply move information around and therefore are inept at generating novelty, that is, new information. Similarly, pure chance cannot produce complex specified information according to Dembski. He contends: "Most biologists reject pure chance as an adequate explanation of CSI. Besides flying in the face of every canon of statistical reasoning, pure chance is scientifically unsatisfying as an explanation of CSI. To explain CSI in terms of pure chance is no more instructive than pleading ignorance or proclaiming CSI a mystery."[44]

Dembski claims that the only possible source of information is an intelligent designer. While it is important to note that the proponents of intelligent design do not name the designer, nevertheless, most of its adherents are Christians.

What should Christians believe about the origin of life?

What are the implications of origin of life science for the Christian, and what are possible responses of the Christian believer to the issues raised by the science? Certainly all Christians believe in the existence of an intelligent designer, but what should we believe about how the designer accomplishes the design? The views of scientifically trained Christians on the questions raised here span a wide spectrum.

There are some who would consider the question of how God made life, posed in terms of origin of life science as we have in the foregoing, as totally irrelevant. These individuals believe that the book of Genesis records in literal terms the what, where, when, and how of life's origins. For them, it is pointless to phrase these questions in scientific terms because current science presumes the development of life to involve process. In contrast, these individuals believe that life was formed via the spoken word of God, essentially instantaneously and quite recently compared to the geological estimates. For want of a better term, we will refer to this position by the commonly used moniker *young earth creationism*.

At the opposite extreme from young earth creationism, among believing scientists, are those who would hold that God created the cosmos and everything within it, but He accomplished these ends through various physical processes susceptible to scientific study. This viewpoint has been expressed in a variety of ways. An American example would be physicist Howard Van Till, who speaks in terms of a "fully gifted creation." Van Till argues that God is intimately involved in his creation, but that the creation has "by God's unbounded generosity and unfathomable creativity, been given all of the capabilities for self-organization and transformation necessary to make possible something as humanly incomprehensible as unbroken evolutionary development."[45] Similarly, a British example would be John Polkinghorne, the particle physicist turned Anglican priest. He writes in various places of a God who engages in both creation *ex nihilo* (out of nothing) as well as *creatio continua* (continuous creation).[46] Polkinghorne characterizes the creation as being invested by God with the power to—so to speak—create itself. Although these physicists have not written specifically on the questions of origin of life science, clearly they would view any scientific advances in understanding the process of life's formation as enhancing rather than diminishing their appreciation of God's creativity. We will refer to this position as *evolutionary creationism*.

Many believing scientists align themselves with the intelligent design movement. They would probably place their position somewhere between young earth creationism and evolutionary creationism. They believe that the origin of life is an important scientific question and should be addressed as such. Intelligent design proponents are generally quite critical of the theories and some of the methods of origin of life science, but unlike the young earth creationism approach, the discussion occurs in terms of the current science. Representative examples would include the numerous works of Dembski,[47] *Darwin's Black Box* by biochemist Michael Behe,[48] and a previously cited book that predates the rise of intelligent design, *The Mystery of Life's Origin* by Thaxton, Bradley, and Olsen.[49]

Within the intelligent design movement, there seems to be a range of opinions on the question of the *mechanism* of life's origins. For example, philosopher of biological science Paul Nelson holds to a recent and presumably essentially instantaneous creation; nevertheless, he places himself in the intelligent design movement.[50] In a recent work, Fazale Rana and Hugh Ross argue for an ancient creation but with an essentially miraculous appearance of life.[51] Meanwhile, the main issue for intelligent design theorists, according to its principal spokesman, William Dembski, is not one of mechanism. He writes:

> Logically, intelligent design is compatible with everything from utterly discontinuous creation (e.g., God intervening at every conceivable point to create new species) to the most far-ranging evolution (e.g., God seamlessly melding all organisms together into one great tree of life). For intelligent design the primary question is not how organisms came to be … but whether organisms demonstrate clear, empirically detectable marks of being intelligently caused. In principle an evolutionary process can exhibit such "marks of intelligence" as much as any act of special creation.[52]

Dembski, in the passage immediately following this quote, is quick to dissociate intelligent design from theistic evolutionism or evolutionary creationism. Nevertheless, the fact remains that, by his own admission, there is no logical basis for such a separation.

Which is the appropriate choice for a Christian in science? Is it young earth creationism, evolutionary creationism, intelligent design, or some combination of these? The choice for a given individual will probably be determined by a combination of factors, including one's religious background and educational training. However, regardless of the position taken, a thinking Christian should be open to and tolerant of opposing views held by other people of faith.

In addition, there is a need for humility with a touch of agnosticism (which literally means an admission of a lack of knowledge), whatever the stance taken. Both the humility and the agnosticism should grow out of the recognition of two important points. One of these points involves the nature and history of science. Science is not a collection of facts, but rather an evolving process. To be sure, there are many examples in the history of science of sudden breakthroughs that resulted in spectacular gains in knowledge. Still, it is a very fallible enterprise, given that humans conduct it. At its best, science is self-correcting, but at any given point in time, even science has been known to get it wrong; and this demonstrates that no one can know with absolute certainty what is wrong and what is right in the realm of science.

The second point involves simply a restatement of emphases made in the earlier discussion of origin of life science. Current origin of life science is riddled with widespread uncertainty. There are vast spaces of untouched territory involving difficult and often fundamental, unanswered questions. Nevertheless, although prospects for major advances in origin of life science may be few and limited, they do exist. For example, claims have been made that smaller, simpler life-forms than the simple bacteria discussed earlier do exist. These organisms are known as *nanobacteria*. Debate continues in the scientific community over the validity of claims for the existence of very small microorganisms and their possible relationship to primordial life-forms.[53] Another area of research that is relatively unexplored involves the chemistry of conditions resembling what exists around hydrothermal vents in the ocean floor. Not much is known about the chemistry of life-related compounds at the extreme temperatures and pressures in the mineral-rich water that exists at great ocean depths, but research continues.[54]

Some people believe that current origin of life science is foundering and that the multiple unanswered questions are, in fact, unanswerable.[55] They might be right; yet, then again, they might be wrong. The possibility exists that the description of life's origin lies beyond the capability of human science, but it may be too early to be sure. Thus it would seem that the appropriate approach to origin of life questions should include an admission of current ignorance, what might be called a healthy agnosticism, along with a spirit that should characterize all Christian enterprise—one of humility.

Did God make life by simply speaking it into existence? Or did he accomplish it through intricate mechanisms, currently only dimly understood or imagined by origin of life scientists? In either case, the accomplishment of the complex design represented in even the simplest living cell is worthy of our praise. *Soli Deo gloria.*

QUESTIONS

1. An important component of NASA's space exploration effort is the search for extraterrestrial life—an ongoing effort to locate extraterrestrial intelligent life with a program called Search for Extra-Terrestrial Intelligence (SETI; see chapter 5 for more information). What would be the theological implications, if any, if this search were successful?

2. The creation of life in the laboratory is the presumptive goal of some scientific research. What criteria should be used to judge success in these efforts? (Consider the meaning of the terms *creation* and *life*.) Would success in these efforts have any theological implications?

3. What is the value of scientific investigations into the origin of life? Is this an area of science that deserves the input of significant resources? Is this an area of science to which a Christian chemist or biologist might worthily give his or her time and effort?

NOTES

31. Viruses can self-replicate but not without assistance. They need to invade a living organism's cell and use its molecular machinery to reproduce. The lack of this self-replicating machinery is generally felt to disqualify viruses from the category of the living.
32. J. William Schopf, ed., *Life's Origin* (Berkeley: Univ. of California Press, 2002), 158–79.
33. For a discussion of the controversy over fossil and chemical evidence for early life, see Richard Corfield, *Chemistry in Britain* 38, no. 9 (2002): 29–31; see also http://www.richardcorfield.com/pages/other_writing/moving_finger/finger_spring_03.htm and http://www.biomedcentral.com/news/20040930/01.
34. C. B. Thaxton, W. L. Bradley, and R. L. Olsen, *The Mystery of Life's Origin* (Dallas: Lewis and Stanley, 1992).
35. R. F. Gesteland, T. R. Cech, and J. F. Atkins, eds., *The RNA World: The Nature of Modern RNA Suggests a Prebiotic RNA* (Cold Spring Harbor, N.Y.: Cold Spring Harbor Laboratory Press, 1999).
36. A book that provides much of the details of current origin of life chemistry is Geoffrey Zubay, *Origins of Life on the Earth and in the Cosmos*, 2nd ed. (San Diego: Academic Press, 2000). For a highly readable, more skeptical account, see Robert Shapiro, *Origins: A Skeptic's Guide to the Creation of Life on Earth* (New York: Summit, 1986).
37. L. E. Orgel, *The Origins of Life: Molecules and Natural Selection* (New York: Wiley, 1973).
38. Manfred Eigen, *Steps towards Life: A Perspective on Evolution*, trans. P. Woolley, (Oxford: Oxford Univ. Press, 1992), 12.
39. See http://www.us.net/life.
40. Stuart A. Kauffman, *Investigations* (Oxford: Oxford Univ. Press, 2000), 29.
41. Stuart A. Kauffman, *The Origins of Order: Self-organization and Selection in Evolution* (New York: Oxford Univ. Press, 1993), 289.
42. Paul Davies, *The Fifth Miracle* (New York: Simon & Schuster, 1999), 141.
43. William A. Dembski, *Intelligent Design: The Bridge between Science and Theology* (Downers Grove, Ill.: InterVarsity Press, 2002), 165.
44. Ibid., 167.

45. Howard J. Van Till, "Theistic Evolution," in J. P. Moreland and J. Mark Reynolds, eds., *Three Views on Creation and Evolution* (Grand Rapids: Zondervan, 1999), 173.
46. John Polkinghorne, *The Faith of a Physicist*: *Reflections of a Bottom-Up Thinker* (Princeton, N.J.: Princeton Univ. Press, 1994).
47. E.g., *No Free Lunch*: *Why Specified Complexity Cannot Be Purchased without Intelligence* (Lanham, Md.: Rowman & Littlefield, 2002).
48. Michael J. Behe, *Darwin's Black Box*: *The Biochemical Challenge to Evolution* (New York: Free Press, 1996).
49. See n. 3.
50. Paul Nelson and John Mark Reynolds, "Young Earth Creationism," in Moreland and Reynolds, *Three Views on Creation and Evolution.*
51. Fazale Rana and Hugh Ross, *Origins of Life*: *Biblical and Evolutionary Models Face Off* (Colorado Springs: NavPress, 2004).
52. Dembski, *Intelligent Design*, 109.
53. Space Studies Board, National Research Council, *Size Limits of Very Small Microorganisms*: *Proceedings of a Workshop* (Washington, D.C.: National Academy, 1999).
54. E.g., J. P. Amend and E. L. Shock, "Energetics of Aminoacid Synthesis in Hydrothermal Ecosystems," *Science* 281 (1998): 1659–62; G. D. Cody et al., "Primordial Carbonylated Iron-Sulphur Compounds and the Synthesis of Pyruvate," *Science* 289 (2000): 1337–40; E. Imai et al., "Elongation of Oligopeptides in a Stimulated Submarine Hydrothermal System," *Science* 283 (1999): 831–33.
55. Many of these individuals are in the intelligent design movement, but not all. Others include those who argue for *panspermia,* the belief that life did not originate on earth, but came via seeding from outer space.

SUGGESTED READING

Davies, Paul. *The Fifth Miracle*: *The Search for the Origin and Meaning of Life.* New York: Simon & Schuster, 1999.
Rana, Fazale, and Hugh Ross. *Origins of Life*: *Biblical and Evolutionary Models Face Off.* Colorado Springs: NavPress, 2004.
Shapiro, Robert. *Origins*: *A Skeptic's Guide to the Creation of Life on Earth.* New York: Summit, 1986.
Thaxton, C. B., W. L. Bradley, and R. L. Olsen. *The Mystery of Life's Origin.* Dallas: Lewis and Stanley, 1992.
Zubay, Geoffrey. *Origins of Life on the Earth and in the Cosmos.* 2nd ed. San Diego: Academic Press, 2000.

How Does Chemistry Impact Human Society?

Peter K. Walhout

What are the main ways that chemistry impacts human society?

Chemistry impacts our society primarily through technology, though there is also an impact of the raw scientific knowledge itself. Our minds are expanded and our souls are nourished simply by understanding the periodic behavior of the elements, by realizing chemical bonds are quantum mechanical phenomena, and by comprehending the complexity of the Kreb's Cycle. However, this raw chemical knowledge itself is beneficial only to those who choose to learn about it. Yet chemical technology impacts all of society in countless ways. Four major areas of technology and society are especially impacted by chemistry: medicine, materials, the food industry, and the environment. These four areas together encompass the basic creature comforts of life, including health, home, food, and recreation. Virtually everything done in every hour of one's life is influenced by chemical technology.

How does research in chemistry help medicine?

Modern medicine relies on a biochemical understanding of human physiology. Most modern advances in medicine are a direct result of advances in knowing how the body works at the molecular level.[56] For example, Rituxan is a drug sold by Genentech to treat non-Hodgkin's lymphoma, which is a cancer of the lymph system. The drug is a "monoclonal antibody" that targets and destroys only the type of white blood cells involved in the cancer.[57] It can do this because its molecular structure has been designed to bind specifically to proteins that appear only in those types of cells. Once bound to the cancerous cells, the body's immune system is called on to "finish the kill." Clearly such a drug would not have been developed if we did not know the chemistry of the human body. Furthermore, modern drugs are synthesized in laboratories using the tools of chemistry. Commercial aspirin and Rituxan are not grown in a field or harvested from trees—they are synthesized from simpler compounds by chemists and chemical engineers. (See plate 16.)

It is worth noting that a lot of "basic research" in chemistry preceded the development of this cancer-fighting drug. Basic research is scientific research that is done more to seek new knowledge and understanding than to develop new technological applications. Basic research is not driven by the desire to invent something or to make a profit, so nonprofit university and government laboratories do most of the work. The development of Rituxan relied on decades of research into protein structure, amino acids, instrumentation, and intermolecular interactions. This basic research was done by thousands of scientists in thousands of different laboratories around the world, even though they had little idea that their work would contribute specifically to a treatment for lymphoma. Basic research is done with only a glimmer of what the knowledge might be used for in the future, and often the uses are a total surprise. Such was the case with basic research fifty years ago regarding the nuclear spin interactions of atoms in a molecule. No one ever imagined it would lead to the technology of medical magnetic resonance imaging (MRI). The quest for new knowledge and understanding invariably generates technology as a by-product.

What does chemistry have to do with the materials used in modern manufacturing?

Manufacturers are always on the lookout for new materials—materials that are stronger, lighter, water-repellant, more flexible, colorful, temperature-resistant, and so on. Chemistry has contributed the most important new material of all to our modern world—plastic. Plastic is ubiquitous, as a quick look around the room you are sitting in will likely attest. The clock on the wall has many plastic pieces, the cover of the book you are reading may have a laminated plastic coating, your clothes likely have some plastic fibers, and the "glasses" you may be wearing are mostly plastic. It was only through carefully controlled chemical reactions that modern synthetic plastics were developed. The raw material for plastic comes from organic molecules found in crude oil. These small molecules (monomers) are strung together into long "polymer" molecules through a variety of chemical reaction schemes that now serve as the backbone of the vast plastics industry. Each type of plastic, whether it is vinyl, polycarbonate, nylon, PET, PVC, or Styrofoam, to name but a few, has its own chemical technology that is unique to its chemical makeup and processing requirements. Synthetic rubbers (elastomers) are also very important modern materials that are not hardened like plastics.

The other important material in our modern world is metal, and one could argue that metallurgy is a more important technology than plastics technology. Chemistry plays a key role in either case, however. Metallurgy is the application of chemical principles to the mining and manufacturing of metals and metal alloys. Steel, for example, is an alloy of iron that is made by mixing in carbon atoms to reinforce the crystal lattice of iron atoms. The iron itself has to be chemically isolated from the iron ore mineral that is mined from the ground. Do not think that steel is old news from the nineteenth century; it is constantly being reformulated and improved. For instance, about 79 percent of the types of steel used in modern automobiles did not exist ten years ago![58]

Chemistry is also involved in many new materials besides plastics and metals. For example, the last few years have seen an explosion of interest in the newly synthesized "nanotubes," which are made entirely of carbon (see figure 9.2). They are essentially sheets of carbon (graphite) that are seamlessly rolled up into cylinders. Nanotubes exhibit tremendous strength and unique electronic properties that have led to a whole new class of materials research.[59] One potential use for them is as a storage container for hydrogen gas, which will be of critical importance as the world pursues alternatives to fossil fuels.[60] As another example, graphite plays a central role in the materials that have revolutionized golf and tennis. Modern clubs

Figure 9.2.

Carbon Nanotubes. Vertically aligned carbon nanotubes about 100 nanometers wide (one 10,000th of a millimeter) and 3 microns tall. Nanotubes are stronger than steel, but the most important uses for these threadlike macromolecules may be in faster, more efficient, and more durable electronic devices.*

Photo courtesy of NASA Ames Research Center.

*Philip G. Collins and Phaedon Avouris, "Nanotubes for Electronics," *Scientific American,* vol. 283(6) (December 2000): 62.

and rackets are typically made from a polymer resin reinforced by graphite fibers, often with other additives such as Kevlar or titanium mixed in. On a different note, modern art materials also exist thanks to chemistry, including photographic film and film processing, paints, plastics, and glass.

Do chemical technology and research affect the food we eat?

Everything about modern food is related to chemistry. The manufacturing of food preservatives, additives, agricultural pesticides, and herbicides; food processing; packaging; and the widespread genetic engineering of plants and animals all involve chemistry.[61] Frozen vegetables, for instance, are prepared and frozen at precisely the right temperature and cooling rate to preserve the quality of the structure and taste of the food upon reheating. Many food researchers worldwide in academia, government, and industry are continually working to improve every aspect of the food industry. For example, two types of food chemistry research programs in New Zealand illustrate the high-tech nature of foods: "Physical chemical factors that influence the melt behaviour and free oil formation in Mozzarella cheese," and "Understanding physico-chemical changes in food during frozen storage."[62]

Besides making and preparing food, chemistry also helps us know which foods are healthy and which are not. Creating a balanced, nutritional diet comes from understanding the constituent chemicals of a food and how those chemicals interact with and affect the biochemistry of our bodies.

Can chemistry help the environment as well as harm it?

It has been left to chemists to understand most of the harmful effects that industry and energy consumption have wrought on the environment. These man-made problems include acid rain, global warming, and the ozone-hole, which was created by the now-banned aerosol additives known as chlorofluorocarbons, or CFCs. Chemistry is also critical in identifying toxic industrial wastes, assessing their danger to society, and providing solutions for their remediation.

On a more positive note, an exciting, emerging field in environmental chemistry is called "green chemistry." Green chemistry can be defined briefly as "the design of chemical products and processes that reduce or eliminate the use and generation of hazardous substances."[63] This includes creatively making alternative products that are not harmful to the environment and minimizing the use of harmful materials in the synthetic process. As an example of this new work, a company called SummerSet Products in Minnesota has developed a "green" herbicide called AllDown Green Chemistry Herbicide. This is an application that will kill unwanted weeds and grasses through dehydration, but because it uses only naturally occurring ingredients, it can be used in large quantities around waterways without fear of contamination.[64] This is an extremely effective herbicide, and it is representative of the new successes chemists are finding by focusing on naturally occurring substances.

Are there additional questions that involve chemistry?

Chemistry is often referred to as "the central science," and it is not hard to see why. Chemistry has contributed to nearly every major technology, whether it is in the form of component materials, production, or conceptual understanding. It also has fascinated centuries of people who are simply curious about how the world works and how they can effect change through physical processes. Many Christians have found a career in chemistry to be a perfect way of answering our call to the stewardship and understanding of God's creation. This call to stewardship through chemistry is one way we can hope to answer many other pressing questions as well:

1. Can we cure common forms of blindness?
2. How can we prevent Alzheimer's disease?
3. Can farm crops be developed that grow in arid regions?
4. How do aerosol particles affect our health and global warming?
5. Can we develop a room-temperature superconducting material?

The list is endless, as is God's work here on earth.

QUESTIONS

1. Is basic research still important, given how much we already know?

2. Can a Christian be "called" to develop a better material? A better golf club?

3. Who should decide whether the potential dangers of a new chemical discovery outweigh the potential advantages?

NOTES

56. Richard B. Silverman, *The Organic Chemistry of Drug Design and Drug Action*, 2nd ed. (San Diego: Academic, 2004).
57. *Rituxan*, October 2004, www.rituxan.com.
58. *Facts and Figures*, October 2004, www.uksteel.org.uk/facts.htm.
59. Charles Lieber, "The Incredible Shrinking Circuit," *Scientific American* 287, no. 5 (September 2001): 58.
60. A. C. Dillon, K. M. Jones, T. A. Bekkedahl, C. H. Kiang, D. S. Bethune, and M. J Heben, "Storage of Hydrogen in Single-walled Carbon Nanotubes," *Nature* 386 (1997): 377–79.
61. Norman N. Potter and Joseph H. Hotchkiss, *Food Science*, 5th ed. (Gaithersburg, Md.: Aspen, 1999).
62. http://www.otago.ac.nz/foodscience/research/research.htm.
63. P. T. Anastas and J. C. Warner, *Green Chemistry: Theory and Practice* (New York: Oxford Univ. Press, 1998), 30.
64. *All Organic Links: The Global Resource for Organic Information*, October 2004, www.allorganiclinks.com/Gardening/Lawn_Care/more2.shtml.

SUGGESTED READING

Emsley, John. *Nature's Building Blocks*: *An A-Z Guide to the Elements*. Oxford: Oxford University Press, 2003.

Goozner, Merrill. *The $800 Million Pill*. Berkeley and Los Angeles: University of California Press, 2004.

LeCouteur, Penny, and Jay Burreson. *Napolean's Buttons: How 17 Molecules Changed History*. New York: Tarcher/Putnam, 2003.

Ratner, Mark A., and David Ratner. *Nanotechnology*: *A Gentle Introduction to the Next Big Idea*. Upper Saddle River, N.J.: Pearson/Prentice Hall, 2002.

Sacks, Oliver. *Uncle Tungsten: Memories of a Chemical Boyhood*. New York: Vintage, 2002.

Schwarcz, Joe. *That's the Way the Cookie Crumbles*. Toronto: ECW Press, 2002.

Somerville, Richard. *The Forgiving Air*. Berkeley and Los Angeles: University of California Press, 1999.

Werth, Barry. *Billion Dollar Medicine*. New York: Touchstone/Simon & Schuster, 1995.

Are Pharmaceutical Drugs Good or Bad?

Jennifer L. Busch

Most, if not all, of us have benefited from some type of pharmaceutical drug. Temporary pain is soothed with a pain-reliever. Heart patients take blood-thinning medication. Many of us realize that pharmaceutical drugs are an integral part of our society, yet we may have preconceived ideas concerning them that stem from personal experiences, stereotypes, hearsay, misunderstandings, or popular literature. New pharmaceutical drugs are becoming available, and their uses will affect the future of our society.

What is a "pharmaceutical drug"?

A pharmaceutical drug is defined as any legal, controlled, medicinal preparation that causes a physiological response. Drugs that fit in this category may or may not be addictive or be FDA-approved, and they may be acquired either with or without a prescription. Illegal, uncontrolled, and/or recreational drugs, such as marijuana or nicotine are not included in this definition.

How do pharmaceutical drugs work?

Pharmaceutical drugs cause physiological responses, changes in the body. To understand how drugs initiate these responses, it is important to know how the body works and how illnesses develop. The body is made of small building blocks called cells. Cells with similar functions form tissues and tissues combine to form organs, such as the heart, lungs, and stomach. Organs must work together to keep the body healthy, and each organ relies on its cells to do their jobs. The ultimate job of the cells is to help the body maintain homeostasis, a level of constancy in a changing environment, by detecting changes in their local environment and sending signals to other cells of the body, instructing these cells how to respond. Cells detect environmental changes or respond to signals through proteins on their surfaces. These proteins, called receptors, interact with specific signals, like certain locks only interact with specific keys, to initiate a series of intracellular reactions called signal transduction. The end result is a cellular response that restores homeostasis to the body.

Blood pressure regulation is an example of cellular signal transduction. Our bodies continually monitor and regulate our blood pressure through cellular communication. If blood pressure rises, baroreceptors (pressure-detectors) on cells within the aortic arch and carotid artery send a signal by way of neurons to the heart and blood vessels. This signal is transduced (interpreted) in the muscle cells of the heart and the blood vessels. The interpretation/transduction happens this way: neurotransmitters[65] are released from the neurons and bind to receptors on the muscle cell surface. Neurotransmitter binding initiates a cascade of intracellular events in the muscle cells that ultimately lowers calcium concentrations ($[Ca^{2+}]$). Decreased $[Ca^{2+}]$ decreases muscle contraction, so the cardiac cells do not contract as forcefully, and a smaller volume of blood is pumped through the circulatory system. The muscle cells lining the interior circumference of the arteries, like a coating on the inside of a hollow rod, also relax, thus increasing the vessel diameter. This decreased cardiac output and increased space within blood vessels lowers blood pressure to a normal level. If blood pressure drops below the normal level, the baroreceptors send signals to increase $[Ca^{2+}]$ within the heart and vessel muscle cells, which increases heart contraction force and decreases the diameter of the vessels; this increases blood pressure.

Amazingly, our bodies remain healthy because of thousands of such constant cellular monitoring and communications. Occasionally, however, this monitoring and communication breaks down and illness results. For instance, hypertension results when the body cannot detect and respond to increased blood pressure. Reasons for this are numerous. The body may retain too much sodium, and since water typically stays with sodium, blood volume[66] increases. The smooth muscle cells lining the blood vessels may be unable to respond to the neurotransmitter, so the diameter will not increase. Perhaps intracellular $[Ca^{2+}]$ remains elevated, so muscle cells of the heart and blood vessels cannot sufficiently relax. Maybe too many neurotransmitters are released from the neurons, and this constant barrage of stimulation abnormally elevates blood pressure.

In each of these examples, some part of the messenger and signal transduction pathway has broken down. Pharmaceutical drugs act as substitutes for, or blockers of, the body's signals[67] and attempt to restore the proper function to the cellular communication system by overriding the problem. If sodium imbalance is a cause of hypertension, diuretics increase sodium excretion and, as a result, increase water excretion. If smooth muscle cells cannot properly relax, nitroglycerin lowers $[Ca^{2+}]$. Calcium channel blockers decrease intracellular $[Ca^{2+}]$, and β-adrenergic receptor blockers, commonly referred to as beta-blockers, reduce the number of neurotransmitters that bind to the muscle cells.

What are some motives for developing and taking pharmaceutical drugs?

Our understanding of whether pharmaceutical drugs are good or bad may be affected by the motivation of pharmaceutical companies to develop and market drugs. In this consumer-driven free-market society, money does drive business, and a company's success is often marked by its profit, prestige, and competitiveness. According to mission and purpose statements of several leading pharmaceutical companies, these businesses also maintain a high focus on people. They are committed to "improve the quality of life and satisfy customer needs" (Merck),[68] to "dedicate ourselves to humanity's quest for longer, healthier, happier lives" (Pfizer),[69] to "enrich the lives of patients, families, communities and other stakeholders" (AstraZeneca),[70] and to "help people live longer, healthier and more active lives" (Eli Lilly).[71] Although the companies' general goal is to positively impact people's lives, certain people do not benefit. The practice of marketing drugs at high prices often excludes the developing world from benefiting from these drugs. Interestingly, a nonprofit pharmaceutical company, the Institute for OneWorld Health, was initiated in 2000 to develop affordable drugs to combat specific diseases in the developing world.[72]

People seem to have three main motives for taking pharmaceutical drugs: to treat an illness, to enhance mood, and to replace personal responsibility. Treating a medical problem is the most obvious and sensible motive. Yet, according to a recent combined press release from several federal agencies—the Office of National Drug Control Policy, Health and Human Services, Food and Drug Administration, and Drug Enforcement Agency—nonmedical use of specific pharmaceutical drugs is prevalent among Americans.[73] Since some abused pharmaceutical drugs bind to the same receptors as do the body's natural positive mood-enhancing molecules, the endorphins, they promote the same desirable feelings. Yet these effects on brain neurons make these pain relievers, tranquilizers, stimulants, and sedatives highly addictive.

Finally, our society seems to be relying on medication to fix problems rather than taking personal responsibility and action for the problems. American contemporary culture emphasizes autonomy, individualism, and progress. These postmodern thoughts infiltrate medicine and society's perceptions of disease. People seek to be in control and, oftentimes, are unwilling to accept responsibility for situations that are "out of control." Human problems or circumstances that hinder progress or interfere with one's sense of self-worth and individuality are often redefined as illnesses.[74] This process, called *medicalization*,[75] redefines the problem and eliminates blame and personal acceptance of consequence. Hypercholesterolemia (high cholesterol) and obesity[76] are examples. Admittedly, uncontrollable high cholesterol or obesity due to heredity warrants medication. Yet high cholesterol or obesity caused by poor diet and lifestyle choices does not. Nevertheless, many patients seek medication for hypercholesterolemia or surgical interventions for obesity without sufficiently altering their lifestyles. People often take medication for prolonged stress-induced high blood pressure, anxiety, or gastric ulcers rather than confront and deal with the root problem.

How should Christians respond to such motives?

Prestige and profit, two motivations for pharmaceutical companies, cause some Christians to balk. After all, they claim, the Bible speaks for humility and against the love of money. Yet, can Christians in good conscience lead and work for companies with two such motives? "Yes," as long as their personal motives remain pure. Christians in pharmaceutical administrative or leadership positions will have profit as one of their goals if they are committed to doing their job well. Money as a goal is not a bad thing as long as it is used wisely and does not override Christian morals. Contentment, humility, and a commitment to excellence to God's glory are not to be surpassed by personal pride and greed. Christians must use their God-given talents and be witnesses for Christ in the workplace. Interestingly, pharmaceutical companies value behavior consistent with Christlike character.[77]

Christians ought not discredit physiological explanations and pharmaceutical remedies, but they should use them responsibly. Graham Haydon, in his essay titled "On Being Responsible," defines responsibility as having choice to act, realizing accountability for choice, and knowing actions have consequences.[78] Responsibility, he says, is fundamental for living morally in the world. Taking individual action for the good of others is echoed in the words of the apostle Paul (Rom. 12:5; 15:1–6).

How do Christians use pharmaceuticals responsibly?

Drugs should not be taken for addictions.[79] Drugs should not be taken to cover up nonphysiological roots of physical, emotional, or mental distress[80] or as alternatives to confronting personal issues of pride, gluttony, greed, or laziness. Many Christians fall into the postmodern trap of medicating rather than confronting root issues. This should not be, for Christians belong to God (Rom. 1:6; 14:8; Eph. 1:4–8; Col. 3:3; 1 Peter 2:9; 1 John 3:1), live in community with others, and are not autonomous. They are not to be driven by personal achievement but by the will of God for His glory (1 Cor. 10:31; Eph. 1:11–12; 2:10). Furthermore, Christians' bodies are the Holy Spirit's temple (1 Cor. 3:16; 6:19–20). Good stewardship of this temple means not covering up physical symptoms that point to a deeper problem. Rather, it means confronting a deeper problem by asking God for strength, communicating with others, going to a brother or sister who has sinned or wronged us, admitting our misdeeds and asking forgiveness, and fellowshipping with other believers for encouragement. Christians are part of a community (Rom. 12:5, and note the "body" imagery of Eph. 4 and 5). This leaves no room for selfish individualism.

Responsible pharmaceutical drug use restores health and well-being; it does not enhance health and well-being.[81] The President's Council on Bioethics puts it this way: "In wanting to become more than we are, and in sometimes acting as if we were already superhuman or divine, we risk despising what we are and neglecting what we have. . . . In seeking brighter outlooks, reliable contentment, and dependable feelings of self-esteem in ways that bypass their usual natural sources, we risk flattening our souls, lowering our aspirations, and weakening our loves and attachments."[82]

Christians must realize the limitations of pharmaceutical drugs. The role of medicine is to "help us be healthy enough to act in ways indicative of a person who knows that the [purpose] of life is not dominating over the restrictions of our natural finitude but living faithfully towards God within the community of faith."[83] Certain "imperfections" cannot or should not be treated with medication; they are used for sanctification (2 Cor. 12:9–10; Phil. 4:11–13).

A proper balance of scientific and theological information is important to how we use technology, such as pharmaceuticals, and integrate it into everyday use.[84] Christians must "recognize the potential goods of innovation, but realistically anticipate and restrict its potential harms. This requires a correct understanding of human nature and of God's ultimate plans for our species that only the gospel can provide."[85] Two ways by which Christians can gain this understanding are first, to be educated by Christian physicians, scientists, and theologians, and second, for churches and medical personnel to help them identify what a good life is, as life within a Christian community of people often contrasts with society's individualistic definition.

QUESTIONS

1. Why should people be prescribed a pill? If for a sickness, who defines what a sickness is? If for enhanced quality of life, who defines the proper quality of life?

2. Are some diseases rooted in sin? If so, should drugs be developed to treat "sinful" diseases? Can sin, in fact, be treated with drugs?

3. Should millions of dollars be spent on developing a new drug that acts similarly to a drug already on the market?

4. Should Christians invest or participate in pharmaceutical research if alternative or natural medicine works?

NOTES

65. *Neurotransmitter* is a term given to chemical signals released by neurons. Examples of such neurotransmitters are acetylcholine and norepinephrine (also called noradrenalin).

66. Blood is 60 percent water, and volume is directly related to pressure. As volume increases, pressure increases.

67. Realize that pharmaceutical drugs prescribed to treat most illnesses interact with protein receptors in much the same way as do the body's innate signals. The chemical structure of many pharmaceutical drugs mimics the structure of the body's signals.

68. The Corporate Philosophy Mission Statement, copyright 2004, http://www.merck.com/about/mission.html.

69. Pfizer Mission Statement, copyright 2002–04, http://www.pfizer.com/are/mn_about_mission.html.

70. AstraZeneca Mission Statement, copyright 2004, http://www.astrazeneca-us.com/content/aboutUs/missionStatement.asp.

71. Eli Lilly and Company home page, copyright 2004, http://www.lilly.com. More information about the mission, purpose, and values of these leading pharmaceutical companies can be found on their respective websites.

72. Institute for OneWorld Health, copyright 2004, http://www.oneworldhealth.org; Gary Stix, "Making Drugs, Not Profits," *Scientific American* 290, no. 5 (May 2004): 42–44.

73. "Non-medical use of narcotic pain relievers, tranquilizers, stimulants, and sedatives ranks second (behind marijuana) as a category of illicit drug abuse among adults and youth; in 2002, 6.2 million Americans were current abusers of prescription drugs; [and] 13.7 percent of youth between the ages of 12 and 17 have abused prescription drugs at least once in their lifetimes." See also "U.S. Drug Prevention, Treatment, Enforcement Agencies Take on 'Doctor Shoppers,' 'Pill Mills,'" Office of Drug Control, March 2004, http://whitehousedrugpolicy.gov/pda/030104.html.

74. Peter Conrad, "Medicalization and Social Control," *Annual Review of Sociology* 18 (2004): 210, 215; Linda L. Layne, "The Cultural Fix: An Anthropological Contribution to Science and Technology Studies," *Science, Technology, and Human Values* 25 (2000): 492; A. M. Weinberg, "Can Technology Replace Social Engineering?" in Albert H. Teich, ed., *Technology and the Future*, 7th ed. (New York: St. Martin's Press, 1997), 57.

75. In this context, medicalization is not meant to include illness with root physiological causes (Conrad, "Medicalization and Social Control," 210).

76. Recently the Department of Health and Human Services and the Medicare agency have come closer to defining obesity as a disease. As a result, Medicare can cover certain obesity-related treatment health costs. Yet, should obesity, which can often be treated with lifestyle changes, be called an illness? For primary sources on this issue, see the following: George A. Bray, "Obesity Is a Chronic, Relapsing Neurochemical Disease," *International Journal of Obesity* 28 (2004): 34–38; Tommy G. Thompson, *Obesity Summit Speech*, United States Department of Health and Human Services, June 14, 2004, http://www.hhs.gov/news/speech/2004/040602.html; Clare Murphy, "Whose Fat Is It Anyway?" *BBC News Online*, July 27, 2004, http://news.bbc.co.uk/1/hi/world/americas/3912711.stm; "HHS Announces Revised Medicare Obesity Coverage Policy," United States Department of Health and Human Services, July 15, 2004, http://www.hhs.gov/news/press/2004pres/20040715.html; "Obesity Is Not a Disease," The International Size Acceptance Association, September 24, 2004, http://www.size-acceptance.org; David Crary, "Fight Bell Sounds for 'Fat Liberation,'" *Chicago Tribune*, August 3, 2004, sec. 1, 8.

77. A stated value of Merck and Co., Inc., is, "We recognize that the ability to excel—to most competitively meet society's and customers' needs—depends on the integrity, knowledge, imagination, skill, diversity and teamwork of our employees, and we value these qualities most highly" (see n. 4).

78. Graham Haydon, "On Being Responsible," *The Philosophical Quarterly* 28 (1978): 56.

79. Joseph R. Bianchine, "Drugs—Use and Misuse," *Pastoral Psychology* 23 (2004): 59.

80. Ibid.

81. Agnieszka Tennant, "Define Better: An Interview with Bioethicist C. Ben Mitchell," *Christianity Today*, January 2004, 42.
82. The President's Council on Bioethics, *Beyond Therapy*: *Biotechnology and the Pursuit of Happiness* (Washington, D.C., 2003).
83. Sansom Dennis, "Why Do We Want to Be Healthy? Medicine, Autonomous Individualism, and the Community of Faith," *Christian Scholar's Review* 23 (1994): 302.
84. Tennant, "Define Better," 34.
85. C. Christopher Hook, "The Techno-Sapiens Are Coming," *Christianity Today*, January 2004, 40.

SUGGESTED READING

For scientific pharmaceutical, pharmacological, or physiological information:

Bennett, P. N., and M. J. Brown, eds. *Clinical Pharmacology*. 9th ed. Edinburgh: Churchill Livingstone, 2003.

Brody, Theodore, Joseph Larner, and Kenneth P. Minneman, eds. *Human Pharmacology*: *Molecular to Clinical*. 3rd ed. St. Louis: Mosby–Year Book, 1998.

Saeb-Parsy, Kourosh, Ravi G. Assomull, Fakhar Z. Khan, Kasra Saeb-Parsy, and Eamonn Kelly. *Instant Pharmacology*. Chichester, Eng.: John Wiley and Sons, 1999.

For sources relating to faith and health:

Groopman, Jerome. *The Anatomy of Hope: How People Prevail in the Face of Illness*. New York: Random House, 2004.

Levin, Jeff. *God, Faith, and Health: Exploring the Spirituality-Healing Connection*. New York: John Wiley and Sons, 2001.

Matthews, Dale A., and Connie Clark. *The Faith Factor*: *Proof of the Healing Power of Prayer*. New York: Viking Penguin Putnam, 1998.

Is There Meaning beyond the Biomolecular?

Greta M. Bryson

Have you ever thought about what really happens when you eat or drink or even breathe? What happens to the food, the drink, the air? How does the body use this material to maintain life? Ultimately, these natural life-sustaining processes, and the control of them, are underpinned by complex molecular reactions and interactions that collectively fall within the purview of biochemistry. Biochemistry is study of the structure, function, and reactions of molecules that are essential for life. These molecules include proteins, lipids, carbohydrates, RNA and DNA, and many others.[86] They do not alone define life, and starting and continuing life is not as simple as adding the right chemicals in the right proportions. Rather, life continues as these molecules interact very specifically. The biochemist's role is to investigate and elucidate the particular ways in which these bioactive molecules function to support life.

What is life? What can biochemistry teach us about life? What can and should we do with our biochemical knowledge? These are highly relevant questions for everyone to consider but perhaps even more for Christians who are scientists. God's creation is "fearfully and wonderfully made" (Ps. 139:14). In Colossians 1:16–17, we read that "by him all things were created. . . . in him all things hold together." God created life and sustains life, and we can admire His awesome work even in the absence of scientific details. However, using the tools and knowledge of biochemistry, we can gain a unique perspective on what we call life as we consider life. God even tells us of ways to begin addressing our biomolecular questions:

> But ask the animals, and they will teach you,
>> or the birds of the air, and they will tell you;
> or speak to the earth, and it will teach you,
>> or let the fish of the sea inform you.
>
> —Job 12:7–8

It is the role of the biochemist to explain life on a molecular level in the manner that the Lord told Job. What is life and what do biochemical studies reveal about life? What are the consequences and implications of such knowledge, especially for Christian believers?

What is life?

Life can be described in a variety of ways, but the definition here will be restricted to using the following characteristics of living organisms: (1) the cell is the smallest unit of a living organism; (2) organisms that are alive have the ability to self-replicate or reproduce; and (3) living organisms have the ability to interact with and respond to their environment, including actions like eating and breathing. Intricate biochemical pathways sustain these characteristics of living organisms found in complex multicellular eukaryotic organisms, such as humans, and in more simple unicellular prokaryotic organisms, such as bacteria.[87]

What can a biochemist "know" about life?

What does life look like on a molecular level? The first characteristic of a living organism involves a cellular nature. If we look within the organism and examine the actions of individual cells, we find that there are molecular changes that occur as cells function and as they interact with each other. Intracellular communication takes place via multiple metabolic pathways.[88] Glycolysis, citric acid cycle, oxidative phosphorylation, and fatty acid oxidation are among the major intracellular pathways integral to supplying the energetic needs of the cell. Enzymes, or catalytic proteins, are central to these pathways, where they mediate the biochemical reactions in which molecules bind, chemically modify, and are themselves modified. For example, many enzymes, when bound to their substrate molecule, (1) change their three-dimensional shape, (2) convert their substrate to a different molecule, and (3) are themselves controlled, or regulated, by the action of other molecules.

Intercellular communication is also facilitated via specific molecular interactions. In neural fibers, neurotransmitters travel between neurons, or nerve cells. Neurotransmitters are small organic molecules that bind very specifically to protein receptors that span the membrane of the neuron.[89] As a result of a neurotransmitter binding to its receptor on the exterior of the cell, a chemical change occurs in the interior of the cell. When the neurotransmitter acetylcholine binds to a specific location on the acetylcholine receptor, the receptor responds by opening its barrel-like structure, forming a channel through which small cations, like sodium (Na^+), can pass into the otherwise ion impermeable cell.[90] When the ion concentration changes in the neuron, it causes a whole-cell response, which includes the release of more neurotransmitters that are able to affect cellular responses in neighboring cells. In these ways, molecular events are translated into cellular responses.

The second characteristic of living organisms is their ability to self-replicate. This is different from viruses and other subcellular units (e.g., prions),[91] which share some characteristics with living organisms but are not able to replicate in the absence of a host. In all known cellular organisms, DNA is the genetic material that is reproduced for the continuation of that organism's existence. The replication of DNA is a complex act that involves scores of protein and nucleic acid components and is subject to multiple biochemical control mechanisms. Furthermore, additional proteins are involved in the repair of DNA that has been erroneously replicated. The proteins that are involved in replication and repair interact with DNA via specific charge-charge, hydrophobic and hydrogen bonding interactions between the amino acids of the proteins and the nucleotides of the DNA. The proteins "recognize" and bind to specific DNA sequences. The tremendous specificity with which certain proteins interact with DNA, for example, is part of what allows organisms to faithfully replicate their genetic material and, when the occasional misincorporation, or mutation, is made, to repair the damage.

Eukaryotes and even many prokaryotes are very faithful in replication with an error rate of 1 in 10^8–10^{10}. Compare this with the error rate of a virus like the Human Immunodeficiency Virus, or HIV, which is estimated at 1 in 10^3–10^4. The inherent inability of HIV—and other viruses—to correct its own replication errors contributes to the development of drug-resistant strains of the virus. This was recently noted as a new multi-drug-resistant and virulent strain of HIV was identified and characterized in an individual in New York.[92]

Finally, living organisms interact with and respond to the environment. Eating, drinking, and breathing are among the ways that an organism does this. In higher animals, eating, and the ultimate digestion of food, while very physiological in character, is still governed by specific molecular interactions. Digestion is the result of breakdown of protein, lipid, and carbohydrate molecules from the diet by enzymes like proteases and lipases.[93] The products of this digestion are then able to enter into biochemical pathways in which these fuels are used to produce energy, much of it stored in the form of adenosine triphosphates, or ATP.

Likewise, the "simple" act of breathing involves a series of molecularly connected events that result in specific physiological outcomes.[94] When humans breathe air in, oxygen binds to the protein hemoglobin that is abundant in the red blood cells, a major component of blood. The oxygen is delivered by hemoglobin to the various tissues of our body, where it plays a vital role in metabolism. Hemoglobin is a protein comprised of two different but related protein chains, referred to as **a** chain (alpha) and **b** chain (beta). In each hemoglobin protein molecule, there are two **a** chains and two **b** chains that are joined together in a manner similar to Velcro—that is, very sticky but not permanently attached. Each chain has a non-protein molecule tightly associated with it that confers the ability to bind oxygen. This molecule, called heme, has an iron (II) atom bound to it. It is the specific interaction between the iron (II) atom and the oxygen molecule that we define as oxygen binding.[95]

In a nonliving system, if iron (II) comes in contact with and interacts with oxygen, the compound that is irreversibly formed is FeO_3, iron (III) oxide, or rust. However, in the context of this marvelous hemoglobin protein framework, the iron (II) that is bound in the heme structure is protected from being oxidized to iron (III), making the binding of oxygen a reversible process. Oxygen can bind and can be released without inflicting permanent change to the iron, the heme, or the protein.

As hemoglobin travels through the bloodstream and reaches various tissues, oxygen is unloaded to other proteins, including myoglobin, primarily a muscle protein. Myoglobin has one polypeptide chain, structurally resembling the **a** and **b** chains of hemoglobin, that has a single heme group with an iron (II) atom that binds oxygen in the same way hemoglobin does. Myoglobin has a greater affinity for oxygen, so that as hemoglobin bound with oxygen reaches the heart, for example, myoglobin, in essence, extracts the oxygen from the hemoglobin. Hemoglobin acts as an oxygen carrier, while myoglobin acts as a receiver. Ultimately, the oxygen is itself reduced to water while supporting the oxidation of fuel molecules, mostly the sugars and fats, that we get from our diet. The oxidation of these fuels results in the production of CO_2, carbon dioxide, which we exhale into the air. The respiratory cycle is oxygen in, carbon dioxide out.

What do we learn from biochemistry?

These few metabolic examples illustrate how wonderfully intricate the chemistry of life is. Yet even understanding the molecular nature of life does not help us to understand what life is or how we should take care of it. As stated at the outset, these molecules and their intriguing specific interactions do not alone define life. We cannot start and continue life by simply assembling all of the right pieces. Certainly we see that life continues as these biologically active molecules interact in very specific ways, and we can learn a great deal about living organisms by studying their biochemical reactions.

Biochemistry, while carefully teasing out the molecular nature and mechanisms of how life functions, does not and cannot satisfactorily explain why or how it is held together. What can we learn beyond the biomolecular to help us understand life? Scripture tells us that in Him "all the treasures of wisdom and knowledge" are held (Col. 2:3). Perhaps, as Romans 1:20 suggests, God's invisible qualities are reflected and understood from what has been made by Him.

Consider the biochemical studies of nonhuman mammals. Respiration, for example, occurs by a mechanism similar to that of humans. Their hemoglobin and myoglobin proteins serve the same functions as described above, with some changes in the sequence of amino acids that comprise their proteins. Some of these changes serve unique physiological functions. For example, whale myoglobin has a much higher affinity for oxygen than human myoglobin does. It binds oxygen more tightly than human myoglobin. This allows the whale to remain underwater for longer periods of time without having to come up to obtain more oxygen from the air. A relatively small change in the amino acid sequence provides a way for the whale myoglobin to facilitate this mammal's way of life. The purpose and plan for which the whale was created included this molecular adaptation, among others.

Not only do all mammals respire in a similar manner, but there are other living organisms that use globin-related proteins to bind and deliver oxygen. Species as diverse as chickens and rainbow trout, both nonmammal vertebrate species, have a hemoglobin-myoglobin system for oxygen delivery. Even invertebrates, like *C. elegans*, a species of worm, and *Tetrahymena*, a protozoan, produce a hemoglobin protein very similar in structure and function to human hemoglobin.[96] Indeed, it seems that all eukaryotic species studied to date share this special relationship with humans who bind O_2 via an iron (II)–heme-binding globin mechanism.

So what is it that the animals, birds, earth, fish—indeed, all of creation—teach humans about life? One thing they reveal to us is that we are molecularly similar. We share a molecular framework that is observed in our metabolic pathways and the molecules that are used to continue life. This also suggests that we are connected to creation.

While it is important for us to recognize and respect the fact that we are linked to creation, we also know that humans are unique. The creation of humankind by God and delineation of the purpose of humankind by God mark a departure from the rest of creation, as we are distinctively made in His image and likeness; we bear the *imago Dei*.[97] Scripture tells us that God "formed the man from the dust of the ground and breathed into his nostrils the breath of life, and the man became a living being" (Gen 2:7). God gave us His creation to use for food (sustenance) and for us to rule, or steward (Gen 1:26–31). Although we have seen a glimpse of how common biochemical pathways and principles connect and unite us with all of His living creation, the life that *we* experience is uniquely appointed by God.

Why is what a biochemist can "know" important?

The animals, birds, earth, and fish—in fact, all of the natural world—teach us that we share some common threads. Many scriptures point to a demand for us to learn about, explore, respect, love and care for creation (Gen. 2:15; Job 12:7–10; Ps. 104:10–30; Isa. 42:5; Rom. 1:20; Col. 1:15–20). As Christians, we are able to capture this concept from a theological point of view. God's creation is fearfully and wonderfully made, down to the molecules that support life (Ps. 139:14).

Ultimately, the goals of science and religion are certainly different but not at all incompatible. There are, however, some "rational boundaries" of scientific and religious efforts to understand the created world.[98] The general goal of Christian theology is to develop knowledge and understanding of the nature of the triune God and our relationship with Him and that which He has created. Part of the purpose of Scripture is to lead us to God, through faith in Jesus Christ by the prompting of the Holy Spirit. Scripture is one of the ways God reveals Himself to us as believers. The Bible is not intended to be a scientific textbook, but it does reveal certain principles about the created order. Still, the Bible does not speak to the details or mechanisms of creation as we have above in our discussion of the biomolecular characteristics of life.

The general goal of science is to develop knowledge and understanding of the nature of the world. For biochemists, this means understanding the chemistry of living organisms in a systematic manner. However, science is often driven by the conviction that scientists will be able to explain everything, including that which was necessary at "the beginning," to establish the living and nonliving world around us.[99] This reductionist approach effectively denies the possibility of more meaningful interpretation of the scientific data. That is, even if biochemistry is ultimately able to explain every single nuance and facet of the function of hemoglobin in oxygen transport, biochemists still will not be able to assign meaning beyond the molecular. To think that this is possible without seeking first the kingdom of God is arrogant and philosophically irresponsible. Augustine of Hippo considered such an effort unwise.

> The man, however, who puts so high a value on these things as to be inclined to boast himself one of the learned, and who does not rather inquire after the source from which those things which he perceives to be true derive their truth, and from which those others which he perceives to be unchangeable also derive their truth and unchangeableness, and who, mounting up from bodily appearances to the mind of man, and finding that it too is changeable (for it is sometimes instructed, at other times uninstructed) does not strive to make all things redound to the praise and love of the one God from whom he knows that all things have their being;—the man, I say, who acts in this way may seem to be learned, but wise he cannot in any sense be deemed.[100]

Our Christian faith demands that "we demolish arguments and every pretension that sets itself up against the knowledge of God, and we take captive every thought to make it obedient to Christ" (2 Cor. 10:5). This verse indicates that even when science has elucidated mechanisms and molecular connections, we are called to bring that knowledge before the Father.

> Whatever has been rightly said by the heathen, we must appropriate to our uses. These, therefore, the Christian, when he separates himself in spirit from the miserable fellowship of these men, ought to take away from them, and to devote to their proper use in preaching the gospel. Their garments, also,—that is, human institutions such as are adapted to

that intercourse with men which is indispensable in this life,—we must take and turn to a Christian use.[101]

What does biochemistry mean to a Christian?

Biochemistry as a field of study has been able to greatly impact life. Our increase in knowledge about the fundamental molecular mechanisms that sustain our metabolic pathways and keep us physically alive has improved our overall health as a species. Biochemical studies of animals, insects, plants, and humans have revealed volumes of information about what is necessary for a life-sustaining diet, identified causes of disease states, and established ways to alleviate disease states, among others. We have been able to learn more about how we should and should not steward God's creation.

We have not yet plumbed the depths of understanding life. Indeed, with all of our knowledge, we have not even approached the limits of comprehension of God's creation. Arguably, one of the important things we have gained from biochemistry is a brief glimpse into our heavenly Father's mind. We have gained and continue to gain the ability to see, demonstrate, and occasionally even prove the intricacy of the work of God the Father, the creator and sustainer of us all. This is a spiritual act of worship. "How many are your works, O LORD! In wisdom you made them all" (Ps. 104:24).

QUESTIONS

1. Society at large has surely physically benefited from biochemical knowledge, but what about the less tangible gains and losses? How has biochemistry changed the way we think about life? Are we doomed to view life as a solely molecular experience? Will we continue to look to tweaking our "biochemical status" to give us advantages in life?

2. With the use of herbicides, humans have the potential to increase crop yields, a benefit to society. At the same time, modified plants have been developed that have genetic resistance to herbicides. What are the theological implications of modifying the genome of a plant? How is our view of the stewardship of creation affected by these developments?

3. With the potential to do both harm and good with biochemical knowledge, is this a viable area of study for a Christian?

NOTES

86. Proteins are polymers of amino acids. Proteins are also called polypeptide chains, in reference to the peptide bond that joins the amino acid monomers. Amino acids are the building blocks of proteins. DNA and RNA are polymers of deoxyribonucleic acid and ribonucleic acid, respectively. Polymers are molecules that are composed of many

smaller units (monomers) that are joined, or bonded, together in a regular fashion. Polymers may be composed of the same units or building blocks, or may be made up from several different kinds of monomers. Lipids and carbohydrates are commonly known as fats and sugars, respectively.

87. A biochemical, or metabolic, pathway is defined as a "series of connected enzymatic reactions that produce specific products" (Donald Voet, Judith G. Voet, and Charlotte E. Pratt, *Fundamentals of Biochemistry* [New York: John Wiley & Sons, 1999], 355).

88. The term *intracellular* refers to those activities that take place in the interior of the cell. The term *intercellular* is applied to actions that occur between neighboring cells.

89. Protein receptors are polypeptides that are imbedded in the lipid bilayer that composes the cellular membrane. The polypeptide chain weaves up and down through the membrane, often assuming a barrel-like structure.

90. Acetylcholine binding to its receptor ultimately causes, among other actions, muscle contraction. Several known nerve poisons, like sarin gas, specifically inhibit acetylcholinesterase, the enzyme that destroys acetylcholine, and ends the signal transmission. In the absence of functional acetylcholinesterase, acetylcholine continues to cause transmission of muscle nerve signals, which can result in heart failure.

91. *Prions* are proteins that occur naturally in brain tissue of mammals. This protein becomes an infectious agent when the three-dimensional structure of the protein is altered. The mechanism by which it changes conformation is currently unknown. Mad cow disease and Creutzfeldt-Jakob disease are well-known brain diseases that are a result of prion infection. See Stanley B. Prusiner, "The Prion Diseases," *Scientific American* 275 (1995): 48–57; and David Westaway and George A. Carlson, "Mammalian Prion Proteins: Enigma, Variation and Vaccination," *Trends in Biochemical Science* 27 (2002): 301–7.

92. Marc Santora, Lawrence K. Altman, and Donald G. McNeil Jr., *New York Times*, February 12, 2005, A1.

93. Proteases are enzymes that catalyze the breakdown of proteins into smaller peptides and amino acid monomers. Lipases catalyze the breakdown of fats into their constituent fatty acids and glycerol backbones.

94. Breathing here refers to respiration, involving consumption and ultimately reduction of oxygen, O_2, to water, H_2O.

95. Christopher K. Mathews, K. E. van Holde, and Kevin G. Ahern, *Biochemistry*, 3rd ed. (San Francisco: Benjamin/Cummings, 2000), 212–30.

96. Ross Hardison, "The Evolution of Hemoglobin," *American Scientist* 87, no. 2 (March 1999): 126–37.

97. John Walton, *Genesis: From Biblical Text ... to Contemporary Life* (Grand Rapids: Zondervan, 2001).

98. James A. Marcum, "Exploring the Rational Boundaries between the Natural Sciences and Christian Theology," *Theology and Science* 1, no. 2 (2003): 203–20.

99. Sir John Eccles, "Modern Biology and the Turn to Belief in God," in Roy Abraham Varghese, ed., *The Intellectuals Speak Out about God* (Chicago: Regnery Gateway, 1984), 50.

100. Augustine, *On Christian Doctrine*, bk. 2, chap. 38, pt. 57 (selections). Translation is from series 1, vol. 2 of the *Nicene and Post-Nicene Fathers*, published 1886–90 and in the public domain (http://ccat.sas.upenn.edu/jod/augustine.html).

101. Ibid., bk. 2, chap. 40, pt. 60.

SUGGESTED READING

Falk, Darrel R. *Coming to Peace with Science: Bridging the Worlds between Faith and Biology.* Downers Grove, Ill.: InterVarsity Press, 2004.

Pratt, Charlotte W., and Kathleen Cornely. *Essential Biochemistry.* Hoboken, N.J.: John Wiley & Sons, 2004.

HOW ARE TECHNOLOGY
AND ENGINEERING RELATED
TO CHRISTIANITY?

The development of technology has affected humanity in immeasurable ways. Technology was important in early cultures and remains a driving force for science and economics. Electronic and digital products dot the landscape of most homes in America, and electronic communication has closed the gaps between continents. The world communicates faster, processes data faster, and creates technostructures where large-scale business and industry flourish. The world of engineers meshes well with technology because engineers design, manufacture, and operate technology. Their influence in creating solutions to problems and making practical applications of technology serves well to enhance and move cultures to higher levels of efficiency.

Even with all the engineering ingenuity of humans applied to the world, there is still nothing that compares with the work of Jesus Christ, the chief engineer.

Should Christians Embrace Technology?

Peter K. Walhout

What exactly is technology?
First appearing in sixteenth-century English from ancient Greek origins, the word *technology* has taken on a larger meaning since the Industrial Revolution as certain aspects of technology have come to dominate our lives. Technology is now colloquially associated not only with the *processes* involved in manipulating nature to create devices and tools, but also with the finished *objects* themselves. For example, the creation of an audio compact disc involves converting analog sound waves into pits on a plastic surface. A CD player later reads these pits as a string of binary data and turns it back into sound waves. This complex engineering process, together with the scientific knowledge that undergirds it, is the technology of CD audio recording. However, in modern usage, the end-product disc and CD player are also called technology.

Sloppiness in using and defining the word *technology* can be dangerous. If the products of technology are lumped in with technology itself, then an assumption that technology is good may cause us to think those products are necessarily good too. Doing so surreptitiously lets economic forces and commercial advertising determine what is valued in our lives.[1] Even if the technology of digital recording is valued, the resultant CD should not *necessarily* be valued. As technological products continue to permeate our economy, culture, and private lives, the challenge is to be discerning in the use of technological objects and to hold on to the important nontechnological aspects of our lives, such as carrying on face-to-face conversation, making music, and worshiping in a church.

What does Christianity teach about the value of technology?

The development and use of technology is a natural, God-ordained human activity that Christians should embrace.[2] David Gelernter has said, "To hate technology is in the end to hate humanity, to hate yourself, because technology is what human beings do."[3] However, one must be wary of how technology is transforming our culture.[4] Because Christians are called to stewardship and holiness, they are also called to be thoughtful, careful users of modern technology.

The Bible obviously does not explicitly deal with technology—there is no verse that says, "Blessed are the design engineers, for they shall create the society of tomorrow." However, technical knowledge and craftsmanship, at least on a small scale, are clearly God-given and valued by God. The construction of both the tabernacle and the temple relied on technology (Ex. 31:3–7; 1 Kings 6; 9:3), and God revealed to Noah the engineering specifications for the ark by which humanity was saved from the flood (Gen. 6:13–18). Christ himself was a carpenter and used woodworking technology on a daily basis to help support his family.

> "Technology is a distinctly human cultural activity in which human beings exercise freedom and responsibility in response to God by forming and transforming the natural creation, with the aid of tools and procedures, for practical ends and purposes."
>
> —from *Responsible Technology*, Stephen V. Monsma, editor

Christian theology also provides a framework to consider the value of technology and the power it bestows on humanity.[5] First, humans were created in the image of God and hence are creative beings. Devising new tools and technologies is one way we manifest the *imago Dei*. Furthermore, these tools can be used to assist humanity with its charge of stewarding creation (Gen. 1:26–29; 2:15). Stewardship involves caring for and maintaining the *shalom* of God's creation, a state of harmony and order within all the earth and between the Creator and his creation.[6] Second, humans and human civilizations are fallen and thus often use technology for purposes that fail to bring *shalom* to the world. A world living in *shalom* would not need to use the technology of atomic fission to create horrible weapons of mass destruction. Third, God redeemed creation through Jesus Christ and His atoning work on the cross. Humanity is no longer bound to sin, but is free and empowered by the Holy Spirit to usher in the kingdom of God here on earth. Redeeming creation involves eradicating disease, feeding the hungry, clothing the naked, and protecting our natural environment. Clearly technology should be used if Christians are serious about striving to accomplish these goals in an effective manner. Harnessing the technology of atomic fission to replace the burning of fossil fuels as a source of energy is an example of such striving. Nuclear energy is a prime example, however, of how new technology inevitably leads to new problems.

Philosopher Albert Borgmann writes that "technology advances and is sustained by regardless power."[7] "Regardless power" refers to the fact that technology, at least in theory, always works regardless of the situation it is embedded in or the particular humans who are using it. Borgmann says a more "careful power" is called for in the use of technology, a restrained use of power that fosters creaturely relationships and improves difficult circumstances.[8] A careful use of technological power will strive to bring its future development and consumption in line with the biblical principles of the Beatitudes, where humility, peacemaking, mercy, and purity of heart are valued over selfishness, conflict, ruthlessness, and greed.

> "America would almost certainly be a happier, better place if TV were to vanish without a trace ... and yet no serious person would ever propose a law to ban TV."
>
> —David Gelernter, *Machine Beauty*

Why should we be wary of technology?

One danger of technology is that it produces consumer products that can easily become idols.[9] An idol is anything that claims the type of loyalty that belongs to God alone. If loyalty is manifested in offerings of time, talent, and treasure, it is obvious that many are guilty of idolatrous behavior toward technological objects. For example, we may spend too much time watching frivolous television shows or spend too much money on lavish stereo systems and upscale automobiles instead of giving to the church. While these examples fall short of overt idolatrous worship of a golden calf, they do illustrate that the best we have to offer God is easily wasted on the trappings of technology.

There are also practical problems with technology that appear at both the individual and the public level. Individual problems are more familiar—reckless driving due to talking on cell phones, carpal tunnel syndrome, and obesity. One must not forget, however, the ill effects of technology endured by society as a whole. These problems include exploitive labor practices, overconsumption, toxic waste, and increased exposure to violence in movies and television. Many technologies fall into both categories. Biotechnology is an example of this as people grapple at both the individual and societal levels with "advances" like the morning-after abortion pill, plastic surgery, and "designer genes" to either predict or control physical aspects of offspring.

Technology is an integral part of our pluralistic culture and inevitably shapes individuals' lives whether they realize it or not. Christians need to be at the forefront of society, asking the difficult questions regarding the ethical use and consumption of technology. While Christians are called to responsibly use technology to further God's kingdom on earth, they also must be alert to the values and patterns of behavior that technology and its attendant economic forces foist on the unsuspecting world.

> "You need a pilot's license to use these."
>
> Dr. Robert Adler, inventor of the TV remote control, on modern remote controls

QUESTIONS

1. Why are the modern technological miracles of modern medicine not accessible to all who need them?

2. Should churches officially advocate abstinence from television?

3. Does technology inevitably cause cultures to become more hedonistic in the use of free time?

NOTES

1. Alan Jacobs has written a series of entertaining essays regarding this phenomenon in the computer industry: "Computer Control: Who's in Charge?" *Books and Culture* 8, no. 3 (2002): 16; "Life among the Cyber Amish," *Books and Culture* 8, no. 4 (2002): 14; "The Virtues of Resistance," *Books and Culture* 8, no. 5 (2002): 22.

2. One who naively opposes technology on principle is pejoratively called a *Luddite*. The term originates from a group of British workers who destroyed machines in the fabric industry during labor unrest between 1811 and 1816. For more, see David Linton, "Luddism Reconsidered," *Etcetera*, Spring 1985, 32–36.

3. David Gelernter, *Machine Beauty: Elegance and the Heart of Technology* (New York: Basic Books, 1998), 134. Gelernter is a professor of computer science at Yale. He was seriously wounded by the man who is called the Unabomber, Ted Kaczynski, an avowed Luddite who is in prison for a string of bombings from 1978 to 1995.

4. See Neal Postman, *Technopoly* (New York: Vintage Books, 1993). Postman's book provides an in-depth analysis of this phenomenon in American culture.

5. Stephen V. Monsma, ed., *Responsible Technology* (Grand Rapids: Eerdmans, 1986), 44–47.

6. Nicholas Wolterstorff, *Until Justice and Peace Embrace* (Grand Rapids: Eerdmans, 1983), 70.

7. Albert Borgmann, *Power Failure* (Grand Rapids: Brazos, 2003), 88.

8. Ibid., chap. 5, "Power and Care."

9. See 1 Cor. 10:23 and 1 John 5:21.

SUGGESTED READING

Berry, Wendell. *What Are People For?* New York: North Point Press, 1990.

Borgmann, Albert. *Power Failure: Christianity in the Culture of Technology.* Grand Rapids: Brazos, 2003.

Gelernter, David. *Machine Beauty: Elegance and the Heart of Technology.* New York: Basic Books, 1998.

Jacobs, Alan. "Harry Potter's Magic." *First Things* 99 (2000): 35–38.

Johnson, Steven. *Emergence: The Connected Lives of Ants, Brains, Cities, and Software.* New York: Scribner, 2001.

Monsma, Stephen V., ed. *Responsible Technology.* Grand Rapids: Eerdmans, 1986.

Petroski, Henry. *The Evolution of Useful Things.* New York: Vintage, 1994.

Postman, Neil. *Technopoly: The Surrender of Culture to Technology.* New York: Vintage, 1993.

Ratner, Mark A., and David Ratner. *Nanotechnology: A Gentle Introduction to the Next Big Idea.* Upper Saddle River, N.J.: Pearson/Prentice Hall, 2002.

Schultze, Quentin J. *Habits of the High-Tech Heart.* Grand Rapids: Baker, 2002.

Does Engineering Contribute to a Better Future?

Stewart M. DeSoto and Gayle E. Ermer

What is engineering?

What do engineers *do*? In a word, engineers *design*. Just about every product we use today has been developed by an engineer or a team of engineers. Engineers continually attempt to invent or improve an object or system that will be superior to all other existing solutions. In a sense, everyone is an amateur engineer. Consider the tasks of choosing and configuring a sound system for your home or organizing an unruly garage. In solving this type of problem, products and materials must be evaluated and chosen to fit some particular set of requirements. For the sound system, these might include complete sound coverage for the room, connectivity with particular components, and aesthetic placement of speakers. For the garage, these might include low cost, high strength, and ease of installation. In the discipline of engineering, these desired properties are called design *specifications*, or *specs* for short. A typical view of the overall process of engineering a new design, from initial brainstorming to marketable product, is sketched in figure 10.1.

Each of these many tasks requires a certain expertise. On the one hand, the initial development stages benefit from creative insights from individuals with the ability to envision new possibilities beyond what already exists. On the other hand, diligent analysis of preliminary results from computer simulations implementing theoretical calculations is essential to assist in choosing among several design alternatives. After the concept is chosen, systematic design methodologies, and very often additional cycles back through the earlier creative stages, are necessary to carefully guide the project to fruition. With the final product in hand, a team of *applications* engineers with strong interpersonal skills is needed to promote the benefits of the innovative new solution and customize it for specific users. To complete a large-scale modern engineering project, hundreds of specialists (e.g., in design, testing, production, applications, and sales) must work closely together. In contrast, a simple engineering project like the garage storage problem may be completed by a single individual capable of performing all of the tasks.

The products that modern engineering teams design and build are incredibly complex. A single automobile is made up of more than 30,000 parts of 4,000 different types. A Boeing 747 aircraft includes 6 million separate components. For this reason, most engineering projects involve large groups of people. Creative problem-solving requires the sharing of ideas. Engineers thus need to be able to interact effectively with others. In addition, the products engineers design have many stakeholders. An electrical grid goes far beyond an individual person, business, community, or even country. Often much is riding on the success of an engineer's design. If the garage shelving system turns out not to be strong enough, some of the

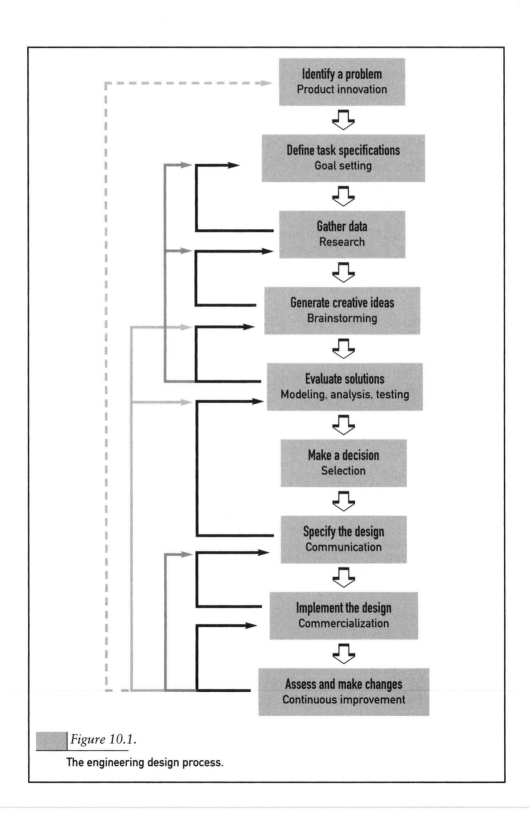

Figure 10.1.

The engineering design process.

tools may fall and break. If an airplane design has a slight flaw, the implications may be far more serious.

Engineers love the challenge of creating useful new products to help improve society. As part of this task, they often ask provocative questions. The garage storage engineer might ask: "Would the shelves sag less in the middle if I could find or create a more rigid shelving material? Could the installation process go faster if there were a more efficient way to fasten pieces together?" Clearly, broad-based knowledge beyond simple "storage technology" is helpful when answering such questions. On the larger scale, professional engineers ask: "What will hydrogen fuel cell cars of the future look like, and what kind of infrastructure will make them practical? Can we build an elevator attached to Earth's equator to ferry people into space? Can lives be saved by making a car's frame *weaker* rather than stronger, reducing impact forces during a collision?" To probe such issues, individual creativity can be as important as specific scientific knowledge. For this reason, engineering is sometimes described as more *art* than science.

> "Technical and scientific work is usually fun. In fact, creative technical work provides much the same satisfaction that is obtained from painting, writing, and composing or performing music."
>
> Jerome B. Wiesner, engineer

At first glance, it may be easy to mistake an engineer for a scientist. A modern engineer is usually an expert in some subfield of science and/or technology. But engineering is not just applied science. Science is primarily concerned with the effort to understand and describe physical reality, and the scientific ideal is to be as objective as possible in this quest. Engineering does supply many of the tools scientists use to study nature (e.g., electron microscopes and particle accelerators). But, in engineering, the final goals of a project are to satisfy one or more *human* needs and desires. Clearly, knowledge of the natural sciences together with leaps of creativity are necessities in achieving this. But without taking into account the psychological, social, and economic realities of the human condition, an engineering project is bound to fail.[10]

For example, the Chicago-based telecommunications company, Motorola, had a vision for a truly global satellite-telephone network named Iridium. The company's idea was to place seventy-seven satellites into orbit, symbolically mirroring the atomic number of iridium, an element found worldwide. This colossal engineering scheme, costing billions of dollars, was actually achieved in 1998. Less than three years later, however, and despite introducing breathtaking new technology, Iridium declared bankruptcy. The financial implosion was due to a much weaker than anticipated demand for the service. The engineers built the system because they *could*, but were shortsighted about the marketplace rewards for doing so.[11]

A brief history of engineering: Was Noah the first engineer?

According to Genesis 6, Noah built a large, three-level boat following a very precise set of instructions, which included among other specifications, the length of the boat and the necessary construction materials. In this case, the design specs came directly from God, although the actual handiwork was left to Noah. Was Noah an engineer? Actually, Noah was a craftsman, or what we may call a *proto-engineer*. Although our modern concept of *engineering* per se did not exist during Bible times, ancient peoples clearly used the range of technologies available to them. In the first pages of the Old Testament, there is already a reference to craftsmen working with brass and iron (Gen. 4:22). The Old Testament temple in Jerusalem was built by many different types of craftspersons and artisans, including stone-cutters, engravers, and workers of gold, bronze, and iron (1 Chron. 22:2; 2 Chron. 2:7). In the New Testament, Paul practiced tent-making, a common craft of that time. Since the time of Adam and Eve, then, knowledgeable master craftspersons have passed down their knowledge and skills to apprentices, the process repeating over countless centuries.

> "The ideal engineer is a composite. He is not a scientist, he is not a mathematician, he is not a sociologist or a writer; but he may use the knowledge and techniques of any or all of these disciplines in solving engineering problems."
>
> N. W. Dougherty, engineer

However, the modern "engineer" didn't appear until the nineteenth century. The so-called golden age of engineering lasted from about 1830 to 1950. It was during this period that the field of engineering differentiated itself from simple craftwork by incorporating numerous innovations, including systematic design planning, newly discovered scientific and mathematical principles, and abstract design tools such as the blueprint.

By the beginning of the twentieth century, engineers were increasingly seen as potential saviors of humankind, and the machines they created were the instruments of salvation. Inventions such as the sewing machine (1830), typewriter (1867), electric lightbulb (1879), and air conditioner (1902) were widely viewed as the first steps toward liberating humankind from the drudgery of manual labor. Moreover, transportation technologies like the steam train (1830s), mass-produced automobile (1900s), and aircraft (1900s) were widely perceived as taking humanity to dizzying new heights by providing unprecedented freedom to traverse the globe. The invention of the telephone (1876), the radio tuner (1916), and the television (1927) revolutionized personal communication and entertainment. It was thought (and not only by engineers) that the engineering profession could help save humanity, not only through the fruits of its labor, but even more so by its modern, logical way of thinking. In 1902 the president of the American Society of Civil Engineers said: "And in the future, even more than in the present, will the secrets of power be in his [the engineer's] keeping, and more and more will he be a leader and benefactor of men. That his place in the esteem of his fellows and of the world will keep pace with his growing capacity and widening achievement is as certain as that effect will follow cause."[12] Based on the achievements of the nineteenth century, his boasts were not entirely ill-founded.

However, in the years surrounding the Second World War, our society's outlook on the notion of technological "progress" darkened dramatically. The atomic bombs unleashed on Nagasaki and Hiroshima had brought a swift end to the war with Japan, and yet at the same time they demonstrated the godlike power of scientists and engineers. This was unnerving to many, and the subsequent arms race with the Soviet Union, bringing potential for global annihilation, catalyzed strong opposition to nuclear weapons and other "dangerous" forms of advanced technology.

Furthermore, awareness of the hazards unavoidably coupled with implementation of technology was not entirely new. In 1642, just after the arrival of the Pilgrims on America's east coast, a Narragansett tribesman charged, "Our fathers had plenty of deer and skins, our plains were full of deer, as also our woods, and of turkeys, and our coves full of fish and fowl. But these English have gotten our land, they with scythes cut down the grass and with axes fell the trees; . . . and we shall all be starved."[13] Recently it has become popular to view such statements as a rejection of all forms of technology and to romanticize peoples with relatively low-technology lifestyles as living "in harmony with nature" and as superior in some ways to our own "advanced" culture. We must realize, however, that Native Americans used all the technologies available to make their lives more convenient and fulfilling (e.g., snowshoes and birch-bark canoes for transportation; traps, hoes, axes, and wooden utensils for food gathering and preparation; bows and arrows for warfare). Even so, the lack of advanced technologies contributed to a decreased life span compared with modern humans.

Is engineering morally neutral?

Does Christian faith have any bearing on engineering? One author has pointedly asked, "Is there such a structure as a 'Christian bridge'?"[14] If so, how would it differ from a "non-Christian" one? Engineering appears to be a natural human instinct, as Henry Petroski, an engineering professor at Duke University, notes in his book *To Engineer Is Human*.[15] Christians affirm this by noting that we are created in God's image. According to Genesis 1–2, God created the solar system, magnetism, water, and chickens all for our benefit. We thus emulate God when we share in the process of design and creation. Since we are finite beings, we cannot create from nothing, but God has entrusted us with the resources of this world to use as our raw materials. Engineering is one of the ways Christians can choose to steward creation or to "fill the earth and subdue it" (Gen. 1:28), which is referred to as the cultural mandate.

Is engineering entirely good?

We must not forget that the fall had an immense effect on humankind and the creation. Technology, part of the created order, has thus also unavoidably been corrupted. The systems developed by engineers are inevitably subject to failure. Sometimes catastrophes happen, as in the explosions of the *Challenger* and *Columbia* space shuttles and the meltdown of the Chernobyl nuclear reactor. The power of technology can also be purposefully used for evil ends—consider the use of jet planes by terrorists to bring down skyscrapers on 9/11. We can never completely anticipate unintended uses or side-effects of an engineered solution. Something that looks benign initially may prove to have catastrophic consequences later. Or it may benefit some people but turn out to be harmful to others.

Technologies are never entirely good or bad. Yet neither can technological artifacts be considered neutral, for they are inherently biased toward specific uses and reflect the values held by both designers and users. For example, an SUV is designed to have extra power for towing and off-road driving, resulting in significantly lower fuel efficiency. Such vehicles, ironically, are most often used for urban transportation simply because consumers desire them for their rugged, recreational image. Some might argue this to be a waste of fuel and therefore an irresponsible use of scarce resources. Knowing this, some question whether the design, promotion, and use of such vehicles is responsible. All individuals, from engineers to marketers to end-users, should assume some degree of responsibility for the actual marketplace uses of an engineered product.[16]

> "Engineering is the art of modeling materials we do not wholly understand, into shapes we cannot precisely analyze, so as to withstand forces we cannot properly assess, in such a way that the public has no reason to suspect the extent of our ignorance."
>
> A. R. Dyke, British Institute of Structural Engineers

Do engineers contribute to a better future?

Are engineers the source of many of the ills our society faces today? Some people insist that something is rotten at the core of our highly engineered technological civilization and that scientists and engineers, as our modern-day "prophets," bear much of the blame. In the *Matrix* movies, a dystopian future is portrayed. In this nightmare, machines originally designed by *engineers* to serve humans become conscious and enslave the human race in a matrix of pods, using their bodies as an energy source. The worst part of the humans' fate is that they are unaware of their true condition because the machines provide a pleasant alternate reality piped directly into their brains. Also, the name of the popular heavy metal band Rage Against the Machine makes their antitechnology worldview obvious, the term *machine* being a metaphor for modern technology and more generally all that is wrong in the world. One of their albums proudly states in all caps: "NO SAMPLES, KEYBOARDS OR SYNTHESIZERS USED IN THE MAKING OF THIS RECORDING." Theodore Kaczynski (the Unabomber), a professor of mathematics at the University of California at Berkeley, became so concerned with the effect of technology on society that he began an eighteen-year terror campaign, sending mail bombs to individuals at the vanguard of technological research. There is an ever-expanding list of technological concerns in the popular culture, including a "grey-goo" of self-reproducing nanoparticles (tiny chunks of matter only nanometers across), genetically modified food (GMO or "frankenfood"), and big-brother surveillance via ubiquitous nano-scale cameras and computer networks.

Intellectuals have also pondered the negative roles of technology in our society. Neil Postman describes contemporary American society as a *technopoly*, in which we have succumbed to "the submission of all forms of cultural life to the sovereignty of technique and technology."[17] In 1973 E. F. Schumacher published the book *Small Is Beautiful*, sharply criticizing the giant-sized, centralized, and resource-depleting technologies of that time and advocating small-scale technological solutions "as if people mattered."[18] Christian thinkers have also considered the role of technology and its place in Christian life and thought. French sociologist Jacques Ellul wrote a powerful critique in *The Technological Society*, questioning whether New Testament Christianity can even coexist with modern society's emphasis on *technique*.[19] Ellul's writing is said to have had some influence on Kaczynski's adoption of his radical antitechnology views.[20]

In contrast to this bleak view of engineering technology, there is a vocal movement that foresees an amazing new world in which science and technology will give us incredible powers. Especially in such emerging engineering fields as nanotechnology (the manipulation of matter at the atomic scale), artificial intelligence, and synthetic biotechnology, proponents of this movement believe the future has no boundaries. They predict the emergence of infinite free energy via solar nanotechnology as well as futuristic Star Trek–type molecular assemblers capable of efficiently constructing electronic devices, clothing, building materials, and even food, all on an atom-by-atom basis.[21] These technology enthusiasts even envision our world returning to its natural pristine state as vast areas presently needed for agriculture are gradually converted back to forests, prairies, and wetlands.

As Christians, what are we to make of two such radically differing visions of the future of our planet? Clearly a careful analysis is called for, all the more so since the

TABLE 10.1. QUESTIONS TO ASK OF A PROPOSED ENGINEERING TECHNOLOGY.[22]

Does the Technology Promote . . .	
Cultural Appropriateness?	Does the technology fit the society in which it will be used, taking into account appropriate cultural constraints?
Transparency?	Is the composition and use of the technology clear to all, and are the risks and benefits honestly communicated?
Stewardship?	Will the resources entrusted to us by God be used frugally and efficiently, minimizing harmful effects on the environment?
Harmony?	Will the design be pleasing and attractive to use and promote healthy relationships?
Justice?	Will the benefits and burdens of a technology be allocated fairly across society?
Caring?	Will the technological solution address real needs and express Christian love to all individuals?
Trust?	Is the technology reliable and worthy of trust on the part of those affected by it?

pace of technological change will only increase in the years to come. Although the creative impulses of humankind have unavoidably been affected by sin, careful discernment may help guide us and give us hope. Since technology impacts individuals and societies in so many varied ways, we need to ask holistic questions when evaluating new technologies, to reflect the entire scope of how people live and interact (see table 10.1). These questions may be helpful for "amateur engineers" in evaluating which technologies to incorporate into their lives or which public policies to support. They are also essential for professional engineers to be mindful of as they guide the process of technology development.

We need to recognize the potential impact of each new technology, acknowledging the inevitable hazards alongside the desired benefits. Some technologies, like chemical weapons or undetectable plastic handguns, are inherently dangerous and lend themselves to morally questionable uses. These kinds of technologies may need to be carefully controlled. Creative redesign may help to reduce the possibility of misuse. For example, a biometric identification system designed into a handgun could allow only the authorized individual to use it. Other technologies (e.g., genetic engineering) may not be as inherently dangerous and may even potentially provide great benefits, but may nevertheless be troubling for Christians. We need to make sure in our development of new technologies that worthy ends never justify unethical means, no matter how wonderful the promises appear at the outset.

> "Engineers ... are not superhuman. They make mistakes in their assumptions, in their calculations, in their conclusions. That they make mistakes is forgivable; that they catch them is imperative. Thus it is the essence of modern engineering not only to be able to check one's own work but also to have one's work checked and to be able to check the work of others."
>
> Henry Petroski,
> *To Engineer Is Human*

Although the task may be difficult, trying to anticipate—and correct—the unintended side-effects of any novel technology is essential. Airbags in automobiles were initially hailed as a powerful lifesaving tool in head-on collisions. An unanticipated side-effect was eventually discovered. The rapid inflation of the airbags was causing occasional fatal injuries for young children. Engineering changes in the airbag design and statements that young children should ride in the rear seat of the vehicle helped to minimize this risk. Engineers try to predict such unexpected outcomes, but anticipating all potential problems is almost impossible. In the real world, there are always tradeoffs in design, for example, between risk and expense. In theory, we could make cars, airplanes, or nuclear power plants extremely safe, but the costs to implement the necessary fail-safe systems would be prohibitively expensive. An important part of an engineer's job is to help make these cost-benefit analyses, which are often literally a matter of life and death to customers, or even the public at large.

Some critical engineering problems are already widely known. Our reliance on the burning of fossil fuels to power our society brings a multitude of negative consequences, including political vulnerability, smog, oil spills, acid rain, and global warming. Most important, a carbon-based energy system is not sustainable. As the nations of the two-thirds world bring their consumption levels up to ours, global energy demands will only increase. The challenge is for engineers to develop new energy strategies while simultaneously anticipating potential negative consequences. These may not be at all obvious. For example, even the seemingly innocuous solution of using the wind to generate power is not without drawbacks. Huge wind turbines may be noisy, land-intensive, a visual blight, and a hazard to birds. Finding a way to meet the world's future power needs is a pressing and extremely challenging problem among many others that our society faces.

As Christians, we know that despite all the apparent progress humanity may make in its quest toward improving life on our planet, we will never experience perfection. In the end, we must put all our hope in God and know that, try as we might, we can never hope to engineer a perfect, painless world. Nevertheless, the earth is truly a worthy place for us to invest ourselves and our lives. Jesus Himself in His incarnation shows this. Technology that facilitates social justice, that helps improve the lives of the poor and needy, and that provides us with experiences that enrich our lives, is in tune with Christ's commands. Much of the history of engineering is about meeting precisely these needs. Careful engineering, with compassionate understanding of the challenges we face, while simultaneously recognizing our limitations, is required. The best scientific engineering practices, encompassing prediction of technological effects in the broadest sense, and the thoughtful exercise of our creative gifts can produce not only great satisfaction and joy for the practicing engineer, but also profound benefits for the future of our world.

QUESTIONS

1. Does our modern emphasis on rational problem solving remove us from our dependence on God? Is faith necessary when we can solve many human concerns via technological methods?

2. Who is responsible for the development of technology? What role do you—as a citizen, as a consumer, and as a concerned Christian thinker—have in creating the world of the future?

3. Can all potential ramifications of a novel product or technology be predicted? If not, should change be avoided at any cost?

NOTES

10. Subrata Dasgupta, *Technology and Creativity* (New York: Oxford Univ. Press, 1996).
11. Iridium was subsequently bought by another company for pennies on the dollar, and that company has become a profitable company.
12. Samuel C. Florman, *The Existential Pleasures of Engineering* (New York: St. Martin's Press, 1976), 3.
13. Carroll Pursell, *The Machine in America* (Baltimore: Johns Hopkins Univ. Press, 1995), 14.

14. Lambert Van Poolen, "Towards a Christian Theory of Technological Things," *Christian Scholars Review* 33, no. 3 (Spring 2004): 367.

15. Henry Petroski, *To Engineer Is Human: The Role of Failure in Successful Design* (New York: Vintage Books, 1982).

16. Charles C. Adams, "Automobiles, Computers and Assault Rifles: The Value-Ladenness of Technology and the Engineering Curriculum," *Pro Rege* (Dordt College) 19, no. 3 (March 1991): 1–7.

17. Neil Postman, *Technopoly: The Surrender of Culture to Technology* (New York: Alfred A. Knopf, 1992), 52.

18. E. F. Schumacher, *Small Is Beautiful: Economics as If People Mattered* (New York: Harper & Row, 1973).

19. Clifford Christians, *Jacques Ellul: Interpretive Essays* (Urbana: Univ. of Illinois Press, 1981).

20. Alston Chase, "Harvard and the Making of the Unabomber," *Atlantic Monthly* (June 2000): 53.

21. See, e.g., Douglass Mulhall, *Our Molecular Future* (Amherst, N.Y.: Prometheus, 2002), 210; also, K. Eric Drexler, *Engines of Creation* (Garden City, N.Y.: Anchor Press, 1986), 14.

22. Derived from the design norms included in Stephen Monsma, ed., *Responsible Technology* (Grand Rapids: Eerdmans, 1986), chap. 9.

SUGGESTED READING

Florman, Samuel. *The Existential Pleasures of Engineering*. New York: St. Martin's Press, 1976.

Monsma, Stephen, ed. *Responsible Technology*. Grand Rapids: Eerdmans, 1986.

Postman, Neil. *Technopoly: The Surrender of Culture to Technology*. New York: Alfred A. Knopf, 1992.

Tobin, James. *Great Projects: The Epic Story of the Building of America, from the Taming of the Mississippi to the Invention of the Internet*. New York: Simon & Schuster, 2001.

CRUCIAL QUESTIONS IN THE APPLIED SCIENCES

Attempting to capture the full influence and intrigue of science is an enormous task. Liberal arts students and faculty enthusiastically engage in the sciences of their choice, and many choose disciplines that allow them to serve human needs. Some choose to develop careers in academia at the elementary, secondary, college, or university level. Some of them then practice science in cultures abroad or on their home continents and have hundreds of careers from which to choose. The editors have chosen to present some cross-cultural influences of science and two major career fields, agriculture and medicine, that encompass diverse technologies and strategies. Helping disadvantaged people by using science is a way to meet their physical needs, and living out and sharing the gospel in their neighborhoods is a means of meeting their spiritual needs.

How Is Science Applied across Cultures?

Paul W. Robinson and Helene Slessarev-Jamir

Is science universal in the questions it asks, the methodologies it employs, and the answers it derives? How can science contribute to sustainable development among the world's poor and marginalized? How can Western Christians develop science that will enhance life in marginalized communities?

Is there a universal approach to science?

"A scientist had a bird in his hand. He wanted to find out in what part of the bird's body its life was and what the life itself was. So he began dissecting the bird. The result was that the very life of which he was in search mysteriously vanished. Those who try to understand the inner life merely intellectually will meet with a similar failure. The life they are looking for will only vanish."[1]

As Christians we humbly acknowledge the limitations of human knowledge, recognizing that while all cultures have some comprehension of the truth, the fullness of God's truth nonetheless eludes all of us. For, "if God is the source of all knowledge, he evidently works redemptively through all human communities, empowering people to find and use information that enhances their ability to support life in their respective cultures."[2] The questions people ask of science and the answers they derive from science are, in significant measure, predicated on their values and concerns. Anthropologist William O'Barr writes: "Science is but one of many systems of thought, and it would do us well to think of it as satisfying the needs of a particular society and culture.... Because it works so well as a system of explanation and prediction in our society, we tend to dismiss alternatives outright."[3] If we accept this statement, then we need to consider what other models that represent other voices contribute to "the human quest to understand causes and effects."[4]

Human cultures are shaped by the specific circumstances in which they have developed and the particular challenges of adaptation and survival that they have encountered, all cultures sharing "a unique ability to adapt to circumstances and resolve the problems of survival."[5] Because cultures view the world and the cosmos in the context of their particular experiences and challenges, each asks different questions that often lead to different answers. For example, while some cultures see the development of new technologies as the goal of science, others may place community concerns more at the center of scientific inquiry. The questions, methods, and values of science and its application carry with them specific cultural concerns. From different perspectives emerge different goals.

Several years ago a Western organization providing health services to communities across Africa commissioned a study that would examine issues relating to health and healing in Africa.[6] The organization was concerned about a growing disaffection of Africans toward the health services (largely organized along Western scientific biomedical principles) offered by the hospitals and clinics it supported. The study revealed that the disaffection was rooted in the different foundational questions that African cultures ask of medicine and the healing professions. African thought (which informs African *science* relating to medicine), understands illness as having social and spiritual as well as natural components. In an African context, therefore, treatment, or the application of knowledge, is based on this understanding of holistic causation. Care relating to the natural causative elements of illness and disease is based on chemical medication (e.g., herbs that are identified, processed, combined) as well as surgical processes. The social and spiritual dimensions are treated through prescriptions that include community-based reconciliatory processes, exorcism of evil spirits, and appeal to ancestors. Treatment includes and is predicated on dealing with all factors as a unified whole, including whatever and whoever are understood to be the causes. In both the diagnostic and treatment aspects of healing, healers are expected to deal with these multiple dimensions. Africans have a rich tradition of medical research and practice yet are at critical points alienated from Western medicine because the Western tradition relies almost exclusively on what they understand to be a narrow and noncomprehensive model that lacks understanding of these other dimensions.

Do different questions lead to different answers?

The study discussed above showed that beginning with different questions will lead to different ways of problem solving (i.e., the types and application of technologies). The underlying philosophy of and approach to health and healing in the Western scientific and biomedical model overwhelmingly looks for causation and cure in the empirical—in viruses, bacteria, and chemicals. It stresses the individual, diagnosing and treating the individual in isolation from his or her community. Most non-Western cultures understand that disease has many dimensions that must be addressed together and so have developed etiologies that include both empirical and nonempirical causation and treatment. They see disease as having both individual and social dimensions, and they look for a restoration of health and treatment within the context of community involvement and support.[7] While biomedicine has become largely focused on individual *cure*, these cultures' approach has been centered on community-based *care*. The focus of Western medicine has been primarily on *disease*, while the center of concern of non-Western cultures is on *health*. Removing the patient from these dimensions and the context of community involvement in healing has led to isolation, alienation, and a perceived lack of wellness.[8] The study on health care in Africa affirmed the influence of culture on the nature and focus of science and its application. Quite simply, culture, and the power that is associated with particular cultural perspectives, often determines what science is done, the questions that are asked, and the technology that is developed.

Do value systems determine the nature and application of science?

A critical issue for contemporary Africa is the HIV/AIDS pandemic that is wreaking untold devastation on the continent. In the current international efforts to address the HIV/AIDS pandemic, Western science, largely funded by Western governments and philanthropic organizations, has been focused primarily on understanding the biology of the HIV virus and developing a vaccine or treatment to prevent its transmission and eliminate it. From an African perspective, this approach will neither eliminate the epidemic nor solve the crisis, for Africans believe that HIV/AIDS has deep social, economic, political, and spiritual causative factors that require broader diagnoses and treatment. Africans believe that HIV/AIDS is as much caused by poverty as it is by a virus; that its spread is propelled by economic structures with roots in colonial policies that are dependent on migrant labor and separate husbands and wives for much of their lives; that it is nurtured by conflict, often supported and funded by corporations and even nations looking to exploit and control access to Africa's natural resources; and that it is abetted by Africa's own political institutions that benefit from these. Africans believe that the reasons for the devastating course of the HIV/AIDS pandemic on their continent are deeply rooted in its poverty, marginalization, and exploitation.

Global development is largely predicated on theories of a linear course of change, progress, and advance. These theories also drive the powerful concurrent process of globalization, in its science and technology. A number of scholars are increasingly asking questions regarding persisting inequalities, poverty, and environmental degradation as "a function of exclusion, abandonment, and disenfranchisement."[9]

They argue that local knowledge, values, and organization systems, growing out of the full historical range of human knowledge, skills, and talent for social and cultural adaptation, have the potential to speak deeply and with sustainability to the challenges facing humanity, provided these are heard.

What are some of the characteristics of different value systems?

A core feature of many non-Western cultures is that of *balance*. Among the world's hunter-gatherer peoples, often described as *immediate return societies*, life is centered in living off the flows of resources that nature regularly renews. This lifestyle required these cultures to develop a comprehensive knowledge of the environments in which they lived, to understand every nuance of resource availability and variability, and to live on daily returns from hunting and gathering without processing or storing food. Within this framework, hunter-gatherer peoples limited their wants and needs and yet at the same time are characterized as "generally well-fed, egalitarian, ecologically sustainable, and socially and intellectually complex and . . . have an abundance of leisure time."[10] In this context, their lives were "spent not at a workplace, away from friends and family, but in talking, resting, sharing, and celebrating; in short, in being humans."[11] The social structures and economies of hunter-gatherer societies addressed questions of knowledge and technology from a perspective at virtually every point counter to *modern* science, and yet avoided "the vicious cycle of resource exhaustion, substitution, technological change, more resource exhaustion, and so on that seems to have been the pattern for human societies over the past 10,000 years or so.[12]

It is widely accepted that global population increases together with human use of rapidly changing and expanding new technologies have impacted the environment in complex and problematic ways. Increasingly it is recognized that questions must be asked that link Earth's carrying capacity with population and the environment, and the assumptions of Western science must be rethought. The key to sustainable development is likely to be in efforts that strengthen and build on local knowledge, processes, and systems, and that are appropriate to specific environments.[13]

On the Kenya-Ethiopian frontier, Gabra pastoralists occupy extremely arid land that is at the very margins of human survivability.[14] They have neither a scientific tradition in the Western sense, nor sophisticated technology. Yet their knowledge and understanding of astronomy, meteorology, and climate are profound, based on generations of careful observation and analysis that are recorded and carried in the living memories of individuals. Though nonliterate, the Gabra observe and mentally record cycles of time and environmental change, including observations on rainfall periodicity, volume, and distribution; plant growth, quality, and location; and numbers, dispersal, aggregation, and migration patterns of multiple species of insects, birds, and mammals. All this they have woven into a resource management system based on livestock and the practice of a form of transhumance that is highly adapted to the harsh environment in which they live and that has survived and prospered over time. They develop and nurture complex relationships that become networks for the free transmission of knowledge from camp to camp, which in turn determine the movement of people and livestock. These networks also ascertain the timing of aggregations of wider communities for ritual and governance purposes and for the sharing and redistribution of livestock. Gabra knowledge and praxis are deeply rooted in a philosophy that stresses living within the natural and cyclical parameters of the rangeland environment they occupy.

The Gabra are part of a broad human cultural model that today numbers at least 23 million people in Africa, Asia, and the Middle East. For millennia they have been successful producers of meat and dairy products in environments that are unsuitable for other forms of food production. In virtually every context in which pastoralists live, their livelihoods, security, and productivity are under threat, and their populations face dislocation, famine, and poverty. Much of this is attributable to linear development paradigms that see no place for this successful human adaptive strategy. Development initiatives directed at transforming pastoralist economies and lifestyles toward sedentarization and agricultural or "ranch" production have for the most part resulted in severely degraded environments, permanent dependency on relief aid, and dramatically decreased food production.[15]

Most often the case has been that when these cultures have come into contact with Western knowledge systems and values, they have been overwhelmed and their survival and prosperity seriously threatened if not destroyed. Gowdy (and many others) argue that the reasons for this are to be found in the organizing principles that guide behavior and explain and justify the way things are.[16] Modern science has been more concerned with research and application that leads to technological advancement and economic growth and has been largely unable, inadequate, or unconcerned with the task of maintaining or restoring ecological and social balance. It is the case that technological advancement and economic growth are often achieved at the expense of ecological and social balance, and that power determines which perspectives succeed. Describing one of the costs of inappropriate science, Kenyan zoologist George Kinoti, observes, "Much environmental degradation has resulted from erosion of traditional environmental conservation practices (e.g., intercropping, fallowing, terracing, nomadic use of pastures) and the adoption of inappropriate or locally untested technologies."[17] As these societies become more integrated into the process of national and international economic exchange, they are confronted with the demand to modify their values and lifestyles while at the same time remaining deeply concerned with the consequences of these changes. In many cases, they become marginalized and their perspectives ignored.

How can Western science respond or incorporate different value systems?

One of the chief purposes of science and its application in its Western paradigm is to improve human well-being. Bruce Bradshaw notes:

Science's leading function is to unfold the empirical nature of creation by "observing relationships between varying natural events, proposing explanations for these relationships, and testing the validity of these explanations by evaluating their ability to predict future events." Technology, an application of science, includes "all those machines, devices, and other physical apparatuses made and used by humans for instrumental purposes, and the physical products of those machines and devices.[18]

Scientific development is intended to enable each human being more fully to reach his or her God-given capabilities. Within this framework it has often been argued that while science can and does contribute to humanity's ability to address the challenges to whole and productive living, it "cannot provide the values to address these ills."[19]

A Nobel Prize–winning economist, Amartya Sen, argues that science should contribute to the quality of life by enhancing human freedom.[20] Sen is concerned with substantive freedoms,[21] of which one of the most elementary is "the ability to survive rather than succumb to premature mortality." Yet the earlier health-care example demonstrates the limitations that science developed in the West encounters when it attempts to transfer its basic methods and assumptions into other cultures. It has been this Western scientific approach that has largely determined the philosophy, approach, and technology of global development. Even today the "world-ordering knowledge" of Western science has difficulty understanding and evaluating what is considered a different reality.[22]

In contrast to Western post-Enlightenment knowledge systems that separate people, nature, and the metaphysical world from each other, many cultures see the essential unity of spiritual and material realities. Writing of Indian knowledge systems, Darshan Shankar summarizes this different approach to problem solving: "The traditional approach ... attempts to solve problems by examining them in their entirety, together with their interlinkages and complexities. This method of solving problems in their natural setting has proved capable of providing balanced solutions."[23] Thus scientists and health-care and development workers who are working within the traditional approach must integrate Western scientific knowledge into the more holistic worldviews of the local people. Often physicians and health workers in technologically less developed countries lack the sophisticated diagnostic equipment found in more developed countries, yet their diagnostic skills are effective because they have learned to rely on a more comprehensive understanding of their patients' social and physical state.[24] As Christians, we ought to be more receptive to worldviews that integrate spiritual and physical realities.

Writing in *The Ecologist*, Seyyed Hossein Nasr notes that modern humanity, through its scientific *secularization* and *segmentation* of nature and its commitment to domination over a segmented nature, has abandoned the core principle by which humanity for most of its history has understood the *order* that governs the cosmos. The fundamental consequence of this shift has been a worldview that has replaced the concept of *balance* and stewardship of creation with mastery over or exploitation of creation. By exercising domination without restraint, not only has nature been deprived of its moral and spiritual value, but survival itself is threatened.[25]

Do all people have equal access to the benefits of science?

Western science often neither addresses nor meets the concerns of marginalized communities, because scientific inquiry is rarely driven by their needs, nor is it congruent with their values. Moreover, the impact of change that is driven by science often results in increased long-term vulnerability. This is true not only in the non-Western societies we have been dealing with above, but in marginalized communities within the developed economies of the West. In many older cities in the United States, vast stretches of former factory sites lie vacant and unused. This has left the older urban communities that once depended on the surrounding factories for their livelihood in desperate straits, with many residents lacking work or steady incomes. At the same time, new warehouses and factories are springing up overnight on the outer edges of these urban centers on what had only recently been farmland. Often the expense of doing environmental remediation on the old factory sites is so high that it is cheaper to plow up cornfields, thereby contributing to urban sprawl and ever greater dependence on the automobile. Yet only in the last ten years have federal research dollars been invested into developing cost-effective technologies to clean up urban brownfields. Previously, budgets for research on environmental remediation were spent on nuclear waste sites and rural groundwater contamination from pesticides. City governments that were left with the burdens of growing unemployment and shrinking tax bases lacked the resources to address ground soil contamination without federal research and support. Only in the mid-1990s were efforts made to develop remediation technologies appropriate to these urban waste sites.

Across the globe, the benefits of scientific knowledge often do not reach a large portion of the world's populations. Scientific knowledge has not increased their capabilities to live freely in ways that people in wealthy countries take for granted. According to the United Nations *Human Development Report 2003*, "Today's world has greater resources and know-how than ever before to tackle the challenges of infectious disease, low productivity, lack of clean energy and transport and lack of basic services such as clean water, sanitation, schools, and health care. The issue is how best to apply those resources and know-how to benefit the poorest people."[26]

Famine remains a reality in parts of the world. With the exception of China, hunger increased in the developing world during the 1990s.[27] Every year more than 10 million children die of preventable diseases—30,000 a day. Around the world, 42 million are living with HIV/AIDS. Tuberculosis remains the leading infectious killer of adults, while malaria now kills a million people every year.[28] More than a billion people lack access to clean water, while 2.4 billion lack access to improved sanitation, both of which can be life and death issues.[29] Throughout much of the developing world, public spending on health care is a woeful six dollars per capita annually.

Hunger and premature death stalk the lives of many Americans as well. Studies have found that urban residents, especially minority populations, are "at greater risk for morbidity and mortality than residents in suburban and rural areas."[30] In 2000 the overall mortality for urban African-Americans was 26 percent higher than for urban whites, while that of Hispanics was 21 percent higher than for whites.[31] Some poor African-American communities on Chicago's West Side have experienced infant mortality rates as high as those found in sub-Saharan Africa. African-American males living in certain cities have a lower life expectancy than men living in China or in the state of Kerala in India. Bangladeshi men have a better chance of living beyond the age of forty than do black men living in Harlem.[32] HIV/AIDS is now the second highest cause of death among young African-American males.

These examples demonstrate the inequalities in access to the benefits of scientific knowledge across the globe. Bradshaw is right in his observation that transformation does not always follow from correct understandings or explanations of problems.[33] Transformation must also involve dealing with issues of access and relationships of power. Without broadening access to its benefits, scientific research and its manifold applications can contribute to the unequal distribution of human capabilities. Issues of access largely lie beyond the immediate boundaries of science itself to the issues of the funding for scientific research, the link between the practice of medicine and pharmaceutical companies, and political invisibility of many marginalized communities.

What would a more integrated approach to science look like?

Practitioners working in marginalized communities across the globe are seeking to develop science that draws on some of the strengths of Western science while simultaneously preserving traditions' values. For example, the Ministry of Agriculture of Nagaland, a tribal state in Northeast India, is working with its farming villages to increase the agricultural production above subsistence level in order to sustain a larger population as well as export some produce. So, while introducing some Western scientific methods to improve upon what has been a "slash and burn" system of cultivation, they are assiduously avoiding the use of any chemical fertilizers, preferring to expand the use of natural fertilizers. Similarly, while allowing for the introduction of "profit" into agricultural production, they are resisting the privatization of what has traditionally been communally held land.[34] What is significant in this example is the presence of local decision makers who are trained in both Western and traditional scientific methods.

Similarly, on Chicago's West Side, Bethel New Life, a community development corporation, built a partnership with Argonne National Laboratories, a research center operated by the U.S. Department of Energy, to facilitate the transfer of technologies used in environmental remediation. Argonne scientists had developed technologies for the cleanup of nuclear waste sites, which were adapted in conjunction with the Bethel New Life staff for application to the cleanup of old, abandoned urban industrial sites. In this case, the transfer of technologies occurred through an unusual partnership built by a small number of people in both institutions who together had recognized the need for remediation of these old industrial sites and the possible application of Argonne-developed scientific research.[35]

How can Christians use science to serve the poor and marginalized?

As Christians we need to learn to see Jesus in the faces of the poor and marginalized, and we need to learn to work and live incarnationally. Furthermore, we must be humble about the limits of our own knowledge and remain open to learning from people who are vastly different in their culture yet spiritually wise.[36] The examples from Nagaland and Chicago point to a necessary synergy between traditional and "modern" understandings and methods of science, and between practitioners in locations at the center and peripheries of power. Moreover, the diversity of human knowledge represented in its multiple cultures brings to science the awareness that science cannot be separated from values and beliefs and ultimately not from the presence, purpose, and activity of God in relation to the cosmos. This is a recognition that is embedded within the interpretive framework of many human cultures. Christian Scripture acknowledges that God is sovereign over all creation, seen and unseen, and that includes cultures, powers, and all social, economic, and civil structures. His purpose is to redeem and reconcile all creation to Himself (Col. 1:9–20). In understanding God's purpose in this context, human communities find their value and mandate.

QUESTIONS

1. What are the implications for your own study and practice of science of the different questions that different cultures ask?

2. Having read this chapter, do you think there are values that Westerners can learn from other cultures about science and its applications?

3. Can you think of other means of addressing the inequalities of access to the lifesaving and life-enriching applications of science in addition to the examples provided in this chapter?

NOTES

1. Sundar Singh, *Wisdom of the Sadhu: The Teachings of Sundar Singh* (Farmington, Pa.: Plough, 2000), 185.
2. Bruce Bradshaw, *Change across Cultures: A Narrative Approach to Social Transformation* (Grand Rapids: Baker, 2002), 197.
3. William M. O'Barr, "Culture and Causality: Non-Western Systems of Explanation," *Law and Contemporary Problems* 64.4 (Autumn 2001): 317.
4. Ibid.
5. John Reader, *Man on Earth* (London: Collins, 1988), 7.

6. This discussion is based on research undertaken in East Africa in 1995–96 by Paul W. Robinson for MAP (Medical Assistance Programs) International's East and Southern Africa office.

7. W. Meredith Long, *Health, Healing and God's Kingdom: New Pathways to Christian Health Ministry in Africa* (Oxford: Regnum, 2000), 118–21; and Daniel E. Fountain, *Health, the Bible and the Church* (Wheaton: Billy Graham Center, 1989), 4.

8. This is, of course, changing. In Western medicine there is an increasing recognition of these dimensions in many aspects of diagnosis and treatment. The growth of hospice care is evidence of this. However, it might be noted that hospice care is predominantly "end of life" focused, coming after technological interventions have been exhausted. See also Fountain, *Health, the Bible and the Church*, 13.

9. Barbara Slayter-Thomas, *Southern Exposure: International Development and the Global South in the Twenty-first Century* (Bloomfield, Conn.: Kumarian Press, 2003), 20–21. See also the writings of Robert Chambers, Jayakumar Christian, Rajni Kothari, Bryant Myers, and Amartya Sen.

10. John M. Gowdy, *Limited Wants, Unlimited Means: A Reader on Hunter-Gatherer Economics and the Environment* (Washington, D.C.: Island, 1998), xviii.

11. Ibid., xxiv.

12. Ibid., xxv.

13. Slayter-Thomas, *Southern Exposure*, 268–69.

14. Discussion of Gabra pastoralism based on Paul W. Robinson, *Gabra Nomadic Pastoralism in Nineteenth and Twentieth Century Northern Kenya: Strategies for Survival in a Marginal Environment*, Ph.D. thesis, Evanston, Ill.: Northwestern Univ., 1985.

15. Elliot M. Fratkin, *Ariaal Pastoralists of Kenya: Studying Pastoralism, Drought and Development in Africa's Arid Lands* (Boston: Pierson Education, 2004), 25–42.

16. Gowdy, *Limited Wants, Unlimited Means*, xvi.

17. George Kinoti, *Hope for Africa, and What the Christian Can Do* (Nairobi: African Institute for Scientific Research and Development, 1994), 65.

18. Bradshaw, *Change across Cultures*, 187.

19. Ibid.

20. See Amartya Sen, *Development as Freedom* (New York: Anchor, 2000).

21. Ibid., 24.

22. John Studley, "Dominant Knowledge Systems and Local Knowledge," paper presented at the Defining Local Knowledge conference of the Community-Based Mountain Tourism organization, May 1998.

23. Darshan Shankar, "The Epistemology of the Indigenous Medical Knowledge Systems of India," *Indigenous Knowledge and Development Monitor* 4, no. 3 (December 1996).

24. For case studies, see: Fountain, *Health, the Bible and the Church*, 9–11, and Long, *Health, Healing and God's Kingdom*, 3–4.

25. Seyyed Hossein Nasr, "The Spiritual and Religious Dimensions of the Environmental Crisis," *The Ecologist*, January 2000.

26. United Nations Development Programme, *Human Development Report 2003* (New York: United Nations, 2003), 3.

27. Ibid., 6.

28. Ibid., 8.

29. Ibid., 9.

30. *Big Cities Health Inventory*, ed. N. Benhow (Washington, D.C.: National Association of County and City Health Officials, 2003), 3.

31. Ibid., 7.
32. Sen, *Development as Freedom*, 23.
33. Bradshaw, *Change across Cultures*, 175.
34. Interview with Dr. Subong Keitzar, director of the Ministry of Agriculture for the state of Nagaland, India, August 11, 2004.
35. This discussion is based on consulting research by Helene Slessarev-Jamir in 1995–96 for the *Urban Sustainable Communities Initiative* at Argonne National Laboratories.
36. Contemporary Christian thinking on transformation and development is increasingly focused on this emerging paradigm. While it is seen as a new model, it nevertheless has deep historical roots. For a sampling of writing on this topic, see James F. Engel and William A. Dyrness, *Changing the Mind of Missions* (Downers Grove, Ill.: InterVarsity Press, 2000); Viv Grigg, *Companion to the Poor* (Monrovia, Calif.: MARC Publications, 1990); Samuel Escobar, *The New Global Mission: Where Have We Gone Wrong?* (Downers Grove, Ill.: InterVarsity Press, 2003); William R. Shenk, *Changing Frontiers of Mission* (Maryknoll, N.Y.: Orbis, 1999); Lamin Sanneh, *Whose Religion Is Christianity? The Gospel beyond the West* (Grand Rapids: Eerdmans, 2003); Mark Gornik, *To Live in Peace: Biblical Faith in the Changing City* (Grand Rapids: Eerdmans, 2002).

SUGGESTED READING

Bradshaw, Bruce. *Change across Culture: A Narrative Approach to Social Transformation*. Grand Rapids: Baker, 2002.

Chambers, Robert. *Whose Reality Counts? Putting the Last First*. London: Intermediate Technology Publications, 1997.

Samuel, Vinay, and Chris Sugden, eds. *Mission as Transformation*. Oxford: Regnum, 1999.

Sanneh, Lamin. *Whose Religion Is Christianity? The Gospel beyond the West*. Grand Rapids: Eerdmans, 2003.

Sen, Amartya. *Development as Freedom*. New York: Anchor Books, 2000.

Thomas-Slayter, Barbara P. *Southern Exposure: International Development and the Global South in the Twenty-First Century*. Bloomfield, Conn.: Kumarian Press, 2003.

What Values and Health-Care Priorities Are Expressed in Our Health-Care Delivery System?

June A. Arnold

The design of health-care delivery systems and the nature of the health professions workforce reflect the values, health-care priorities, and resources of a nation. The American health-care delivery system is complex, and providing health care in the twenty-first century is demanding. Navigating the health-care delivery system to see your primary care physician (PCP) of choice or to receive needed health care may be difficult and frustrating. The context of health-care delivery entails legal, economic, political (e.g., health policy), social, and ethical aspects. The design may or may not be a response to citizens' actual medical needs. But, in some way, the medical infrastructure of each nation must form an answer to similar questions about access to health care and about maintaining sustainable health strategies.

Historically, medicine was primarily a physician providing care for an individual patient. Today many health-care providers (e.g., the health-care team) collaborate in the care of a patient. Health care has expanded to include a wider array of services (e.g., geriatric psychiatry and rehabilitation medicine). Additionally, the national health-care network includes health-care facilities, research institutions, pharmaceutical companies, biotechnology firms, and federal agencies. Consequently, health-care requires a larger workforce with more specialists. The health-care team is comprised of a variety of health professionals and allied health professionals. Some health professionals are involved in direct patient care, others in health-related or medically related occupations.[37] Health occupations may be categorized by the services they provide in the context of a health-care facility: therapeutic, diagnostic, informational, and environmental.[38]

Health professions of long tradition include medicine, dentistry, and nursing. More recently, proliferation of health careers includes physician extenders, such as physician assistants. Advance practice nurses, such as nurse practitioners and certified registered nurse anaesthetists, are finding their niche in the workforce. Allied health professions include physical therapy, occupational therapy, pharmacy, optometry, public health, and many others. Veterinary medicine, a health profession in which the provider cares for animals, is intricately involved in health issues related to humans (e.g., mad cow disease).

How shall our health-care providers be prepared and educated?

The basic sciences (biology, chemistry, physics) and mathematics are essential for adequate preparation to enter medicine and many of the health professions. To diagnose, develop a treatment plan, and conceive good medical decisions, physicians must possess an intimate knowledge and understanding of human anatomy, physiology, genetics, and cell and molecular biology. The medical school curriculum provides instruction in the sciences that underlie medical practice and in the application of those sciences to health care.[39] Thus medicine, and by extension the health professions, are applied sciences. Some health professionals engage in research, thereby contributing to the body of medical knowledge (evidence) that makes clinical applications possible. As undergraduate students planning to enter medical school gain research experience, their problem-solving skills are enhanced, and ultimately, their ability to practice evidence-based medicine is honed. A health professional's proficiency in the basic sciences can contribute to embracing the conviction that malfunction in virtually every cellular process will eventually be recognized as contributing to human disease.[40] Proficiency is also required in disciplines such as ethics, law, humanities, and the social sciences. These disciplines lay the foundation for human interactions as characterized by the doctor-patient relationship. Additionally, they facilitate the administration of a medical practice, relationships with colleagues, and delivering quality care in the context of society.

What is the impact of research on health-care delivery?

Scientific discoveries, in addition to increasing our understanding of disease, also contribute to research and development. New technologies and new therapies to be used in the practice of medicine are the result of basic research and clinical trials. The "technological imperative," the notion that if a technology exists, we should use it and take advantage of its benefits, led to the advancement of medicine. However, that perspective (or value judgment) certainly generates difficult ethical dilemmas in the process. Health-care delivery is modified in response to changes in technology. As more specialists are required to implement the developing technology, the complexity of the health-care delivery system increases. For example, organ transplantation brings the gift of renewed life and vigor to many patients. However, it generates ethical dilemmas in the areas of prolonging life, in futility, and in allocation of scarce health-care resources. New fields are emerging, such as human donation sciences to prepare human organ procurement coordinators.[41] Xeno-transplantation (taking cells, tissues, and organs from animals and transplanting them into humans) developed, in part, as a response to the shortage of human organs. The U.S. Food and Drug Administration (FDA) is one of the federal agencies in the United States Department of Health and Human Services (see the "Federal Agencies under the Secretary of Health and Human Services" sidebar).[42] This federal regulatory agency is charged with protecting public health concerns brought about by xenotechnology.

What are the obligations of health-care professionals?

Physicians are obliged to their patients to keep current with these new technologies and developments in order to facilitate effective medical decision making. Physicians have obligations to individual patients, to patient populations, and to society to provide competent and compassionate care. This contract with society is based

FEDERAL AGENCIES UNDER THE SECRETARY OF HEALTH AND HUMAN SERVICES

Administration for Children and Families (ACF)
Administration on Aging (AoA)
Agency for Healthcare Research and Quality (AHRQ)
Agency for Toxic Substances and Disease Registry (ATSDR)
Centers for Disease Control and Prevention (CDC)
Centers for Medicare and Medicaid Services (CMS)
Food and Drug Administration (FDA)
Health Resources and Services Administration (HRSA)
Indian Health Service (IHS)
National Institutes of Health (NIH)
Program Support Center (PSC)
Substance Abuse and Mental Health Services Administration (SAMHSA)

on professionalism and necessitates accountability.[43] Though the contract has been eroded by managed care and litigation, it generates high societal expectations. Most Americans believe that health-care providers should provide care for patients in need of medical care regardless of whether they can pay. Important questions come into focus as we consider these dimensions of health care. Is medical care in the United States a right based on need or ability to pay, or is it in fact rationed?

How does health-care delivery in the United States compare with that of other countries?

Cross-national comparisons of health-care systems are helpful because systems of health-care delivery and health-care priorities reflect values held. In the British system, the government administers the health-care system. Cost containment occurs by global budgeting.[44] Health-care delivery by the British National Health Service (BNHS) occurs according to the results of studies outlined in the White Paper of 1990. Needs assessment, services provided, and funding are determined so there are defined roles for the various BNHS authorities. The general practitioner makes referrals to specialists. The BNHS provides a predetermined level of health-care benefits for each of its citizens. That is, all citizens are entitled to health care even if it is a limited amount.[45]

In contrast, the United States does not have universal coverage or a national health-care plan. Health care is considered a privilege and a commodity. Directives are a mixture of decentralized federal and state regulations. There are three tiers of patients: insured, underinsured, and uninsured (i.e., no health-care coverage). Private sector health insurance is primarily employer-based. In the public sector, the federal government provides assistance in the form of Medicare, health-care insurance for the elderly and the disabled. Additionally, both federal and state government monies support Medicaid, which provides limited health insurance for the poor. Nevertheless, some citizens "fall through the cracks" and do not have access to affordable health care. They are the unemployed or small-business owners who are too poor to buy health insurance but not poor enough to receive Medicaid. The lack of health insurance receives considerable attention because approximately 45 million Americans are uninsured (see plate 17).[46] Financing health care has been a major issue in political campaigns. Over the years, many health-care reform proposals have sought to rectify the problems of the medically underserved.

How can these economically disadvantaged people receive good health care?

The Bible portrays a clear picture of how we are mandated to care for widows, orphans, and the poor since they cannot fully care for themselves (Deut. 15:7–11; James 1:27). Can health professionals who seek to abide by the Scriptures decide not to accept patients into their practice who have no health-care insurance? Can they choose not to accept patients on Medicaid? What obligations do they have to provide health care for illegal immigrants? Some would suggest that the illegal immigrant has no right to the services of the host country (e.g., health care), and the case is a human rights issue.[47]

As the demographics (e.g., the aging of society) and the cultural diversity of our nation change, new patient populations form with unique medical needs (e.g., immigrants, refugees). David Hilfiker is a physician who left a practice in the Midwest to serve the homeless population in Washington, D.C. He describes how neither medical school nor his background in science prepared him for the psychosocial and cultural issues he faced in providing health care for the poor. Hilfiker feels the need for poverty medicine *results from a society that collectively agrees it is acceptable that some people remain poor.*[48] Clearly, then, health professionals need a broader range of capabilities.

How is health education reformed to prepare health-care providers?

Changes in health-care delivery (e.g., managed care, litigation), patient preferences, and sophisticated technology have each, in their turn, precipitated changes in what is required to prepare health-care providers for the twenty-first century. Medical education reform is occurring in areas other than the basic sciences to address current needs. Physicians are traditionally service-oriented and compassionate individuals, but resolving conflicts about whom to serve and how best to serve them is difficult. To help ensure that medical practice incorporates virtues in the practice of holistic medicine whereby healing occurs in body and mind, health professionals need to learn specific knowledge and skills. Additionally, they need to demonstrate certain desirable attributes, attitudes, and values important for physicians and other health professionals to possess. These should be promoted and developed preprofessionally.[49]

Since the Hippocratic oath of long ago, medical ethics has been required as a part of the formal curriculum. Health professionals need to be effective in ethical decision making. National professional associations, such as the American Medical Association and the American Nurses Association, provide a code of ethics to guide practice as well as guidelines for the education and accreditation of their practitioners. To address some of the psychosocial and cultural issues, medical anthropology and medical sociology may be included in the curriculum. Efforts to increase the cultural competency of health professionals should be intentional and incorporated in curriculum design.[50] As the patient population becomes more diverse and multicultural, efforts to consider the health beliefs, practices, and traditions of the patient are important. Health professionals need to be cross-culturally effective. Increasing diversity in the health professions' workforce is one of the best ways to facilitate cross-cultural effectiveness. A commitment should be made at all levels of the educational pipeline to increase diversity in the health professions schools through admissions and retention of underrepresented minorities so as to move closer to racial and ethnic parity with the U.S. population.[51] Additionally, early in 2005 the American Association of Medical Colleges (AAMC) recommended an annual increase in medical school enrollment to avoid a future physician shortage.[52]

When dealing with difficult issues such as suffering, grief, and death, health professionals need more than relational skills. Literature, the visual arts, history, music, and other disciplines within the humanities are expressions of the human condition. One medical school established the major objectives of integrating the medical humanities with the study of the basic sciences and of sustaining the study of the medical humanities throughout the preclinical years.[53] Just as studying science improves problem-solving skills, studying medical humanities improves other skill sets used in the practice of medicine (e.g., observe, reflect, interpret). Reading literature about aging or viewing joy and suffering in a film impacts the practitioner and changes his or her way of relating to patients.

Should patients be educated in a manner similar to the good doctor?

Physicians are trained to practice evidence-based medicine, and no one questions whether future practitioners should study science. But can patients take charge of their own care without any instruction or familiarity with scientific inquiry and methodology or the scientific process? The depth of patients' understanding of the scientific enterprise may determine in part how well they understand information they are given about their medical condition or health status. A foundation in science may not only enable patients to be better partners when making informed choices on the basis of evidence-based health information, but may be necessary.

Traditionally patients were willing to follow the recommendation of their physician. Nowadays, patients, after visiting the Virtual Hospital, a digital library of health information,[54] (1) may self-diagnose using the Internet as well as many other sources and (2) may even suggest the treatment plan they have decided on when they hand their self-diagnosis to their physician. An advertisement showing a woman on the examining table of a clinic had this caption: "There are 126 schools in the country that teach you how to be a physician but not one that teaches you how to be a patient."[55] The sponsor of the advertisement was encouraging patients to apply the concept of self-care and personal responsibility for their health. They encouraged patients to make informed choices using evidence-based health information.

As the trend toward even greater use of the Internet for obtaining medical and health information increases, critical-thinking skills are necessary for the evaluation and careful selection of websites. Since no agency has been given the authority to regulate, standardize, or ensure that medical information on the Internet is accurate, users cannot always be certain the information is reliable.

How do public health professionals practice their profession?

Health information comes from a variety of sources. Health education has been disseminated in the United States in a variety of ways. Educating populations by promoting healthy lifestyles and injury prevention has been one of the roles of public health professionals. Health care may not always be delivered to an individual patient per se. Health care may be delivered to a population with specific medical needs (e.g., the underserved or the chronically ill). Public health is a population-based form of preventive and protective health care; objectives are directed toward improving community health.[56]

Sometimes a very large population, a city, or an entire nation must deal with a disaster like HIV/AIDS or the 9/11 terrorist attacks that affects, even overloads, local health-care systems. Preparedness is important and so is the ability to deal with aftereffects. C. Everett Koop, M.D., Sc.D., a former U.S. surgeon general, dealt proactively with HIV/AIDS, tobacco use, and obesity.[57] To launch a mass campaign educating citizens and helping them understand the at-risk and safe behaviors related to AIDS, he had a brochure mailed to every household in America.[58] Parents were encouraged to discuss the contents with their children, thereby providing a measure of sex education. This need for health education and health promotion still exists. International response to the AIDS pandemic has been called for and emphasized in many publications like *Science*, where research papers are regularly published and demographic studies (e.g., HIV/AIDS in Asia) emphasize again the need for scientific literacy to help future generations understand health (as a tangible effect of science literacy).[59] Similar initiatives are needed in our approach to tobacco, drug use, and obesity.

Is there a national/international health agenda?

The World Health Organization (WHO) is an organization particularly concerned with health and access to health care in the global community. On the global level, the policy "health for all in the twenty-first century" is to be implemented through regional and national initiatives, policies, and strategies. Health, as defined by the WHO, is *a state of complete physical, mental, and social well-being and not mere*

HEALTHY PEOPLE 2010—LEADING HEALTH INDICATORS

1. Physical activity
2. Overweight and obesity
3. Tobacco use
4. Substance abuse
5. Responsible sexual behavior
6. Mental health
7. Injury and violence
8. Environmental quality
9. Immunization
10. Access to health care

absence of disease or infirmity.[60] The WHO strategy—Health 21—is a population-based, public health model of health care. The strategy employs a primary care model that is community oriented.[61]

The Healthy People 2010 program is the closest thing to a national health agenda or strategy found in the United States. This program, coordinated by the office of the surgeon general, has focus areas, established objectives (to be met by 2010), and indicators of health status (see "Healthy People 2010" sidebar). The program seeks to improve health and eliminate health disparities. Although there is no particular way to ensure implementation, the objectives are designated health-care priorities.[62]

Are there other examples of setting health-care priorities?

Methods for priority setting abound for patient selection (e.g., waiting list for a transplant), budgets, and even how much time to spend with one patient. Priority setting is a necessary part of the macroallocation (societal priorities) and micro-allocation of scarce health-care resources. For example, the role of health research in fighting poverty and the global burden of disease is complicated by the fact that most research occurs in the industrialized nations. Much of that research is not targeted toward diseases that are more prevalent in the developing nations, yet these diseases account for the heavier portion of the global burden of disease. Specific methodologies for setting priorities have been constructed in a way that could help correct the global inequities.[63] Additionally, the Task Force on Health Research for Development defined seven elements for implementing essential national health research; priority setting was one of the seven elements.[64]

Grassroots movements in the United States have from time to time brought about change based on the outcomes of establishing health-care priorities. In Oregon, health-care priorities were determined by polling citizens. The cost-benefit analysis to rank priorities was a QALY–based method (quality–adjusted life–years). Ultimately, the community value clusters discovered were used to guide resource allocation decisions in revamping Medicaid entitlements (i.e., set the minimum-benefits package).[65]

Health-care priorities may also differ because of value conflicts that arise regarding the efficacy of different models of care. Western biomedicine is considered to be mainstream conventional medicine. Physicians have been trained in allopathic medical schools (M.D.s). Western biomedicine is evidence-based medicine and traditionally biased toward curative care. Physicians trained in schools of osteopathic medicine (D.O.s) are common as well.

But along with self-care there has come a renewed interest in other treatment modalities that have existed through time. Complementary and alternative medicine (CAM) includes dietary supplements, herbals, naturopathy, homeopathy, acupuncture, mind-body interactions, and a host of other therapies. When the National Center for Complementary and Alternative Medicine was established, health professionals were encouraged to become more knowledgeable about

CAM.[66] There are four schools in the United States specifically for naturopathic medicine (whose graduates are doctors of naturopathy [N.D.s]), but only a few states are currently licensing practitioners in naturopathic medicine. The ideal is integrative care that blends and encompasses both conventional allopathic and more unconventional treatments in the best interests of the patient (whole person).[67]

One pragmatic issue continues to be how health-care practitioners can help patients with their spiritual needs during difficult times—when they are suffering or at the end of their life, when they feel helpless, alone, and vulnerable. Health-care writer Linda Gundersen looked at the relationship between the domains of medicine and religion and concluded that in an atmosphere of evidence-based medicine, research geared toward striving for definitive evidence of health benefits from spiritual interventions may be a limited endeavor. Gundersen also noted that if the research is geared toward natural explanations, measuring the effects of supernatural forces has limited usefulness. Gundersen found that the variables from the two domains being compared were not consistent among research projects. When investigators assessed the relationship between the two domains in a patient's recovery, they compared: faith and healing, health and religion, intercessory prayer and severity of condition, religiosity and improved health, spirituality and health.[68]

How can practitioners provide support for patient's spiritual needs?

Parish nursing exemplifies one form of faith-based care. Parish nursing combines practicing a health profession with serving a faith community while promoting whole-person health care. The parish nurse has the congregation as the patient population and the church/parish as the practice setting (church-based health ministry). In this way, the nurse may serve as health advocate for a local congregation.[69] Members of the congregation may even assist with community health screenings or serve as lay health advisors.[70]

But what about faith-based care in health-care facilities? Historically, many hospitals have been faith-based institutions, and the hospital chaplain has served as the primary agent of spiritual care. Even today health professionals may make a referral to the chaplain. Some health professions schools now include spirituality and health somewhere in the curriculum. They are seeing the value of the spiritual dimension of health. They are finding medical parameters that are influenced by patients' religious beliefs, practices, and the social support they obtain in their communities of faith. Additionally, health professions' schools may teach their students how to take a spiritual history as part of the patient history.[71] Efforts are directed toward patient-centered care of the whole person.

What is the sacred task of the Christian health professional in the delivery of faith-based, biblically based health care?

Traditionally, the "good doctor" is held to be the ideal to which health professionals should aspire. A step beyond is to use Jesus Christ as the exemplar. Jesus as "the great physician" has always affected how Christians view the practice of medicine.[72] The gospel stories about Jesus healing the blind, lame, and lepers are a rich resource of principles for health professionals to infuse into their lives and into their clinical practice. Medical interventions are viewed as only a part of restoration to wholeness. Medical ethicist Kenneth Vaux, in speaking about healing, says, "Healing blends self-awareness, prevention, and life-style health maintenance; the skill of the physician; the therapy of medicaments—all are viewed as manifesting the single healing desire of God."[73]

Wherever health professionals practice in the global context, they can provide a drop of anointing oil (see James 5:13–16). Since health professionals are with the patient in the midst of their condition, whatever that is, their presence is reassuring. Henri Nouwen in speaking about compassion says: "Compassion asks us to go where it hurts, to enter into places of pain, to share in brokenness, fear, confusion, and anguish. Compassion means full immersion in the condition of being human." He makes these statements in relationship to Christ as Immanuel ("God with us") and to the radical quality of the command to be compassionate as our heavenly Father is compassionate.[74] When Jesus had compassion on the crowds, He healed the sick (Matt. 14:14). Compassion is clearly a necessary response from a health-care practitioner of the twenty-first century.

Christians entering the health professions, therefore, have a set of sacred tasks. Whether they serve wealthy patients in a suburban practice or bring medical care to a poverty-stricken region of the globe, they can practice medical missions wherever they are. They can treat patients with respect because both are made in the image of God. They can be good stewards of health-care resources. They can be careful to set health-care priorities based on biblical values and principles rather than on the dominant cultural values (e.g., care for the poor) and to set priorities that will reduce health-care disparities. They can be agents of change, improving health-care delivery wherever they practice. Jesus gave His disciples power and authority and He sent them out to preach the kingdom of God and to heal the sick. The disciples responded; they set out and went from village to village preaching the gospel and healing people everywhere (Luke 9:1–6). The tradition that began long ago is carried on today by Christian health professionals who are servant-leaders delivering health care in villages around the globe.

QUESTIONS

1. Consider the doctor-patient relationship. What virtues, attitudes, and competencies are expected from health professionals?

2. How are integrative therapies (alternative or complementary) based on evidence gleaned from scientific research?

3. When the health care required is related to lifestyle choices (e.g. obesity, alcoholism, violence), how would you describe individual respon-

sibility and social responsibility? What incentive/disincentive structures could be used to implement preventive measures that would improve individual and social responsibility?

NOTES

37. Peggy S. Stanfield and Y. H. Hui, *Introduction to the Health Professions,* 3rd ed. (Boston: Jones and Bartlett, 1998).

38. Shirley A. Badasch and Doreen S. Chesebro, *Introduction to Health Occupations*: *Today's Health Care Worker* (Englewood Cliffs, N.J.: Prentice Hall, 2004), 16.

39. American Medical Association, *Graduate Medical Education Directory 2004–2005* (Chicago: AMA Press, 2004), 9.

40. Catherine D. DeAngelis, ed., *The Johns Hopkins University School of Medicine*: *Curriculum for the Twenty-first Century* (Baltimore: Johns Hopkins Univ. Press, 1999), 61.

41. Human Donation Sciences, Medical College of Ohio, August 11, 2004, http://www.mco.edu/allh/donation_science/index.html.

42. United States Department of Health and Human Services, About HHS, March 25, 2004, http://www.hhs.gov/about/index.html#agencies.

43. American Medical Association, *Declaration of Professional Responsibility*: *Medicine's Social Contract with Humanity*, August 30, 2004, http://www.ama-assn.org/ama/pub/category/7491.html. Drafted in response to the needs of September 11, 2001. Adopted by the House of Delegates of the American Medical Association in San Francisco, December 4, 2001.

44. Carl M. Stevens, "Health Care Cost Containment: Some Implications of Global Budgets," *Science* 259 (January 1, 1993): 16.

45. Barbara Connah and Ruth Pearson, eds. *NHS Handbook*, 7th ed. National Association of Health Authorities and Trusts (London: Macmillan, 1991).

46. Carmen DeNavas-Walt, Bernadette D. Proctor, and Robert J. Mills, U.S. Census Bureau, Current Population Reports, P60–226, *Income, Poverty, and Health Insurance Coverage in the United States*: *2003* (Washington, D.C.: U.S. Government Printing Office, 2004). Also available at http:www.census.gov/prod/2004pubs/p60–226.pdf.

47. Dwyer, James, "Illegal Immigrants, Health Care, and Social Responsibility," *Hastings Center Report* 34, no. 5 (January–February 2004): 34–41.

48. David Hilfiker, *Not All of Us Are Saints*: *A Doctor's Journey with the Poor* (New York: Hill and Wang, 1994), 144.

49. Patricia M. Etienne and Ellen R. Julian, "Identifying Behaviors of Successful Medical Students and Residents," *Analysis in Brief* (American Association of Medical Colleges, Washington, D.C.) 1, no. 4 (November 2001).

50. American Medical Association, *Cultural Competence Compendium* (Chicago: American Medical Association, 1999); Rachel E. Spector, *Cultural Diversity in Health and Illness*, 6th ed. (Englewood Cliffs, N.J.: Pearson/Prentice Hall, 2004), 301–4.

51. Institute of Medicine. *The Right Thing to Do, the Smart Thing To Do*: *Enhancing Diversity in Health Professions*, Summary of the Symposium on Diversity in Health Professions in Honor of Herbert W. Nickens, M.D. (Washington, D.C.: National Academy Press, 2001), 206.

52. Press release, "AAMC Calls for Modest Increase in Medical School Enrollment," from American Association of Medical Colleges, March 7, 2005, at http://aamc.org/newsroom/pressrel/2005/050222.htm.

53. Therese Jones and Abraham Verghese, "On Becoming a Humanities Curriculum: The Center for Medical Humanities and Ethics at the University of Texas Health Science Center at San Antonio," *Academic Medicine* 78, no. 10 (October 2003): 1010–14. Issue was devoted to the humanities and medicine and reported on forty-one U.S., Canadian, and international programs.

54. Virtual Hospital is a digital library of health information from the University of Iowa Health Care. It can be accessed at http://www.vh.org.

55. *Daily Herald, USA Week-End* (McClean, Va.: Gannett Co., Inc., May 7–9, 2004), 8–9.

56. Harry A. Sultz and Kristina M. Young, *Health Care USA: Understanding Its Organization and Delivery*, 4th ed. (Boston: Jones and Bartlett, 2004), 367–94.

57. C. Everett Koop, *Shape Up America!* July 22, 2004, http://www.shapeup.org/general/koop.htm.

58. *Understanding AIDS (A Message from the Surgeon General)*. HHS Publication No. (CDC) HHS–88–8404. Washington, D.C.: U.S. Government Printing Office: 1988–532–152.

59. "Landmark AAAS/UNESCO Forum Explores Science Education," *Science* 304, no. 5679 (June 25, 2004): 1921.

60. Preamble to the Constitution of the World Health Organization as adopted by the International Health Conference, New York, June 19–22, 1946; signed on July 22, 1946, by the representatives of sixty-one states (Official Records of the World Health Organization, no. 2, p. 100) and entered into force on April 7, 1948. The definition has not been amended since 1948.

61. *Health 21: An Introduction to the Health for All Policy Framework for the WHO European Region*, European Health for All Series, no. 5 (Copenhagen: World Health Organization, 1998).

62. *Healthy People 2010*, conference ed. in 2 vols. (Washington D.C.: Department of Health and Human Services, January 2000).

63. Andres de Francisco, "Priority Setting in Health Research," in *The 10/90 Report on Health Research 2003–2004* (Geneva: Global Forum for Health Research, WHO, 2004), 67–108, available online at http://www.globalforumhealth.org/filesupld/109004_chap_4.pdf.

64. "A Decade of Implementation: COHRED's Impact on Health Research for Development," *Research into Action: The Newsletter of the Council on Health Research for Development*, special ed. (September 2004), http://www.cohred.ch/documents_COHREDweb/Newsletters/SpecialEdition.pdf.

65. Martin A. Strosberg et al., *Rationing America's Medical Care: The Oregon Plan and Beyond* (Washington, D.C.: Brookings Institution, 1992).

66. *Cultural Competence Compendium* (Chicago: American Medical Association, 1999), 245.

67. Victor S. Sierpina, *Integrative Health Care: Complementary and Alternative Therapies for the Whole Person* (Philadelphia: F. A. Davis, 2001); Harold G. Koenig, M.D., *Spirituality in Patient Care: Why, How, When, and What* (Philadelphia: Templeton Foundation Press, 2002). Koenig is a founder and director of the Duke University Center for the Study of Religion/Spirituality and Health.

68. Linda Gundersen, "Faith and Healing," *Annals of Internal Medicine* 132, no. 2 (January 18, 2000): 169–72.

69. Phyllis Ann Solari-Twadell and Mary Ann McDermott, eds., *Parish Nursing: Promoting Whole Person Health within Faith Communities.* (Thousand Oaks, Calif.: Sage, 1999).

70. Mission Possible: Health Care among the Poor: A National Meeting of the Christian Medical and Dental Society with Participation from Christian Community Health Fellowship, Luke Society, Inc., MAP International, Nurses' Christian Fellowship, Parish Nurse Resource Center, Chicago, October 1–3, 1993.
71. Victor S. Sierpina, *Integrative Health Care: Complementary and Alternative Therapies for the Whole Person* (Philadelphia: F. A. Davis, 2001).
72. Hessel Bouma III et al., *Christian Faith, Health, and Medical Practice* (Grand Rapids: Eerdmans, 1992).
73. Kenneth L. Vaux, *Health and Medicine in the Reformed Tradition: Promise, Providence, and Care* (New York: Crossroad, 1984), 120.
74. Henri J. M. Nouwen, Donald P. McNeill, and Douglas A. Morrison, *Compassion: A Reflection on the Christian Life* (New York: Doubleday, 1983).

SUGGESTED READING

Daniels, Norman, and James E. Sabin. *Setting Limits Fairly: Can We Learn to Share Medical Resources?* New York: Oxford University Press, 2002.
Hilfiker, David, M.D. *Not All of Us Are Saints: A Doctor's Journey with the Poor.* New York: Hill and Wang, 1994.
Koop, C. Everett, M.D. *Koop: The Memoirs of America's Family Doctor.* Grand Rapids: Zondervan, 1992.

Just Agriculture?

Robb De Haan and Ron Vos

What is agriculture? What makes it unique?

Agriculture is the management of ecosystems to provide food, fiber, and other products for society. Agriculture is always practiced in a cultural setting, whether by the hunter-gatherers of the past or agricultural producers of the present. Since agriculture involves management of ecosystems, it requires energy and other inputs. Agriculture is unique in that it requires a land base for its operations and is very dependent on biological and climatic factors for its success.

So what is agriculture today really like? How is the majority of the food in North America produced?

The current North American food system produces a wide range of plant and animal products; everything from corn, soybeans, and hazelnuts, to fish, milk, and pork. The production systems for the goods are equally diverse, but mainstream agriculture has many common themes.

One of these themes is rapid change. Farm size is increasing, farm numbers are declining, and industrialization (product standardization, farm specialization, and centralization of control) is occurring rapidly. These processes are changing crop and livestock production practices, the lives of people involved in food production, and the entire rural landscape. A closer look at corn, the most widely grown grain in the United States, and at swine, a representative livestock species, will give us a better idea of how the agricultural system in the United States functions.

In 2004 field corn was planted on 81 million acres of land in the United States. The other major crops were soybeans at 75.2 million acres and wheat at 59.7 million acres.[75] Corn yields were predicted to average 160.4 bushels per acre in 2004, for total corn production of 11.8 billion bushels, the largest crop ever recorded.[76] These record yields are a result of favorable weather, classical plant breeding work, genetic engineering, and changes in crop production practices. The development of genetically modified corn hybrids created to be resistant to herbicides, European corn borers, and corn rootworms have made it easier to grow corn. Farm machinery has become larger and more precise, and fertilizer application techniques have been fine-tuned. As a result, it takes fewer hours of human labor to grow an acre of corn today than at any time in the past, and that acre is more productive than it has ever been. This corn crop is being used for livestock feed (55 percent), exports (18 percent), food and seed (13 percent), fuel alcohol (11 percent), and stored reserves (3 percent).[77]

These changes sound positive, but they don't tell the whole story. Because agriculture requires less labor, the populations of rural nonmetro counties in the Great Plains (those that lacked a town of at least 2,500 people) lost more than a third of their population base between 1950 and 1996.[78] Rural people are also more likely to be poor than urban people. "In 2002, 14.2% of the non-metro population, or 7.5 million people, were poor, compared with 11.6% of the metro population."[79] The average age of residents of rural counties is significantly older than the average age of people in urban counties.[80] In addition, agricultural pollutants (sediments, nutrients, pesticides, minerals, and pathogens) are significant problems and reduce environmental quality in agricultural areas.[81]

So what is happening on the livestock side of agriculture? In 1981 there were 585,500 farms raising hogs in the United States. By 2003 that number had dropped to 73,600, an 88 percent decrease.[82] In 2001, one percent of the hog farms in the United States were producing 60 percent of the animals.[83]

The majority of pork for sale in the United States today comes from hogs produced in confinement facilities known as concentrated animal feeding operations (CAFOs). The animals in the CAFO are usually fed a ration that is a mixture of genetically modified corn and soybean meal. Since most of Europe does not accept genetically modified grains into its markets, these grains are utilized in North America either as feed for animals or in the human food chain.

Confinement hog production facilities are generally managed by professionals working out of a central office. They may be responsible for thousands of animals at multiple sites and for many employees who do the day-to-day work. These employees generally have repetitive jobs that require little formal education, do not pay well, and involve difficult working conditions. Because these employees follow fixed operational procedures, there are limited opportunities for classical animal husbandry.

Studies done in Mississippi observed that large CAFOs were unevenly distributed and occurred in greater numbers in geographical areas that had a higher percentage of African Americans and a higher percentage of persons in poverty than areas without CAFOs. The clumped distribution of large production facilities may have adverse environmental impacts, such as increased human health risks.[84]

Increases in the geographic concentration of hog production have led to water pollution through spills and leakage from high numbers of very large manure storage lagoons.[85] When manure is applied inappropriately, large amounts of nitrogen and phosphorus enter the environment through runoff, percolation into groundwater, and volatilization of ammonia from CAFOs. Many CAFOs are located in nutrient-sensitive watersheds where the wastes contribute to eutrophication of lakes and pollution of streams and rivers.

A PIG'S LIFE?

In a conventional confinement hog facility, mature female pigs (sows) are housed in large, slatted-floor (which allows manure to fall through), power-ventilated buildings with hundreds or thousands of other sows, all of which are fed a restricted diet to minimize excess weight gain, and watched closely for signs of heat (ovulation). Animals in heat are fertilized using artificial insemination (a person uses a special tool to insert semen collected from a superior boar [mature male]). Once the sow becomes pregnant, she is moved to a gestation crate just large enough for her to stand up and lay down, for about 110 days. The last few days of her pregnancy, she is moved to a birthing crate, in which she gives birth to eight to fifteen piglets. The crate restricts the sow's movement, decreasing the likelihood that she will roll over and accidentally crush her young. Shortly after birth, the eye-teeth and tails of the piglets are clipped, and the males are castrated. Each piglet is also given an iron shot and vaccinated for common diseases. At ten to twelve days of age, the young are weaned and moved to a nursery facility at a separate site, and the sow is prepared for another reproductive cycle. In a well-managed herd, the average sow will give birth to a litter of pigs every five months and produce a total of four litters before being culled. Young pigs are raised to 40 to 50 pounds in the controlled environment nursery building and then are moved to a finishing building at another site. Animals are often shipped a hundred miles or more between sites, depending on facility arrangements. The typical finishing building houses 1,200 or more animals separated into pens of about fifty animals each. Animals are monitored daily for health and treated when necessary. Feeding and watering are completely automated. Market weight is approximately 260 pounds and is attained about 180 days after birth. Manure from sow, nursery, and finishing facilities is stored in liquid form in pits below the buildings, or in outside lagoons. It is typically applied to surrounding cropland in the spring and/or fall of the year.*

*For a more detailed description of conventional and alternative swine production systems, see University of Minnesota Extension publication no. BU–07641, "Hogs Your Way: Hog Production Systems for the Upper Midwest," available online at http://www.extension.umn.edu/distribution/livestocksystems/DI7641.html.

How did we arrive at the present agricultural situation in North America?

The history of North American agriculture can be examined by reviewing the development of social contracts between those producing food and fiber and those consuming these items. In this context, the term social contract means an unwritten understanding between various groups within society.

Native Americans practiced an extensive (using a large area with minimal disturbance) form of agriculture prior to the arrival of Europeans. They had a very complex system of agriculture that was successful chiefly because it worked in harmony with the God-ordained cycles of creation. Although substantial differences existed among tribes, there were some common characteristics. In general, they viewed land as something that could not be bought, sold, or owned individually. It was considered sacred and was to be well cared for so that all might benefit. In order for everyone in the village to be fed, crops were grown to supplement hunting and fishing. Game and crops were shared with everyone in the village based on elaborate systems that had developed over time.

The Puritans are associated with the next social contract. In many ways, their view of land and creation was the opposite of the Native American view. Their goal was to establish the kingdom of God in the new world. They believed God was a God of orderliness. Therefore, forests and other "wild" ecosystems needed to be removed so that crops could be planted, whereas the Indians planted their crops in open spaces between trees. The Puritans viewed land as something that could be owned, bought, and sold.

The next social contract in United States agriculture was outlined by Thomas Jefferson and can generally be called *agrarianism*.[86] In the narrow sense of the term, agrarianism can be described as the belief that farming is the best way of life and the most important economic endeavor. Newer forms of agrarianism take a broader view and include important concepts of community and justice in both rural and urban settings.[87] Jefferson wrote with hyperbole that "those who labor in the earth are the chosen people of God, if he had a chosen people" and "cultivators of the earth are the most valuable citizens. They are the most vigorous, the most independent, the most virtuous, and they are tied to their country and wedded to its liberty and interests by the most lasting bonds."[88]

The agrarian social concept has guided (and still influences) United States agriculture, although it has been challenged. Alexander Hamilton and James Madison, contemporaries of Jefferson, believed that the United States would be best served by concentrating power in an elite, educated class of gentlemen whose financial interests would be tied to large landed estates. They felt that "common" citizens would shirk their responsibility for public good and only press for personal interests. The Civil War in one sense was a war over whether the philosophy of Jefferson or Hamilton would be the guiding principle for United States agriculture.

The last two social contracts for United States agriculture are both products of the twentieth century and often conflict. The first is the industrialization of agriculture. This started with the advent of World War I and in some sectors is still going on today. The concept here is to produce food and fiber with the fewest people possible. Early on, this freed up people to help in war efforts; later it freed them up to pursue a "better life." Labor is considered costly and therefore is an input to be minimized. Education is thought to be the ticket to the "better life."

A social contract that is often in conflict with industrialization is society's expectation that farmers and others involved in the food system should maintain open space, clean air, and clean water for the benefit of all of society. The expectation of mutual benefit is often at odds with the trend toward industrialization. This creates a tension that frequently surfaces in contemporary agricultural debates.

What criteria should Christians use to evaluate the present system?

Many Christians are hesitant to question the status quo in agriculture. They realize that by doing so they may end up critiquing family, friends, or fellow Christians who are part of the system as either producers or consumers. This situation makes them uncomfortable. According to Scripture, however, followers of Christ are called to evaluate all aspects of life. In Philippians 1:9–11, the apostle Paul says, "And this is my prayer: that your love may abound more and more in knowledge and depth of insight, so that you may be able to discern what is best and may be pure and blameless until the day of Christ, filled with the fruit of righteousness that comes through Jesus Christ—to the glory and praise of God." Paul is saying that if we are to deepen our relationship with Christ and maximize the glory and praise we bring to God, we need to carefully examine our culture and identify those aspects that are good as well as those that need to be changed. Followers of Jesus Christ are not constrained by the culture in which they live; rather, they should seek to transcend and reform the culture in which they live (Rom. 12:2; 2 Cor. 5:17; James 4:4).

It is one thing to accept a task, but another thing entirely to figure out how to do it and do it well. What criteria should Christians use to discern God's intentions for food systems? How do we know which practices reflect obedient responses to God's call and which reflect disobedience and rebellion? The will of God for creation can be found by searching the two great books of Scripture and creation.

Theoretically, we should be able to tell the difference between Christians and non-Christians by the food choices they make and by the way they farm. Practically, however, this is not easy. Obviously, if we are going to evaluate our food system we need to begin by articulating some Christian principles that can be used as plumb lines (Isa. 28:17).

A foundational principle is that the earth belongs to God (Lev. 25:23; Ps. 24:1) and exists to give Him praise and glory and honor (Gen. 6:5–8; Ps. 19). God, not people, is the owner of all things. Creation doesn't exist primarily to meet human needs and wants. Its ultimate purpose is to give God glory and honor—to "sing" His praises. Humans were created to direct the earthly choir (following God's leading) by serving it and caring for it (Gen. 1:28; 2:15).

This understanding has practical implications. It means that normative food systems will help maintain the vast array of creatures made and owned by God Himself and that these food systems will enable each of these creatures to live as God created them to. In other words, these systems will maintain the integrity of the choir (not cause the loss of members via extinction) and will enable all the members to "sing" (function in God's world) as God has created them to (Job 38–41). This means that good agricultural systems must leave room for God's wild creatures and that all the plants and animals in the system, both wild and domestic, must be encouraged to express the full range of characteristics that God has given them. These characteristics include things like forming social groups, finding mates, pollinating, reproducing, caring for young, migrating, and finding food. Good agricultural systems, therefore, will do much more than produce protein, carbohydrates, fiber, or energy for human utilization. Christian systems will help all of the creatures in them live as God designed them to live and thus enable these creatures to bring praise and honor to their Creator.[89]

This principle gives us some guidance regarding the biotic aspects of food systems, but what about economic and social aspects? One of the major themes of Old Testament law is justice and care for the weak and socially vulnerable in society. God commanded the Israelites to make sure that aliens, widows, the fatherless, and the poor were treated fairly and provided for (Ex. 22:21–27; 23:6–12). This principle clearly applies to contemporary agricultural systems, even though the specific regulations and penalties do not. The application of this principle in today's food system might mean adequate pay and benefits for migrant workers, government policy that favors small (powerless) farmers rather than large and powerful ones, and food subsidies for low-income families (Deut. 24:19–21).

A second social and economic principle is that a good food system must be based on deep and genuine interpersonal relationships. The importance of relationships is underscored by Jesus' summary of the law. In Mark 12:30–31 Jesus says that the most important commandment is to "'Love the Lord your God with all your heart and with all your soul and with all your mind and with all your strength.' The second is this: 'Love your neighbor as yourself.' There is no commandment greater than these." The striking thing about Jesus' summary of the law is that it is entirely relational. In Luke, the summary of the law is followed by the parable of the good Samaritan (Luke 10:29–37), in which the loving neighbor shows mercy to the man in need. At the conclusion of the parable Jesus commands the expert in the law to "Go and do likewise." Clearly, when Jesus commands us to love our neighbor as ourselves, He means actions, not just feelings.

If we are to take Jesus' command to love our neighbor seriously, we must have a relationship with that neighbor. If a farmer knows the individuals consuming the food he or she produces, the farmer can express love by producing safe and nutritious food and selling it at a fair price. A consumer who knows the farmer can request and purchase food products that allow the farmer to make an adequate living, enjoy a healthy lifestyle, direct creation's choir with care, and have meaningful and challenging work. The key to the expression of love in the food system context is a relationship between the producer and/or processor and the person eating the food. A good food system will facilitate the development of meaningful relationships between those who participate in it and encourage those involved to truly "love their neighbor as themselves."[90]

How has sin impacted North American agriculture?

Sinful people (all of us) miss the mark individually, but we also join together with other sinful people and create broad social structures and policies influenced by sin.

Individual farmers might sin by allowing their soil to erode, paying employees inadequately, preventing their animals from living as God designed them to, contributing to water quality problems, eliminating wildlife habitat from their farms, or in many other ways. Consumers can sin by demanding either too much food or too much variety, by failing to support farmers who are living out their faith, or by purchasing agricultural products produced in unethical ways. Sin on this level involves a personal response to God and His calling for our lives.

Sin also affects agricultural markets, financial institutions, farm suppliers, and national farm policy. Sin on these levels becomes part of the structure of agriculture, part of the overall context within which farmers and consumers must function. Structural sin may limit market access for smaller producers, promote genetic manipulation motivated by a utilitarian approach to creation, or ignore global climate change. It may also allocate agricultural production in questionable ways (as with corn) or make it very difficult for producers to allow their land and animals to take a Sabbath rest. These impacts of sin are very difficult for individual farmers or consumers to deal with. An effective response requires the identification of the societal structure that needs to be changed and the mobilization of many citizens.

Sin at both levels often has at its root the anthropocentric belief that creation is here primarily for our benefit.[91] People have a persistent tendency to believe that they have the authority to decide which parts of creation have value and which do not, to make themselves judges of creation's worth. Psalm 148 makes it clear that God is the One who gives creation its value. When people at individual and societal levels forget this truth, the outcome is tragic. Examples include the destruction of 99.9 percent of the tall grass prairie ecosystem in the state of Iowa,[92] large oxygen depleted zones in the Gulf of Mexico,[93] and a lack of animal husbandry.[94]

Is anyone attempting to establish a "good" food system? What can Christians do to support these efforts?

Many individual farmers and consumers are working to make the United States food system more consistent with a God-centered point of view. Some Christian farmers have set aside land for wildlife and changed production practices to control soil erosion and to improve water quality by reducing nutrient and pesticide loads. Others have modified their livestock production practices to enable the animals they care for to express their God-given characteristics. The market for organically produced food is growing by about 20 percent per year. In general, organic production practices are preferable to conventional ones. Christian farmers are also selling, and consumers are buying, food at local farmers' markets. Others have set up and joined community supported agriculture organizations explicitly designed to connect producers and consumers and to promote creation-friendly production and consumption patterns. The United States Department of Agriculture (USDA) has set up the Alternative Farming Systems Information Center (AFSIC). It is available for viewing at http://www.nal.usda.gov/afsic/csa. Several organizations are also promoting food system changes that are generally consistent with a Christian perspective. Some of these are listed in the Suggested Reading section at the end of this chapter.

What can Christians do to support the development of good food systems? We can start by making it a matter of sincere prayer. We can follow that up by finding out where our food comes from. Once we know, we can consciously decide to support farmers, processors, wholesalers, and retailers who share our Christian values and bring them to life in their day-to-day business practices. We can also talk to friends, relatives, people in our churches and our schools, and advocate for a Christian food system. Structural changes are needed as well. We can vote, volunteer to help with an election campaign, or become politically active ourselves. Some of us may even decide to pursue a career in some part of the food system. God is clearly at work in this part of His Kingdom. He wants Christians to join Him in the redemptive work of developing a truly good food system that brings praise, honor, and glory to the Creator.

QUESTIONS

1. How do you think God designed cattle to live? How about elk or a native grass like little bluestem? What kind of a system would it take for all three to coexist and express their God-given abilities?

2. What changes in the agriculture-food system can and should be made by producers? Which ones need to be supported or demanded by those who purchase food?

3. To what extent should congregations, denominations, and/or parachurch organizations get involved in the issue of food system reform? Explain.

4. Christians may be tempted to separate reality into sacred and secular domains. This might be expressed by ignoring how food is produced and focusing on more "spiritual" topics. What do the following passages have to say about this dichotomy: Micah 6:8; Isaiah 56:1–7; Jeremiah 7:1–11?

5. Define and compare biocentric, theocentric, and anthropocentric worldviews of creation. Examine the effect that each worldview has on the design of food production systems. (See Roger W. Elmore, "Our Relationship with the Ecosystem and Its Impact on Sustainable Agriculture," *Journal of Production Agriculture* 9, no. 1 (1996): 42–45.)

NOTES

75. U.S. Department of Agriculture, National Agricultural Statistics Service, *Field Crops Graphics* (January 2005), available at http://www.usda.gov/nass/aggraphs/crops.htm.

76. Ibid.

77. U.S. Department of Agriculture, *USDA Agricultural Baseline Projections to 2013*, Economic Research Service, Publication No. WAOB–2004–1 (February 2004), 38. Also available at http://www.ers.usda.gov/publications/waob041/.

78. Richard Rathge and Paula Highman, "Population Change in the Great Plains: A History of Prolonged Decline," *Rural Development Perspectives* 13, no. 1 (July 1998): 19–26.

79. U.S. Department of Agriculture, Dean Jolliffe, *Rural Poverty at a Glance*, Economic Research Service, Rural Development Research Report No. RDRR100 (July 2004). Available at http://www.ers.usda.gov/publications/rdrr100/.

80. Jeffry Walser and John Anderlik, "Rural Depopulation: What Does It Mean for the Future Economic Health of Rural Areas and the Community Banks That Support Them?" Federal Deposit Insurance Corporation, October 15, 2004, http://www.fdic.gov/bank/analytical/future/fob_04.pdf.

81. U.S. Department of Agriculture, Ralph Heimlich, *Agricultural Resources and Environmental Indicators, 2003*, Economic Research Service, Agriculture Handbook No. AH722, October 22, 2003, http://www.ers.usda.gov/publications/arei/ah722/dbgen.htm.

82. "Number of Hog Operations, United States," April 30, 2004, http://www.usda.gov/nass/aggraphs/hgoper_e.htm.

83. Ron Plain, "Number of U.S. Farms Raising Hogs Declined in 2001," ThePigSite Latest News, February 2002, http://www.thepigsite.com/LatestNews/Default.asp?AREA=LatestNews&Display=2972.

84. Wilson Sacoby, Frank Howell, Steve Wing, and Mark Sobsey, "Environment Injustice and the Mississippi Hog Industry," *Environmental Health Perspectives*, no. 110 (2002): 195–201.

85. Rich Wesh, Bryan Hubbell, and Chantal Line Carpentier, "Agro-food System Restructuring and the Geographic Concentration of US Swine Production," *Environment and Planning Abstracts* 35, no. 2 (2003): 215.

86. R. Douglas Hurt, *American Agriculture: A Brief History* (West Lafayette, Ind.: Purdue Univ. Press, 2002), 72.

87. See Eric T. Freyfogle, *The New Agrarianism-Land, Culture, and the Community of Life* (Washington, D.C.: Island, 2001).

88. Thomas Jefferson, "Writings: Thomas Jefferson," in *Literary Classics of the United States*, ed. Merrill D. Petersen (New York: Library of America, 1984).

89. Robert De Haan, "Production Principles for 'Good' Agriculture," in *Biblical Holism and Agriculture: Cultivating Our Roots* (Pasadena, Calif.: William Carey Library, 2003), 81–97.

90. Ronald J. Vos, "Social Principles for 'Good' Agriculture," in *Biblical Holism and Agriculture*, 43–63.

91. Roger W. Elmore, "Our Relationship with the Ecosystem and Its Impact on Sustainable Agriculture," *Journal of Production Agriculture* 9, no. 1 (1996): 42–45.

92. Fred Samson and Fritz Knopf, "Prairie Conservation in North America," *Bioscience*, 44, no. 6 (June 1994): 418–21.

93. Nancy N. Rabalais, R. Eugene Turner, and Donald Scavia, "Beyond Science into Policy: Gulf of Mexico Hypoxia and the Mississippi River," *Bioscience* 52, no. 2 (February 2002): 129–42.

94. Bernard E. Rollin, "Hog Heaven: Preaching to Swine Farmers," *Christian Century*, June 19, 2002, 10–11.

SUGGESTED READING

Evans, D. J., R. J. Vos, and K. P. Wright, eds. *Biblical Holism and Agriculture—Cultivating Our Roots*. Pasadena, Calif.: William Carey Library, 2003.

Van Dyke, F., D. C. Mahan, J. K. Sheldon, and H. B. Raymond. *Redeeming Creation: The Biblical Basis for Environmental Stewardship*. Downers Grove, Ill.: InterVarsity Press, 1996.

Online Resources:

The Center for Rural Affairs—http://www.cfra.org/

The Christian Farmers Federation of Ontario—http://www.christianfarmers.org/index.html

Farm Bureau—http://www.fb.org/

Institute for Agriculture and Trade Policy—http://www.iatp.org/

National Farmers Union—http://www.nfu.org/

National Sustainable Agriculture Information Service—http://www.attra.org/

Practical Farmers of Iowa—http://www.practicalfarmers.org/

Sustainable Agriculture Research and Education—http://www.sare.org/

HOW SHOULD THE CHRISTIAN'S FOUNDATIONAL BELIEFS SHAPE THE WORK OF SCIENTISTS?

E. David Cook

This book is about questions that arise as we practice our Christian faith and proper scientific work. The reader has been able to walk with practicing scientists as they have encountered the crucial questions that arise as scientific work is conducted. These scientists have not tried to avoid difficult areas or issues; rather, they have honestly and professionally shown how scientific work and Christianity are not in conflict but are intertwined and mutually enhance each other. We can focus on what we have learned by trying to articulate the fundamental questions that have emerged at the points of intersection between the Christian faith and the practice of science. The profound questions and answers at these intersections force Christians to ask tough questions and to harmonize the faith truths with the natural world.

What have we learned about the nature of the world?

As scientists undertake their scientific work, they realize that to do science at all requires assumptions about the way the world is and how we know about it. It is amazing that, for all of the different scientific enterprises explored in this book, there is universal agreement among scientists around the world that the world is ordered and can be understood by humanity.

Of course, some might argue that ordered nature is just the way the world is and humans are, so ordering of the cosmos is all left to chance. Others claim that there is no real order in the world and what we call science is really just human beings forcing their perceptions on the world and making it seem ordered when in fact it is not ordered at all.

Regardless of the difficulty in making these views fit the facts, historically and practically, there is no doubt that science is possible only when we assume that there is an order to and in the world; hence, the more we research the nature of reality, the more we see the order. What is inevitable, however, is that in finding such order, we ask about the origin of that order—whether it is just chance or there by itself or the result of some divine creation. Scripture strongly affirms that the earth is the Lord's and that everything in it comes from and is sustained by Him.

Christians in science approach their work believing that God created the world and imparted order to that creation. The world is intelligible, and the more we develop our scientific understanding, the more we learn of the order and purpose in the world. The world is not self-explanatory, and in seeking explanations for the world, we find that the Christian account fits well with the way the world is and the way it functions.

The world is real and makes sense. That is not to say that we do or even ever will understand all there is to know about the world, but we have learned extraordinary amounts of information about the nature of the world. We also trust that our information is more accurate than that discovered in past centuries. The success of science is not just that the descriptions scientists offer match what we find as we go about the work of science, but is also that the results and findings of scientific experimental work allow us to direct, control, and benefit from these scientific discoveries. Science works.

Technology demonstrates the validity of our scientific understanding of the world from the subatomic and genetic level to the behavior of the solar systems and ecosystems. Science is dynamic, and the progressive nature of science is shown in our scientific descriptions and our technological applications that are constantly being refined and reapplied as we discover more about the world and its nature.

What have we learned about the nature of the divine?

Everything we do requires that we make assumptions about who we are, what we do, and the context and content of what we are doing. Christians believe not just that the world makes sense and that we can make sense of it, but also that the order of the world and our capacity to discover order arises directly from the God who created the world and all that is therein. Christians believe that God reveals Himself in the world that He has made, in the process of history, in the special revelation of Jesus Christ, and in the Bible, God's Word.

The nature of God is revealed in the fact and nature of creation. The world tells us that we can know the good God who created and sustains the world and humanity. In this we learn that God is a revealing God. He helps humanity understand that He exists and what He is like. He is a creative God who made the world out of nothing. There was no preexistent reality with which He worked. In His almighty power, He created the world, but He does not leave it to work on its own. In God's goodness, He maintains its being and operation. When the psalmist says that the heavens declare the glory of the Lord, we realize that God is not just creative, all powerful, and good, but He is worthy of worship and praise. He deserves worship because of the wonderful works He has done and what He continues to do. He enables humankind to grasp the ordered nature of the world. If the world is intelligible, God has also made us intelligent enough to make sense of what He has made. This is part of knowing the goodness of God.

The world is just right for human life. A delicate balance of nature enables human life to grow, develop, and flourish. The conditions of the world at every biological, chemical, and physical level have been designed to sustain life. God is also a revealing God who helps us understand the world, who we are and what God is like. A frailty of humanness is the inability to hold on to all knowledge and all understanding with our limited and fallen human minds. However, even if humans cannot know everything, that doesn't mean that we cannot know a great deal and act on the basis of that information.

The created order and the world are the important context and arena where the drama of human salvation takes place. God entered into time and space in the incarnation of Jesus Christ. In that action, God affirms the goodness of the physical realm and begins the crucial actions of redemption that culminate in the death and resurrection of Jesus Christ. The raising of Jesus from the dead by God as the actual and symbolic manifestation of redeemed and restored humanity shows the worth and value of the created world. It also substantiates God's commitment to and love for the world and everything in it. He has created, and His providential daily care and provision for humanity are matched by the particular revelation of His love in the giving of His Son, Jesus. Jesus Christ brought humanity from the sin that affects each person into a restored, living relationship with God, who created and sustains creation. Studies in science, reflected on by rational minds that ask metaphysical questions, teach us a great deal about the loving, creating, sustaining, and providential nature of God. The responses of humans to revelations about God's creative nature and provision for humankind should result in adoration, wonder, and worship of the loving God who designed and made humans.

What have we learned about the nature of humanity?

The psalmist reminds readers that when the heavens, the stars, and all the fruits of God's work are considered, we readily see that humanity is limited in the grand scheme of things. The more learned we become, especially in engaging the scientific process, the more we discover human limitations and frailty. Human lives are limited and fragile. Death can occur at any moment. Knowledge about the natural world is incomplete, and it is constantly corrected and refined as science yields more insights. Human nature is not viewed as "ideal." The apostle Paul complains that the good we know we ought to do and follow, we fail to do, and the evil we know we ought to avoid, we still go ahead and do (Rom. 7:14–20). Human beings are sinful people. What humans do to the delicate balance of nature and to harm our environment is scandalous, but that is put in the shadows as the evil done to our fellow human beings is revealed. Note, for example, the ways in which humans abuse scientific knowledge and build conventional, nuclear, chemical, and biological weapons of individual and mass destruction.

The Bible affirms the value and worth of humans when it says that people are created in God's image and that Christ died for humanity. Humans are created and destined for glorious relationships with God, each other, and the redeemed and restored harmonious world that God has designed for those who love and worship Him. Human beings are made from dust and destined for glory.

Humans are seekers. They want to know and understand who they are and all they can learn about the world around them. That natural curiosity is as much a part of human nature as human weaknesses, failings, and shortcomings—our sinful nature. Even though we are sinful creatures, God has given us the capacity to understand and direct the world and to care for ourselves, each other, and the world surrounding us. God has entrusted His world to humans to steward. People are responsible and are able to make a response to God while bearing the moral responsibility for words, thoughts, and actions as well as shortcomings, failures, and omissions. Part of our relationship with the Creator is that all of us will be required to give an account before the judgment seat of God for all we have done and have failed to do. Life is serious and complicated for humans because they are their brothers' and sisters' keepers, stewards of the world, and answerable to God their Creator.

Humankind's abilities can be used to benefit the world and its inhabitants or to destroy it. The good news is that God lovingly displays His commitment to humanity and intervenes by sending His Son to be the Savior. That salvation will be completed when the new heaven and earth fulfill and express all that God intends for human good.

What is the relationship between the world and humanity?

In reading the descriptions of an absolute beginning in the early chapters of Genesis and in exploring the effect of human beings on the world and in the practice of science, we learn that there is a close and powerful relationship between humanity and the world. Everything is equally created. Either something is created or it is not. A person cannot be more or less created. Thus there is equality in creation. Humans share the same world, and all human beings affect the world. Everything that happens in the world affects human beings. Interdependence is a fundamental characteristic of life. Humans not only share the same ecosystem with the rest of creation, but they are also part of that ecosystem. Humanity and the world are mutually interdependent.

That, however, does not mean that everything is just the same and of the same value. In making humans in His image and giving them specific responsibilities for care of the world and the other creatures He had made, God indicated that human beings are distinguishable from the rest of creation. This distinction is not a basis for pride but a commissioning by God to be responsible stewards of His creation.

Science is crucial because it enables humans to engage properly in the God-given task of caring for creation. Unfortunately, environmental science has reiterated what the early chapters of Genesis affirm—human beings are sinful, and all we do affects the world and our environment. Clearly, there are better and worse ways of treating the world and animals. Science helps humans discern what enables the created order to flourish and what harms it. This is not some idiosyncratic perspective; it is a matter of life and death for many species, humans, and even the world itself.

Science enables humans to develop a vision for their relationship to the world of which they are part and on which they depend, so that they and their children will be able to enjoy a good life in a flourishing world full of variety.

How should we be good stewards of all God has given us?

There can be no doubt that God's image bearers are called to be good stewards of all that God has given. Yet there also is no doubt that humans are abusing and quickly using up vital resources. Therefore, we must ask, "How shall God's people live in light of God's commands and the desperate state of the world and environment?"

Science is essential to discerning the parts of creation that need attention and to developing strategies to preserve the creation. Good scientific information is vital to develop priorities to conserve God's good earth. Stewards are responsible not just for conserving the created order, but also for developing the well-being and potential of species and the world. Although stewards are allowed to live off the world and enjoy its fruits, that is no charter for exploitation and abuse. When we consider how humans live in the world, we must consider actions and behavior in light of and in relation to God. Since humans are answerable to God for all they do, they should make clear decisions, assessing behavior and presenting a rationale for what has been done and will be done in light of God's standards and will.

The church tradition of natural law is often expressed as creation ordinances or creation ethics. This tradition is a reminder that there are good reasons why God made the world as He did, and even though sin has affected that order, signs remain of God's intentions in the way the world operates. Accordingly, we should explore the nature of how things individually and together flourish as we try to follow God's endowed purpose and plan. As we learn more about the rich diversity of plant life on Earth, it is no surprise to discover the natural goodness contained in so many of these plants, which was often known by indigenous people, whose wisdom has been lost as modern medicine has advanced. The full circle has led back to homeopathic remedies based on God's generous provision for human well-being. The natural sciences provide insight into the delicate balance of all things living together in proper relationship. Living in harmony is part of the *shalom* God intended from the start in Eden and promised will be fulfilled in the New Jerusalem, the redeemed heaven and earth.

Our stewardship responsibility is delegated by Christ Himself, for all things have been created by Him and are His. Christ expects His stewards to use intellect to rule over the natural world. The principles involved in stewardship of nature are also useful for guardianship of our minds, spirits, and bodies. In Jesus' parable of the talents, He made his expectations clear. His servants should not bury their talents, but should make extraordinary advances in caring for the resources entrusted to them. Christ gives significance to how humans use what they have been given in this life. As His servants, they are responsible for the welfare of the resources of the current generation and for their legacy to future generations. Truly serving Christ is a noble role motivated by love for Him with a promise for the great commendation, "Well done good and faithful servant."

How do we establish ethical guidelines for study of the natural realm?

The practice of science is not just science; it also considers social and cultural settings and is undergirded by particular presuppositions. Not least of these are ethical presuppositions about the nature and practice of science and what should be done in light of scientific knowledge. Thus, the practice of science requires some ethical guidelines. When there is a report of a new scientific discovery in a scientific journal, the reader believes it represents the actual work of the people presenting the new discovery. They have not stolen the theory or pretended that it is their own work when in fact it belongs to someone else. The reader has confidence that the writers are telling the truth, that their results can be replicated, and that there are no negative results that have been hidden or ignored.

Science proceeds on the assumption that those involved are part of a community of women and men of good faith who are honest and trustworthy. Scientists are asked to declare conflicts of interest and reveal sources of funding so that the results and the implications drawn from them are not dishonestly influenced. Commercial interests might influence scientists to slew results in certain financially favorable directions rather than to simply tell the truth, especially when large sums of money are involved. Similarly, science ought to proceed on the basis of respect, whether for nature itself, humans, animals, plants, or even insects. Humans interfere with God's plan for nature at their own peril. Therefore, they should work with and in nature using holistic methods that are genuinely for the benefit of all concerned. If there is a cost to nature, it should be carefully weighed as worthwhile and a proper price paid.

Society also recognizes that scientists must not be left to their own devices. In medical research, there is a simple rule about how to limit such research. Previously, the question asked was, "Would a scientist do this to himself or herself?" But history has shown that some scientists would do anything to themselves for the sake of their theory. Later a different question was introduced: "Would a scientist do this to a member of his or her own family?" Likewise, tradition has shown that scientists would do anything to their family for the sake of their theory. In recent years, ethics committees and institutional research boards have been introduced to oversee scientific research experimentation. Society has set legal and institutional review boards in place to ensure that animals and people are safeguarded in scientific research and experiments.

Clear ethical guidelines have been delineated to protect animals and humans. These guidelines are based on such values as protecting privacy, minimizing harm, avoiding unnecessary research and exploitation, securing fully informed, valid consent, and ensuring that research facilities are humanely run and organized.

When research is conducted on nature, the ethical guidelines lie within the individual scientist, the community of scientists, and the social, legal, and cultural context of the scientific enterprise. Increasingly, codes of ethics are being drawn up and ethics is being taught as part of science courses. The scientific community recognizes that it must set its own house in moral order, and institutions recognize that they must create a highly ethical climate for the practice of science. Moreover, there is an overwhelming move toward forming ecological guidelines in the practice of science. Environmental concerns now feature greatly in how nature and animals are treated as understanding of their functions is disclosed. A simple set of guidelines might include determining principles that undergird the research, the motives involved, the actual process itself, who and what are affected, and the likely consequences of the research.

Scientists increasingly accept responsibility for the knowledge they discover and how they apply the fruits of their research. They make tremendous good and evil possible. Once scientific knowledge is in the public domain, that knowledge and the uses to which it is put must be carefully monitored. A totally free market economy in science would lead to extreme vulnerability for all except those who had the most money and research clout.

QUESTIONS

1. How is the practice of science loving God with our minds?

2. To what lengths should scientists and science be controlled by society and law?

3. If Christian values are rejected, what kind of moral rules can be agreed upon for scientific practice?

SUGGESTED READING

Cook, David. *The Moral Maze.* London: SPCK, 1994.

Reichenbach, Bruce R., and V. Elving Anderson. *On Behalf of God: A Christian Ethic for Biology.* Grand Rapids: Eerdmans, 1995.

Van Dyke, Fred, David C. Mahn, Joseph Sheldon, and Raymond H. Brand. *Redeeming Creation: The Biblical Basis for Environmental Stewardship.* Downers Grove, Ill.: Inter-Varsity Press, 1996.

CONCLUSION

Great expectations: What we hoped for at the start

When we start something new or begin a new journey, we often have high expectations. The same is true when we pick up a book we haven't read. When this book was conceived, the editors' expectations were that the various authors would produce a book not only worth reading, but that fulfilled our hopes. Two intentions focused our attention. The book should represent good science and a good expression of the Christian faith. We hoped for a good integration of Christian faith and science. We began stressing that what scientists do is not just science. It is an expression of their worldviews and of society's and culture's needs and expectations, and the product of a particular historical context and tradition. Science does not arise in a vacuum. It is firmly contextualized. Science is an important part of how societies attempt to understand the world. Societies use that understanding to improve humanity in care of health, living conditions and the well-being of Earth itself, the environment and the animal and plant kingdoms, and for Christians, to worship God.

Good science enables and facilitates appropriate control and direction of all that the world has for the good of all. The authors of this book are people who are committed to the reality of the living triune God and His relationship in the creation and sustaining of the universe and of humanity. They also acknowledge the truth and authority of the Scriptures, which point us to the saving life, death, and resurrection of Jesus Christ, and the calling of every Christian to understand, relate with, and behave properly toward God's world and each other.

These authors believe that God has given humanity the gift of minds for intellectual engagement, understanding, and superintending knowledge. Our minds enable us to grasp the nature and purpose of the world and all that is in it. As part of the creation mandate that God gave our human parents, Adam and Eve, knowledge remains part of our human responsibility and stewardship to God for His and our world and everything in it.

The world around us reveals details about the ways human beings affect the world. We can help it flourish and be nurtured, or we can abuse and destroy it. The early chapters of the book of Genesis are confirmed by the lessons from ecology and should be seen in the context of the creation of a new heavenly and earthly realm as vividly pictured by the prophet Isaiah (Isa. 35) and by the apostle John in the final chapters of the book of Revelation.

The more we understand and engage in scientific work and research, the more we do justice to who God is and what science is all about. The aim throughout this book is to proclaim that God is God—Creator and Lord of all. We have sought to disclose scientific truth and the limitations of scientific knowledge while clarifying understanding and purporting a healthy perspective and celebration of truth. Every writer has tried to blend his or her scientific understanding and practice with a grasp of biblical truth and insight.

Inevitably, this means that our anthropology and worldview have been expressed. Part of that is a view of humanity that is both realistic and optimistic. Human beings can indeed understand and direct science, scientific wisdom and knowledge, and the application of science. We have seen how scientific knowledge can be used for good and ill. The same scientific grasp that enables the discovery of new advanced medical treatments and cures for horrific diseases can also produce frightening weapons of mass destruction that affect not just human beings but also the very world itself for generations to come.

Not just science in perspective: What we learned along the way

The history of the rise of Western science shows clearly that the Christian faith encouraged and enabled the development of good science and that many good scientists were fine Christians. That remains true today, when so many engaged in scientific teaching and research find no conflict between their personal Christian faith and the science they practice. For many of us, it is extremely odd and very sad that those who are most critical of the boundary of science and Christian faith write in such negative terms, misunderstanding both the nature of Christianity and the relationship of Christian faith and science. It is not science that leads to conflict, but the worldviews, presuppositions, and philosophies of life they bring to and express in their account of science.

Each worldview has a particular explanation of what it means to be human. As we have recounted the scientific account of particular sciences and their applications, we have seen time and again that human beings are both wonderful and awful. What humanity has discovered and created is remarkable. How we have been guilty of abusive destruction of animals and our fellow human beings is shameful. Such insights into human nature are not a reason for beating our breasts and tearing out our hair, but rather for realizing again our responsibility as human beings for how we conduct science and for what we do with the scientific knowledge we acquire.

In our commitment to the process of education in institutions of higher learning, churches, and other venues, we acknowledge that education is not just about abstract, theoretical learning, but about how we apply what we know in our lives. That is why the application and practice of science has been part of every section in this book. The descriptions we present affect deeply the prescriptions we follow in light of that understanding.

Science cannot and ought not to be divorced from ethics. What scientists do and how they do it matters crucially to how science is viewed and how society deals with scientific knowledge and its practitioners. The Bible is very clear that we are known and judged by our fruits. What we do and how we live reveals the true nature of our knowledge and the quality of our true nature. Good science must be integrated with high ethical standards. We have seen this not only in the standards expected of and practiced by the scientific communities, but also in the applications of scientific knowledge to the problems, challenges, and issues facing society and the world. The integration of high ethical standards with the application of science is literally a matter of life and death for our ecosystem and the human race.

Knowledge can be pursued for its own sake, but in reality, human nature seeks to know things in order to do something with that knowledge. Knowledge gives us more control over what is happening and makes us less victims of circumstances. Natural disasters, disease, and environmental degradation all affect humanity, and we look to science to alleviate the effects of all three. Science has drawn our attention to the way weather creates hurricanes and tornadoes and the way the crust of the earth shifts in earthquakes. It has revealed that our various fossil fuels, fishing stocks, and natural resources are being depleted at an alarming rate. Scientific knowledge has shown the relationships between genes, bacteria, viruses, and disease. Without the benefit of good science, we would remain ignorant of all of these things.

We also look to science to help us find solutions for problems, cures for diseases, strategies to limit the harm, and creative insights into new ways to move forward. All of this matters because scientific knowledge has value not only for its own sake, but for the sake of the world, for our own sakes, and for God's sake. What we have learned along the way is that all scientific knowledge and practice can be seen in light of and come under the control of the sovereign creator God who rules all things. It is no wonder that as the various scientists described their science and the questions raised at the intersection of their Christian faith and their practice of science, notes of rejoicing in their work kept peeking through. This rejoicing is matched by the notes of praise and worship that underlie implicitly, and often are made explicit, in their accounts of the relationships of the scientist, humanity, and the natural world with God Himself. Time and again the very contemplation of the universe and its wonders has led to a sense of the wonder and awe humanity has felt and tried to express in poetry and literature. For Christians that natural realm cannot be separated from the creator God who continues to uphold and sustain reality and humanity. He is indeed worthy of all praise and honor.

What should we do with what we have learned?

When asked to summarize the message of the book, the editors replied that it was one of confidence in practicing science as Christians. To be properly educated in liberal arts requires that each of us has some grasp of the sciences and their potential and limitations. Everyone, Christian and non-Christian alike, should be able to confidently approach the sciences with understanding and recognize the significance that knowledge has for all of humanity.

Christians engaged in the daily work of science can be confident that their work is a proper fulfilling of a God-inspired vocation that is for the good of humanity and a fulfillment of God's unique calling of humankind. It is no wonder that good science has often been done and is being done by fine, committed Christian people, for there is no fundamental conflict between good science and being a good Christian. We have nothing to fear from doing our scientific work well. Nor need we fear what science will produce. We can have that assurance because of who God is—the creator, sustainer, and source of all truth—and because we recognize that science and scientific knowledge are inherently limited, provisional, and open to revision. On this side of eternity, there will be no final, closed scientific conclusions, because our science, our scientific understanding, our expressions of that understanding, and our very human nature are all limited and less than perfect. The good news is that there is always more to know and to be known. In that sense, science will be with us always.

This book has been a communal undertaking. It consists of many different voices with many differing experiences, traditions, and specializations. Each one is committed to good science and sound Christian truth and practice. We are involved in and committed to the kind of education that is called Christian liberal arts, believing that such an education best prepares all of us not only to live in the twenty-first century but to be knowledgeable and careful members of the human community. This book and your reading of it prove that we cannot do our educational and scientific work in isolation. It is not a do-it-yourself business. Neither is Christianity. The practices of science and of the Christian faith are fundamentally community based. We learn and discover, apply and modify, and use and abuse our knowledge and our wisdom together.

Jesus gave two key pictures of how Christians are to behave in the world. They are to be salt and light. That requires involvement and commitment. Our prayer is that many who read will be encouraged to develop a career in the scientific community as committed Christians, knowing that in science they will show that what they do is not just science but part of glorifying and loving God with our hearts, minds, and strength, and our neighbors as ourselves.

ACKNOWLEDGMENTS

We are grateful to all who have contributed to this book. Those contributions include the gifts of finances, prayer, and expertise. May God receive the glory for all that is good in this book. For the errors and weaknesses herein, we acknowledge our own fallenness.

Personal thanks go to Kathleen Cook, who has been a great encourager and has supported this effort in many ways through conversation and the provision of delicious meals over which rich discussions have occurred.

Excellent contributions from many segments of the academic community have influenced this book. The cataloging and managing of the large amounts of material and details of the entire book have been carefully directed by Vicki Totel, who has extended her expertise and much generosity of spirit and goodwill. Special thanks go to her for lending her competence and the greatest Christian graces toward us as we have undertaken this project. Many have contributed to editing, reading, and helping us shape the book. For their intellectual and Spirit-led contributions that have stimulated the academic content of the book, we acknowledge those who have inspired or helped the authors bring this project to completion: Greg Aldin, Robert Brabenec, David Bruce, Katherine Cooper, Jeff Davis, Dillard Faries, Devin Goulding, Cary Gray, Jeffrey Greenberg, Deborah Haarsma, John Hayward, Arthur Holmes, Brian Howell, David Ianuzzo, Stanton Jones, Tim Larsen, Alvaro Nieves, Maggie Noll, Kristen Page, Lisa Richmond, Nadine Rorem, Joe Sheldon, Dan Treier, Samantha Turner, Fred Van Dyke, and William Wharton. Thanks also go to many students who have encouraged and stimulated their faculty. In addition to his contribution of a manuscript, we are grateful to Terence Perciante, who has assisted us with many technical details. Special thanks go to the PEW Charitable Trust for its support of a faculty seminar on "Christology" in 1996, attended by Dr. Joseph Spradley, where he developed some of his ideas for his manuscript.

We are grateful to Stan Gundry, vice president and editor-in-chief at Zondervan; Jim Ruark, senior editor-at-large; and all the personnel at Zondervan for their global contributions to Christian reflection.

Venues and niches for Christian faculty who serve in public and private higher education cannot be left out of the list of those to whom we owe thanks. The discourse that occurs on campuses, in particular, that shapes and maintains the vision for thinking "Christianly" about all fields of enquiry, is provided by the rich heritage of educational institutions. For Wheaton College and other Christian liberal arts colleges, we give thanks for the settings and commitment of all things "for Christ and His kingdom."

Dorothy F. Chappell
E. David Cook

SPECIAL THANKS

Special thanks go to Anita and George Speake, loyal supporters of higher educa-tion, especially the sciences, for their support of this project. They have been excep-tionally generous in helping bring the dream of this project to reality.

The Editors

When I attended Wheaton College as a physics major in the early 1960s, I did not find it strange that some classes focused on God's truth as revealed in the world and others on God's truth as revealed in the Word and that many classes dis-cussed the integration of both. The fact that one should expect to find one truth, God's truth, revealed in both His general and special revelation seemed quite rea-sonable.

Graduate school and three decades in the aerospace industry saw that unity drift out of focus. There was no specific conflict, just the bifurcated focus on the phys-ical world of science and engineering during the week and the Word on Sunday. Moral issues ran through the week; doing the right thing, making the right choices continued seven days, but issues of meaning in science and engineering rarely had a moment to raise their heads.

By 2000 I had retired and finally found some time and thought I'd revisit the unity of God's world and Word. The few books and articles I found and discus-sions with friends seemed woefully unbalanced. Some misquoted science; others seemed decades out of date. Many developed shallow straw men to be easily knocked down on either the scientific or sacred side of the dialogue. In fact, there was no dialogue, only one-sided, weak, unsupported positions.

I easily found people who would gladly discuss the advances of modern science and their moral implications as seen by a secular society; I found others who would gladly reject modern scientific advances based on what seemed to be well-inten-tioned application of shallow, uncritical Christian belief but with no understand-ing of the scientific issue or its true impact. Nobody wanted to do the hard work of really looking at tough questions.

In 2001 I was having a discussion with Dr. Dorothy Chappell, Dean of Natural and Social Sciences at Wheaton College. I told her of my interest in taking a criti-cal look at what I thought were the pressing issues raised by the developments of science in the last twenty or thirty years. Cloning has been a hot issue that has raised questions about scientific ethics or lack thereof. And there have been many other issues inside and outside biology, including issues from the fields of astronomy and cosmology, physics, geology, medicine, and engineering, to name a few. The question is not about what is going on in science, but about how current issues in science impact the Christian scientist or the Christian not in the sciences but who cares about the integration of God's truth.

A few nudges and words of encouragement to Dr. Chappell and hard work by several dedicated Christian faculty over the last three years have led to the book you now hold in your hands. I am not particularly aligned with or opposed to any specific chapter, although I have my favorites, but I am passionately committed to the dialogue the collected chapters represent. The issues should help us focus on the intersection of God's world and His Word and the implications of that intersection for Christians in the sciences today. Go ahead and dig in. It's hard work, but it's fun. I hope you enjoy it!

George Speake

THE AUTHORS

THE EDITORS

Dorothy F. Chappell is Dean of Natural and Social Sciences at Wheaton College (IL). She has served as President of the American Scientific Affiliation, on the Board of Trustees of the Phycological Society of America, on the Board of Advisors of The John Templeton Foundation, on the Board of Trustees of Wheaton College (IL), and as Academic Dean of Gordon College (MA). She is a Fulbright Research Scholar Alumna in Australia, Fiji, New Zealand, and her interests include cell biology of algae, theological and practical approaches to bioethics, and trends in higher education. She is the author of papers on the cell biology of green algae, the distribution of some vascular plants, and bioethical issues.

E. David Cook is currently Holmes Professor of Faith and Learning at Wheaton College (IL); Fellow of Green College, Oxford; and Professor of Christian Ethics, Southern Seminary, Louisville. He is a well-known author, broadcaster, and conference speaker throughout the world. He speaks regularly in the media, especially on medical ethics issues, has had his own television and radio series, and has been part of a weekly topical debate program on the BBC. His latest books include *Question Time* and *Blind Alley Beliefs*, both published by InterVarsity Press. His book *The Moral Maze* is in its tenth edition. He is a member of the UK Xenotransplantation Interim Regulatory Authority and advises the Archbishops of the Anglican Church on medical ethics issues. He has given evidence to both House of Commons and House of Lords working parties on genetics and euthanasia. He divides his time between Chicago and Oxford.

THE CONTRIBUTORS

Dean E. Arnold is Professor of Anthropology at Wheaton College (IL). He was a Fulbright Scholar in Peru and Mexico, a Visiting Fellow at Clare College, Cambridge, and three times a visiting scholar at the Department of Archeology at the University of Cambridge. He is a fellow of the American Association for the Advance-

ment of Science and has received the Society of American Archeology's Award for Excellence in Ceramic Studies. His two books, *Ecology of Ceramic Production in an Andean Community* and *Ceramic Theory and Cultural Process*, both published by Cambridge University Press, and many articles attest to his interest in modern potters, the hermeneutics of material culture, and integrative issues concerning human origins, missions, and anthropology.

June A. Arnold is the Coordinator of Health Professions at Wheaton College (IL), where she advises and mentors students of pre-health professions. Her membership in the National Association of Advisors in the Health Professions and teaching experience in the Department of Biology at Wheaton attest to her expertise as teacher, advisor, and mentor to many students. Currently Ms. Arnold teaches the "Health Professions Seminar/Internship," a course designed for pre-health profession students. Previously, while teaching "Contemporary Issues in Biology," she developed an interest in health-care issues, specifically methods of fostering pre-professional formation and development in undergraduates as they determine their pathway to the health profession of choice. Her interests also include global health and how health-care priorities are expressed in health-care delivery systems.

Vincent E. Bacote is Assistant Professor of Theology at Wheaton College (IL). He is the author of the book *The Spirit in Public Theology: Approaching the Legacy of Abraham Kuyper*. He is president of the Christian Theological Research Fellowship and is a member of both the Evangelical Theological Society and the American Academy of Religion. He has a PhD in Theological and Religious Studies from Drew University, an MDiv from Trinity Evangelical Divinity School with an emphasis in Urban Ministry, and a BS from The Citadel.

Greta M. Bryson is Assistant Professor of Chemistry at Wheaton College (IL). She received her PhD in chemistry from Purdue University and a BS in chemistry from Spelman College. Dr. Bryson is a former Ford Foundation Predoctoral and Post-doctoral Fellow. She teaches general chemistry, a course on drugs and society, and a number of biochemistry courses and labs. Her biochemical research focuses on protein tyrosine phosphatases, enzymes that are involved in signal transduction processes.

Jennifer L. Busch is Assistant Professor of Biology at Wheaton College (IL) with a PhD from Vanderbilt University. She teaches college biology and a variety of physiology courses. Her academic research involves molecular regulatory mechanisms in physiology.

James A. Clark is Professor of Geology at Wheaton College (IL). His research, funded by NASA and NSF, analyzes satellite observations of global sea-level change possibly associated with global warming. His publications are extensive and attract international attention. He also works with Lifewater International, bringing plentiful clean water to African villages.

Robert (Robb) L. De Haan is Associate Professor of Environmental Studies at Dordt College (IA), where he serves as Department Chair. His graduate training is in plant breeding and genetics and in agricultural ecology. He currently teaches ecology and field biology, agroecology, genetics, avian biology, and senior seminar courses. His interests include the ecology of prairie ecosystems, agricultural sustainability, and the intersection of faith and landscape management practices.

Stewart M. DeSoto is Associate Professor of Physics at Wheaton College (IL) and received his PhD from the University of Illinois. He has worked as a design engineer for Texas Instruments. At Wheaton he has taught classical and modern physics, analytical mechanics, experimental physics, mathematical methods, and biological physics. He has published extensively, with emphasis on nuclear magnetic resonance, superconductivity, and integrated circuit design.

Gayle E. Ermer is Associate Professor of Engineering at Calvin College (MI). She teaches "Mechanical Engineering," specializing in manufacturing systems and machine dynamics. She is the author of papers on engineering ethics and women in engineering. She also teaches the core course "Developing a Christian Mind" with a focus on responsible technology.

Larry L. Funck is Professor of Chemistry at Wheaton College (IL). He has supervised the General Chemistry program at Wheaton during his entire thirty-five-year career. He has served in numerous chemical education capacities, including working as a consultant in the Advanced Placement Program for the Educational Testing Service and on several examination committees of the American Chemical Society. He is a Fulbright Alumnus and Lecturer from programs in Lesotho in southern Africa. His interest in origin-of-life chemistry stems in part from his participation in the "Theories of Origins" interdisciplinary course at Wheaton.

Loren Haarsma is Assistant Professor of Physics at Calvin College (MI). He has written several articles and book chapters on the intersection of science, philosophy, and Christian theology and organizes a regular series of seminars on these topics at Calvin. His scientific training is in the fields of experimental atomic physics and neuroscience.

Raymond J. Lewis is Associate Professor of Biology at Wheaton College (IL). His research on the physiology and reproduction of marine algae has been published in various scientific journals. He teaches college courses in advanced plant biology, marine biology, environmental science, environmental ethics, and theories of origins. His interests include research in the reproductive biology of brown algae and Christian environmental ethics.

Stephen O. Moshier is Associate Professor of Geology at Wheaton College (IL). Previously he served on the faculty of the University of Kentucky and as a petroleum geologist with Mobil Oil Corporation. He regularly teaches general science classes in physical geology, natural disasters, oceanography, and theories of origins. His classes for geology majors include Earth history and stratigraphy, general petrology and petrography, biogeology, and geoarchaeology. He has published research on North American and Middle Eastern limestone deposits, petroleum source rocks in Canada, and most recently, the geoarchaeology of ancient Egypt. He has served as president of the Geological Society of Kentucky and the Affiliation of Christian Geologists.

Robert C. O'Connor serves as Chair of the Department of Philosophy at Wheaton College (IL). His research interests have centered on the intersection between science and Christian faith, with a special interest in how understanding the methods of science can help Christians understand the support available for their theology. His most recent work has focused on the argument from design, especially as formulated by the Intelligent Design movement.

Terence H. Perciante is Professor of Mathematics at Wheaton College (IL). His recent work with an international team of writers and researchers has resulted in numerous books, articles, and other publications in the area of fractal geometry and chaos theory. Because he enjoys computer programming for classroom purposes, he has authored multiple educational computer software packages for elementary, middle school, high school, and college teachers. He is a frequent speaker at National Science Foundation institutes and symposia as well as other professional meetings.

Paul W. Robinson is Director of the Human Needs and Global Resources (HNGR) Program and Professor of History at Wheaton College (IL). He grew up in the Democratic Republic of the Congo and Kenya and has lived and worked for forty years in those countries. His scholarly interests center on the dynamics and challenges of international development and culture change, particularly in the arid and semi-arid regions of Africa. For twenty-five years he has developed and led international educational study programs for university students, and his passion is to foster understanding and relationships across cultures and to build global Christian community. He currently serves on several international boards, including Bread for the World, Africa Exchange, Tanari International, and The Congo Initiative.

Helene Slessarev-Jamir is Director of the Urban Studies Program and Associate Professor of Politics and International Relations at Wheaton College (IL). She coauthored a book on federal job training policies in the 1980s and is author of *The Betrayal of the Urban Poor* (Temple University Press), an examination of the failures of American federal anti-poverty efforts. Her current research examines the work of American faith-based organizations in seeking justice for the urban poor and in supporting the upward mobility of new immigrants. She has also done extensive consulting work with Chicago-based educational, civil rights, and community organizations.

Stephen R. Spencer is Blanchard Professor of Theology at Wheaton College (IL) and received his PhD from Michigan State University. He has written on medieval and Reformed scholasticism, the history of biblical interpretation, evangelicalism, eschatology, and apologetics. He has contributed to reference works and symposia, including the *Dictionary for Theological Interpretation of Scripture*, *Evangelical Dictionary of Theology* (2nd Edition), *The Encyclopedia of Christianity*, the *Historical Handbook of Major Biblical Interpreters*, and *Later Calvinism: International Perspectives*. His areas of teaching and research include theological method, theological interpretation of Scripture, Thomas Aquinas, and John Calvin.

Joseph L. Spradley is Professor of Physics at Wheaton College (IL). After completing his BS, MS, and PhD degrees in engineering physics at UCLA and four years of research at Hughes Aircraft Company, he has taught "Physics," "Astronomy," and "History of Science" at Wheaton. He also served as Science Chair and Acting President at Haigazian College in Beirut, Lebanon, from 1965 to 1968; USAID Science Specialist and Senior Lecturer at Ahmadu Bello University in Zaria, Nigeria, from 1970 to 1972; Visiting Professor of Physics at American University in Cairo, Egypt, from 1990 to 1991; and Visiting Professor at Daystar University, Kenya, in 1988, 1998, 2001, and 2004.

Ralph Stearley is Professor of Geology at Calvin College (MI) and received his PhD from the University of Michigan. During 1991–92 he was a research scientist at the Illinois State Museum. Since 1992 he has taught geology, oceanography, and paleontology at Calvin. He has published scientific papers on marine invertebrate ecology and paleoecology, the evolution and systematics of salmonid fishes, fish skeletal remains in archeological sites, and the biogeography of Ice Age mammals. In 1999 he directed the excavation of an American mastodon in Cascade, Michigan. He is currently collaborating with Davis Young on an update of the book *Christianity and the Age of the Earth*.

William M. Struthers is Assistant Professor of Psychology at Wheaton College (IL) and received his PhD in Biopsychology from the University of Illinois at Chicago. He has authored scientific papers for the journals *Brain Research*, *Physiology & Behavior*, and

NeuroReport as well as theoretical papers in *Perspectives on Science and Christian Faith,* the journal of the American Scientific Affiliation. He is an active member of the Society for Neuroscience, Faculty for Undergraduate Neuroscience, and American Scientific Affiliation. His laboratory research interests are in the neural mechanisms that underlie behavioral arousal and the processing of novel environments, which employs the use of stereotaxic surgery, immunochemistry, and behavioral manipulations to investigate gene expression in the cingulate cortex and basal ganglia. His theoretical study focuses on consciousness and the neural substrates of worldviews.

 Randy Van Dragt is Professor of Biology at Calvin College (MI), where he chairs the Biology Department and oversees the college nature preserve. He is on the faculty of the AuSable Institute of Environmental Studies and has been active in environmental preservation and ecological restoration for the last twenty years.

 Thomas J. VanDrunen is Assistant Professor of Computer Science at Wheaton College (IL). His main research interest is programming languages and compilers. He has published papers on compiler optimization and has also worked on the design of programming languages at the intersection of object-oriented and functional programming. Some of his additional interests include virtual machines, software engineering, and instruction in computer science.

 Ronald (Ron) J. Vos is Professor of Agriculture at Dordt College (IA), where he serves as Department Chair. His graduate training is in environmental studies, agronomy, agricultural policy, and agricultural economics. He currently teaches "Soil Fertility," "Field Crop Production," "Perspectives on Agricultural Policy, History, and Economics," and "Farm Management." His work on agricultural sustainability has taken him to several foreign countries. His other interests include operating a small farm and dealing with policy and justice issues as they apply to agriculture.

 Peter K. Walhout is Assistant Professor of Chemistry at Wheaton College (IL), where he teaches courses in Physical Chemistry and General Chemistry. He has taught the "Chemistry Capstone" course, which involves in-depth reading and discussion of matters related to the integration of faith and scientific knowledge. His graduate work at the University of Minnesota was in the area of ultrafast laser spectroscopy, and he did post-doctoral research in polymer physics at the University of Wisconsin. His current research utilizes various laser-based experimental techniques to study the physical properties of polyelectrolyte multilayered thin films.

 Peter H. Walters is Associate Professor in the Department of Kinesiology at Wheaton College (IL). He has offered and presented papers on progressive resistance training, the effects of sleep deprivation on cognitive and psychomotor function, and measures of anxiety among athletes. He is a certified strength and conditioning specialist, an Olympic weightlifting club coach, and a certified educational trainer for the National Strength and Conditioning Association, American Council for Exercise, and the American Fitness Association. His interests include strength training, health and sport psychology, and challenging adventures.

 Jennifer J. Wiseman is an astronomer who has studied star-forming regions of our galaxy using radio, optical, and infrared telescopes. She studied physics at MIT for her BS, discovering the comet Wiseman-Skiff in 1987. She then earned a PhD in astronomy at Harvard University in 1995 with a thesis on the dynamics of the Orion interstellar cloud. She accomplished subsequent research as a Jansky fellow at the National Radio Astronomy Observatory and as a Hubble Fellow at Johns Hopkins University. In addition to research, Dr. Wiseman is also interested in public science policy. She was selected as the 2001–2002 Congressional Science Fellow of the American Physical Society and served on the staff of the Science Committee of the U.S. House of Representatives. She is now the Program Scientist for the Hubble Space Telescope at NASA Headquarters in Washington, DC. Dr. Wiseman is a Fellow of the American Scientific Affiliation, a professional organization for Christians in the sciences. She is an adult Sunday School teacher and lay speaker at her church.

We want to hear from you. Please send your comments about this book to us in care of zreview@zondervan.com. Thank you.

GRAND RAPIDS, MICHIGAN 49530 USA

WWW.ZONDERVAN.COM